W9-BMD-274

Praise for
"You're Going to Love This Kid!"
Second Edition

"Paula Kluth 'gets it' when it comes to understanding and educating individuals with autism/ Asperger's! A spectacular work, filled with thought-provoking wisdom that cultivates an appreciation for the positive potential inherent in every child on the autism spectrum, and practical suggestions for helping these kids shine! You're going to LOVE this book!"

—**Veronica Zysk**
Managing Editor
Autism Asperger's Digest Magazine

"Full of great ideas and excellent strategies . . . . Every teacher and parent should have multiple copies—one to keep and the rest to loan out!"

—**Lynn Kern Koegel, Ph.D., CCC-SLP**
University of California
Santa Barbara

"This second edition provides the same incredibly practical information as the first and then some. This new edition is a very positive and upbeat state-of-the-art resource that goes well beyond including students with autism and presents solid advice on best practices for a wide range of students."

—**June E. Downing, Ph.D.**
Professor Emeritus
California State University, Northridge

"This book provides a wealth of knowledge, strategies, and resources to assist all educators in successfully understanding the value of inclusive education for all learners. Sharing real experiences from students with autism and their families only strengthened my resolve to build deeper and more collaborative relationships with my students and their families. Each chapter in this book said, 'Believe.' The teacher who believes that each child has the ability to learn will possess the power to break down barriers to inclusive education and build highways of learning."

—**Patricia Mack-Preston**
Special education teacher
Howard County, Maryland

"I loved this book! Paula Kluth clearly takes the time to listen to and understand our students so that we can truly work with them rather than just attempt to manage behavior. Respect and empathy infiltrate every chapter of this book and inform us how to appreciate and include all kids. It is this kind of thoughtfulness that allows teachers to truly connect with and educate their students."

—**Jed Baker, Ph.D.**
Director of the Social Skills Training Project
Author
*No More Meltdowns: Positive Strategies for
Managing and Preventing Out-of-Control Behavior*

"With this updated version, Paula Kluth has once again supplied practitioners with solid, practical, and realistic ideas on how to successfully include and educate students on the autism spectrum. In all her work, Dr. Kluth demonstrates an unwavering philosophy about respecting human dignity and taking a person-centered approach. Her insights and information are uplifting and extremely positive. Every teacher should have the opportunity to experience Dr. Kluth's wit, clarity, and wisdom."

—**Cathy Pratt, Ph.D.**
Director, Indiana Resource Center for Autism
Board Chair, Autism Society

"I thought it practically impossible that a new version could be better than the first. Paula's book was a masterpiece—well conceptualized and well written. I freely admit I was wrong. Whatever superlative exceeds *excellent* should be given to this new edition. It is simply fabulous!"

—**Brenda Smith Myles, Ph.D.**
Consultant
The Ziggurat Group

"Paula Kluth has, astonishingly enough, improved upon a unique and wonderful book. It is filled with strategies to *personalize* effective strategies for teaching and learning from students who are too often known only by their label. Here, every page has ideas and ways to get to know and meet the unique needs of each student. You're going to love the book as I do."

—**Anne M. Donnellan, Ph.D.**
Director
Autism Institute
University of San Diego

"Excellent! Paula brings clarity to complex issues, makes tangible the values and vision of inclusive education, and advances education toward wonderful new possibilities. Your students and colleagues are waiting for you to read this book!"

—**Michael McSheehan**
Clinical Assistant Professor
Communication Sciences & Disorders
Project Coordinator
Institute on Disability
Durham, New Hampshire

"You're Going to
Love This Kid!"

"You're Going to Love This Kid!"

Teaching Students with Autism in the Inclusive Classroom

SECOND EDITION

by

Paula Kluth, Ph.D.

with invited contributors

·P·A·U·L·H·
BROOKES
PUBLISHING C°®

Baltimore • London • Sydney

Paul H. Brookes Publishing Co.
Post Office Box 10624
Baltimore, Maryland 21285-0624
USA

www.brookespublishing.com

Copyright © 2010 by Paul H. Brookes Publishing Co., Inc.
All rights reserved.
Previous edition copyright © 2003.

"Paul H. Brookes Publishing Co." is a registered trademark of
Paul H. Brookes Publishing Co., Inc.

Typeset by Integrated Publishing Solutions, Grand Rapids, Michigan.
Manufactured in the United States of America by Sheridan Books, Inc., Ann Arbor, Michigan.

Every effort has been made to ascertain proper ownership of copyrighted materials and obtain permission for their use. Any omission is unintentional and will be corrected for future printings upon proper notification.

Excerpted material from pp. 57–58 from A SLANT OF SUN: ONE CHILD'S COURAGE by Beth Kephart. Copyright © 1998 by Beth Kephart. Used by permission of W.W. Norton & Company, Inc.

Excerpted material from pp. 64 and 184 from *Schooling Without Labels: Parents, Educators, and Inclusive Education* by Douglas Biklen. Used by permission of Temple University Press. © 1992 by Temple University. All Rights Reserved.

Excerpted material from p. 115 from OUT OF SILENCE: An Autistic Boy's Journey into Language and Communication, © 1994 by Russell Martin. Reprinted by permission of Henry Holt & Co., LLC.

Excerpted material from pp. 137, 140, 153, 168, 180, and 230 from A REAL PERSON: LIFE ON THE OUTSIDE by Gunilla Gerland. Copyright © 1996 by Souvenir Press Ltd.

The individuals described in this book are composites or real people whose situations are masked and are based on the authors' experiences. In all instances, names and identifying details have been changed to protect confidentiality.

Cover illustrations by Barbara Moran. Ms. Moran is a graphic artist, a presenter, a self-advocate, an advocate for people with disabilities, and a person with autism. Her artwork has been displayed across the country. Her unique and captivating drawings are available for purchase from http://www.karlwilliams.com/moran.htm

Purchasers of *"You're Going to Love This Kid!" Teaching Students with Autism in the Inclusive Classroom, Second Edition,* are granted permission to photocopy forms in the text for clinical or education purposes. None of the forms may be reproduced to generate revenue for any program or individual. Photocopies may only be made from an original book. *Unauthorized use beyond this privilege is prosecutable under federal law.* You will see the copyright protection notice at the bottom of each photocopiable page.

Library of Congress Cataloging-in-Publication Data

Kluth, Paula.
"You're going to love this kid!" : teaching students with
autism in the inclusive classroom / by Paula Kluth, Ph.D.
with invited contributors. —2nd ed.
     p.   cm.
Includes bibliographical references and index.
ISBN-13: 978-1-59857-079-3
ISBN-10: 1-59857-079-X (pbk. : alk. paper)
1. Autistic children—Education—United States.   2. Inclusive education—United States.   I. Title.
II. Title: Teaching students with autism in the inclusive classroom.
LC4718.K58 2010
371.94—dc22   2010004746

British Library Cataloguing in Publication data are available from the British Library.

2021   2020   2019

10   9   8   7   6

Contents

About the Author

Paula Kluth, Ph.D., is one of today's most popular and respected experts on autism and inclusive education. Through her work as an independent consultant and the high-energy presentations she gives to professionals across the country, Dr. Kluth helps professionals and families create responsive, engaging schooling experiences for students with disabilities and their peers, too. An internationally respected scholar and author, Dr. Kluth has written or cowritten several books for Paul H. Brookes Publishing Co., including *Pedro's Whale* (in press), *From Tutor Scripts to Talking Sticks: 100 Ways to Differentiate Instruction in K–12 Classrooms* (2010), *"A Is for All Aboard!"* (2010), *"A Land We Can Share": Teaching Literacy to Students with Autism* (2008), and *"Just Give Him the Whale!" 20 Ways to Use Fascinations, Areas of Expertise, and Strengths to Support Students with Autism* (2008). Learn more by joining her fan page on Facebook or by visiting her popular web site: http://www.paulakluth.com.

About the Contributors

Kelly Chandler-Olcott, Ed.D., is Associate Professor and Chair of the Reading & Language Arts Center at Syracuse University, where she also directs the English Education programs. She was a high school English teacher in her native state of Maine before becoming a teacher educator. At Syracuse, Dr. Chandler-Olcott teaches courses in English methods and literacy across the curriculum. Her research interests include adolescents' technology-mediated literacy practices, classroom-based inquiry by teachers, content literacy, and approaches to literacy pedagogy for inclusive classrooms. She has coauthored five books and published numerous articles in journals such as *Reading Research Quarterly, Journal of Literacy Research, English Education, Journal of Adolescent & Adult Literacy, Reading Research & Instruction, Journal of Teacher Education,* and *The Reading Teacher,* among others.

Christi Kasa-Hendrickson, Ph.D., is Assistant Professor in the Department of Education at the University of Colorado. Her teaching, research, and consulting are guided by her passion to create successful inclusive schools for all students. Dr. Kasa-Hendrickson teaches both graduate and undergraduate classes focusing on differentiated instruction, best practice for inclusive schooling, and communication strategies for people with significant disabilities. She began her career teaching in the public schools of California as a general education teacher, special education teacher, and an inclusion facilitator. Her expertise is in the area of supporting students with significant disabilities to access general education curriculum and engage in meaningful participation in the inclusive classroom. Dr. Kasa-Hendrickson's published works have appeared in *Journal of The Association for Persons with Severe Handicaps, The International Journal for Inclusive Education,* and *The American Educational Research Journal.*

Eileen Yoshina, M.Ed., a writer and educator, is an instructor at the South Puget Sound Community College in Olympia, Washington. Ms. Yoshina holds a masters of education in human development and psychology from Harvard University and specializes in diversity issues. A former elementary school general education teacher, Ms. Yoshina has taught in inclusive schools and believes in using an inclusive and social justice orientation in her teaching and educational writing.

Foreword

Paula Kluth is probably the best person around to write a book about how to support children with autism in public schools. She knows the first three rules of education as well as anybody I can think of.

Rule number one is to listen before you talk. And by listen, I don't just mean pretend to listen, but really listen as if you are ready to be told an important secret. The second rule is to love your students. And by love I don't mean like a mom or a pet owner; I mean the love between two people who need each other to make their way through the hard times and the easy times together. The third rule is that there are no rules. And that doesn't mean that nothing really matters; it means that people matter too much to try to make rules about what they need.

So, welcome to this wonderful book. By the time you finish it, you will know what a blessing you might become for a child who has the good luck to meet you.

Eugene Marcus
Syracuse, New York

Author's note: Eugene Marcus is a man with autism who believes in his own rights and those of others with and without disabilities. He is a product of Syracuse's inclusive school system. He is co-teaching undergraduate courses at Syracuse University, where he also serves as an associate of the Facilitated Communication Institute. He lectures frequently on communication, inclusive schooling, autism, and the rights of people with disabilities.

Preface

On the morning of my first day of teaching, I was told I would be working with a 6-year-old student with autism named Jacob. I was given dozens of files to review. I marveled at the stacks of reports, evaluations, observations, clinical assessments, work samples, and standardized test results. I couldn't believe a child so small could have so many "credentials." As I reviewed the files, my feelings changed from stunned to overwhelmed to terrified. Jacob's paperwork was filled with information about his inability to be a student or a learner. The documents detailed his challenging behaviors, skill deficits, and communication problems. I was dazed—I was scarcely 22 years old, I had only recently graduated from my teacher preparation program, and I remembered little from the one or two lectures I had attended on autism.

Before I could complain to my colleagues or sneak out the back door of the building, I heard my name on the loudspeaker and was beckoned to the school office. I grudgingly made my way down the hallway only to be met halfway by a grinning and extremely animated school administrator. Dr. Patrick Schwarz seized me by the shoulders and said, "So, you're going to be Jacob's teacher! That's fantastic. You're going to LOVE this kid!"

This inspirational leader could not have been more accurate in his assessment of Jacob or the future I would have with this young student. In the next few years, Dr. Schwarz, the school principal, my general education colleagues, Jacob, and the other students in the school all collaborated to create an inclusive environment and experience in the first-grade classroom. The first few weeks of school were a challenge, but the school community worked together to create success for this young man. Administrators shifted classroom schedules to accommodate Jacob's need for a recess break early in the day; students worked to learn Jacob's communication system; teachers created materials and invented lessons that intrigued and engaged their new student; Jacob's family shared their expertise and gave suggestions for making him comfortable in his new school; and Jacob worked daily to meet new friends, learn classroom routines, and participate in lessons.

Although Jacob did not speak, occasionally struggled with challenging behaviors, and needed a wide range of adaptations to engage in curriculum and instruction, he was soon participating and succeeding in all aspects of school life. Through this energetic, precocious, and unique 6-year-old, I learned how to be a teacher—not only of students with autism but also of all learners with and without disabilities in the inclusive classroom.

An important piece of this story is obviously the role of my former administrator, Dr. Schwarz. His positive attitude and encouraging behaviors influenced my impression of Jacob; inspired me to learn about students in holistic ways; and prompted me to study more about autism, behavior supports, instruction, communication needs, and curriculum development.

Unfortunately, the perspective and attitude offered by Dr. Schwarz seem to be rare. The dominant paradigm in educating students with autism has been and continues to be based on labels, deficits, and clinical understandings of difference. This paradigm was verified by the information in Jacob's files and is exemplified in much of the educational literature, college textbooks, and popular media sources that introduce preservice teachers to autism.

I believe Jacob's story is an appropriate way to illustrate an alternative approach to educating students with autism. Dr. Schwarz's understanding of Jacob was based on a positive, individualized, and inclusive ideology instead of only on student needs, failures, and struggles. This anecdote portrays the possibilities that exist when educators see students as part of the school community, view inclusive schooling as a possibility for all learners, and understand support as a process.

The book provides concrete examples of how to plan lessons, engineer a safe and comfortable classroom, provide communication opportunities, and support challenging behaviors. Drawing on classroom observations as well on as my own experience as an elementary and high school teacher, I explore pragmatic ways of making schools safe, challenging, and accessible for students on the autism spectrum. The chapters are designed to highlight how *any* student can be supported to participate in academic instruction, school routines, and the social activities of the inclusive school.

As readers of the first edition will notice, this second edition is longer and physically larger. The reason for making the book longer was simply to add in more examples and illustrations of suggested strategies. The reason for making the book physically larger was to transition *"You're Going to Love This Kid!"* from just a textbook into a textbook and workbook combined. I did this because so many readers of the first edition asked me follow-up questions such as, "What would a portfolio look like?" "Do you have a form to use in assessing my inclusive school?" and "Can you provide examples of the adaptations you describe in the book?" Teachers (and many parents) were looking for concrete examples of ideas presented. To respond to these individuals, I added reproducible forms, checklists, charts, photographs, figures, and space for taking notes in the second edition. Those looking for more guidance will be able to immediately see that the book now provides a more detailed "game plan" for assembling supportive learning environments and crafting inclusive lessons.

As in the first edition, the book consists of 12 chapters. Each chapter is concerned with a different school issue/structure (e.g., lesson planning, collaboration) and provides concrete examples of how learners with autism can be supported:

Chapter 1 includes definitions and characteristics of autism and illustrates how those on the spectrum experience differences.

Chapter 2 provides information about how teachers and school leaders can work toward inclusive education in both elementary and secondary schools. This chapter also outlines the federal laws related to special education.

The role of the teacher is reviewed in Chapter 3. This chapter explores some of the values and beliefs that support the development and sustenance of inclusive schools.

Chapter 4, coauthored with Eileen Yoshina, features the voices of families and gives ideas for partnering with mothers, fathers, siblings, and other family members in respectful and meaningful ways.

In Chapter 5, I share specific strategies helpful in the creation of a positive and comfortable educational environment. Ideas for arranging and organizing classrooms are provided, as is information on adjusting classroom lighting, seating, and space.

Chapter 6 contains ideas for building classroom community and supporting the development of social relationships for all students.

If students do not have reliable communication or struggle to express themselves effectively, every other aspect of their education program is at risk. Chapter 7 illustrates different ways that student communication can be bolstered and supported in the inclusive classroom. Different types of augmentative and alternative communication are also described in this chapter.

In Chapter 8, I explore with my coauthor, Kelly Chandler-Olcott, why students with autism may not be receiving the literacy instruction they need or deserve, and we explore several recommendations for teaching literacy to students with autism.

The focus of Chapter 9 is behavior. Here, behavior is explored from an alternative perspective. Instead of examining how to stop or "treat" behaviors, I present it as something that must be understood in context and interpreted carefully. Positive ways to support a range of behaviors are provided throughout the chapter.

Chapter 10 contains tools and structures to assist educators in planning lessons appropriate for students with autism and for all learners in inclusive classrooms. A step-by-step process is provided for teaching a wide range of learners in diverse schools.

Chapter 11, "Teaching Strategies," is coauthored with Christi Kasa-Hendrickson, a professor of education and a former elementary classroom teacher. This chapter is a collection of classroom-tested ideas that can be used either with all students in the classroom; with a handful of students; or with any individual student who needs something extra or different in terms of classroom materials, daily instruction, or curriculum.

Collaboration and co-teaching are the focus of Chapter 12. This chapter gives educators suggestions for working with all team members and tips for structuring the collaborative classroom.

I believe this book is unique in that most texts related to teaching students with autism

- Do not include information or ideas useful for today's diverse, inclusive classrooms

- View autism from a medical model or a deficit perspective

- Treat communication, behavior, and learning problems as things that "belong" to students instead of as issues that must be understood in context and within relationships

- Lack perspectives, ideas, and suggestions from individuals with autism, Asperger syndrome, and their families

"You're Going To Love This Kid!" alternatively

- Focuses exclusively on inclusive schooling

- Views inclusion as both an ideology and a pedagogy

- Proposes sensitive new ways to see and understand students with autism

- Stresses how students with autism can participate in the curriculum and instruction in the inclusive classroom if appropriately and creatively supported

- Includes frameworks, approaches, and strategies useful for teachers, administrators, and other school personnel (e.g., therapists, counselors, volunteers)

- Prominently features the voices of those with autism and Asperger syndrome

Despite the progress that has been made across the country in inclusive schooling, too many students with autism are still being excluded from public schools. In many cases, teachers want to support these learners but do not have the support, knowledge or skills to do so. This book is written for this audience—those committed to inclusive schooling and looking for answers.

Acknowledgments

I am indebted, first and foremost, to all of the students with whom I have worked, but especially to Jason, Andrew, Franklin, Paul, Caleb, Kelsey, and Michael. You were the first to teach me about autism.

Many other friends and colleagues on the spectrum have helped me to think critically about disability, ability, and autism, including Roy Bedward, Jamie Burke, Stephen Hinkle, Hesham Khater, Jon Micheal, Barbara Moran, Christie Sauer, Stephen Shore, Sean Sokler, Mark Van Boxtel, and Lianne Holliday Willey. The families of individuals with autism have also been incredibly generous with their time and energy; their stories and teachings have been invaluable.

I would like to thank the staff of Kruse Education Center in Orland Park, Illinois. The teachers at Kruse taught me how to teach and crafted many of the strategies shared in this book. I am especially grateful for the support of Barbara Schaffer and Peg Sheehan. Unending gratitude also goes to Patrick Schwarz, who first told me, "You are going to love this kid!" My colleagues at Stoner Prairie Elementary School in Verona, Wisconsin, also taught me a great deal about inclusive schooling—especially my second-grade team and, specifically, Erin DiPerna. More recently, my work has been inspired by educators at the John J. Audubon School in Chicago, Illinois, and those who participated in the Cayuga-Onondaga BOCES autism grant project (2002–2004). Most of the new examples in this second edition of the book come from these teachers.

My work in this book is inspired by several mentors. Lou Brown, Alice Udvari-Solner, Sue Rubin, Eugene Marcus, Anne Donnellan, Douglas Biklen, and Mayer Shevin. I am so grateful for their contributions to the field.

I am indebted to the friends who read pieces of this manuscript and gave thoughtful feedback: Kelly Chandler-Olcott, Christi Kasa-Hendrickson, Tracy Knight, Gail Gibson, Matt Grant, Kathy Kurowski, Lori and Bernie Micheal, Janna Woods, Sally Young, Nancy Rice, Kate Zagorski, and Eileen Yoshina.

Big love and lots of affection to my mother, Mary (Madee), who shamelessly promotes all of my projects and gives nothing but loving encouragement. I thank her for her faith in this project and in me. To my sister, Victoria: You are the best fan and now, the best partner, in my writing endeavors. Erma and Willa, thank you for your hugs and kisses of support; I hope you will continue to write your own books for the rest of your life! And, finally, a big "I couldn't have done it without you" to Todd. Your tech support is second to none. Your grace is unmatched. And your ability to put up with markers and manuscripts everywhere is astounding. I love you so much.

Finally, I am grateful to those at Paul H. Brookes Publishing Co. for the care that they invested in this book (again)! Thank you to Rebecca Lazo (who not only cares about the books but about teachers and kids as well), Leslie Eckard (who shares ideas, stories, *and* edits), Steve Plocher (who fixes everything before it needs to be fixed), and Melanie Allred (who has been as collaborative as she has been creative).

To Franklin Wilson, a gifted and patient teacher,
and to Pat Wilson, my teacher's teacher

1

Defining Autism

Autistic children don't deserve to be molded into someone they are not.
They deserve to learn and grow, and feel comfortable about themselves.
Their worlds can expand to include new experiences, and they can become teachers,
opening others to their viewpoints. (O'Neill, 1997, p. 1)

A teacher called me to ask a question about a new student, a young woman with an autism diagnosis, in her eighth-grade classroom. The teacher shared that she wanted to know more about autism and wanted other students to feel comfortable with their new classmate. For these reasons, the teacher asked me if I thought it would be a good idea to have the social worker do a classroom presentation on autism or to have the student's parents come in and answer questions about disabilities. I asked her if the student had a reliable way to communicate. The teacher told me that, yes, the student could speak and was actually quite verbal and engaging. Then I asked the teacher about the student's needs and ideas. Specifically, I wanted to know if the student *wanted* the social worker or her parents to visit the classroom. The teacher answered, "I don't know, I didn't ask her."

Too often, teachers forget to tap into the most important resource of all: students with autism and their families. Mr. Rusch, one of my former colleagues, learned this lesson when he was told that he would have a student with autism in his third-grade classroom. For weeks, he called me on the telephone, pestering me to send him a textbook about autism. I resisted, fearing that he would have one of two responses. He would either 1) see the medical and/or technical definitions and fear he was "not qualified" to teach a student with autism, or 2) read the text and declare himself quite ready to serve as an expert on the topic. Neither of these outcomes, I reasoned, would be good news for Ronnie, his new student.

Before I could figure out how to properly support Mr. Rusch, he called to tell me that Ronnie's family had invited him to dinner. Mr. Rusch accepted the invitation and

---

[1] I generally use the terms *autism* or *autism spectrum* throughout this book when referring to students with any label related to autism; all of the information, suggestions, ideas, and recommendations also apply to students with Asperger syndrome, pervasive developmental disorder-not otherwise specified (PDD-NOS), and other disabilities that I have highlighted in this chapter.

when he came back to school the next day, he was feeling far more confident about teaching Ronnie. He told me all about Ronnie's need for an alternative communication system (a series of signs and gestures), his ability to play complex video games, and his interest in building card houses.

In getting to know Ronnie as an individual, my colleague was practicing what Kliewer and Biklen called *local understanding*, which is "a radically deep, intimate knowledge of another human being" (2001, p. 4). The intimacy of the relationship, these researchers claimed, is important because "it allows those in positions of relative authority or power to see in idiosyncratic behavior demonstrations of understanding that are otherwise dismissed or disregarded by more distant observers" (p. 4). This means that getting to know Ronnie in a personal way and seeing him as an individual helped Mr. Rusch generate effective supports. It also helped him serve as an advocate for Ronnie. When the technology teacher suggested that instruction using computers would be too difficult for Ronnie, Mr. Rusch objected, citing the student's video game prowess as an example of his abilities in problem solving, fine motor control, and complex thinking. The technology teacher agreed to include Ronnie in the lessons and was pleasantly surprised when Mr. Rusch and Ronnie proved him wrong.

In Chapter 1, I introduce readers to the topic of autism but also encourage every teacher reading this book to note the lesson that can be taken from Mr. Rusch's engagement with Ronnie. That is, only so much can be learned about autism; the rest of the education comes from the individual students with autism labels who enter your classroom. Therefore, in this chapter, I will not only define autism from the medical model but also share interpretations of it from people who know it best—those on the spectrum themselves. Following that, I will explore labels themselves and discuss what the language and descriptions of autism really mean. Finally, I look at the main characteristics of autism, complete with quotes, perspectives, and reflections from individuals on the spectrum.

What Is Autism?

Often, one of the first things a teacher wants to know when he or she learns that a student with autism is coming into the classroom is "What is autism?" *Autism* is a difficult term to define because the disability is complex. As Kathy Xenia Grant, a woman on the spectrum, shares in the documentary film *"We Thought You'd Never Ask": Voices of People with Autism* (Hussman, Kluth, Strong, & Tweedy, 2009), no two individuals with the label of autism experience it exactly alike: "Autism is so complex because it's a spectrum disorder. It's like saying, 'Define the Middle East.' What country? Iran? Iraq? Syria? Autism is the same way."

Although many people with the label of autism have much in common, they tend to have more differences than commonalities. For example, some individuals with autism appear to welcome touch; others find it painful. Some students crave social interaction; others need more space and time alone. Some are extremely talkative; others cannot use speech reliably. It is critical to remember that students with autism vary widely in experiences, skills, abilities, interests, characteristics, gifts, talents, and needs. If you know one person with autism, you know ONE person with autism. For these reasons, I offer several descriptions of autism and many interpretations of the disability from different perspectives.

What the Experts Say

I begin with the most important and useful definitions of autism—those that come from people with autism, experts who experience sensory, movement, and communication differences every day, who know what it feels like to have a disability label, and who struggle with societal notions of normalcy:

Autism isn't something a person has, or a "shell" that a person is trapped inside. There's no normal child hidden behind the autism. Autism is a way of being. It is pervasive: It colors every experience, every sensation, perception, thought, emotion, and encounter, every aspect of existence. It is not possible to separate the autism from the person—and if it were possible, the person you'd have left would not be the same person you started with. (Sinclair, 1993, p. 1)

Eagerness to be like others didn't make Pinocchio real—it turned him into a donkey! And eagerness by parents to cure autism or retardation or compulsiveness will not drive great distances toward the final solution to the actual problem. Because the person who believes "I will be real when I am normal" will always be almost a person, but will never make it all the way. (Marcus, 1998, p. 2)

When I learned that autism was neurological and was related to sensory processing, that made sense to me because so many things bothered me that didn't bother other people. I just didn't develop and function like other people did. And I learned that the reason it was hard for me to control my behavior was because life was much more intense for me.... (Moran in Hussman, Kluth, Strong, & Tweedy, 2009)

Autism means having to watch how I feel every second that I am awake. Autism means having challenges when I leave the room fearing that others will say unkind things about me to other people. Autism means being dateless on weekends as well as constant loneliness, only watching TV on Saturday night. Autism means not being able to fit in on social peer relations. However, autism, in my case, means that I have a calendar memory for birthdays, being articulate and having skills. I, all in all, would rather be autistic than normal. (Ronan, as cited in Gillingham, 1995, p. 90)

Some aspects of autism may be good or bad depending only on how they are perceived. For example, hyperfocusing is a problem if you're hyperfocusing on your feet and miss the traffic light change. On the other hand, hyperfocusing is a great skill for working on intensive projects. This trait is particularly well suited to freelancers and computer work. I would never argue that autism is all good or merely a difference. I do find that my autism is disabling. However, that doesn't mean that it is all bad or that I want to be cured. I may not be altogether happy with who I am, but that doesn't mean I want to be someone else. (Molton, 2000)

Perhaps the most striking aspect of the definitions put forward by people with autism is that they often look and sound so different from those espoused by the medical and scientific communities. Although people on the spectrum often note their struggles in defining autism, they also commonly describe some associated gifts or abilities. Certainly, this way of seeing autism is not true for every individual on the spectrum, but I highlight the optimism that *some* put on their definitions because these perspectives get too little attention. Consider a few ways in which some individuals on the spectrum describe the gifts associated with their "dis/ability":

I believe Autism is a marvelous occurrence of nature, not a tragic example of the human mind gone wrong. In many cases, Autism can also be a kind of genius undiscovered. (O' Neill, 1999, p. 14)

I like being different. I prefer having AS [Asperger syndrome] to being normal. I don't have the foggiest idea exactly what it is I like about AS. I think that people with AS see things differently. I also think they see them more clearly. (Hall, 2001, p. 15)

We can describe a situation like no one else. We can tell you what intangibles feel like and secret flavors taste like. We can describe for you, in unbelievable depth, the intricate details of our favorite obsessions. (Willey, 2001, p. 29)

I think Asperger syndrome is another perspective on the world. It's certainly helped me with the mathematical side of things. I find it very easy to think in highly abstract terms. I can solve a Rubik's Cube in two minutes. (Molloy & Vasil, 2004, p. 40)

Glancing at the ground as I walked along, I noticed some movement at my feet and saw the last exit moments of a cicada crawling out of a hole in the ground. I watched this creature transform before my eyes from a dull brownish-green bug into a beautiful bright green and gold, singing creation. The process took only one and a half hours. I have since heard that people thought my standing in the heat for one and a half hours to watch an insect was a crazy thing to do. I think it is they who are crazy. By choosing not to stand and watch, they missed out on sharing an experience that was so beautiful and exhilarating. (Lawson, 1998, p. 115)

The Medical Model

As of 2010, when this book was published, no biological markers were associated with autism; therefore, the categories and descriptions provided have been constructed and reproduced based on the judgment and opinion of scholars, researchers, and the medical community. Put more succinctly, the following definitions or labels represent efforts to categorize and consider the difficulties individuals may encounter, the behaviors they may exhibit, and the experiences they may report, but they are limited in that they can give us little information about individual learners and their needs. Therefore, a student's label should *never* drive curriculum, instruction, and supports; any child's educational program should be based on his or her individual characteristics and abilities. A label can certainly be helpful but only in that it can give teachers a starting point for learning about a student's needs.

The Autism Spectrum

Autism is often referred to as a *spectrum disorder*—a disorder in which symptoms can occur in many varieties and with varying degrees of intensity. Autism, first described in the 1940s by American psychiatrist Leo Kanner, is one of the most common developmental disabilities in children. According to the Centers for Disease Control and Prevention, approximately 1% of American children are on the autism spectrum. This rate is significantly higher than the 2007 estimate of 1 in 150 (Centers for Disease Control and Prevention, 2009).

Autism typically appears before a child reaches the age of 3, although it is not always diagnosed until the child is age 4 or older, if ever. It is commonly reported that autism is four to five times more likely to occur in boys than in girls, but some researchers are challenging these numbers, claiming that spectrum-related differences may look or "present" differently in girls than they do in boys (Attwood, 2007; Hill, 2009; Nichols, Moravcik, & Tetenbaum, 2009). Girls, for instance, may not show the extreme interest in trains, gadgets, or computers that boys do but may be fascinated instead with pop stars or television programs. The social differences they experience may look different or not stand out as much. A girl on the spectrum who struggles with social situations may constantly retreat to her room or to a corner of the classroom or even to the edge of the playground to read or to write. Some argue that this type of behavior is simply noticed more often and seen as more unusual in boys than in girls; thus, it might inspire questions about a spectrum diagnosis for a child of one sex more than another.

Autism traditionally has been defined by terms outlined in medical literature. According to the *Diagnostic and Statistical Manual of Mental Disorders, Fourth Edition, Text Revision* (*DSM-IV-TR*, American Psychiatric Association, 2000), a reference book designed to provide guidelines for the diagnosis and classification of mental disorders, individuals with autism have "delayed or abnormal functioning" in at least one of the following areas:

- Social interaction
- Communication
- Patterns of behavior (e.g., restricted, repetitive, stereotyped), interests, and activities

Table 1.1 provides more details of the *DSM-IV-TR* diagnostic criteria for autism.

Asperger Syndrome

Asperger syndrome is another label that may be given to learners who fall within the autism spectrum. Students with Asperger syndrome typically report communication differences (e.g., avoiding eye contact, struggling to maintain a conversation) social differences (e.g., difficulty reading social cues), sensory differences (Attwood, 2007), struggles with change and transitions, and the tendency to have one or more absorbing areas of interest at any given time. These students often have excellent rote memory skills (e.g., figures, facts, dates) and may exhibit repetitive motor patterns such as hand or finger flapping. Many also have exceptional interest and ability in math and science. Students who are labeled with Asperger syndrome may go undiagnosed for years and may be seen by others as simply quirky or eccentric. Table 1.2 provides more details of the *DSM-IV-TR* diagnostic criteria for Asperger syndrome.

Although Asperger syndrome was once seen as a disability or label distinct and separate from autism, it is now understood as a variant of it. Some characterize Asperger syndrome as mild autism, but, as Luke Jackson, in his autobiographical work *Freaks, Geeks, and Asperger Syndrome: A User Guide to Adolescence,* indicates, this explanation may not take into account the complexities of looking typical but having subtle, hidden, or misunderstood differences:

AS [Asperger syndrome] is usually described as a mild form of autism but, believe me, though the good outweighs the bad there are some bits that most certainly are not mild. AS people reading this, do you feel as if you only have a "mild" problem when you are having one of those days where you feel as if you may well be from another planet? (2002, p. 21)

Kalen Molton agrees with Jackson. She has shared that those who discount the significance or influence of her Asperger syndrome have caused her great stress:

Some people have called Asperger syndrome "nerd disorder" as a way of minimizing it. There is a fine line between "normal but odd" and "very high functioning autistic." My personal opinion is that the line is where the traits become disabling. I have a very good "guest mode" where I can appear quite normal; however, being forced to sustain guest mode for an extended period can, and has, led to a serious breakdown. My ability to behave near normally at times has led others to believe that I can do it all the time and if I don't then I am lazy, unmotivated, manipulative, and deliberately annoying. No one expects a tightrope walker to do it all the time. (2000)

Table 1.1. *DSM-IV-TR* definition of autism

The *DSM-IV-TR* defines autism as follows:

A. A total of six (or more) items from (1), (2), and (3), with at least two from (1), and one each from (2) and (3):

    (1) qualitative impairment in social interaction, as manifested by at least two of the following:

        (a) marked impairment in the use of multiple nonverbal behaviors, such as eye-to-eye gaze, facial expression, body postures, and gestures to regulate social interaction

        (b) failure to develop peer relationships appropriate to developmental level

        (c) a lack of spontaneous seeking to share enjoyment, interests, or achievements with other people (e.g., by a lack of showing, bringing, or pointing out objects of interest)

        (d) lack of social or emotional reciprocity

    (2) qualitative impairments in communication, as manifested by at least one of the following:

        (a) delay in, or total lack of, the development of spoken language (not accompanied by an attempt to compensate through alternative modes of communication such as gesture or mime)

        (b) in individuals with adequate speech, marked impairment in the ability to initiate or sustain a conversation with others

        (c) stereotyped and repetitive use of language or idiosyncratic language

        (d) lack of varied, spontaneous make-believe play or social imitative play appropriate to developmental level

    (3) restricted, repetitive, and stereotyped patterns of behavior, interests, and activities as manifested by at least one of the following:

        (a) encompassing preoccupation with one or more stereotyped and restricted patterns of interest that is abnormal either in intensity or focus

        (b) apparently inflexible adherence to specific, nonfunctional routines or rituals

        (c) stereotyped and repetitive motor mannerisms (e.g., hand or finger flapping or twisting or complex whole-body movements)

        (d) persistent preoccupation with parts of objects

B. Delays or abnormal functioning in at least one of the following areas, with onset prior to age 3 years: (1) social interaction, (2) language as used in social communication, or (3) symbolic or imaginative play

C. The disturbance is not better accounted for by Rett's disorder or childhood disintegrative disorder.

Reprinted with permission from the Diagnostic and Statistical Manual of Mental Disorders, Text Revision, Fourth Edition (copyright 2000). American Psychiatric Association.

Other Disability Labels Related to Autism

A few other labels in addition to autism and Asperger syndrome are given to people who have "autism-like" characteristics. Sometimes students do not meet the *DSM-IV-TR* criteria, but they do have learning, communication, behavioral, or other differences and need supports similar to those provided to students on the spectrum. These learners have other labels such as *pervasive developmental disorder–not otherwise specified (PDD-NOS)* and *childhood disintegrative disorder.*

Students with Rett syndrome, Williams syndrome, fragile X syndrome, and Landau-Kleffner syndrome also share characteristics with those on the spectrum. Students with these diagnoses may have some of the same needs as those with the label of autism and may benefit from the strategies and ideas shared in this book.

Diagnosis and Labeling: Important Considerations

Diagnostic labels such as *autism, Asperger syndrome,* and *PDD-NOS* can be very helpful; they can provide individuals with disabilities, families, educators, and researchers with a common language and framework and connect people to resources, funding, and services. In addition, labels can provide a starting point for educators in terms of making connections and having

Table 1.2.   *DSM-IV-TR* definition of Asperger syndrome

The *DSM-IV-TR* characterizes Asperger's Disorder as follows:

A.   Qualitative impairment in social interaction, as manifested by at least two of the following:

  (1)   marked impairment in the use of multiple nonverbal behaviors, such as eye-to-eye gaze, facial expression, body postures, and gestures to regulate social interaction

  (2)   failure to develop peer relationships appropriate to developmental level

  (3)   a lack of spontaneous seeking to share enjoyment, interests, or achievements with other people (e.g., by a lack of showing, bringing, or pointing out objects of interest to other people)

  (4)   lack of social or emotional reciprocity

B.   Restricted, repetitive, and stereotyped patterns of behavior, interests, and activities, as manifested by at least one of the following:

  (1)   encompassing preoccupation with one or more stereotyped and restricted patterns of interest that is abnormal either in intensity or focus

  (2)   apparently inflexible adherence to specific, nonfunctional routines or rituals

  (3)   stereotyped and repetitive motor mannerisms (e.g., hand or finger flapping or twisting, or complex whole-body movements)

  (4)   persistent preoccupation with parts of objects

C.   The disturbance causes clinically significant impairment in social, occupational, or other important areas of functioning.

D.   There is no clinically significant general delay in language (e.g., single words used by age 2 years, communicative phrases used by age 3 years).

E.   There is no clinically significant delay in cognitive development or in the development of age-appropriate self help skills, adaptive behavior (other than in social interaction), and curiosity about the environment in childhood.

F.   Criteria are not met for another specific pervasive developmental disorder or schizophrenia.

Reprinted with permission from the Diagnostic and Statistical Manual of Mental Disorders, Text Revision, Fourth Edition (copyright 2000). American Psychiatric Association.

conversations. An overreliance on these labels, however, can serve as a barrier to understanding students as individuals and can lead teachers and others to believe that disability categories are static, meaningful, and well understood when in fact they are none of these things.

Because labels are subject to change at any time and because they are in many ways experimental, many families and professionals now use the broader term *autism spectrum* as a way of including all of the labels that are connected to autism. Although this label has many of the same problems as others, it may help educators move away from understanding autism, Asperger syndrome, PDD-NOS, and other labels as distinct and separate. The more that is uncovered about autism, the more unclear the distinctions among types of autism become. Because we are learning new facts about the autism spectrum every day, at this point we can only be sure of three things: 1) We have very little information on autism; we *don't* know more than we *do* know (Anne Donnellan, personal communication, October 20, 2008); 2) we will have new definitions, terminology, understandings, and conceptual knowledge in the near future; and 3) many of the things we feel we understand will prove to be wrong. For these reasons, it is important to be aware of some of the cautions or problems associated with defining autism and labeling students.

Consider: (How Much) Does a Particular Diagnosis Matter?

Some debate exists as to the usefulness of differentiating one "type" of autism from another. For example, some question the usefulness of using so many different labels to discuss the same types of characteristics. Other professionals insist that using the right label is crucial to understanding student concerns and characteristics and to providing appropriate supports. Labeling, however, is a tricky business. Because autism and Asperger syndrome cannot be diagnosed by medical tests, labels are assigned based on questionnaires, rating scales, psychological tests, and other subjective instruments and tools. Therefore, there is a large degree of judgment, personal opinion, and even bias in diagnosis and labeling.

I have heard stories of families going from one professional to the next looking for clarification on their child's label: Is it autism? Is it Asperger syndrome? Is it PDD? One mother asked me to observe her daughter and then proceeded to ask me if I thought she had autism or Asperger syndrome. I told her that diagnosing and testing children wasn't something I normally did as an educator. I then asked her to tell me what *she* thought about her daughter's label. As we ended the conversation, I asked her only one question: "What would you do differently tomorrow if you called this autism instead of Asperger syndrome?" In most cases (but not all), the answer is "nothing"; the supports do not change, and the types of programs or services to which the learner has access do not change. This doesn't mean parents should not seek answers, but they should always understand the very tenuous nature of these assignments, categories, and assessments.

In other words, practitioners must keep in mind that diagnosis does not necessarily provide families, teachers, or other professionals with relevant information about what needs or abilities a student has or how to teach him or her most effectively. Furthermore, this label—no matter what it is—does not indicate the milestones he or she will reach or the abilities he or she will be able to develop; it is critical, then, that labels never be viewed as limits.

What Do We Learn from Assessments?

In many cases, assumptions are made about students based on their performance on diagnostic tests. Use of these tools is a problem for many students with autism for a variety of reasons. Some have difficulty manipulating materials, communicating, or responding to directions in typical ways. For example, a student with autism may be asked to draw a triangle as part of an assessment. The student may well know what a triangle is but be unable to draw it due to motor planning problems or even anxiety. In this situation, the test will not reveal what the student knows; the assessor will learn only that the student cannot draw a triangle on command. Likewise, a student being assessed might be asked to examine pictures of animals and choose "the one that lives in a barn." Again, if the child knows the answer (e.g., cow) but has no reliable pointing response or cannot process the question quickly enough, she will fail that item. The problem with so many of these instruments is that they purport to assess student knowledge or skill but what so many end up evaluating is how autistic the pupil is! In other words, many students who struggle with these tests are being assessed not on intellectual ability but on how efficiently their body works; how significant their movement, sensory, or communication problems are; and how well they deal with novel tasks and people.

When I was a student teacher in a high school, I was asked to accompany Caleb, a teenage boy with autism, to an evaluation. One instrument used during the evaluation was a nonverbal, multiple-choice test designed to evaluate an individual's receptive knowledge of vocabulary. The test required students to study four pictures at a time and answer increasingly difficult questions about the pictures. Early questions in the test simply required the students to identify a picture (e.g., "Which one is the tree?"). Subsequent questions tapped into higher order thinking and required the test taker to know about properties, qualities, or uses of the items and/or things pictured (e.g., "Which one eats grass?"). Caleb did not make it to the complex, higher order questions. He got most of the items in the first five questions wrong because he failed to point at anything, and, in response to the next two questions, he stabbed his finger at the wrong pictures.

During the entire assessment, Caleb, who also had low vision, wiggled in his seat and flapped his arms. He tried to leave the room once and at least two times he placed his cheek against the testing materials and giggled. It was difficult to tell if he was uncomfortable, excited, confused, or frustrated, but Caleb did attempt to engage in the assessment despite the task and the examiner being completely unfamiliar to him. For most of the assessment, Caleb pointed at pictures without seeming to even look at them (perhaps because he could not clearly see them). On the last test item, however, the examiner asked Caleb to point to the light bulb. He was asked to choose from four pictures (e.g., horse, dollhouse, umbrella, light bulb). Caleb put his face close to the pictures again. Then, he grabbed the table lamp in front of him and shook it wildly. The examiner took the lamp from Caleb and gently asked him to continue with the test. Again, she asked him, "Show me the light bulb," and again Caleb grabbed and shook the lamp.

I suggested to the examiner that Caleb might be showing her the light bulb in the only way he could due to both his motor planning problems and his low vision. She agreed, but explained that she could not know for sure. She did make some notes in the testing materials about the incident but, in the end, Caleb received a very low score on the assessment. Although the examiner caught glimpses of Caleb's potential ability and saw that the assessment was an inappropriate measure of his ability, those who look at his records will see that his receptive vocabulary is that of a 2-year-old.

As illustrated in Caleb's story, assessment is problematic when the tools used do not take into account the unique needs of the student on the spectrum. This situation is exacerbated when the examiner does not know the child. In these instances, collaboration is key. Consider the story of Wendy Robinson, who took her son to the doctor's office for an assessment only to be questioned and ultimately insulted by the professional assessing her son:

> She asked me lots of questions and gave Grant simple tests to do. He failed miserably at most things. He was not in the mood today to perform in his usual contrary way. She asked me if he held his hands in the air when I removed his clothes before bath or bed.
> "Yes," I replied.
> "Are you sure?" she retorted. "I can't believe he does that." (2003, p. 21)

Of course, many professionals are conscientious and well understand the need to collaborate with other professionals and families, but even the most sensitive educators should reflect on what types of values and beliefs they are bringing to an assessment. Everyone involved in the process should be committed to a team approach that is student- and family-centered. Furthermore, students should be assessed using a range of tools including observations across environments; interviews with family members; and, if possible, interviews with the student.

Where Do Most Definitions of Autism Come From?

In *Autism: A New Understanding*, Gail Gillingham challenged the ways in which most definitions of autism have been constructed. The primary flaw in most definitions, she contends, is the lack of "direct experience" that has informed descriptions of autism. Comparing the definition of depression with that of autism, Gillingham pointed out that only the former seems to have been informed by the perspectives of those diagnosed:

> When we look at the criteria for depression, we find it includes symptoms such as recurrent thoughts of death, markedly diminished interest or pleasure in all activities, and feelings of worthlessness. The criterion for Social Phobia includes the symptoms of a marked and persistent fear of social situations, the recognition that this fear is excessive and irrational and that exposure to the feared situation provokes anxiety. None of these symptoms can be determined without taking the actual experience of the person who is diagnosed into account.

Gillingham goes on to explain that this honoring of the "insider" experience does not happen with autism or Asperger syndrome. Instead, she shares, the professionals have relied on their own observations and interpretations:

> Do we see an impairment in communication? Do we experience an impairment in social interaction? The repetitive and stereotypic behaviors are observed and measured directly from our viewpoint. No one has taken the time or effort to include anything from the actual experience of the autistics. I assume this is because we do not believe that they are capable of sharing anything useful. However, if the direct experience of those who are diagnosed with depression or social phobia is considered valuable information, why are we not accessing the same from those who have autism? I expect that this lack of input from direct experience invalidates the whole process of diagnosis . . . I am certain [the definition of autism] would not look the same if [people on the spectrum] had the opportunity to add their comments. (2000, p. 169)

Indeed, the *DSM-IV-TR* and other standard definitions of autism appear to communicate not only an "outsider" perspective but also one that is too heavily focused on impairments. In reading most definitions of autism, one learns only what a person cannot do and little about possible strengths or abilities. Are there strengths or abilities related to aspects of autism? Are there things that people on the spectrum do better than some of us, or most of us? These are pieces of the autism puzzle given far too little attention.

The language used in definitions and diagnosis is problematic for another reason. Leary and Hill (1996) pointed out that diagnostic language is often filled with assumptions that can be incorrect or even damaging. For instance, for the purpose of diagnosis, behaviors are often described with phrases such as "prefers to" or "unusual interest in" without specifying what particular symptoms may lead to that impression.

As Leary and Hill indicate, how can an observer (especially one who does not have an intimate knowledge of the child) know if a child "prefers" to play alone? Perhaps the child prefers to play with his sister but is playing alone because he cannot tolerate the smell of a lotion that his sister is wearing. Or, perhaps he is playing alone because he is not sure how to enter the game she is playing. Teachers, especially those who conduct student evaluations, must always be aware of the impact of the language they use and the assumptions they make. Is the learner hyper or active? Is the student demonstrating avoidance behaviors or is he taking a break? Does he prefer spending time with adults or does he just lack the skills to initiate social interactions?

Liane Holliday Willey, a woman with Asperger syndrome who disagrees with the ways in which she is often characterized, proposed a more sensitive and hopeful way to see individuals with autism spectrum labels:

> I only accept the term "disability" because it is the password that opens the doors to the support and intervention services we Aspies [people with Asperger syndrome] need if we are to meet our potential. If it was practical, I would wish the word away, at least when it is used in a sentence with AS. The word comes with too many negative images. Picture—powerless, incompetent, weak, helpless, pathetic, useless, and incapable. Think—hopeless and doomed. I will not buy into the notion that AS is a dead-end diagnosis. I like to say Aspies are not defective but that we are simply different; differently able, if you will. Yes, we have learning inefficiencies, but never are we without the ability to learn, grow, cope and progress. Pushed further, I would assert we Aspies are fine like we are, or at least we would be if only society would learn to be more accepting and empathetic toward the atypical. (2001, pp. 138–139)

Common Characteristics of Individuals with Autism

Although no two students with autism look, behave, communicate, or learn in the same way, students with autism do share some general characteristics. Some of the most significant characteristics are shared in this section, including movement differences, sensory differences, communication differences, social differences, learning differences, and interests and fascinations.

Movement Differences

Movement differences describe symptoms involving both excessive, atypical movement (Ringman & Jankovic, 2000) and the loss of typical movement. These difficulties may impede postures, actions, speech, thoughts, perceptions, emotions, and memories (Donnellan & Leary, 1995; Leary & Hill, 1996; Nayate, Bradshaw & Rinehart, 2005). Individuals with movement differences may walk with an uneven gait, engage in excessive movements (e.g., rocking, hand flapping, pacing), produce speech that is unintentional, stutter, or struggle to make transitions from room to room or situation to situation.

Many individuals with autism experience these movement problems constantly. As Kathy Xenia Grant shares, even the smallest tasks can take effort by those on the spectrum:

We don't realize how complex movement is. How complex of a movement just picking up a pen is. What parts of the body it goes through and what parts of the brain. A lot of us on the spectrum [have these] motor planning problems. (Hussman, Kluth, Strong, & Tweedy, 2009)

Although many people without autism struggle to combine thoughts and movements, engage in excessive pencil tapping or nail biting, get lost in repetitive or obsessive thoughts, or sing the same tune repeatedly without realizing it, they are seldom significantly affected by these experiences, but some students with autism may find these behaviors to be incredibly distracting and even overwhelming at times.

A movement difference can cause difficulties with the dynamics of movement such as in starting, executing (e.g., speed, control, target, rate), continuing, stopping, combining, or switching movements. The complexity of disturbed movements may range from simple to those affecting overall levels of activity and behavior. Many individuals who experience movement disturbance also report differences in internal mental processes such as perception, attention, consciousness, motivation, and emotion. For instance, Sue Rubin, a woman with autism, claims, "Autism is a way of life awash in emotions. Emotions rule me" (Hussman et al., 2009).

And different ways of moving are not only frustrating for the people who experience them but often confusing for those who observe them. According to Donnellan and Leary, atypical movements often mask the competence of individuals who exhibit them and may have an impact on a person's ability to communicate, relate to others, and be seen as competent. For example, they noted, "Delay in responding or inability to regulate movements may affect the ability to turn attention from one event to another in a timely fashion, or use conventional signs of communication" (1995, p. 42). In many cases, these movement differences are assumed by observers to be symptoms of intellectual impairment when they are actually problems with the body (Donnellan & Leary, 1995).

Understanding and recognizing movement differences can help teachers to better support students and to prevent them from making damaging assumptions about learners with autism. For instance, a teacher who is unaware of a learner's movement problems might assume that a student who is gazing up at the ceiling or pacing in the back of the room is not attending to a lecture. A teacher who is aware of the student's movement differences, however, may not jump to such a conclusion. A friend of mine, Christie, will stand up, screech, and run around the room when she gets together with her extended family. Because the family has become familiar with Christie's movement problems and because Christie has been able to explain some of her behavior, they do not assume she is asocial or unable to participate in the family's conversations. Instead, they assume that Christie is very interested in being part of the group but, because of the noise and commotion of the big group, she is struggling to keep her body quiet and organized. In other words, they recognize her activity as a physical problem, not an intellectual, behavioral, or emotional one.

Understanding movement problems like Christie's can help teachers interpret a student's actions sensitively, and, perhaps most critically, avoid making harmful assumptions. Consider, for example, how some people with autism describe their movement differences:

> I never really know when sounds are coming out of my mouth or when my arms need to move or when my legs need to run and jump. I also have a hard time controlling my thoughts when someone is not helping me focus. You see my mind is very active and thoughts jump around like popcorn being popped. I have very interesting thoughts. It's just that they keep firing off so fast that it's hard to stop them unless someone helps to focus my attention on something. You can imagine how hard it is to get anything done with a roller coaster mind without any clear destination. My eyes are unable to move up and down and left to right at will without me moving my head in the directions I'm facing. I can see things really well from the corner of my eyes. When I look at someone facing me sometimes I see three eyes instead of two, and it looks scarey [sic] so I avoid directly looking at people sometimes. This makes it hard for people to know whether I'm paying attention. (Fihe, 2000, p. 1)

> How to conduct myself when the body is constantly trying to find some stability? By this I mean to say that some times I felt that my body was made of just my head while sometimes I felt that it was made of just my legs. It was very difficult to feel the complete body when I was not doing anything. (Mukhopadhyay, 2000, p. 73)

> At school I was more direct in how I expressed my irritation and scorn, getting flushed, giggling uncontrollably, running around the room and biting my hand. (Blackman, 2001, p. 127)

> Stereotypical movements aren't things I decide to do for a reason; they're things that happen by themselves when I'm not paying attention to my body. (Cessaroni & Garber, as cited in Donnellan & Leary, 1995, p. 53)

> Constantly asking questions was another of my annoying fixations, and I'd ask the same question and wait with pleasure for the same answer—over and over again. If a particular topic intrigued me, I zeroed in on that subject and talked it into the ground. (Grandin, 1996a, p. 35)

> Sometimes I am just not able to contain my actions and myself. Ninety percent of an autistic person's efforts while in public are spent trying to avoid inappropriate behaviors that "normal" people seem to be able to easily suppress. One place where I had a terrible time trying to sit still and not make noise was in the small theater watching the play The Diviners.
> I didn't have a terrible time at the play, quite the contrary. In fact, I loved this play. Deep into the drama, I relaxed my guard and was soon a noisy, rocking back and forth in my seat, spectator. Good things don't often cause this reaction, so we might say that the

Ian Weatherbee behavior-o-meter registered a four-star reading for The Diviners and its excellent cast. (Weatherbee, 1999, p. 2)

> But I am not hurting anyone when I scream
> and I need to do it so much to get my balance
> perhaps one day I won't need it but now I am sure it
> is still important. (Sellin, 1995, p. 216)

Clearly, examining the concept of movement differences can bring new understanding to the struggles, abilities, and tendencies of people on the spectrum.

Sensory Differences

People with autism tend to have unusual sensory experiences. Students may exhibit hypo- or hyper-responses to visual, auditory, olfactory, gustatory, tactile, vestibular, and proprioceptive sensitivities; all of these can have an impact on a student's classroom performance and behavior (Kern et al., 2006; Myles et al., 2004). Among the sensory "violations" that people on the spectrum report are fluorescent or intense lighting, food with unappealing textures or tastes, speech that is too loud or too fast, unexpected or painful sounds, perfumes or strong odors, chaotic visual fields, rooms that are too warm or too cool, and scratchy clothing (Janzen, 2003; Myles, Cook, Miller, Rinner, & Robbins, 2000). To make matters more complicated, responses to sensory stimuli will change throughout the day, depending on each individual's "sensory threshold" (Aquilla, Yack, & Sutton, 2005, p. 202) or level of tolerance.

Jared Blackburn, a man with autism, described what these differences feel like and how they can cause discomfort, anxiety, and even pain:

> One common effect of these heightened senses is that autistic people are vulnerable to sensory overload with continued low-level bombardment. This may also result from too much emotional or social stimulation. Autistic people may become overloaded in situations that would not bother (or might even entertain) a normal person. When overloaded, autistic people have trouble concentrating, may feel tired or confused, and some may experience physical pain. Too much overload may lead to tantrums or emotional outburst. Another result of too much overload may be "shutdown," in which the person loses some or all of the person's normal functioning. Shutdown may feel different to different people, but is extremely unpleasant. (1997)

A student's sense of hearing, touch, smell, sight, or taste may be more sensitive or less sensitive than is typical. Remember, too, that every student will have a different sensory profile. So, although Blackburn's experiences may not be unusual for a person on the spectrum, his concerns may be very different than another person's concerns. To provide insight on sensory challenges that may be experienced in the classroom, I share some details on some of them here.

Tactile Sensitivity

One of my students could not tolerate being touched in a gentle way. If I brushed his hand or tried to guide him somewhere by lightly grasping his shoulder, he screamed as if in pain. If, instead, I gave him a firm handshake or thumped him on the back, he appeared unaffected. This is just one example of how tactile sensitivity can affect students with autism. Tactile sensitivities may be apparent across activities and environments and may affect the way students use space (e.g., avoiding touching or working near others), work with supplies (e.g., avoiding or preferring certain materials), and interact with others (e.g., craving or avoiding hugs).

Auditory Sensitivity

The hearing of individuals is also often affected by their autism. Students may be bothered by sounds that teachers cannot even detect. Tyler Fihe, a young man with autism, reported that he hears things other cannot:

For example, I can be in one room of the house and hear what my mother is saying on the telephone even when she has the door shut. There are also certain sounds that are painful to listen to like the microwave, the telephone ring, lawnmowers, leaf blowers, the blender, babies crying, vacuum cleaners, and my mom's VW Vanagon when it just starts up. (Fihe, 2000, p. 1)

As Fihe pointed out, a range of noises and sounds may cause a person with autism distress, including those that may seem benign to most. For instance, a student might be completely distressed by the sound of an eraser rubbing on paper or frightened by the hissing of a radiator. Many people with autism also have trouble understanding conversation or verbal directions. My friend, Kathy Xenia Grant, for example, has noted that, for her, conversation partners often sound like the wordless teacher in Charlie Brown's classroom (Hussman et al., 2009).

Visual Sensitivity

Students with autism may be sensitive to certain types of light, colors, or patterns. As one individual with autism described, visual sensitivity may not only have a negative impact on the person's sensory system but can also cause him or her to become fearful or anxious:

It may be because things that I see do not always make the right impression that I am frightened of so many things that can be seen: people, particularly their faces, very bright lights, crowds, things moving suddenly. Large machines and buildings that are unfamiliar, unfamiliar places, my own shadow, the dark, bridges, rivers, canals, streams, and the sea. (Jolliffe et al., as cited in Attwood, 2007, p. 285)

Teachers should watch to see if a student seems bothered by things she sees in the classroom (e.g., a certain poster, a bulletin board). Even the color of the walls in the classroom can bother a student's sensory system.

Olfactory Sensitivity

Students with autism also may have a heightened or otherwise different sense of smell. The individual may find some smells unbearable and others pleasant, helpful, or calming. For instance, one of my former students avoided any teacher who wore perfume but loved to smell the hair of a fellow student who used strawberry shampoo. Students with olfactory sensitivity may struggle with any number of odors in the school, including art or craft supplies, class pets, cleaning products, food, and science chemicals.

Communication Differences

Many students with autism have communication differences that affect speech and language, and many use few or no spoken words. For students who do speak, their speech may have unusual qualities. For instance, a student may have atypical speech intonation or use repetitive speech (echoing the words of others). Furthermore, conversational timing and rhythm may be difficult for someone with autism to learn or use. Students might also struggle with using language. Some students, for instance, have difficulties using pronouns or learning the rules of conversation. Others may find figurative language (e.g., jokes, metaphors) hard to decipher.

Students with autism may have difficulties with expressive or receptive communication. That is, they may have trouble sharing thoughts and ideas or struggle to understand what they hear or see. Many students experience difficulties with both receptive and expressive communication.

Individuals with autism are increasingly finding communication success through the use of various teaching strategies and technologies, including facilitated typing and writing, picture communication systems, and augmentative and alternative communication devices (see Beukelman & Mirenda, 2006; Biklen, 1990, 2005; Bondy & Frost, 2002; Crossley, 1997; Mukhopadhyay, 2003; Stoner et. al, 2006; Thunberg, Sandberg, & Ahlsén, 2009). These techniques, interestingly, are not only giving students access to words, but in many cases are also changing the ways educators, families, and researchers think about the abilities and potential of students with autism.

Social Differences

A common stereotype is that students with autism are not interested in social relationships. John Elder Robison, the author of the runaway bestseller, *Look Me in the Eye*, explains that in his case, nothing could have been further from the truth:

> Many descriptions of autism and Asperger's describe people like me as "not wanting to connect with others" or "preferring to play alone." I can't speak for other kids but I'd like to be very clear about my own feelings. *I did not ever* want *to be alone*. And all of those child psychologists who said, "John prefers to play by himself," were dead wrong. I played by myself because I was a failure at playing with others. I was alone as a result of my own limitations, and being alone was one of the bitterest disappointments of my young life. (2007, p. 211)

Daniel Tammet* shares a similar sentiment about social concerns:

> People with Asperger syndrome do want to make friends but find it very difficult to do so. The keen sense of isolation is something I felt very deeply and was very painful for me. (2006, p. 78)

Stories such as these are more common than some might believe. The characterization of the person on the spectrum as aloof or disconnected is as pervasive as it is potentially damaging. Although some individuals with autism do report that they need time alone or find some social situations challenging, some of these same individuals also claim that they crave social interaction and friendship. That is, it is possible for a person with autism to both struggle with and want relationships. In fact, some individuals with autism claim that being with people is not challenging but it is the social settings themselves that make being with others difficult. For instance, my friend, Theola, values the one-to-one relationships she has with her sisters, nieces, and nephews but cannot tolerate family events such as weddings, birthdays, and graduation parties because of the noise, the bright lights, and the confusion of the games, dances, and rituals that go with the celebrations.

Others find social situations difficult because they lack the skills necessary for successful social interactions. For instance, individuals with autism may not be very good at reading subtle social signals. If a person begins putting on his or her jacket, most people would read this as a signal that the individual is getting ready to end the conversation and go home. For some individuals with autism, reading these signs is a real challenge.

---

*Reprinted with permission of The Free Press, a Division of Simon & Schuster, Inc., from BORN ON A BLUE DAY: Inside the Extraordinary Mind of an Autistic Savant by Daniel Tammet. Copyright © 2006 by Daniel Tammet. All rights reserved.

Another common social problem for individuals on the spectrum is understanding pragmatics or the use of language in a social context. John Elder Robison, the man who lamented social perceptions others had of him earlier in this section, shares his many social struggles throughout his book. One that he explains in great detail is his inability to master small talk and to engage in the types of polite questions acquaintances sometimes exchange:

Normal people seem to learn certain stock questions and utter them to fill a conversational void. For example, when meeting someone they have not seen in a while, they say things like:
"How's your wife?"
"How's your son?"
"You're looking good—did you lose weight?"
Normal people will emit statements like this in the absence of any provocation, or any visual indication that there may have been a change in the wife or son or the weight. Some people I've observed appear to have dozens of these stock questions at their command and I have never been able to figure out how they choose a particular phrase for emission at any given moment. (2007, pp. 192–193)

Other challenges that students with autism may have with pragmatics include difficulty shifting topics and initiating and repairing conversations, not seeing how and when others initiate conversations, providing the appropriate level of detail or information during a conversation, and reacting to or integrating the comments or reactions of conversation partners when speaking in a group.

It must also be noted that misunderstandings and social confusion are not only problems of those on the spectrum. At times, students with autism may also struggle socially because those around them don't understand their attempts to be social or to interact. For example, one of my former students, Donna, often ripped paper from her notebook, crumpled it into a ball, and tossed it at her classmates. Students reprimanded Donna for this behavior and told her repeatedly, "Donna, don't throw garbage at your friends." When I told Donna's mother about the behavior, however, she gasped and then laughed. She then explained that Donna was imitating her brothers; when her older brothers wanted to play with her, they crumpled paper into little balls and pretended to shoot baskets through hoops they made with their outstretched arms. In Donna's house, play could be initiated by throwing paper in someone's direction; the appropriate response, of course, was to arc your arms to make a "basket" for the shooter. From Donna's perspective, she was behaving perfectly appropriately; it was her classmates who lacked social awareness!

Lucy Blackman, a woman with autism, emphasized the importance of realizing the different ways that students initiate social contact and interaction:

For me, successful "social" contact depended on someone else interpreting my own signals. Some of my attempts at communication were fairly conventional, as when I put my arms up towards a person with my hands stretched up because I desperately needed to be picked up or lifted over an obstacle. However Jay noted that if I turned my hands outward when I put my arms up to her, I was asking for a boost for a somersault, rather than some help in climbing up. If she interpreted wrongly, things could get very noisy. (2001, p. 11)

Blackman illustrates the need to exercise caution when interpreting any behavior. In her case, what may have seemed like a simple request to be moved or helped actually meant, "Play with me!," a sweet social request likely often missed by those who did not know her intimately.

Learning Differences

As well as the communication, sensory, movement, and other differences autism can cause, many individuals on the spectrum report that they have learning difficulties or learning differences. For example, Donna Williams, an author with autism, related that she has many different types of processing difficulties. She refers to one category as "sorry, wrong address" or "misfires":

Messages can be sorted inefficiently so that they are related badly. This is like putting a call through to the wrong number or the next-door-neighbor's house instead of your house.

These are what I call "misfires." Some examples of these in my own life have been where I've come up with words or names that have a similar shape, pattern or rhythm to one I am trying to recall without being similar in meaning. I've had this trouble with names such as Margaret and Elizabeth because they seem to have the same feel and seem similar to me.

In the same way, I've said things like "I want my shoes" when I meant "I want my jacket" and been surprised to get things I apparently asked for. (1996, p. 89)

And Sue Rubin, a woman with autism, reported that she has significant problems with memory:

I have a deficit in my thinking and I don't know if it is common in autism or is just unique to me. When I remember events, I can't tell if they really happened or I imagined them. I can actually picture events in my mind and I am sure they are real until someone points out that they couldn't have happened. Awash in embarrassment, I realize that I imagined the event. I even worry about imagined events that I think really happened. Waking nightmares may be a good description. Lasting problems can result from this. The problem with my memory does not affect my schoolwork. I learn what is in my books, what the professor says, and what everyone says in class. I admit I still have problems with assignments. I need someone to write them down for me because I cannot recall them. Assume my forgetting assignments is much worse than normal people's forgetting. (1998, p. 3)

Although many of the problems students have traditionally had are assumed to be problems with intellect, they are, in fact, remarkably similar to the types of struggles reported by individuals with learning disabilities (Gilroy & Miles, 1996; Kurtz, 2006; Mooney & Cole, 2000; Smith & Strick, 1997). In other words, teachers may assume that a student does not or cannot give a correct answer or respond to a direction correctly because he or she is incapable of understanding the task. In many instances, however, the student does not or cannot perform because of the way in which the information is presented, heard, or processed.

Interests or Fascinations

Many individuals with autism have a deep interest in one or a variety of topics. Some interests are commonly seen across individuals with autism (e.g., transportation, electronics); others seem more unique to an individual person (Kluth & Schwarz, 2008; Winter-Meissiers, 2007). For instance, Sean Barron, a man with autism, once had a great interest in the number 24. At another point in his life, he became fascinated by dead-end streets (Barron & Barron, 1992). Phil Dougherty (2006) shares that his daughter, Jenny, has been, at different times, fascinated with slugs, fire alarms, and recycling symbols.

Unfortunately, these special "loves" that students bring to schools are not always celebrated or sometimes even tolerated. Many a meeting has been planned and many a behavior program has been written to squelch a student's fascination. As a person with more than a few compulsions of my own—hoarding Sharpie markers, watching the same action movie several times a month, obsessing about anything made of taffeta—I cannot and do not want to imagine what it is like to have another person manage my "favorites" for me.

Willey cautioned that it can be dangerous for people without autism to pass judgment about someone else's special interests. In fact, she noted, in many ways and in many circles, having intense interests is considered positive and even admirable.

At the base I have to wonder, are we so very different from marathon athletes, corporate presidents, bird watchers, or new parents counting every breath their newborn takes? It seems lots of people, NT [neurotypical] or otherwise, have an obsession of sorts. In my mind, that reality rests as a good one, for obsessions in and out of themselves are not bad habits. There is much good about them. Obsessions take focus and tenacious study. They are the stuff greatness needs. I have to believe the best of the remarkable—the artists, musicians, philosophers, scientists, writers, researchers and athletes—had to obsess on their chosen fields or they would never had become great. (2001, p. 122)

Luke Jackson criticized that it seems okay for people without disability labels to have these interests in our society, but not those with labels:

I have a question for teenagers here.

Q: When is an obsession not an obsession?
A: When it is about football.

How unfair is that? It seems that our society fully accepts the fact that a lot of men and boys "eat, sleep, and breathe" football, and people seem to think that if someone doesn't, then they are not fully male. Stupid! (2002, p. 47)

Jackson noted the rigidity of society when it comes to issues of difference and normalcy:

I am sure if a parent went to a doctor and said that their teenage boy wouldn't shut up about football, they would laugh and tell them that it was perfectly normal. It seems as if we all have to be the same. Why can no one see that the world just isn't like that? I would like everyone to talk about computers all day actually, but I don't expect them to and people soon tell me to shut up. (2002, pp. 47–48)

In keeping with the suggestions from Willey and Jackson, teachers may want to allow the student with a specific fascination the time and space to pursue it if it is not disrupting the student's education or hurting him or her. Students often need favorite materials, activities, behaviors, and interests to relax, focus, or make connections with others. In addition, students often will find their own ways of regulating their compulsions when left to do so.

Of course, some students want and need help restricting behaviors or time spent with fascinations, especially if they are dangerous or inappropriate (e.g., touching the clothing of other people). Some individuals with autism will have a desire to spend less time with or to get rid of these interests; in these instances, the teachers should support the student in doing so. It is important to emphasize, however, that this process should be done in a respectful way and always in collaboration with the student.

Willey suggested talking to the student with autism about the "good and bad parts of obsessing." She shared a story of how she has helped her daughter, who has Asperger syndrome, learn how to live in concert with her interests.

Slowly, patiently, with tiny steps we are trying to help her find the good and the bad parts of obsessing. "It is good to play with your monkey collection when you feel badly about something that happened at school," we tell her. "Of course you can buy that book about monkeys because you worked hard to control your temper this whole week," we will say. "No, you cannot sort your monkeys right now, not until your homework is finished," we remind her. In time, she will do these things for herself. In time, she will know on her own how to share her life with her obsession. (2001, p. 125)

If the student is not interested in moving away from his or her interests, the teacher should proceed with caution. In many cases, some people in the student's life may want an interest to recede when the student does not. Eugene Marcus, a writer, teacher, and advocate with autism, has indicated that fascinations and interests often serve important purposes in the lives of individuals with autism. He has stressed that, when possible, individuals with autism should be allowed to assess and control their own interests, compulsions, or fascinations:

My own view is that my life is enriched and made livable by the habits that enslave me. My feeling is that my enslavement is a voluntary one in that nobody else forces me to be compulsive, or even gives me permission to be compulsive.

My wish is to one day be free of my compulsions, but not any day soon. By being an inconvenient and loud slave to compulsion, I have learned things I never would have through silent cooperation. I have tested the limits of my real and unreal friends (even those people who wanted to be my friends, but only when I was play-acting a role—not being myself). My compulsive behavior has allowed me to set my own agenda in situations where the most I could have hoped for was "eats and treats." My compulsive behavior is a long-playing defense against well meaning people who cannot guess what I really am thinking of or wishing for. How can I be a non-compulsive person but also not compulsively agreeable? Because I can see that in compulsive agreeing is a big risk of losing my path and my dreams. (2002, p. 8)

The Social Construction of Autism

This chapter would not be complete without considering the role society plays in "constructing" disability. Many individuals with autism have experienced difficulties due to societal and cultural ideas of how people should look, communicate, interact, move, and behave. That is, autism is—in part—a social construction; it is a phenomenon that is created and recreated by popular media, schools, the medical community, and many other entities and influences.

Although most people with autism will tell you that "it" is real, that they do experience things in different ways, that their bodies are uncooperative, or that they have sensory or communication problems, it might also be suggested that autism is in some ways exacerbated by an inflexible society. For instance, people may feel that they have more or less of a disability on any given day based on whether appropriate supports are provided for them or whether they are expected to communicate in a conventional way. Jonathan McNabb, a man with autism, suggested that "neurotypical" individuals (people without autism) stop assuming that difference means deviance and start understanding the autistic experience from those who live with it:

Personally I find the basic stumbling block on which all the other issues stem is the assumption most Neurotypical people have that Neurotypical worldview is neutral and normative. The Neurotypical world is presented as a given. I would be very surprised if many would be aware of it being an issue. Autism is then seen in contrast to this given, natural, neutral, and normal society. The person with autism is then judged on his or her ability to conform to the values and standards of society.

The autistic person is then in the position of being in a society which does not understand autism and where the defining of autism [is] controlled by those who have regularly not helped the position of autistic people and indeed much of the time have hindered them. The autistic person is then placed in position of how to cope within such a society. There are numerous solutions, some which are better for the person than others. Many are forced to take the pioneer role. (2001, p. 1)

In other words, disability is created or illuminated when we have rigid values about the "right way" to do things, when we fail to provide appropriate support, or when we expect all individuals to need the same things.

When an individual's participation or inclusion seems impossible, it often is because a context has not been created for participation. When a student with autism needs space to relax, extra time to make the transition between classes, or support from a peer, and these accommodations are provided, ability is emphasized and disability is diminished.

To illustrate the narrow ways in which individuals without identified disabilities often perceive ability, the "Institute for the Study of the Neurologically Typical," a parody web site assembled by people with autism and Asperger syndrome, offers another way of seeing autism (http://isnt.autistics.org). The creators of the site have imagined a world where autism is the norm and being so-called "typical" is a problem. Sit for a moment on the other side of the teacher's desk and consider this passage from the site:

Neurotypical syndrome is a neurobiological disorder characterized by preoccupation with social concerns, delusions of superiority, and obsession with conformity. Neurotypical individuals often assume that their experience of the world is either the only one, or the only correct one. NTs find it difficult to be alone. NTs are often intolerant of seemingly minor differences in others. When in groups NTs are socially and behaviorally rigid and frequently insist on the performance of dysfunctional, destructive, and even impossible rituals as a way of maintaining group identity. NTs find it difficult to communicate directly, and have a much higher incidence of lying as compared with persons on the autistic spectrum. NT is believed to be genetic in origin. Autopsies have shown the brain of the neurotypical is typically smaller than that of an autistic individual and may have overdeveloped areas related to social behavior. (Institute for the Study of the Neurologically Typical, 2002)

Summary

Until the movie *Rain Man* (Johnson & Levinson, 1988) was released, few people knew what autism was and fewer still knew a person with that label. Although the much-acclaimed motion picture gave the average person a glimpse into this little-understood diagnosis, it also provided Americans with a range of stereotypes about autism. In the wake of the film, many viewers came to believe that everyone with autism could recite the phone book or count cards like a Las Vegas professional. Today, more than 2 decades after the movie's debut, people's awareness of the autism spectrum has increased greatly. Because of widespread deinstitutionalization; the growth of community living and employment for people with disabilities; the expanded use of assistive technology and augmentative and alternative communication for individuals on the spectrum; the proliferation of advocacy groups both nationally and in local communities; and more accurate and varied accounts of people with autism in biographies, autobiographies, magazines, motion pictures, and television; Americans understand more about autism than they ever have before. And, because of the inclusive schooling movement, an increased emphasis on learning about differences in the classroom, and more accurate and varied accounts of students with autism in preservice textbooks and in teacher preparation classes, more classroom teachers are learning about how to educate students with autism.

As I share in the introduction to this chapter, many educators are also learning about autism from their students. This chapter can certainly serve as a primer, but the best way to find success with a learner with autism is to get to know that individual and his or her family. If a student can express him- or herself through speech or writing, this can be an avenue for meeting the student and learning something about autism. If the student cannot communicate reliably, the teacher will learn about the student by observing, teaching, and interacting with him or her. As Jasmine Lee O'Neill pointed out, getting to know students, honoring their individuality, and helping them to feel at home in the classroom is as important as anything else teachers may do:

> Many autistic people affectionately, humorously refer to themselves as aliens. They feel displaced on a vast planet, which has a code of life, and understanding they can't ever quite subscribe to. If they are welcomed, however, and cherished as the individuals they are, then there wouldn't be as much dissension on both sides. Aliens can become more comfortable and less paralyzed in fear, while still remaining who they are. Their essence stays the same. Then they don't have to despise their alien status, as if it were forced upon them. Instead, they can enjoy their uniqueness, just as others enjoy theirs. (1999, p. 125)

FOR MORE ANSWERS AND INFORMATION

📖 Books

Attwood, T. (2007). *The complete guide to Asperger's syndrome.* Philadelphia: Jessica Kingsley.

Biklen, D. (2005). *Autism and the myth of the person alone.* New York: NYU Press.

Carley, J.M. (2008). *Asperger's from the inside out: A supportive and practical guide for anyone with Asperger's syndrome.* New York: Perigee Trade.

Donnellan, A., & Leary, M. (1995). *Movement differences and diversity in autism/mental retardation: Appreciating and accommodating people with communication and behavior challenges.* Madison, WI: DRI Press.

Kluth, P. (2009). *Teaching students with autism and Asperger's syndrome in the inclusive classroom* [laminated reference guide]. Port Chester, NY: National Professional Resources.

Kluth, P., & Shouse, J. (2009). *The autism checklist.* San Francisco: Jossey-Bass.

McGinnity, K., & Negri, N. (2005). *Walk awhile in my autism.* Cambridge, WI: Cambridge Book Review Press.

Parish, R. (2008). *Embracing autism: Connecting and communicating with children in the autism spectrum.* San Francisco: Jossey-Bass.

Shore, S. (Ed.). (2004). *Ask and tell: Self-advocacy and disclosure for people on the autism spectrum.* Philadelphia: Jessica Kingsley Publishers.

Willey, L.H. (2003). *Asperger syndrome in adolescence.* Philadelphia: Jessica Kingsley.

(continued)

(continued)

🛍 Web Sites

The Autism Acceptance Project
http://www.taaproject.com

> This is a rich and varied web site that contains articles and artwork written by people with autism and a blog written by Estée Klar-Wolfond, the mother of a child with autism.

Autistics.org
http://autistics.org

> This must-visit web site is filled with resources for learning about autism through the eyes of those with the label. It contains several essays and offers blogspace for those on the spectrum.

GRASP (The Global and Regional Asperger Syndrome Partnership)
http://www.grasp.org

> GRASP's mission is to improve the lives of those on the spectrum; the site is a great resource for teen students on the spectrum as well as for teachers.

Neurodiversity.com
http://neurodiversity.com

> This web site was created to help reduce the difficulties experienced by children and adults with autism, who often "face extraordinary challenges . . . made more difficult by others' unrealistic expectations and demands, negative judgments, harassment and economic marginalization."

NOTES: _____

_____

_____

_____

_____

_____

_____

_____

_____

_____

_____

Understanding Inclusive Schooling

The idea of school inclusion can be a lousy or a lovely happiness. It's really all in the hands of the teachers along with the permission of the big boss, the superintendent. Teachers must be willing to not just give me a desk and then leave me to fill the chair. I need to be asked questions, and given time for my thoughtful answers. Teachers need to become as a conductor, and then guide me through the many places I may get lost. (Burke, 2005, p. 253)

Inclusive schooling stresses interdependence and independence, views all students as capable and complex, and values a sense of community (Doyle, 2008; Falvey, Givner, & Kimm, 1995; Sapon-Shevin, 2007). According to Udvari-Solner, it also promotes civil rights and equity in the classroom.

> [Inclusive schooling] propels a critique of contemporary school culture and thus, encourages practitioners to reinvent what can be and should be to realize more humane, just and democratic learning communities. Inequities in treatment and educational opportunity are brought to the forefront, thereby fostering attention to human rights, respect for difference and value of diversity. (1997, p. 142)

Like Udvari-Solner, I define inclusive education as something that supports and benefits all learners. I also see it as a social action and political movement. If "inequities in treatment and educational opportunity are brought to the forefront," for instance, teachers and community members might question practices such as tracking and standardized testing that segregate, stratify, and often harm students. If schools create "more humane, just, and democratic learning communities," then all students will be valued and seen as essential members of the school, including students from all racial and ethnic groups, students new to the school, students using English as a second language, and students who identify themselves as gay or lesbian. Inclusion is more than a set of strategies or practices, it is an educational orientation that respects and builds on the uniqueness that each learner brings to the classroom.

Characteristics of Inclusive Schools

Although every inclusive school will have a different look and feel, schools dedicated to serving all students will share some characteristics. Specifically, these schools will have committed leadership, democratic classrooms, reflective educators, a supportive school culture, engaging and relevant curricula, and responsive instruction.

Committed Leadership

Administrators, school board members, and teachers in leadership positions (e.g., department chairs) play a critical role in inclusive schools (Keyes, 1996; Riehl, 2000; Theoharis, 2009) by articulating a vision for inclusive schooling, building support for the vision, and working with the school community to implement strategies and principles that make the school successful. (See Table 2.1 for a list of practices, beliefs, and values for diverse, inclusive schools.) In fact, Trump and Hange (1996) found that administrative leadership was considered by teachers to be the greatest support or the greatest obstacle to the success and development of inclusive schooling.

In a study conducted by Udvari-Solner and Keyes, administrators who were identified as leaders of inclusive education claimed that they needed to have courage to "relentlessly pose the difficult, the contrary, the controversial, and the seemingly unanswerable questions" (2000, p. 450). In addition, these principals and central office administrators stressed the importance of expressing their own personal values. Sue Abplanalp, a principal in the study, shared that she felt that being open and honest about her own beliefs was critical to the development of an inclusive community in her school:

> I guess the most important thing I can do is be an advocate by voicing my opinion, modeling and letting teachers know about best practices, and [by continuing to ask] myself the same question when I am not sure about what to do: is this in the best interest of the child? . . . I have a desire to be an advocate for equality, regardless of age, disability, race, religion, sexual orientation, ability, gender, and anything else I forgot. It's part of my vision for justice. (2000, p. 442)

Administrators and other leaders help students, staff, and the local community understand inclusion as a philosophy or ideology that will permeate the school; they help staff members when new ways of "doing business" are adopted; they provide encouragement and support as teachers take risks and try new approaches; they educate families and community members about the school's beliefs and their inclusive mission; and they help to celebrate day-to-day successes and problem-solve day-to-day struggles (Theoharis, 2009; Van Dyke, Stallings, & Colley,

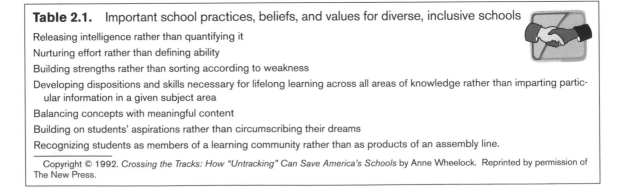

Table 2.1. Important school practices, beliefs, and values for diverse, inclusive schools

Releasing intelligence rather than quantifying it

Nurturing effort rather than defining ability

Building strengths rather than sorting according to weakness

Developing dispositions and skills necessary for lifelong learning across all areas of knowledge rather than imparting particular information in a given subject area

Balancing concepts with meaningful content

Building on students' aspirations rather than circumscribing their dreams

Recognizing students as members of a learning community rather than as products of an assembly line.

Copyright © 1992. *Crossing the Tracks: How "Untracking" Can Save America's Schools* by Anne Wheelock. Reprinted by permission of The New Press.

Table 2.2.   Questions that can be used for staff interviews in K–12 schools

What are your beliefs about inclusive education?

What does our school's mission statement mean to you?

What experiences have you had teaching and supporting students with [autism, intellectual disabilities] in inclusive classrooms?

In your past job, describe your role on collaborative teams for students with disabilities.

Do you have examples of lesson plans or other materials that reflect your skills in inclusive practices?

From Jorgensen, C.M., McSheehan, M., & Sonnenmeier, R.M. (2009). *The beyond access model: Promoting membership, participation, and learning for students with disabilities in the general education classroom* (p. 212). Baltimore: Paul H. Brookes Publishing Co; reprinted by permission.

1995). They also communicate their commitment by putting inclusive schooling and "success for all" front and center in hiring decisions. After all, it will be impossible to cultivate an inclusive school if new teachers do not support and even embrace the existing vision. See Table 2.2 for examples of questions that can be used for staff interviews in K–12 schools.

One example of how administrators can inspire and shepherd change comes from a Chicago Public Schools team I have supported for several years. When new leaders were hired, they brought a team together to discuss the school's inclusive schooling model. The administrators and staff members discussed general and specific goals and objectives, talked about their dreams and nightmares for their school, watched DVDs on school reform, had various staff members share ideas for increasing collaboration and honing skills in differentiated instruction, and celebrated with food and conversation. They continued meeting in this manner for three consecutive summers to continually tweak and enhance their model and their services. In this school, a philosophy of inclusion and the valuing of diversity was apparent from the first day that new leaders took their positions. This belief system was then actualized daily as the team worked on shared goals, aligned their instruction with these goals, and increased the capacity of staff members to coach and support one another. See Figure 2.1 for a form that this team and these leaders used to develop and polish their inclusive practices, and see Table 2.3 for more ideas administrators can use to improve and grow their inclusive schooling models.

Democratic Classrooms

Cunat defined democratic education as "the vital and dynamic process of a learning community that recognizes and validates the individuality and responsibility of each participant" (1996, p. 130). He argued the following:

> The overall purpose of democratic education is to engage individuals in a process that will help them develop the skills and attitudes necessary to become people who can and will contribute to the making of a vital, equitable, and humane society. (p. 130)

Table 2.3.   Actions administrators can take to improve their inclusive schooling models

Integrate the elements of inclusive schooling into your school improvement plan.

Attend local, regional, and national conferences related to inclusive schooling (e.g., TASH, PEAK, PEAL, Inclusion Works!).

Present at local, regional, and national conferences related to inclusive schooling.

Visit other inclusive schools, and invite faculty members from other inclusive schools to visit your school.

Organize a teachers' book club with selections related to inclusive schooling.

Write about inclusion for blogs, newsletters, magazines, newspapers, or other publications.

Develop a web site about inclusion.

Ask students how to make the school more inclusive.

Ask the parent–teacher organization to address issues related to barriers, school culture, and collaboration.

Write a grant to launch an inclusion-related project or reform.

Inclusive School Goal Setting

Instructions:

- Consider what outcomes you want to achieve in the coming year. Be as specific as you can. For instance, it is more clear to state that you "want every staff member to co-teach a lesson" than to say that you want to "increase the amount of co-teaching at your school."

- Keep in mind academic goals (e.g., increasing test scores), social goals (e.g., decreasing bullying-related incidents), goals related to school climate or culture (e.g., increasing community building opportunities), goals related to school structure (e.g., eliminating special education spaces), and goals related to enrollment or placement (e.g., getting more students into inclusive classrooms).

Goal	Date we will achieve our goal	Date to review or update our goal	Individual(s) who will assess our progress
Educate all students with disabilities in their neighborhood schools	September 1, 2010	January 14, 2011	Dr. Kim & principals

Figure 2.1. Goal-setting form for inclusive schools.

How does this kind of democracy look in practice? In a democratic classroom, students often "run the show." Consider a lesson in which the teacher works with small groups of students to present different aspects of content to each. The teacher serves as a coach or advisor to the groups as students work to construct materials and design instruction that inspires and educates their peers. Students are active in constructing knowledge as they move from searching the web at the computer station, to interviewing local experts on their cellphones, to reading primary sources, to developing a three-dimensional model that will eventually be used in a presentation their group makes to the class. Throughout these activities, the teacher consults with students, asking them how much time they should spend on the projects, engaging them in critical conversation about their work, and prompting them to evaluate the experience.

Students in democratic classrooms often share ideas, make rules, question classroom practices, help to create curriculum, and make decisions about their learning and their environment. A teacher interested in making his or her classroom more democratic might ask the following questions (Kluth, Diaz-Greenberg, Thousand, & Nevin, 2002):

- How are rules set and enforced? Are rules constructed collaboratively by the teacher and the students?

- What does the classroom environment look like? When a visitor glances around the room, does the space appear to be a teacher's space (e.g., work displayed is chosen by the teacher) or a space shared by a classroom community?

- Can students question decisions made by the teacher? Are students viewed as decision makers in the classroom?

- Who makes decisions regarding curriculum? Does the teacher make all of the decisions? Do students ever construct curriculum?

In democratic classrooms, students and teachers work as a team to educate one another and to co-create understanding of their shared world (Scarlett, Ponte, & Singh, 2009; Singer, 2009). Thus, a student with autism might educate her teachers about her own needs and strengths. She might write a letter to teachers on "how to help me in the classroom," create a podcast about her challenges and desired supports, or make her own adaptations for certain lessons.

Reflective Educators

When one enters an effective inclusive school, teachers can often be seen asking critical questions, observing one another, critiquing lessons, and sharing stories of their practice. To put it another way, teachers in inclusive schools are reflective. According to Henderson, this means

> They willingly embrace their decision-making responsibilities, and they regularly reflect on problems they confront, and maybe they make mistakes, but they never stop trying. They are sincere and thoughtful professionals who constantly learn from their reflective experiences. They understand that receptiveness to further learning is the key to continued professional development and validity. (1992, p. 2)

In essence, this means, the reflective teacher is above all else . . . teachable!

Although most teachers reflect on their work often—as they are driving to school or while they are working with a student—these incidents do not always result in learning or a deeper understanding of their work. Reflective teaching as it is being discussed here is not just the practice of remembering, rehashing, or musing. John Dewey (1910) suggested that those engaging in reflective action must bring to the act openmindedness, responsibility, thoughtfulness, and caution.

Nirua Regiane Henk proposed a sequence for reflection that can help teachers move beyond the logical and rational. She suggested beginning with an area of focus and selecting tools (e.g., journal, video clips) to help with the study of the issue or event. Next, the teacher should describe the event or focus area in as much detail as possible. This process is followed by asking "why" questions about the event in order to understand it from different perspectives. Although some of this work can be done effectively by individuals, many teachers enjoy and prefer to engage in these exercises with colleagues. To encourage reflective teaching, some schools are now sponsoring discussion groups, professional reading circles, action research projects, peer teaching and mentoring, and other unique professional development activities that inspire contemplation.

Supportive School Culture

Often, the culture of a school is apparent to visitors the moment they walk in the front door. School outsiders can learn a lot about a school by the ways the walls are covered, the types of teacher conversations overheard in the hallways, and the ways in which students are engaged. All of these elements are aspects of school culture (Beaudoin & Taylor, 2004; Fullan & Hargreaves, 1996; Peterson & Deal, 2009).

Fullan and Hargreaves described school culture as the

> Guiding beliefs and expectations evident in the way a school operates, particularly in reference to how people relate (or fail to relate) to each other. In simple terms, culture is the way we do things and relate to each other around here. (1996, p. 3)

If the school culture is open, accepting, and caring, inclusive schooling can thrive. If the school culture is competitive, individualistic, and authoritative, however, teachers will find it impossible to grow inclusive schooling. Cultivating a safe, positive, and robust school culture may be the most difficult piece of creating an inclusive school, but it is also, perhaps, the most critical piece. School leaders and educators concerned with creating an inclusive school culture might implement the following practices:

- "Advertise" their commitment to celebrating diversity and valuing the participation of all (see Figure 2.2 for an example of this).

- Hold informal brown-bag lunches with small groups of teachers, staff members, students, and parents.

- Invite parents and community members to visit classrooms, help with projects, and serve as resources.

- Use suggestion boxes or host electronic discussion boards to give the community opportunites to give input.

- Make time for school celebrations, both small and large.

Peterson (2002) shared the story of how one principal was able to shape the culture of a new school by bringing her staff together to celebrate professional growth. Shelby Cosner, the first principal of Wisconsin Hills Middle School in Brookfield, Wisconsin, scheduled regular "D" Days (staff development days) every other week. The teachers shared food, a symbol of collegiality and celebration, as they studied new approaches to differentiating instruction.

Figure 2.2. Poster on the wall of an inclusive school.

During these meetings, staff also shared personal and professional stories. Eventually, the storytelling became a competition, with the teachers voting for the best story of the day.

Engaging and Relevant Curricula

Teachers in inclusive classrooms must design curricula and instruction and engineer classroom activities that are personally and culturally appropriate, and engage a range of learning styles suitable for learners with various talents and interests. This is critical not only for students with autism but for every learner in the classroom.

Children undoubtedly grow and learn from the daily curricula and also from the ways in which schools respond to difference. Therefore, teachers demonstrating good inclusion practices design curriculum and engage in pedagogy that reflects the diversity found in classrooms and communities. Units of study must be meaningful, themes of investigation must be motivating, and content must be appropriately challenging. Classroom materials should also be engaging to a wide variety of students. The classroom library must include books written by and about people with individual and group differences, for example. Furthermore, classroom lessons should include information about the diverse groups represented by the students. A teacher might achieve this by providing information about Patton's learning challenges during a lesson on World War II or by discussing the complexity and diversities of Chinese cultures when exploring the work of author Amy Tan.

Responsive Instruction

Teachers in inclusive classrooms are concerned about reaching and motivating all learners. In the best cases, they are versed in adapting materials, lesson formats, instructional arrangements, curricular goals, and teaching strategies (Tomlinson & Strickland, 2005; Udvari-Solner, 1996; VanSciver, 2005) and can meet both the academic and social needs of students. Therefore, a teacher in an inclusive classroom might give a struggling student some leadership opportunities in the school, find a community internship for a student needing enrichment, give personal checklists to those who need help with organization, structure cooperative learning lessons so active learners have time to move and share, or give a student with autism opportunities to complete an independent project based on a special interest area.

The idea that students learn in different ways or different styles is now widely accepted within the literature, if not uniformly implemented in practice (Armstrong, 1997; Cole, 2008; Gardner, 2006; Kliewer, 1998; Ladson-Billings, 2009; Nieto & Bode, 2008; Sprenger, 2008; Taylor & Dorsey-Gaines, 1988). The "myth of the average learner" has been shattered, and teachers are recognizing the need to individualize and honor the unique profiles of all students. Inclusive schooling has been a catalyst for such a model and has prompted educators to differentiate instruction and attend to diverse learning styles as they plan and implement daily lessons.

Inclusive Schooling as Education Reform

Although many have understood inclusive schooling to be a reform implemented for the benefit of learners with disabilities, most of its proponents understand it as a movement that concerns every learner and see it as a path to better educational experiences and outcomes for all (Hyatt, DaSilva, Iddings, & Ober, 2005; Kluth, Biklen, & Straut, 2003; McLeskey & Waldron, 2006). Some schools, for instance, are using a move toward inclusive schooling to inspire more collaboration and co-teaching, to encourage community-building, and even to streamline and make the most of available resources (Henderson, 2001; Hyatt et al., 2005). Teachers also commonly report that they become more skilled at their craft as a result of teaching a wider range of students. Farmer (1996), for example, wrote about how the inclusion of Amy, a student with autism, in her middle-school language arts classroom, helped her become more reflective:

> [My colleague] and I have learned many things from Amy's inclusion in language arts. We have learned to be more flexible and patient with learners who have special needs. We have learned to modify or let go some of the curriculum in order to allow more time. We ask ourselves about what Amy has accomplished instead of what she didn't get done. More important, we have learned not to underestimate her learning or any student's learning. (p. 30)

Curriculum and instruction also commonly change in inclusive schools. Although students with disabilities, especially those with more significant needs, may require more creativity and invention on the part of classroom educators, this creativity often benefits all learners in the classroom and teachers, who not uncommonly report that they become better at their craft after expanding lessons to meet the needs of a wider range of students. For instance, I once worked with a high school team who found that one student could inspire new ways of teaching and learning for all. Anne, a young woman with autism, did not have a reliable communication system, often vocalized audibly during classes, and struggled with traditional sit-and-listen lessons. Her American History teacher, a popular instructor (and frequent lecturer), was frustrated with her presence in the classroom; he had been using the same lessons for years and was not prepared to make changes "just for one student." The special education teacher offered to work with the history teacher to create opportunities for Anne to participate in daily lessons.

At the time, the class was studying the Vietnam Conflict. In order to teach this particular unit, the teacher was using a textbook; a range of popular films about Vietnam such as *Apocalypse Now* (Coppola, 1979), *Platoon* (Stone, 1986), and *Hamburger Hill* (Irvin, 1987); newspaper clippings from the late 1960s and early 1970s; and a few fictitious accounts of the war. Although the materials were varied and interesting, the instructor's lessons were not always appealing to all. The teacher, although very entertaining and funny, delivered instruction through a lecture format every day. Although students did have opportunities to ask and answer questions during the lectures, they were not able to interact with each other, explore materials in depth, solve problems independently, or create products. Some students were able to stay attentive during this format; however, many others, including Anne, could not. By the end of the daily lesson, many students were dozing, writing notes to friends, or staring out the classroom's wall of windows.

The special educator suggested that once a week, while the teacher was showing video clips, a few students would be offered an alternative activity. The general educator, they decided, would stay back in the classroom and supervise the movie viewing, while the special educator would accompany a small group of students around the high school, seeking staff members and other adults in the school who would be willing to be interviewed about their memories of the war. For the first few weeks, the special educator took the students on the school tour; five students, including Anne, made their way through the halls, canvassed the teacher's lounge, and searched the hallways for school visitors. Because Anne could not easily communicate, her job was to operate the audio recorder (a new skill she acquired at the onset of the project). She introduced the group to the person to be interviewed via a communication card reading, "We are conducting a history project related to the Vietnam Conflict. We are interested in interviewing people who remember the Vietnam era. Do you mind if we ask you a few questions?" Anne also participated in the interview process by handing question cards to the interviewees (e.g., "What do you remember about the news coverage at this time?")

After 3 weeks, the history teacher decided he wanted to accompany students to the interviews and asked his special education partner to stay back in the classroom and supervise the film. He also decided that *every* student would need to participate in the interviews during the unit. The teachers then designed a formal interview schedule for the class. Through the course of 6 weeks, the students interviewed seven parents, three custodians (one of whom did three tours of duty in Vietnam), all four secretaries, the school nurse, six cafeteria workers (one of whom lost a brother in the war), nearly every teacher in the building, and the police officer assigned to the high school.

The teachers and the students became so excited about the project that they spent 2 extra weeks on the unit, with the teachers adding questions to the interviews to spur new learning. Participants were excited, too; some teachers even signed their friends up to be interviewed. As the students shared the results of their interviews, the class discussed, researched, and investigated topics ranging from women's roles in the 1960s to Watergate to the Black Panther Movement.

Both educators were pleased with the unit and the history teacher claimed that all of his students learned more, even those who could "handle" the lectures. He saw more complexity in all of his learners and felt that the interview activity allowed him to tackle more complicated subject matter and give students more opportunities to think critically. He did not have Anne in any of his classes the following semester, but he continued to use the interviews as a central focus of the unit. In subsequent semesters, all students worked in groups to choose a specific focus for their interviews. Furthermore, students were no longer asked to skip the film; all learners went out into the school and neighboring community to conduct interviews during the class period.

This unit was important for Anne. She was able to address all of her individual learning needs in an authentic context and during a standards-based lesson. She needed more experience using her communication system, interacting with others, and making choices. She was able to practice all of these skills within the context of the project. In addition, she acquired some new skills as a result of the unit. She learned how to operate the audio recorder and later used this skill to listen to music on the school bus and during study hall. Anne also learned about Vietnam, something she probably would not have learned had her teachers decided that the class was inappropriate for her.

Anne's story is just one example of how inclusive practices can inspire changes that profit all. Personally, I have found that it is students with the most significant needs who often stretch teachers' ideas of what it means to reach all learners. Although a teacher can meet the needs of all students without ever having a student with disabilities in his or her classroom, these learners are often a catalyst for change and creativity. Specifically, including students with autism may help teachers think more carefully about the choices offered to students, the design of the lesson, the comfort and safety of all, and the ways in which students can participate in teaching and learning. To learn more about the tenets of inclusive schooling, see Figure 2.3; this checklist can serve as a guide for schools interested in growing their inclusive schooling model and potentially for using inclusion as a tool for comprehensive school reform.

Inclusive Schooling and the Law

Even though inclusion has been part of American schooling since at least 1975, many students with autism and other disabilities are still separated from their peers without disabilities for all or most of the school day (Smith, 2007). This is a frustrating reality considering that students with autism stand to gain so much when they are given access to standards-based lessons in general education settings.

Students educated in inclusive classrooms not only have opportunities to meet individual goals and objectives but also get access to and support in learning grade-level standards, curriculum, and instruction (Fisher & Frey, 2001; Jorgensen, McSheehan, & Sonnenmeier, 2009; Kasa-Hendrickson & Kluth, 2005; Kinney & Fischer, 2001; Kliewer, 2008; Kluth, 1998; Martin, 1994; Rubin et al., 2001; Ryndak, Morrison, Sommerstein, 1999; Savarese, 2007). In addition, teachers often find that communication skills blossom when learners have regular opportunities to interact, share, and express themselves (Jorgensen, McSheehan, & Sonnenmeier, 2009; Kluth, 1998; Martin, 1994; Savarese, 2007). Finally, students stand to make gains in social skills and competencies in inclusive classrooms (Martin, 1994; Ritter, Michel, & Irby, 1999).

An example of how students can make gains in all three of these areas comes from Sonnenmeier, McSheehan, and Jorgensen's (2005) case study of the use of augmentative and alternative communication by Jay, a fourth grader with autism. One of Jay's communication systems featured overlays, or menus, of key vocabulary words paired with pictures on a VOCA (a voice output communication device). Jay's classmates had a copy of the core vocabulary overlay and were encouraged to use it during discussions, writing activities, and teacher-directed lessons. The classroom teacher also had an enlarged copy of the same overlay to use as a visual support during lessons. Other members of Jay's team, including the teaching assistant, the special educator, and the occupational therapist, used his device and his overlays to provide modeling and restatements of things that Jay communicated. This approach of not only valuing Jay's alternative form of communication but of having all members of the class use the system gave everyone new opportunities to learn language and experiment with technology while giving Jay time to practice social skills. Jay not only made impressive gains in his communication during this year but also made many meaningful connections with his classmates due to the structure of daily lessons and the community that was cultivated in the classroom.

These benefits alone should serve as motivators for decision makers to create more opportunities for students with autism and related labels to receive instruction in inclusive classrooms. If more inspiration is needed, however, federal law can help.

The Individuals with Disabilities Education Act

In 1975, Congress passed the Education for All Handicapped Children Act (PL 94-142), guaranteeing for the first time that all students with disabilities would be provided with a public education. The act promoted a free appropriate public education (FAPE) for all and mandated that students with disabilities be placed in the least restrictive environment (LRE) to receive this education.

This law revolutionized American education policy. PL 94-142 was also developed to protect the rights of students with disabilities and their families (e.g., due process in decision making about providing education and related services), to assess and ensure the effectiveness of special education at all levels of government, and to financially assist state and local governments in educating students with disabilities through the use of federal funds. Requirements of PL 94-142 included

- Procedures for referring children suspected of having a disability

- A team comprised of personnel from varied disciplines to determine eligibility

- Team development of an individualized education program (IEP)

- Specialized instruction and placement in an educational setting appropriate to the child's needs

- Procedures for parental notification and participation

- Time limits on how rapidly the eligibility/referral process happens

- Periodic reassessment of the student's eligibility

- Procedures for resolving disagreements and disputes

PL 94-142, later reauthorized as the Individuals with Disabilities Education Act (IDEA) of 1990 (PL 101-476), began a movement toward civil rights for students with disabilities and set the stage for inclusive schooling.

In subsequent decades, the spirit of the law has essentially remained unchanged and its primary provisions are intact. In 1997 IDEA was amended, however, to include, among other things, a legal requirement to include students with disabilities in general state- and districtwide assessments with appropriate accommodations and modifications. Furthermore, IDEA '97 includes a requirement for states to develop alternate assessments and guidelines for students whose disabilities preclude them from participation in general assessments. IDEA '97 also required that IEPs must include how a child will be involved in the general curriculum, including goals related to meeting the child's needs so that the child can progress in the general curriculum (PL 105-17, 111 Stat. 37).

Seven years later, in IDEA 2004, more changes were made in an attempt to better meet the needs of students, families, and teachers. For instance, new language was added to ensure that children with disabilities are taught by highly qualified teachers and receive research-based instruction. It also authorized 15 states to implement 3-year IEPs on a trial basis (PL 108-446, 118 Stat. 2647).

Checklist: Is Your School Inclusive?

	Yes	No	If no, we need to:	Who is responsible for next step(s)?
Is there a school philosophy or mission statement in support of inclusion?			__ Get more info __ Draft a plan __ Get resources __ Get outside help __ Assign a "to do"	
Do staff development opportunities reflect an inclusive philosophy?			__ Get more info __ Draft a plan __ Get resources __ Get outside help __ Assign a "to do"	
Does the school leadership promote inclusion through written materials, presentations, and so forth?			__ Get more info __ Draft a plan __ Get resources __ Get outside help __ Assign a "to do"	
Do teachers use language that reflects the philosophy of inclusive education (e.g., "our students" versus "your students" or "my students")?			__ Get more info __ Draft a plan __ Get resources __ Get outside help __ Assign a "to do"	
Do students with disabilities attend their neighborhood schools (the schools they would attend if they did not have a disability)?			__ Get more info __ Draft a plan __ Get resources __ Get outside help __ Assign a "to do"	
Are students being educated in classrooms with their same-age peers?			__ Get more info __ Draft a plan __ Get resources __ Get outside help __ Assign a "to do"	
Are all students participating meaningfully in curriculum and instruction?			__ Get more info __ Draft a plan __ Get resources __ Get outside help __ Assign a "to do"	
Do students use the same transportation as students without disabilities, whenever possible?			__ Get more info __ Draft a plan __ Get resources __ Get outside help __ Assign a "to do"	
Do students use the same school spaces (e.g., lockers, entrances, lunch tables) as those without disabilities?			__ Get more info __ Draft a plan __ Get resources __ Get outside help __ Assign a "to do"	
Do all students participate in extracurricular activities?			__ Get more info __ Draft a plan __ Get resources __ Get outside help __ Assign a "to do"	
Do curricular and extracurricular activities encourage interactions between peers with and without disabilities?			__ Get more info __ Draft a plan __ Get resources __ Get outside help __ Assign a "to do"	
Do special and general educators collaborate to ensure the participation of all students in general education classrooms?			__ Get more info __ Draft a plan __ Get resources __ Get outside help __ Assign a "to do"	

Figure 2.3.   Is Your School Inclusive? Checklist.

(continued)

"You're Going to Love This Kid!" Teaching Students with Autism in the Inclusive Classroom, Second Edition, by Paula Kluth
Copyright © 2010 by Paul H. Brookes Publishing Co. All rights reserved.

	Yes	No	If no, we need to:		Who is responsible for next step(s)?
Do special and general educators collaborate to address IEP objectives of students with disabilities?			__ Get more info __ Get resources __ Assign a "to do"	__ Draft a plan __ Get outside help	
Do special and general educators collaborate to ensure the adaptation of the core curriculum for students with unique learning characteristics?			__ Get more info __ Get resources __ Assign a "to do"	__ Draft a plan __ Get outside help	
Do special and general educators collaborate to ensure that effective instructional strategies (e.g., active learning) are implemented to support students with unique learning characteristics?			__ Get more info __ Get resources __ Assign a "to do"	__ Draft a plan __ Get outside help	
Do teachers promote self-determination (e.g., student-led IEP meetings)?			__ Get more info __ Get resources __ Assign a "to do"	__ Draft a plan __ Get outside help	
Are special educators, general educators, paraprofessionals, and related service professionals co-planning and co-teaching?			__ Get more info __ Get resources __ Assign a "to do"	__ Draft a plan __ Get outside help	

"You're Going to Love This Kid!" Teaching Students with Autism in the Inclusive Classroom, Second Edition, by Paula Kluth
Copyright © 2010 by Paul H. Brookes Publishing Co. All rights reserved.

Free Appropriate Public Education

The central focus of PL 94-142 and its subsequent revisions is the guarantee of a free appropriate public education (FAPE) for children and youth with disabilities; this means that every student with disabilities can receive educational supports and services at public expense. The passage of the law was a major victory for people with disabilities and their families because prior to 1975, many students were either not educated at all or were educated at the expense of their parents or guardians. In 1970, American schools educated only one in five students with disabilities, and more than 1 million students were excluded from public schools. Some states even had laws excluding certain populations of learners, including those who were blind, deaf, or labeled "emotionally disturbed" or "mentally retarded" (National Council on Disability [NCD]; Back to School on Civil Rights, January 25, 2000; http://www.ncd.gov/newsroom/publications/2000/pdf/backtoschool.pdf).

Individualized Education Program

The IEP is the cornerstone of the law, providing a framework for the student's curriculum and instruction; it can be viewed as the educational road map for students with disabilities. The IEP outlines the student's goals for the year and how he or she will be supported to reach those goals.

An IEP also includes the student's current level of functioning and a clear statement of all special services that the student will be receiving. The IEP team for each student with a disability must make an individualized determination regarding how the child will be involved and progress in the general curriculum and whether the child has any other educational needs resulting from his or her disability that also must be met.

Least Restrictive Environment

Another important tenet of IDEA is that students with disabilities must be educated in the least restrictive environment. The proper forum for making the decision regarding LRE is the IEP team. In deciding, the team must consider the individual needs of the student and must take both academic and nonacademic needs into consideration. Specifically, schools are supposed to ensure

> That to the maximum extent appropriate, children with disabilities, including children in public or private institutions and other care facilities, are educated with children who are not disabled, and special classes, separate schooling, or other removal of children with disabilities from the regular educational environment occurs only when the nature or severity of the disability of the child is such that education in regular classes with the use of supplementary aids and services cannot be achieved satisfactorily. (IDEA 1990, PL 101-476, § 612[a][5])

These phrases from the law mean that schools have a duty to try to include students with disabilities in general education classes. The language of the law can be confusing, however, and is often criticized for being ambiguous. For this reason, it can be helpful when considering LRE to look to the courts for clues in understanding the intent of IDEA. In one of the best-known cases, Rachel Holland and her family spent years fighting in court for her right to be educated in a general education classroom (*Sacramento City School District v. Rachel H.*, 1994). The parents challenged the district's decision to place their daughter half-time in a special education classroom and half-time in a general education classroom; they instead wanted their daughter in the general education classroom full-time. The district court ordered an aide and special education consultant to work with Rachel's teacher and held that she should be placed in a general education classroom. The school district appealed this decision all the way to the Supreme Court; when the Supreme Court refused to hear the case, the lower court's decision was thus affirmed. The Holland family pursued an inclusive education for Rachel for more than 5 years (King-Sears, 1996; Villa & Thousand, 2000; Yell, 1995).

Not all notable cases have favored inclusive placements for students with disabilities, however. In the case of *Beth B. v. Van Clay,* for instance, the court was very conservative in its ruling and refused to venture beyond the wording of IDEA. The court stated that if the student's education in the regular classroom was "satisfactory," then the school district would be in violation of IDEA by removing her, but if the setting was not "satisfactory" (and according to the district it was not), then the placement of the special education classroom could stand (Howard, 2004).

Still, it seems despite important decisions having been rendered both for and against inclusion, the courts—since the 1990s—still generally demonstrate a preference for inclusion (Howard, 2004; Russo & Osborne, 2007; Yell, 1995). However, the circuits still differ upon how far to extend this preference and to what extent nonacademic benefits (e.g., social opportunities) should be considered. The result, at this time, is that children with less significant needs are more likely to be included than in the past, but recommendations for those with more severe disabilities still vary widely across the circuit courts (Howard, 2004). This means that advocates for inclusion must be sure to fight not only for inclusive placements for also for *quality* inclusive placements where stakeholders can clearly see and understand the benefits to learners with autism.

Implementation of IDEA

Just as in *Brown v. Board of Education* (1954), the court decision that integrated schools in the 1950s, getting schools to systematically implement the federal law is proving to be a lengthy and not-so-linear process. Although many schools and districts have successfully been educating students with disabilities in inclusive settings for years, nationwide implementation of IDEA has been slow:

> In the period between 1977–1978 and 1989–1990, there was little or no change in placements of students with disabilities as a group at the national level. In 1977–1978, 68% of students with disabilities were in general education class and resource room environments compared with 69.2% in 1989–1990. Placement of students with disabilities in separate classes was 25.3% in 1977–1978 and 24.8% in 1989–1990. Separate public school facilities and other separate environments educated 6.7% of students with disabilities in 1977–1978 and 5.4% of students with disabilities in 1989–1990. (Karagiannis, Stainback, & Stainback, 1996, p. 23)

The NCD (2000) released similar findings in their independent report, *Back to School on Civil Rights*. The Council found that every state was out of compliance with IDEA requirements and that U.S. officials are not forcing compliance. The investigators also found that children with disabilities often are taught in segregated classrooms and that, in many cases, schools are not following regulations meant to protect students from discrimination. And Smith (2007) found that as a country, the United States is actually regressing when it comes to including students with intellectual disabilities in general education classrooms.

Is Anyone Paying Attention to the Law?

More than 3 decades after the passage of PL 94-142, many educators and administrators remain unclear about how the law should be implemented and what responsibilities schools have to students with disabilities, their families, and school communities. In some cases, districts may be moving slowly toward inclusive education in order to make the transition smooth for families and students alike. Although this strategy can be an effective way to comfortably introduce teachers and students to some changes, "moving slowly" cannot be a rationale for denying the placement a student requires. As Reed Martin (2001), a disability-rights attorney, stressed, students and their families have been patient. It is time for schools to learn the law and for government agencies to hold schools accountable:

> Our kids and their families are still having to fight to get simply what they are entitled to in public schools. They are not asking for charity, or asking for schools to feel sorry for them because they have a disability. The accommodations that we fight for are not "I can't be expected to do as much as typical kids do so you have to go easy on me." Our kids have a right to an end to the illegal and unconstitutional discrimination that every day bars students with disabilities from access to what typical students receive. (p. 1)

Common Questions and Answers Related to the Law

By answering a few questions about special education and the law, I will illustrate how the law affects schools, how the law has been interpreted, and how teachers can work toward offering an inclusive education to their students. These questions are, "Can schools choose to offer inclusion?"; "Is inclusion right for students with significant disabilities?"; "Won't students with autism be better off learning with other students with autism?"; and "What if educators do not feel ready to teach students with autism?"

Question: Can schools choose to offer inclusion?

Answer: I often hear teachers and families talking about inclusion as if it is something schools can choose to adopt (or reject). For instance, I met a teacher who told me that her school had been inclusive but they felt it was not working well and, therefore, decided to move back to a more restrictive model. Similarly, a parent sent me a letter explaining that she wanted her child to have an inclusive education but her neighborhood school "doesn't have it."

In both of these situations, the law is not clearly understood. If a student with disabilities can be successfully educated in a general education setting (with the appropriate supports and services), then the student's school *must* provide that experience. Schools cannot claim that they do or do not "offer" or "do" inclusion. Special education is not a program or a place and inclusive schooling is not a way of doing business that schools can dismiss outright. As the law indicates, students with disabilities should only be removed from general education "when the nature or severity of the disability is such that education in regular classes with the use of supplementary aids and services cannot be achieved satisfactorily" (IDEA, PL 101-476, § 612[a][5]). Therefore, in cases in which students can be educated in general education "satisfactorily," the school must "offer" inclusion.

Question: Is inclusion right for students with significant disabilities?

Answer: A special education teacher recently told me that she was really interested in inclusive schooling and that she decided to "try it" with one of her students. Patricia, a young girl with significant disabilities, began first grade that fall but was moved back into a special education classroom by November. The teacher told me how difficult the decision to move Patricia back to the special education classroom had been and explained why educators had changed Patricia's placement: "The kids really liked her and she loved first grade . . . but she just wasn't catching on with the reading. She couldn't keep up or even come close to keeping up with the other kids."

Some parents and teachers assume that some students with disabilities cannot be provided an inclusive education because their skills are not similar enough to those of students without disabilities. This is perhaps the most common misconception about the law (and about inclusion itself) that exists among families and teachers. Students with disabilities do not need to keep up with students without disabilities to be educated in inclusive classrooms; they do not need to engage in the curriculum in the same way as students without disabilities; and they do not need to practice the same skills as students without disabilities. In sum, *no prerequisites are needed for a learner to be able to participate in inclusive education.*

Consider the ways in which Malcolm, a student with multiple disabilities, is included in his middle-school social studies unit on the Constitution. During the unit, the class writes its own Constitution and Bill of Rights and reenacts the Constitutional Convention. Malcolm participates in all of these activities even though he does not have reliable communication and is just beginning to demonstrate literate ability (e.g., identifying single words). During the lesson, Malcolm works with a peer and a speech-language therapist to contribute a line to the class Bill of Rights; the pair uses Malcom's augmentative and alternative communication (AAC) device to write the sentence. Malcolm also participates in the dramatic interpretation of the Constitutional Convention. During the reenactment, students—acting as Convention participants—drift around the classroom introducing themselves to others. Because he is largely nonverbal, Malcolm (acting as George Mason) shares a little bit about himself by handing out his "business card" to other members of the delegation.

Other students are expected to submit three-page reports at the end of the unit, but Malcolm will be assessed on a shorter report (a few sentences) that he will type on his communication device using a picture-based software program. He will also be assessed on his participation during the class activities, on the demonstration of new skills related to using his communication device, and on how well he initiates social interactions with others during the Constitutional Convention exercise (Kluth, Villa, & Thousand, 2001).

The Constitutional Convention example illustrates how students with disabilities can participate in general education—though not necessarily in the same ways as students without disabilities—without having the same skills and abilities others in the class may have. In addition, this example highlights ways in which students with disabilities can work on individual skills and goals within the context of general education lessons. It is also important to note that the supports and adaptations provided for Malcolm were designed by his teachers and put in place to facilitate his success. Malcolm was not expected to have all of the skills and abilities possessed by other students in order to participate in the classroom. Instead, Malcolm's teachers created a context in which Malcolm could "show up" as competent. This is, without question, why some learners succeed in inclusive classrooms while others "fail."

In order for Malcolm to be successful in his classroom, his teachers need to provide him with a range of "supplemental aids and services." Aids and services might include curriculum that is differentiated to meet the needs of the learner, paraprofessional support, tutoring from peers, assistive technology, instruction from a therapist, different seating, modified tests, adapted materials (e.g., talking books, visual organizers, computer touch-screen), or any number of other strategies and approaches. Although schools do not need to provide every support available, they do need to provide those required by the student to meet his or her IEP goals.

The 1992–1993 case, *Oberti v. Clementon*, illustrated the responsibilities schools have to provide "supplemental aids and services." A U.S. Circuit Court ordered Raphael Oberti, a student with Down syndrome, to be educated in a general education classroom after the court determined that Raphael's school had not supplied him with the supports and resources he needed to be successful in an inclusive classroom. The judge also ruled that appropriate training had not been provided for his educators and support staff. The school was, therefore, required to make greater efforts to educate Raphael in his classroom or explain why they could not. In upholding Raphael's right to receive his education in his neighborhood school with adequate and necessary supports, the court placed the burden of proof for compliance with IDEA's inclusion requirements squarely on the school district and the state (instead of on the family). That is, the school had to show why Raphael could *not* be educated in general education with aids and services; his family did not have to prove why he could. The judge who decided the case endorsed inclusive education by writing, "Inclusion is a right, not a special privilege for a select few."

Question: Won't students with autism be better off learning with other students with autism?

Answer: Years ago I went to my neighborhood school to vote. I was directed down a long hallway near a classroom marked *AUTISTIC CENTER*. I approached a teacher and asked about the sign. She told me that the room was used to educate all of the students with autism in the district; this teacher was responsible for educating 11 students with autism.

Across the country, many school districts are still operating and, in some cases, developing new educational programs for discrete groups of students. Programs and separate classrooms exist for students with certain labels (e.g., emotional disabilities, physical disabilities) and for students with perceived levels of disability. For instance, some districts have programs for students with severe disabilities. In many cases, students are being placed in these specialized environments without being provided with an opportunity to attend a general education classroom with appropriate supports and services. Oddly, students also often are placed in such "specialized" programs without regard for their needs and abilities; that is, students with autism are often educated together because they share a *label*, not necessarily because they have common needs. It is important to remember that a classroom full of students on the spectrum may be as diverse as and likely is *more* diverse in needs and abilities than a typical general education classroom.

In 1993, the *Roncker v. Walter* case challenged the assignment of students to disability-specific programs and schools. This case addressed the issue of "bringing educational services to the child" versus "bringing the child to the services." The case was resolved in favor of an inclusive placement and established a principle of portability. That is, "If a desirable service currently provided in a segregated setting can feasibly be delivered in an integrated setting, it would be inappropriate under PL 94-142 to provide the service in a segregated placement" (700 F.2d.at 1063). The judge in the case stated

> It is not enough for a district to simply claim that a segregated program is superior: In a case where the segregated facility is considered superior, the court should determine whether the services which make the placement superior could be feasibly provided in a non-segregated setting (i.e., regular class). If they can, the placement in the segregated school would be inappropriate under the act (I.D.E.A.). (*Roncker v. Walter*, 700 F.2d at 1063)

The *Roncker* court found that placement decisions must be individually made. School districts that automatically place children in a program or school solely on the basis of their disability or perceived "level of functioning," rather than on the basis of their educational needs, are likely in violation of federal laws.

Question: What if educators do not feel ready to teach students with autism?

Answer: Although many general educators may feel unprepared when they begin teaching students with disabilities, all educators—no matter their subject matter or assigned grade level—need to see themselves as teachers of inclusive classrooms. At any point, any general educator may be called on to teach and support a student with autism. Therefore, it is the responsibility of districts and building administrators to prepare all staff members—not just those best suited to or most enthusiastic about teaching students with disabilities—to work with diverse learners, and it is the job of teachers to acquire new skills and develop new competencies as their student body evolves.

In fact, the IDEA Amendments of 1997 (PL 105-17) call on general educators to participate more actively than ever before in the education of students with disabilities. For too long, general educators have been asked to participate in the education of students with disabilities but have not been given sufficient opportunity, in most cases, to engage in the planning for and evaluation of learners with disabilities. Finally, the law is respecting the work of general educators and including them as full participants in the education of students with disabilities.

The federal law demands that general educators participate directly in the development of the

> Statement of the special education and related services and supplementary aids and services to be provided to the child, or on behalf of the child, and a statement of the program modifications or supports for school personnel that will be provided for the child. (20 U.S.C. 1414[d][1][A][iii])

For students with more than one general educator (e.g., students in middle and high school), at least one teacher who has actually worked with the student must participate. As an attempt to make administrative work more manageable for teachers, IDEA 2004 provided two ways that team members can be excused from attending the IEP meeting. They are 1) if the member's area of the curriculum or related services is not being modified or discussed in the meeting and 2) if, when the member's area of curriculum or related services is being discussed, the member submits written input to the parents and the team prior to the meeting (Cortiella, 2008). All stakeholders should keep in mind that the parent must agree to either of these exceptions in writing and that, ideally, all team members will attend the IEP to be sure that learners get what they need and that these needs are determined by a dedicated, multidisciplinary team.

Summary

Teachers in both elementary and secondary schools are finding that students with autism, including those labeled as having "significant disabilities," can be successfully included in general education classrooms (Biklen, 1992; Downing, 2005; Farlow, 1996; Hedeen, Ayres, Meyer, & Waite, 1996; Jorgensen, 1998; Kasa-Hendrickson, 2002; Kluth, 1998; Schmidt, 1998). If success is possible for students with a wide range of needs, why is inclusive schooling not a reality for more students in the United States? I believe that one central reason for this discrepancy is the way in which most teachers view inclusive schooling. Consider the possibilities that exist when educators view inclusive schooling as a verb—something we do—versus viewing it as a noun—something we have. Too often, inclusion is used as a noun, as in "We have inclusion here, but this child isn't successful in our inclusive classrooms."

An action-oriented understanding of inclusive education can push teachers to refine their practices continually and to become increasingly successful with their students. Seeing inclusion as an action may prompt educators to make inclusive schooling happen when they meet a student with significant communication, behavior, and learning needs—a student who challenges their notion of who gets included in schools. Furthermore, teachers who see inclusion as a process might expect to have struggles; they expect progress for some students to be bumpy at times and appreciate the learning that may occur with such terrain.

Although understanding inclusive education, the laws related to it, and practical strategies are important, nothing is more helpful in learning about inclusive schooling than doing it. Teachers in today's schools must make a commitment to value the participation of all and to work toward quality inclusive practices every day. It is my hope that readers will understand this chapter as a call to action, begin to see inclusive schooling as "something we do" instead of "something we have," not only for those on the spectrum but also for every learner in inclusive schools. As one teacher commented, this is the real essence of inclusion: "I don't call it inclusive because of [my students with autism]. I call it inclusive because . . . I am a teacher for all kids" (Kasa-Hendrickson, 2002, p. 145).

FOR MORE ANSWERS AND INFORMATION

Books

Anderson, W., Chitwood, S., Hayden, D., & Takemoto, C. (2008). *Negotiating the special education maze: A guide for parents and teachers* (4th ed.). Bethesda, MD: Woodbine House.

Downing, J. (2008). *Including students with severe and multiple disabilities in typical classrooms* (3rd ed.). Baltimore: Paul H. Brookes Publishing Co.

Johnson, M.D., & Corden, S.H. (2004). *Beyond words: The successful inclusion of a child with autism.* Knoxville, TN: Merry Pace Press.

(continued)

(continued)

Jorgensen, C.M., McSheehan, M., & Sonnenmeier, R.M. (2009). *The beyond access model: Promoting membership, participation, and learning for students with disabilities in the general education classroom.* Baltimore: Paul H. Brookes Publishing Co.

Kluth, P., Straut, D., & Biklen, D. (2003). *Access to academics for all students: Critical approaches to inclusive curriculum, instruction, and policy.* Mahwah, NJ: Lawrence Erlbaum Associates.

Sapon-Shevin, M. (2007). *Widening the circle.* Boston: Beacon Press.

Schwarz, P. (2006). *From disability to possibility.* Portsmouth, NH: Heinemann Publishing.

 # Web Sites

Inclusion: School as a Caring Community

http://www.ualberta.ca/~jpdasddc/incl/intro.htm

A fantastic web site filled with tips from general and special educators. This site may be especially helpful for secondary education teachers.

Inclusive Schools Network

http://www.inclusiveschools.org

Visit this site to learn more about Inclusive Schools Week and to get their free monthly newsletter.

Inclusive Solutions

http://www.inclusive-solutions.com

Every teacher will find something helpful, interesting, or inspiring on this web site. It is packed with short articles, video clips, and training ideas.

National Inclusion Project

http://www.inclusionproject.org

Newly formed in 2009, this organization supports inclusive programs and creates awareness about inclusive schooling and communities. Get on their mailing list to learn about upcoming inclusion-related news and events.

Patrick Schwarz's web site

http://www.patrickschwarz.com

Schwarz's site contains a definition of inclusive schooling, recommendations for teachers, and a list of useful links.

Paula Kluth's web site

http://www.paulakluth.com

My web site has dozens of articles on inclusive schools, a link to my blog, and other resources.

The Role of the Teacher

People are always looking for the single magic bullet that will totally change everything. There is no single magic bullet. I was very lucky to receive very good early intervention with very good teachers, starting at age 2 ½ years. I cannot emphasize enough the importance of a good teacher. A good teacher is worth his or her weight in gold. (Grandin, 1996b)

In every classic example of students finding "unexpected" success, we find a teacher who believes that all students can learn and who implements practices in order to make this expectation come true (Clark, 2004; Esquith, 2007; Keller, 1954; Ladson-Billings, 2009; Matthews, 1988; Meier, 2002; Moses & Cobb, 2001; Savarese, 2007). Clearly, teachers have incredible power to inspire learning and create important change in schools and in communities. Haim Ginott summarized the amazing charge of teachers in this often-quoted philosophy:

> I have come to the conclusion that I am the decisive element in the classroom. It's my personal approach that creates the climate. It's my daily mood that makes the weather. As a teacher, I possess a tremendous power to make a child's life miserable or joyous. I can be a tool of torture or an instrument of inspiration. I can humiliate or humor, hurt or heal. In all situations, it is my response that decides whether a crisis will be escalated or de-escalated and a child humanized or de-humanized. (1972, p. 13)

It is true that many teachers in inclusive schools—especially those who are the first in the building to support a student on the spectrum—are responsible for creating the climate that will either serve the student with autism or put him or her at risk. In Ralph Saverese's illuminating book *Reasonable People: A Memoir of Autism & Adoption*, he recalls the admirable job his son's first teacher did of "making the weather" and using influence and attitude to create change:

> The woman had possessed the same power so many other teachers possess *and use* to remove children from their classes, but she had never, ever used it. Nor, finally, had any of DJ's other teachers at [the school], even when legitimately provoked. Mrs. Thompson, however, had welcomed hope when hope seemed most alarming. (2007, p. 113)

This chapter is dedicated to the role of the teacher as an educational leader and change agent and stresses how central are the attitudes, beliefs, and actions of teachers to the cultivation of inclusive education. In these pages, I outline 10 ways in which teachers can support students with autism while promoting inclusive schooling and, perhaps in doing so, can be—in Ginott's words—an "instrument of inspiration."

Ten Ways to Support Students with Autism and Promote Inclusive Schooling

Although these 10 are not the only habits that will help teachers succeed with learners on the spectrum, they are certainly some of the most important. I sometimes call this list of 10 the *intangibles* because they represent the good but invisible "stuff" teachers believe, do, or practice to help their learners succeed. The 10 ideas are 1) recognize differences; 2) interrogate the use of labels; 3) reconfigure expertise; 4) preserve student dignity; 5) look for complexity; 6) serve as an advocate and teach advocacy; 7) act as teacher and learner; 8) listen; 9) take necessary risks; and 10) practice subversive pedagogy, if necessary.

1. Recognize Differences

Sometimes, seeing and understanding differences are complicated concepts for a teacher. Teachers often say, for example, "I don't see disabilities; all of my students are special," or, "If you walk into my classroom, you can't tell which student has autism." Although these statements may be well intentioned, they are often misguided. It is, I believe, impossible to "not see" disability or ethnicity or race or the other differences that make up all of our lives; these elements are real and important; they are an integral part of who we are as individuals and as members of our communities. As Sapon-Shevin pointed out, accepting all learners is key, but ignoring differences may not be a desirable way to show such acceptance:

> If differences are minimized or covered up to meet a goal of making all students look the same, what messages are communicated to students about differences? Is it better to talk about Nadia's hearing aides and what kinds of help and support she needs, or should we discourage the other students from noticing that she wears them or that they sometimes squeak or that she has obviously missed a verbal cue? Is it best to accommodate Tim's diabetes and special dietary needs by inconspicuously giving him different treats at snack time so as to spare him the embarrassment of needing a special accommodation? (2001, p. 24)

"Not seeing" is not a positive response to difference. Recognizing, however, and doing our best to really understand how differences affect students' lives and educational experiences, helps us to better know and serve each individual learner.

In inclusive schools, students are encouraged to express their individuality and to acknowledge "not only what is good and enjoyable in their lives but also what is painful and hard" (Sapon-Shevin, 2010, p. 35). As Sapon-Shevin stressed, teachers need to encourage students to feel comfortable with their differences; but to do so, they must first create a context for differences to be exposed and accepted:

> We want to create chances for students to share all aspects of themselves: the good, the laudable, the troublesome, and the confusing. Because community and cultural values and standards concerning what's appropriate to share are apt to vary considerably, it is important for teachers to be extremely sensitive in respecting children's differences. (1999, p. 36)

The inclusive schooling movement has inspired a paradigm shift in the field of education. This critical education reform has helped teachers conceptualize differences as essential and valued aspects of classrooms. Inclusive teachers desire differences in the classroom. In good inclusive schools, "the view that differences among individuals in education pose difficulties and need to be fixed, improved, or made ready to fit (i.e., homogenized) is replaced by the recognition that differences are valuable assets to capitalize on" (Stainback, 2000, p. 508).

2. Interrogate the Use of Labels

Teachers in diverse classrooms must recognize the benefits of celebrating student differences while working to know students as individual learners. During busy classroom days, teachers may rely on stereotypes, assumptions, and perceptions in their daily social interactions with students and in the planning of curriculum and instruction. Educators may also fall into the trap of using labels or simple descriptions of students (e.g., "the two autistics in my health class," "the slow kids in the ninth grade") in conversations with colleagues, in educational reports or other types of communication, and even in interactions with students themselves.

The labeling of differences presents a challenge. Although labeling and identity politics can certainly result in benefits such as self-affirmation, positive self-image, and connectivity with others (Shore, 2004), teachers must take care not to use labels in ways that limit or harm their students. In certain contexts, labels can be constricting and limiting, and relying on them to describe students can lead teachers to see a student's autism before or instead of seeing the individual student. As Nancy Burns, a woman with a disability, pointed out, labeling can result in "othering":

As someone with a disability, I don't want to be thought of or treated like I'm special, stupid, a freak, different, the village idiot, an alien from outer space, a second class citizen or invisible. Treat me with the same amount of respect and consideration you would give to someone else—no matter what. Get to know the person on the inside and not just by the disability. I bet you'll find they are not that much different from you. (1998, p. 12)

In the staff lounge, at faculty meetings, and in educational reports, students are often described in one-dimensional and often unflattering ways. Consider the story of Xang, a first-grade student. One of his teachers gave me a report that made Xang sound very needy and incompetent: "Xang is very disruptive in class. He needs help to complete even the simplest of tasks. Academically, Xang is also experiencing problems. He is struggling in reading and writing in Hmong and in English." In this report and in conversations, Xang was often seen as the slow English language learner student instead of as the active, inquisitive, bilingual, and biliterate youngster that he was. Similarly, James, a student with autism in the same school, was often seen as antisocial, obsessed, and "in his own world" when he wrote and solved his own math equations. His mother and siblings, however, saw him as a brilliant academic learner.

Ayers (2001) called this way of speaking and thinking "toxic." He illustrated the need to examine and carefully critique the ways in which students are described and ultimately perceived:

It's as if supervisors, coordinators, and administrators have nothing better to do than to mumble knowingly about "soft signs," "attention deficit disorder," or "low impulse control," and all the rest of us stand around smiling, pretending to know what they're talking about. The categories keep splintering and proliferating, getting nuttier as they go: L.D., B.D., E.H., T.A.G., E.M.H. It's almost impossible for teachers today not to see before them "gifted and talented" students, "learning disabled" youngsters, and children "at risk." (p. 29)

To combat labeling that is harmful, teachers must work to understand the uniqueness of each student. This might mean spending time with students one-to-one or asking them to share personal information during class. To see each student as an individual, the teacher should also consciously speak about the person with autism as an individual. Instead of comparing and contrasting descriptions of students with autism and talking about these learners as if they are one homogeneous group, teachers who resist the overuse of labels will share information about "Nathan's accomplishments," "Kevin's abilities," and "Anne's successes."

3. Reconfigure Expertise

Too often, students with autism are told about their lives instead of having opportunities to craft their own stories. In order for inclusive education to thrive, teachers must be curious about and interested in the expertise and experiences of individuals with autism. Furthermore, teachers must act on the education they receive from students. Teachers should consider, also, the gifts and strengths that children with autism bring to the classrooms. True inclusive education looks at all students as individuals who can benefit from each other. It is not a specialized program meant to help only a few. The unique perspectives that children with autism can share with others can help their peers and teachers see the world in a new light.

In inclusive classrooms, the teacher looks at the students as the experts, asks them what they would like to learn, and invites them to teach and lead in the classroom. In doing so, the teacher examines his or her own expertise and power. Kliewer and Biklen called for such shifts in practice in their article on the democratization of disability:

> A part of the disability rights agenda has been to reconfigure the meaning of *expert* [italics added]. It demands that no research be conducted on, nor policy implemented for, people with disabilities without their participation. This is certainly a radical democratic stance, but one that comes on the heels of years of subjugation, objectification, and outright silencing at the hands of scientists and policymakers. In effect, people with disabilities are proclaiming to the scientific and policy communities, "Our rights are not yours to give away. The reach of professional prerogative stops at the tenets of democracy." (2000, p. 198)

Teachers must keep in mind that such shifts in power can cause discomfort. Danforth and Rhodes pointed out that "seeking, hearing, and taking seriously the words and ideas of the persons served by special programs, although seemingly innocent enough, is often disruptive" (1997, p. 363).

Dan Reed (1996) relayed an example of such a disruption in his book, *Paid for the Privilege: Hearing the Voices of Autism.* He shared the story of Randy, a man who often hit others in his day treatment program. Reed explained that Randy was not a mean person; rather, he was easily startled and if someone surprised him, he might hit the person. When the hitting began, the staff would immediately "get in Randy's space" to protect him and any others in the area. After learning to communicate using an augmentative communication system, however, Randy was able to tell his team how to better handle the hitting outbursts: GIVE ME ROOM TO BREATHE, Randy typed (on his communication board). The staff of the program decided to honor Randy's expertise and changed their intervention. Instead of moving toward Randy to intervene when the hitting started, the staff moved away and let him have room. Reed reported that "almost without fail, he calms down in a few seconds—no interventions, no head-butts, no more loss of dignity" (p. 113).

Clearly, listening to students is not simply a matter of giving attention and providing opportunity; educators and others who support individuals with autism must respond to the voices of these individuals even when they present information or ideas that challenge authority or criticize institutional structures. Although Randy's request did, in a sense, challenge the way the staff had been responding to crises in the program, staff members were able to hear that challenge and use it as a learning experience. And even though the suggested intervention was a significant departure from the typical interventions used in settings such as schools and group homes, this staff honored the suggestion and gave Randy the ability to help design his own supports.

4. Preserve Student Dignity

Although every teacher, undoubtedly, wants to protect students and help them to build self-respect and self-esteem, these goals are sometimes inadvertently put on the educational "back burner" during busy classroom days. Ironically, when students are not achieving or participating, it is often because we have neglected our personal relationships with them. It is, indeed, in those moments when we pause to listen to our students and learn about who they are and what they need that we do the most to facilitate their learning.

Hutchinson suggested that "dignity requires that the creating of one's life be honored" and that "marginalization is the antithesis of dignity" (1999, pp. 63–64). If we subscribe to Hutchinson's version of dignity, it stands to reason that it is the teacher's job to find space and time for students to shine and to reveal their complexities to others. It is also the teacher's job, then, to consider the ways in which students are marginalized and forgotten and to challenge the structures and practices that hurt students and prevent their full participation and membership in the school community.

Teachers who create comfortable and supportive classrooms in which students can be themselves allow for the preservation and sustenance of all students' dignity. In such classrooms, intimidation, taunting, and name-calling of students who look, communicate, or behave somewhat differently from the "norm" are questioned by teachers and students alike (Bailey, 2001; Mahaffey & Newton, 2008). As Nieto and Bode pointed out, behaviors that threaten student dignity can even be turned into a classroom lesson on social justice:

> The name-calling that goes on in many schools provides a tremendous opportunity for teachers and students to engage in dialogue. Rather than addressing these as isolated incidents or as the work of a few troublemakers, as is too often done, making them an explicit part of the curriculum helps students understand these incidents as symptoms of systemic problems in society and schools. Making explicit the biases that are implicit in name-calling can become part of a "circle" or "sharing time," or can form the basis for lessons on racism, sexism, ableism [i.e., prejudice toward those with disabilities], or other biases. (2008, p. 366)

Even students in the most supportive classrooms, however, may need extra help. Some students with autism have experienced embarrassment, frustration, and even trauma in their educational history. Some, for instance, may have been physically punished by a teacher or excessively teased by peers. Students without identified disabilities may need support, as well. Shy students, students new to the classroom, or those who are experiencing difficulties of some kind may need more encouragement and attention than others. For these students, it may be especially important that teachers find ways to show compassion and caring. For example, dignity can be preserved when educators cultivate and maintain personal relationships with students. Students should feel comfortable showing their uniqueness in the classroom and bringing their personal life to the teacher and to classmates.

As Cummins pointed out, the heart of effective teaching is knowing students: "Good teaching does not require us to internalize an endless list of instructional techniques. Much more fundamental is the recognition that human relationships are central to effective instruction" (1996, p. 73). Likewise, Jasmine Lee O' Neill, a woman with autism, believes that the best professionals are those who want to know students as individuals:

Good professionals in the field spend a lot of time getting to know each new autistic client or pupil. They respect that sensitive person's characteristic to live like a shy sea creature inside a vibrant, colourful, self-containing shell home. They are interested in each one as a human being. They delight in the surprises that unfold as they get to know the autistic individual. (1999, p. 22)

5. Look for Complexity in Learners

Educators must constantly be scouting for student talents and seeking situations that highlight the abilities and support the needs of diverse learners. Teachers of students with autism must believe that students *are* competent, and then they must "set the stage" for students to perform competently. For instance, I once worked with a high school teacher who taught Scott, a student with autism, in her computer class. This learner had limited speech and experienced significant struggles with movement; he often entered her classroom running, and during lessons, he typically paced up and down between the computer tables. Scott, however, was very skilled at certain computer games and very much enjoyed working with his peers.

Scott's teacher realized he was a complex student; he had many struggles but also many strengths she could capitalize on. She, therefore, set up her daily lesson to complement Scott's needs and abilities and to keep all learners engaged and interested throughout the 55-minute period. All students spent the first 20 minutes of class listening to the teacher explain and demonstrate a new skill or concept. During the next 35 minutes, students worked individually or in teams to practice the skill. Scott was given a different schedule of activities to follow, however. Scott started the class by listening to the teacher discuss the new concept as he paced in the back of the room. Then, when students began working on their own, Scott was allowed to pace between tables and stop at two or three different groups to teach his classmates some of the computer skills or games he had mastered. In exchange, students would review the daily work with Scott in a one-to-one format.

The arrangement seemed to benefit all students in the class. Scott's classmates appreciated learning something fun every week, and Scott had an opportunity to learn skills and concepts in a relaxed, small-group situation, which appeared to boost his understanding of the content. As important, Scott's classmates had opportunities to see their peer's talent for learning new software and mastering computer games. Students who had never seen Scott excel at any activity were amazed at his quick reflexes and problem-solving abilities.

In another classroom, a teacher became curious about the behavior of Billy, a student with autism. Billy would come into Spanish class every day and stare at the map of Mexico. It took several reminders to get him to move away from the map and take his seat at the beginning of class. During the second month of school, Billy's behavior still had not changed. Instead of taking the map down as a colleague had suggested, Billy's teacher put a map of Spain next to the one of Mexico. Billy became equally interested in that map. A map of Puerto Rico followed until more than a dozen maps filled the walls of the room. The teacher then gave Billy smaller versions of the maps to keep at his desk so he would be able to study the countries when he was listening to a lesson.

These examples illustrate how teachers built learning experiences and increased student motivation when they looked for complexity and saw their students as learners. The teachers built experiences from student strengths so that their learners with autism would succeed and so that all in the classroom community would be able to appreciate those strengths. Teachers can look for complexity in learners in many ways—by helping an individual student shine during a lesson, studying a student's learning style and teaching to it, or exploring how a student expresses him- or herself and carving out a place in the classroom for that form of expression. Teachers looking for competence and complexity in learners should constantly consider at least the following questions (Kluth, Biklen, & Straut, 2003):

- Who is this student?

- Under what circumstances does this student thrive?

- What gifts, skills, and/or abilities does this student have?

- What is this student's awareness of him- or herself as a learner?

- What effort or potential does this student bring to the classroom?

- How can I help this student find success?

- What prevents me from seeing and/or helps me to see this student's competence?

- How does this student learn?

- What does this student value?

- How and what can I learn from this student?

6. Serve as an Advocate and Teach Advocacy

One of the most important roles a teacher can adopt is to advocate for students. In many cases, teachers who have students with disabilities in their classrooms become responsible for teaching other educators about inclusive education or about specific disabilities. These teachers may also be responsible for answering the questions that families, the PTA, or the local community may pose about inclusive education. For these reasons, it is important that teachers remain aware of the laws as they relate to inclusive education and become familiar with some of the research related to inclusion and educating diverse learners. Teachers should also become familiar with advocacy groups such as TASH, the Autism National Committee (AUTCOM), and the Autism Society of America (ASA) (see the "For More Answers and Information" section at the end of this chapter for more on these groups).

In order to truly make a difference, however, teachers and students must be committed to inspiring change in a way that respects and values all participants equally. This means that in addition to serving as advocates, teachers must promote student self-advocacy (Reiff, 2007; Wehmeyer, 2007). All students are capable of making contributions to their own education, and they must, because most teachers do not know enough about experiencing disability to begin to answer to the multiplicity of issues that students face in their educational lives.

Self-advocacy involves students acting or speaking on their own behalf. To encourage self-advocacy, teachers might encourage students to run for student council, give them opportunities to present information about autism to teachers, help students find ways to contribute to their IEP meetings and to other educational planning meetings, make sure students are given choices and consulted regarding the decisions related to their education (e.g., daily schedule, extracurricular activities), and provide them with opportunities to articulate their preferences and needs.

7. Act as Teacher and Learner

Schools need ways of bringing learners and teachers together and of becoming communities in which participants learn from each other. Teachers must have ways of renewing themselves, of being open to new ideas, and of trying out different strategies and approaches to learning. Some teachers may prefer to continue learning through professional development seminars or college or university courses. Others may seek opportunities in their own buildings. For example, one school I visited held "Share an Idea" workshops every month. Every staff person in the building was invited to present and to attend. A different teacher or team presented one idea during each session. Topics ranged from "Using Writing Workshops in the Inclusive Classroom" to "Co-teaching with Your Speech Therapist" to "Stress Relief at 3:00 p.m." This gave teachers ways to grow as practitioners and helped the school to move forward with progressive practices.

Some schools have instituted book clubs for teachers and other staff members (Kooy, 2006). In one of the schools in which I taught, the book club chose both professional selections (e.g., a book on cooperative learning) and personal favorites that were not directly related to schools and schooling. These experiences allowed teachers to keep current with professional reading and also provided opportunities to socialize and develop a community. In another school, I started a book club focused specifically on autism. This school had an unusually high number of students with autism, and the teachers were constantly seeking opportunities to learn more and to exchange ideas on the topic. We initially focused on autobiographies of individuals with autism, and then teachers took turns suggesting other texts that would help them in their work. (For book club selection ideas, see the "For More Answers and Information" sections at the end of the chapters, and for discussion questions for this book, see Appendix A.)

For those teachers or educational teams who seem to lack common time to meet, web-based discussion boards might be used to share information. Discussion boards can be used to brainstorm lesson ideas, share positive behavioral supports, or post teaching questions and success stories. During a school year when I worked on a grant project with a group of educators that spanned 12 different schools and 7 different districts, the administrators of the project set up an Internet discussion group to encourage conversation and idea sharing. Teachers shared a range of success stories (e.g., "Dan ate his lunch with peers today"), questions (e.g., "What ideas do folks have for helping a student who likes to fidget during classes? What kinds of gadgets have others used?"), and thoughts (e.g., "I have started talking to students in a softer voice and they are responding. I am going to try it with Dottie today. I'll let everyone know how it works"). This structure not only gave our group a way to communicate ideas but also served as a way to build a support system among educators who shared values and a common purpose but seldom had opportunities to meet face to face.

8. Listen

Teachers who are good listeners often find that students are able to provide them with an exceptional education about teaching, learning, and dozens of other topics. For example, consider this description of the perfect school written by Jamie Burke, a teenager with autism:

A school of good soft seats and desks that held wonderful books that told of love and kindness to each other. Kids would need to behave in a most kind manner and teasing would be a detention time. Everyone would be asked to join all clubs if desired and pleasing music would play everywhere. The teacher, good and many of them, would only be as we choose. Not assigned by computers. Courses chosen by love of subject and teachers must be excellent in that class. If homework was told to be done time more than one day is given. Lunch would be served in a room far from cooking so smells are not sickening. The lunch would be a time for peaceful eating and not loud talking and annoying bells and whistles which split my ears as a sword in use of killing monsters. All of the new kids would be treated to a monster movie. Dear parents are welcomed to meet really good all dear teachers to tell of kids powers. But my school is very good and people try both teaching and loving me and my autism. So I think I am fearing less now than younger times of my life and joy in life as a boy in a journey to a happy life is even a dream now seen. Respect comes with love and understanding each kid's abilities and the desire to teach so therefore teachers must have a desire to teach everyone. They must realize that their dreams are not ours. Ask us what we will need to be an independent person later in our life. Teach good skills in a respectful way. Conversations with me will tell you if I'm happy. (Burke, 2005, pp. 249–250)

This passage is important for at least two reasons; first, it provides teachers with concrete ideas for supporting Jamie. An educator who is willing to learn from this student will carefully consider the seating used in his or her classroom or the types of materials available. Second, this description of school is incredibly poetic and introspective. A teacher who listens to Jamie's ideas is also learning about his talent for writing and expression.

Listening is particularly critical when it comes to supporting students with communication needs. Teachers and students in the inclusive classroom will need to consider how they might listen fully and generously to those who do not speak, those with limited English, those with different accents or linguistic styles, and those who struggle to be expressive in whole or small-group situations. Teachers might work with students to create listening adaptations in order to encourage the voices of all. For example, the classroom community might agree to make a very conscious effort to respond to the verbalizations and gestures of peers who do not speak. If a student with disabilities laughs or yells out, peers might turn and say, "You sure seem to have a strong feeling about that. Can you tell us more using your communication device?" Adapting to all learners might also mean working as a group to learn more about the diverse communication styles and approaches in the classroom. The entire class might communicate for an afternoon using only written words, learn storytelling gesticulations, or use sign language greetings and conversation starters.

Another way teachers listen is by tuning into students as they work and socialize. Teachers who participate in casual conversations at lunchtime or who "hang out" in hallways can learn about students in more holistic ways. What makes students excited? Worried? What are they knowledgeable about? Interested in?

Teachers may find keys to teaching and learning and discover ways to better support students by listening carefully during extracurricular activities. For example, my friend Eileen, a fifth-grade teacher, found ways to listen to her students by forming an "anyone-is-welcome" poetry club. She benefited as a teacher not only by participating in a social activity with students but also by eliciting their voices through the poems they wrote. Other teachers listen to students by hanging out at the store, coaching a sport, chaperoning a dance, playing with them at recess, or finding moments to connect with them individually in the classroom.

9. Take Necessary Risks

When I suggest that teachers ask questions and take risks, I do not mean that they should be contrary or that they should constantly challenge the status quo, but I do feel it is important for educators to speak up when students' needs are not being met or when there are injustices that should be addressed. For instance, a teacher who is an advocate for inclusive schooling will want to speak up when his school district considers reorganizing classrooms and resources in order to cluster students with autism into two district schools (instead of keeping all learners at their home schools and in their own neighborhoods). This may mean attending school board meetings, talking to parents, or even offering to problem-solve with leaders.

Risk taking and question posing do not just have to be about big issues such as school restructuring. One of my colleagues, Cara, moved from a school known for its inclusive services to one that was only beginning to include students with autism in general education classrooms. On the first day of school, Cara noticed that all of the students with disabilities ate lunch at the same table. She immediately talked to the lunch assistants about it; the women informed her that this arrangement had been in place for years. She then talked to her coworkers about it, who didn't see it as a problem. Finally she talked to her principal, who also seemed unconcerned. Cara promptly went back to her colleagues and asked them if they minded if she tried playing games with the students at lunch time. Nobody objected. The following day, Cara had the fourth and fifth graders sit according to their birthday months and gave them questions to discuss about their birthdays (e.g., favorite gifts). The next day, Cara had them all sit according to their favorite type of music (six choices were offered). After repeating this for a week, Cara was able to demonstrate the benefits of all learners socializing together; students with disabilities didn't need nearly as much adult support, they had many more opportunities to socialize and communicate, and all students got better acquainted with one another. Cara continued to play the game with the group every Friday, and based on Cara's "intervention," students with disabilities no longer ate at their own table. Just as satisfying to Cara was that two of her colleagues agreed to take turns running the seating game with her.

10. Practice Subversive Pedagogy, if Necessary

Janna, a special education teacher, was asked to set up a behavior management program for Will, a new student with autism. Will often bit his hands or screamed; he seemed to engage in this practice most often during transitions or when there were unexpected changes in his schedule. Janna was told by a district behavior specialist that the biting and screaming were "attention-seeking" behaviors and that she should, therefore, ignore Will if he engaged in them. If the young man was able to refrain from biting his hands and screaming for more than 20 minutes, Janna was to reward him with a baseball card.

Janna refused to implement the program. She believed the student's hand biting and screaming were happening because he was uncomfortable with transitions, frustrated by schedule changes, and uneasy in his new school, in general. Furthermore, she feared that ignoring the behaviors would negatively affect her relationship with the young man. Janna was very concerned about her student and was determined to learn more about the cause of the behaviors.

In rejecting the specialist's program, Janna was practicing what some might call subversive pedagogy. That is, Janna was rejecting common institutional practices in favor of those she saw as more humane and appropriate. Teachers who practice subversive pedagogy "question the policies, procedures, and practices of those who employ them and of these institutions that prevent individual opportunity and growth" (Lasley, Matczynski, & Rowley, 2002, p. 387).

Another example of subversive pedagogy comes from my own teaching experience. During a short period of time when I was teaching in a district that did not support inclusive education, I attended an uncomfortable meeting with a family and an administrator. The mother and father wanted their son to be educated in a general education fifth-grade classroom. The administrator told the family that it would be too difficult to provide the child's education in such an environment. She gave them several reasons but told them it was primarily a staffing issue; she did not have a general education teacher knowledgeable enough or even willing to support a student like their son. The family seemed disappointed when they left the meeting but appeared to accept the administrator's answer. When I tried to talk to the administrator (my boss) about the issue, she made it clear that the decision had been made. I left her office, went back to my room, found a "Parents' Rights in Special Education" booklet in my files, highlighted the sections of importance, and anonymously sent it to the family in the mail. Days later, the parent advocate the family had hired called the administrator to discuss inclusive schooling again.

Subversive pedagogy is not a new phenomenon; there is a long tradition in education of teachers resisting practices and structures deemed oppressive and/or harmful to students

(Ashton-Warner, 1963; Ayers, 2001; Baumgardner & Richards, 2005; Freire, 1970; Holt, 1967; Kozol, 1967; Ladson-Billings, 2009; Paley, 1979). Teacher Bill Ayers reported that he once clipped the wires of the classroom intercom after a stream of senseless announcements disrupted his teaching. Students were able to learn in peace after this act of "creative insubordination," as the intercom was not repaired for 3 years (2001, p. 125).

Teachers in Ladson-Billings's (2009) study of successful teachers of African American students also supported learners by resisting policies and structures deemed oppressive. The researcher explained how the educators worked "in opposition to the school system" at times and felt it was necessary to challenge structures with action:

> They are critical of the way that the school system treats employees, students, parents, and activists in the community. However, they cannot let their critiques reside solely in words. They must turn into action by challenging the system. What they do is both their lives and livelihoods. In their classrooms, they practice a subversive pedagogy. (p. 140)

These teachers in Ladson-Billing's study did everything from rejecting the classroom materials they were told to use (e.g., using trade books and literature instead of textbooks) to quietly sidestepping school policies they deemed inappropriate or damaging to their students. Ladson-Billings pointed out that even though it is sometimes difficult business to struggle against oppression, teachers must not "legitimate the inequity that exists in the nation's schools, but attempt to deligitamize it by placing it under scrutiny" (p. 142). She went on to point out that sometimes "working in opposition to the system is the most likely road to success for students who have been discounted and disregarded by the system" (p. 142). When working with students with autism, then, subversive pedagogy may involve challenging IEPs or reports that contain insensitive or negative language; resisting behavior programs and plans that are undignified, hurtful, or fail to consider the student's individual needs and strengths; rejecting curriculum that does not engage or challenge the learner; or pursuing inclusive education when administrators discourage such actions.

Summary

Although a good teacher certainly needs to know how to develop lesson plans and draw students into learning, the teacher's orientation toward the students is typically the most powerful predictor of success in the classroom. A teacher's beliefs matter. Her politics matter. Her language matters. Her relationships with students matter. Her values matter. In fact, these things matter in very real and very practical ways. Students surely know when and if the teacher believes they will learn and be successful. Consider the words of Stephen Shore, a man with Asperger syndrome:

> I was usually behind in math and reading by at least half a grade. The first-grade teacher said that I would never be able to do math. Nevertheless, somehow I learned and have even taught the subject at the college level. I believe this teacher would be shocked to learn that I went on to study calculus and statistics in college. (2003, p. 53)

Sadly, Shore achieved in mathematics *despite* instead of *in concert with* his teacher's expectation. There is no room for such pessimism in education. As Haim Ginott shares in a quote at the start of this chapter, the teacher's belief in the learner is central to success in the classroom. The best lessons, curricular adaptations, and teaching strategies are useless if a teacher does not expect the learner to achieve; consistently question assumptions; and constantly reflect on the attitudes, values, and actions he or she brings to the daily work of teaching and learning.

FOR MORE ANSWERS AND INFORMATION

📖 Books

Ashton-Warner, S. (1963). *Teacher.* NY: Simon & Schuster.

Ayers, W. (2001). *To teach.* New York: Teachers College Press.

Johnson, L. (2005). *Teaching outside the box: How to grab your students by their brains.* San Francisco: Jossey-Bass.

Ladson-Billings, G. (2009). *The dreamkeepers* (2nd ed). San Francisco: Jossey Bass.

Paley, V. (1990). *The boy who would be a helicopter.* Cambridge, MA: Harvard University Press.

🚪 Organizations

Autism National Committee
http://www.autcom.org
> This advocacy organization is dedicated to "social justice for all citizens with autism." AUTCOM works to protect the human and civil rights of people on the autism spectrum.

Autism Society of America
http://www.autism-society.org
> The goal of the Autism Society of America is to increase awareness about the common issues faced by people on the spectrum. Check out their many local chapters as well.

TASH
http://www.tash.org
> TASH's focus is on those people who are most at risk for being excluded from the mainstream of society, are perceived by traditional service systems as being most challenging, and who have significant disability labels.

🖱 Web Sites

Broadreach Training & Resources
http://www.normemma.com
> The professional site of Norm Kunc and Emma Van der Klift is Broadreach Training & Resources. You will find a lot about the services offered by these two talented professionals but also many great free resources. Check out the great audio interviews, for instance.

Disability Is Natural
http://www.disabilityisnatural.com
> The mission of Kathie Snow's site is to encourage new ways of thinking about developmental disabilities. Disability Is Natural is popular with people with disabilities, families, care providers, and teachers alike. Snow has a blog, a newsletter, and several free articles available to users.

(continued)

(continued)

Responsive Classroom
http://www.responsiveclassroom.org
> The Responsive Classroom is a teaching approach that emphasizes emotional goals as well as academics. Check out the free newsletter for teaching tips.

Teaching Tolerance
http://www.tolerance.org
> Although the focus of this site is typically race, culture, and sexual orientation, the activities and writings featured are related to inclusiveness and creating a safer and more enriching school experience for all.

NOTES: _____

_____

_____

_____

_____

_____

_____

_____

_____

_____

_____

_____

_____

_____

_____

_____

_____

Connecting with Families

with Eileen Yoshina

"Mom," I said, "I'm autistic too, aren't I?"
"Yes," she said. We sat very still and looked at each other for a long, long time.
I had the strangest feeling, one that was entirely new to me. All at once I knew that I
could ask Mom anything, say anything I wanted, and that it would be all right—she
would understand me. (Barron & Barron, 1992, p. 229)

Teachers must work closely with the families of students with disabilities, not necessarily because it is considered "best practice" or because they will often be the most willing and open collaborative partners to whom we can turn. These reasons are relevant, of course, but the most compelling reason to build a strong home–school partnership is related to the intimate relationship that exists between children and their families; the parents of our students know them in ways teachers do not. Parents also *see* students in ways teachers do not. They can provide more rich and detailed information about a student than any professional we can ask or any report we can read.

Consider the story of Beth Kephart (1998), the mother of a child with the label of pervasive developmental disorder (PDD). Kephart tried to enroll her son in a preschool. When Jeremy showed up to visit the school, however, the principal followed him around with a clipboard, making marks each time he struggled. His mother could only look on anxiously:

Jeremy tries—valiantly—to go along with the morning routine. Sits at the computer beside another boy, then attempts to take on the software himself. It's new to him. He fails, gets frustrated. The principal, watching from the corner of the room, strikes a check across her clipboard, and we're asked to move on and join the children in another room who are convening for a snack. There's only one slight problem with the principal's worthy plan—all but Jeremy have special, placarded chairs. When the principal asks Jeremy if he wants something to drink, he circles the room looking for space at the table, offers no answer, returns to me, hurt and teary-eyed. Another check, and we move on.

Kephart then chronicles how the students all move to circle time and the short-sighted assessment continues. As the preschool children gather to sing favorite songs, looking "normal and zesty," Jeremy is lost because these are not songs he knows:

He watches with magnificent patience and I am immensely proud, until the principal asks him if he wants to be the farmer in the dell, and pulls him to the center of the room. *What's a dell?* his eyes seem to be imploring, and what can he possibly do if he doesn't know the answer and the principal's not saying and the other children giggle until Jeremy finally sits down? Another mark on the despicable clipboard, and I throw a spear of hatred across the room.

After the observation, it is finally time for a recess break. Kephart writes that Jeremy, relieved for the break, begins to gallop around the school yard, climb the equipment "with abandon," and dance "to his own dervish tune—demonstrating the grace and balance he's exhibited from his start" but, Kephart notes, "it doesn't really matter":

The performance falls on dead eyes. I am ready for the principal when she approaches with her news. "I've been thinking," she tells me, with a sugary, grandmotherly smile, "that we simply don't have room. The child with diabetes is taking all our extra time, and that means we could never do right by your son." (Kephart, 1998, pp. 164–165)

In this preschool scenario, it is clear how much the perspective of a parent matters. Without Kephart's interpretations, the teachers may not know that using new software will be a challenge for Jeremy or that he *can* successfully participate in the school's snack time if given information about where to sit and how to engage in the routine or that he *does* know how to sing songs (just not those particular songs). Furthermore, it seems that only the parent sees Jeremy's "grace and balance" and knows how very hard he is working to be successful in the preschool activities.

Harry (1992) suggested that teachers must constantly ask the question "Do we assume that professional efforts constitute the only legitimate source of opinion, and that the role of parents is to give permission for professional activities and automatic approval for professional decisions?" If the answer to the question is yes, then changes are essential, as a true partnership with families cannot grow from such a belief system. If families are ignored, dismissed, or otherwise prevented from participating in the education of their child, the student's program will suffer—skills and knowledge gained in the classroom may not be reinforced in the home; any competencies the child demonstrates in the home will not be practiced and, perhaps even seen, in the classroom; and new learning inspired by the synergy of a home–school partnership will never be realized.

This chapter is purposely near the beginning of this book; in placing it before the chapters on curriculum, instruction, communication, behavior, friendship, and other topics, we hope to communicate the idea that building partnerships with families is as or more important than anything else teachers can do in the classroom. The ideas outlined in this chapter are designed to push teams to work with families in new and creative ways and to move beyond

As a parent with multiple children with many different learning abilities, I believe inclusive education shouldn't be thought of as just another thing a teacher has to try and do to accommodate a minority of students. Reaching all students with all kinds of abilities is the goal, and using curricular adaptations and a wide range of materials and strategies can help a teacher create the perfect classroom for all students. If a teacher used these creative ways to reach every student my son could succeed along with every other child in his classroom.

—Lori Micheal

collaboration that is passive or partial. We have divided our information and recommendations into two sections: learning about families and building effective school–home partnerships.

Learning About Families

The first and most important step toward getting connected to students is learning about their families and the lives they share with those families outside school walls. Specifically, we recommend that teachers make an effort to learn more about all of the individuals that make up a family, recognize the diversities that families bring to the classroom, and rethink the idea of "difficult" families.

Think Beyond Mom and Dad

Some students are parented by an aunt. Others live with foster families. Still other students may come from homes with two mothers or two fathers. The one-mother, one-father nuclear family is no longer the norm in American life. Extended family members, friends, or even organizations (e.g., group homes) may serve as guardians or primary caregivers for students in today's schools and should, therefore, be seen as part of the school community in the same way parents are. If students with autism receive respite care or part-time foster care, the individuals providing this care should also be viewed as part of the home–school partnership. Community institutions may be part of the family structure in some cultural groups and neighborhoods; these relationships should be honored as well. A church may play a central role in the life of the family, for instance (Carter, 2007).

The role that siblings play in the life of a student with autism should also be considered when working with families. Siblings might be asked to contribute thoughts or ideas to formal meetings or to give their parents suggestions to bring to discussions about their brother or sister. Often, siblings have a connection with the student with autism that others do not. Siblings of individuals with autism may even have knowledge the parents do not have. For example, one woman told us an amusing story about her son, Peter, and how his siblings support and understand him when his mother and father cannot. The family was having dinner when Peter, who has the label of PDD, yelled out "phooey" and spit a mouthful of chili all over the table. The woman and her husband were surprised and annoyed by this behavior and thought that Peter was trying to impress his brothers by misbehaving. Peter's brothers came to his rescue as they burst out laughing and told their parents that he was only imitating a Scooby Doo videotape he had watched that day. Peter frequently acted out scenes from his favorite car-

As a mother of a college-age child with Asperger's, all I can say is "we did it." When my son was 2 he scored a 72 on an IQ test and we were told he was minimally retarded. His ability to count, add and multiply at an incredibly early age were described as "splinter skills." We saw signs of intelligence and encouraged him to build on it. Math was always his strength. He scored an 800 on his Math SATs. Lots of therapy, lots of love, and a tremendous amount of social counseling have formed my son into the person he is. Some individuals with Asperger's tend to accumulate vast amounts of knowledge about topics that interest them. My son's focus is basketball. He has incorporated this interest into his education. At Seton Hall, he is majoring in sports management and is one of the student managers of their basketball team. He plans on taking his hobby and turning it into a profession.

My son's success did not just happen. We, meaning, my husband and I, his teachers, therapists, and so forth all built on the positives. Most of his teachers modified their social and behavioral expectations for my son well before differentiated learning and inclusion were even thought of as educational jargon. Our elementary school principal paved the way for him to take advanced math classes at our local middle and high school. It took teamwork in "our village" to make this work.

—Linda Malinsky

toons and often used these scenes to communicate with others. The woman and her husband felt differently about Peter's behavior when they got this piece of information and were able to talk to Peter about "how dogs eat hot chili differently than little boys do."

Recognize the Diversity of Families

In many schools in the United States, especially those in urban areas, the differences in culture, language, and life experience among students and teachers can be significant. The teaching force in the United States remains overwhelmingly Caucasian (Epstein, 2005), while the United States and, therefore, the student population of this country, is becoming only more racially and ethnically diverse (Delpit, 1995; Hernandez, 1989; Lapkoff & Li, 2007).

Social, racial, and cultural mismatches between teachers and students are problematic; every student in today's schools—including Caucasian students—would benefit from having more teachers of color. This is not to imply that Caucasian teachers cannot be effective teachers of students of color, but to do so, they must be committed to seeing and valuing the cultural, linguistic, and ethnic differences students and their families bring to the classroom (Howard, 2007; Knight, 2003; Ladson-Billings, 2009; Villegas & Lucas, 2007).

When teachers do not recognize and understand such differences, they are likely to jump to conclusions that are inaccurate and that threaten the home–school partnership. The dangers of rushing to judgment are highlighted in this reflection from a novice teacher who admits it was a "culture shock" to teach at a diverse school:

Even though I felt like a competent teacher, I went through some changes because the children were different. Mai and Dou were both my students and one year apart in age. Mai would come to school tired, inadequately dressed, with dirty hair...while her brother was always rested, neat, and clean. I knew about gender differences in Asian cultures but I was thinking, "When in Rome do as the Romans do." I lost it—got so angry—when she came to school on a snowy day with a T-shirt, shoes with holes in the bottom and without the coat I had gotten for her from a local charity. I asked where her coat was and she said that her mother had given it to her sister. I called and sent notes home but received no word back. I felt they were neglecting this child. Finally, the school social worker, a translator and I made a home visit. In the end, I was wrong...the mother was newly immigrated, did not speak English, was very concerned about both of her children, respected the expertise of teachers, and needed some help getting acclimated to a new world where her cultural practices were easily construed as abuse. (Knight, 2003, pp. 61–62)

Delpit (1995) observed that central to connecting with families is attending to the ways in which they talk about and see themselves instead of trying to guess or, even worse, insisting that we know and understand who they are. Teachers must listen to families and work to understand their experiences, traditions, histories, and beliefs. Teachers will benefit from learning to understand how families view themselves, the students' school experiences, and the partnership between the school and the home.

Teachers should also explore how the family views the student's disability. In some cultures and, therefore, in some families, disability may be seen as a natural human difference; whereas in other cultures, the same disability may be seen as a medical problem. Locust pointed out, for instance, that

Most traditional Indian languages do not have words for mentally retarded or disabled or handicapped and, rather than using such categories, may assign names of individuals that are descriptive of the disability, such as One-Arm, or One-Who-Walks-with-a-Limp. (as cited in Harry, 1995, p. 46)

Knowing how a student's family understands the disability can help the teacher make appropriate choices in designing supports, talking about the student and his disability, and making suggestions for supports and services outside of the classroom. Some families, for instance, feel more comfortable than others in talking about their child's differences as a disability. These preferences should, of course, be honored.

Rethink "Difficult" Families

Teachers sometimes muse about the "difficult" parents of students with disabilities. This label is often given to parents who call or visit often; ask a lot of questions; or often seem uncomfortable with or critical of the school, the teachers, or their child's educational program. Although some of the clashes teachers have with families may be because of personality conflicts or differences of opinion, other struggles occur because teachers do not understand a family's history. Some students with autism and their families come to the classroom with the "baggage" of bad education-related experiences. Families may have felt unwanted in other schools, been treated with indifference or contempt, or been made to feel unimportant in some way. As one parent reports, "I was adversarial with Laura's educational system all the way through, but I had lots of questions that I couldn't get answers to" (Egel, 1989, p. 200).

As Harry (1992) pointed out, many parents become "difficult" because their views are dismissed and their membership in the educational partnership is threatened. In these situations, parents feel that they have no way to express their views or to be heard except to be "difficult."

The mother that calls twice a day to ask questions and criticize may be accustomed to years of feeling brushed aside. The father that starts a conversation with a threat of legal action may fear that a placement he fought years for is at risk. Teachers must keep in mind that many families come to the classroom having dealt with individuals and systems that have misunderstood or even rejected their child. It may take a lot of reassurance and effort to earn the trust of parents who have been insulted, ignored, or otherwise hurt.

One of the most powerful ways to support a wounded family is to listen to them and their stories. Asking the family to share their experiences might help them to feel heard, but these accounts can also help a teacher understand the history that a student brings to the classroom. Biklen (1992) shared the story of a young man with disabilities who, every day at lunchtime, would scream and throw things. At first, the educational team and the child's mother were stumped by the behavior. Eventually, however, the mother realized that her son was upset by the small cans of pudding distributed in the cafeteria. These cans were the exact kind used to reinforce the young man's behavior when he had lived in an institution months

Inclusion has been ongoing and authentic in the case of my daughter's education. Credit goes to the staff in her inclusive environment, as independence has always been an important goal. To that end many learning opportunities have been afforded to Chelsea and peers have been drawn in to support her in those situations. One of the best outcomes has been her social growth and learning. She has not only participated in a high school drama class but with the encouragement of her drama teacher and classmates, she auditioned for and performed a dramatic interpretation of Lewis Carroll's "Jabberwocky" in the school talent showcase. I was initially worried about the after-school rehearsals. Who would supervise? "The staff couldn't possibly be asked to stay after school on their own time, could they?" As it turns out my worries were unnecessary as staff and students had already taken all of these factors into consideration and the event went off without a hitch. This positive exposure led to many more peer contacts in the days after the event.

—Arlene M. Smerdon

earlier. The cans triggered the young man's memory of the institution, a place he greatly feared. Without the input of the family and the knowledge of the student's past, the teachers likely would have never guessed that the lunch problem stemmed from the past trauma and might have worked (unsuccessfully) on solving the problem for months.

Teachers and other educational team members should show the family of any student with a difficult educational history that they value the home–school relationship. Furthermore, the team should seek ways to demonstrate their commitment to the family through action, namely by working to create an effective partnership in the current school and situation.

Elements of an Effective School–Home Partnership

In order to design appropriate strategies and approaches, the elements of an effective school–home partnership must be developed. We suggest five basic elements that must be in place for educators and families to establish positive and productive relationships and collaboration structure: a welcoming school; the belief that all students are valued; open, constant, and productive communication; willingness and interest in learning from families; and clear structures for information and knowledge sharing.

A Welcoming School

Even if a teacher is warm and accepting, parents still may not feel at home in a school if the building and the staff are not welcoming to all families. Promoting an inclusive philosophy is an important part of this process of welcoming families. As one mother shared in a study conducted by one of this chapter's authors, inclusion is not only about providing space for students, it is about communicating a message of belonging:

> I mean there are some schools saying, "We're going to do inclusion" and they're grumbling and they're doing it . . . just because they have to. There are other schools that truly embrace it. [Our new] principal, I mean she has made a huge effort not only to include kids inschool but to make it a community wide kind of thing. (Kluth, Biklen, English-Sand, & Smukler, 2007, p. 50)

Unfortunately, families are still fighting to find schools with this type of commitment. Although this phenomenon is less common today than it was 20 years ago, families across the United States are still struggling to find schools that accept and understand their children with autism (Kluth et al., 2007). Davern (1996) suggested that building relationships with families will involve long-term schoolwide plans to offer full membership to all students, not just offers to set up programs for students in response to the requests of individual parents.

Families should be made to feel that they are valued members of the school community; this is especially true in schools where inclusion is a new phenomenon. In these schools, families may need extra support, as many will be unaware of some of the norms and traditions of a "regular" school; they may be inexperienced in networking and meeting families of students without identified disabilities; and they may not be well connected to some of the typical child-centered community and neighborhood activities. If a family does not have other children without disabilities, they may need help breaking into the "soccer parent" circle or the carpool group. For example, when a family one of us knew came to the school to enroll their young son (who happened to have autism), the principal of the school immediately suggested to the family that they join the PTA and reminded them to attend the open house, which was to occur on the following evening. When the family explained that their son was likely to "get very active" during the open house, the principal reassured them, "This is a school, not an art museum. We expect kids to be themselves here . . . and to act like kids. Please join us tomorrow night."

The family must also feel that the student with autism is seen as a member of the school and classroom. The student should be invited to participate not only in the classroom but also in the life of the school, including extracurricular activities, evening events (e.g., dances, concerts, the school carnival), and before- and after-school rituals and routines (e.g., hanging out in the hallway with friends, visiting the school store).

Our family is very close-knit. If our son is having a bad day, the whole family feels it. Early in our son's high school experience, our oldest daughter was also a student at the high school. She would often express concern when hearing her brother in the hallway during a meltdown. She would excuse herself from class to see what was wrong only to be sent back to class. We would hope that educators would see siblings as a resource. After all, the siblings might bring another outlook to the situation. Most of all, compassion is needed everyday—an understanding that you can make a difference. You have the power through compassion to make every day a good day.

—The Van Boxtel family

The Belief that All Students Are Valued

Families should be able to expect that teachers will value their child and see him or her as an individual and as an important person. One of the most significant messages that can be communicated to a family is "We feel your child has something important to contribute to the life of the school." These types of messages are best communicated through actions. A mother we know, for example, was thrilled when the physical education teacher called the family to ask them if their son, Gordon, could join the after-school weight lifting team. As Gordon's mother shared, "It was the first time something really fantastic happened for Gordon that we didn't need to ask for."

Another way teachers can communicate their respect for a student is to think about the language they use in conversations, meetings, and written documents. If every meeting begins with a description of a student's struggles and if every report written fails to include a student's strengths and gifts, it will be hard for a parent to believe that the teacher appreciates the student and sees him or her as a contributing member of the classroom. Consider the ways in which one mother describes the IEP meetings she endured that were deficit and program driven:

> The room would be filled with too many people, sometimes as many as 21, all eager to push for their own agendas. The meeting would begin with evaluations, present levels, and a list of things that Andrew could not do. . . . Goals had been written by specialists who discussed how they were going to "fix" Andrew's problems, with the hopes of "getting him ready for a regular classroom" (7 out of 10 times, with 85% accuracy). (Dixon, as cited in Contract Consultants, Inc., 1997, p. 61)

Contrast that description with the meetings this same family attended after they moved their son into an inclusive educational setting and began working with professionals who believed meetings should be positive and focused on discussions of student strengths:

> We talk about a beautiful child and his gifts, the things he is learning and what other children are learning from him. When we set goals, no one cares that Andrew doesn't isolate his index finger on command 2 out of 3 times. We care that he is doing the same things as the rest of the class. We depend upon our dreams to set goals for Andrew that will help him succeed in society when his school days are over. (Dixon, as cited in Contract Consultants, Inc., 1997, p. 61)

As Biklen reported from his study of parents of students with disabilities, most families simply want people to care about and recognize the uniqueness of their children:

> The parent of a child with severe autism remembers her trepidation about sending him to a nursery school. Although her son is now nineteen, she still remembers vividly that she "didn't have to beg for entry; they wanted us." The director and the teachers felt that Neil would be "good for the other children. They never made me feel I had to be grateful [to them] for taking him in." Furthermore, "they made it abundantly clear that they enjoyed and cared for Neil. I never had that 'if only I were the child's mother' feeling that one can get from professionals." (1992, p. 53)

Likewise, in a study by Davern (1996), parents reported that they valued the "ability of teachers to see different aspects of a child's personality aside from academic achievement." One parent shared, "For teachers to say to me, 'I really like your kid,' or 'You know, he really has a great sense of humor' . . . lets me know that they really care about him as a person" (p. 61). Another parent shared that she was impressed with teachers who focused on the progress of individual students rather than comparing learners to each other: "So our child's not going to be the top of her class in gym. We understand that. Just take her for who she is. Find space for her" (p. 61).

Open, Constant, and Productive Communication

Communicating with families should be a centerpiece of education. When working with the families of students with disabilities, communication may be even more critical. Several reasons exist for this increased need for communication:

- Some students cannot communicate reliably; therefore, all of the home–school communication must take place between the teachers and the family.

- Students may have special needs that require frequent exchange of information (e.g., sharing information about the impact of medications).

- When working with students with unique learning characteristics, families will often have valuable information about the learner and the disability that teachers cannot get from another source.

One of the most obvious ways to improve communication is to create opportunities and structures for sharing information and giving and getting support. In some partnerships, the stakeholders meet for coffee once per month; in other situations, the parties communicate back and forth with a weekly or daily notebook entry. Still other families and teachers may share information through e-mail, which is an ideal option for busy families and teachers. No matter how information is shared, the team should be sure to have an explicit conversation about the process. Some families cannot field telephone calls at work; others have many children and do not have much time to read and respond to daily notes. The communication systems put in place should meet the needs of all members of the partnership. Other ways that communication can be enhanced are offered here.

Take the Time to Talk

Most communication problems start with parents feeling out of the loop. A parent may feel especially dependent on the school if a student does not have a reliable way to communicate or if he or she has speech or language difficulties. A mother of a kindergarten student was especially frustrated when her child's teacher called her at work to ask why her daughter, Lanie, who is nonverbal, did not have a lunch or permission slip for the day's field trip. The mother was frustrated because she had never been informed about the field trip. It is time-consuming to call parents on a regular basis, but it is worth the investment if the teaching team can avoid misunderstandings down the road. In the case of the mystery field trip, for example, consider that preparing the family for the field trip in advance would have taken approximately 10 minutes. Repairing the damage of a missed communication, however, took far longer and put a strain on the teacher–family relationship for weeks.

Setting aside 15–20 minutes each week or every other week to call parents for a friendly update can build bridges between school and home and provide an avenue for working through concerns or hatching future plans in small and manageable amounts of time. Teachers may call different parents every week, leaving messages for some and having a 5-minute exchange with others. A colleague of ours engages in this practice religiously and makes it a point to call the parents of every student in his sixth-grade classroom at least once during the year. For students with disabilities or other needs, the calls may be more frequent or supplemented with other communication systems.

Involve Families in Solution Building

When parents have a problem or concern, the teacher or a few members of the educational team should sit down and brainstorm a variety of possible solutions. When possible, educators should allow the family to make the final choice; the teacher or administrator might review all of the possibilities with the family and ask, "Which of these options are you most comfortable with? Which seems most doable to you?" Whereas the family might have come in feeling powerless, they would now be leaving with at least a few solutions at their disposal, a clear plan of action, and the final decision over their child's education.

Sharing solution building also divides the responsibility for the situation between school and home. Often, parents want to act but don't know how; this can lead to frustration and feelings of helplessness. If a parent helps to build solutions, the brainstorming process is likely to be more meaningful. When the family and the school work as partners rather than as adversaries, it can make a significant difference in how the family feels and how a student is perceived. For example, one parent shared the following:

In the past few years, I have been told that my son with autism "could be better served in a more specialized program, like a special school." I believe that it was this attitude that hindered his progress. Based on this past experience, we knew it was imperative to have the support of a regular education teacher with an open mind.

I used to believe that the most important component of a good, effective inclusion program was the special education teacher. Although I believe every member of an educational team is an important one, I now feel that the support of the regular education teacher is critical.

David's teacher this year has been just that. His regular education teacher has accepted him as a full participating member of her classroom community. She treats him like all of the other students, is able to be flexible, and makes accommodations if necessary. She accepts us, the parents, as equal members of the team and encourages our input. Most importantly she believes my son can not only learn from his nondisabled peers but that he has a lot to offer them in return.

David not only is happier this year but is progressing both academically and socially. We are extremely grateful for the support and acceptance of his classroom teacher, to whom we attribute this success.

—Jo Anne Califana

Brainstorming together is an energizing process. It can make assessment and planning look more like a celebration and less like a funeral. The focus of the discussion becomes giving families normal life opportunities rather than creating "near normal" children. (Rocco, 1006, p. 57)

Accentuate the Positive

A mother we know claims that she tenses up at work whenever her cell phone rings. Because her son's school is one of only a few parties who have that particular number, she worries she will receive bad news as soon as she answers the call. This pattern has become so regular and predictable that this mother has grown to hate talking on the telephone at all because she associates the ring with frustration, anger, and pain.

Many problems are inherent in this woman's story. Certainly, the school should reconsider the reactive nature of the relationship; a family–school partnership will surely fail if parents are only contacted to respond to negative situations. Furthermore, any telephone call made to a family member should be done with compassion. If a student's behavior or health is in such a state that a telephone call home is warranted, the parent will obviously be disappointed or even distraught to hear the news. The stress of such a situation should always be considered; there is a huge difference between calling a parent to report, "You need to come over here. Tom is having a bad day again," and calling a parent to say, "Do you have time to help us? Tom is biting himself and we can't seem to calm him down. Do you have any ideas?"

Another way to build better relationships and avoid the fear-of-the-telephone phenomenon is to avoid communicating ONLY in difficult moments. Telephone calls, conferences, and notes home should be conduits for sharing all types of news—good as well as difficult. Teachers and administrators should write or call periodically to report on achievements, ask questions, and share ideas that seem to work. This practice is effective not only for sustaining relationships but also for encouraging proactive conversations and helping teachers craft better supports for students. Your team might even consider adopting the practice of one team who conducted "WFF" summits in between IEP meetings; in these gatherings, each team member could share thoughts and celebrate successes and, therefore, get a "warm fuzzy feeling" that things were on track (Kluth & Shouse, 2009).

A Willingness and Interest in Learning from Families

Teachers who do not connect with families and seek expertise or concrete strategies from them may miss all of the rich opportunities for building on skills that are already acquired and fail to capitalize on the important links that can be developed among parents, communities, schools, and students (Hess, Molina, & Kozleski, 2006; Kozleski et al., 2008; Taylor & Dorsey-Gaines, 1988). Through families, teachers can learn about materials that are familiar and valued, strategies that are effective, situations that prompt learning, topics of conversation and discussion that spur discovery and interest, and activities and issues that are relevant and have meaning in students' lives.

Students with autism are incredibly unique, and their needs are unlike others with the same diagnosis. For this reason, teachers need to rely on experts who know the needs and abilities of the individual child

My son's teacher is a very patient and sensitive person. She has called me numerous times at home, and I am pleased to say that the communication between school and home has been wonderful, and I have been very impressed with how difficult situations have been handled at school. I am a teacher myself, and I would understand how difficult it would be to have a student with challenging behaviors. Thanks to the kindness and patience of Yuuki's teacher, along with accommodations made by the administration, my son is able to succeed in school.

There have been occasions when Yuuki has hit, and at that time he was suspended from school for 3 days. My son Yuuki loves school, and we've all come to the conclusion that when there is a break from school, he gets upset because he is such a creature of habit and he doesn't like having a break from school. If Yuuki is expelled, everyone has to go through the trauma of once again having to get used to the school routine when he gets back. I appreciate the school's efforts to work with me and my son.

—Midori Aoki

they are expected to teach. Parents are virtually the only resource with this kind of expertise and knowledge, and educators must therefore use and learn from their ideas and suggestions.

One effective (and too-seldom used) way to learn from families is to get to know them outside of the classroom. Many teachers make it a practice to at least visit the communities of all students in their classes— some teachers even try to visit the home of each one of their students. This practice may be particularly necessary for students with disabilities.

When one of the chapter authors (Paula) was a new teacher, she visited the homes of all of her students right before school started and then 1 week after school had been in session. These meetings were invaluable in getting to know families and in setting up partnerships with them. Furthermore, she was able to see students playing, communicating, and socializing in a natural setting. At the beginning of her career, she knew little about autism, and her administrators and colleagues didn't seem to know much more; therefore, she relied on these parents and siblings to teach her as quickly and as thoroughly as possible. One mother invited her to dinner and showed her how she was struggling to get her son to eat at the dinner table; she was instantly able to see what he could do (e.g., open his napkin, pour his milk) and what was hard for him (e.g., staying seated). Another family allowed her to sit on the floor and play a favorite card game with their son; she immediately went out and bought this same game so this young man would have a familiar activity waiting for him in his new classroom.

As the year progressed and she got to know the families a bit better, she began conducting IEP premeetings in their homes. This gave her a chance to talk casually to the family about ideas for new goals before all of them met with the full IEP team and were faced with the formality of paperwork and protocols. These meetings seemed quite effective; parents started coming to IEP meetings as more active participants, ready to share ideas, ask and answer questions, and give information to other team members.

Keep in mind that learning from families means that we learn not just about their children but that we listen to the family members and value their ideas in general. For instance, at John J. Audubon School in Chicago, Illinois, it was a group of parents who challenged the annual celebration of National Inclusive Schools Week in their school. These parents felt that the school should do more than just acknowledge "inclusion" or the presence of difference; they felt the community should honor it. The group felt a more comprehensive label was appropriate and, therefore, suggested the school celebrate

I believe that for inclusion to have a real chance to be successful, a working partnership must be established between educators and parents. If each is willing to admit that they don't have all the answers, then they should also be willing to admit that they can learn from each other.

Much like success in any interpersonal relationship, here, too, there needs to be a foundation established on mutual respect and trust. Parents should acknowledge the teacher's expertise, dedication, and value. At the same time, parents should be prepared to demonstrate what they know that teachers don't. As a parent I have an insight into my child's unique learning style and the characteristics of my child's underlying condition. I also know that my child can learn, can effectively relate with others, and can fit in . . . if just supported and given the chance. I know this because I have already successfully included my child into my family and my community.

As a parent of a child that learns differently from his peers, what keeps me up at night are the unknowns in my child's future. As an adult will my child fit in? Will he find a job? Will he marry and have kids of his own? Will he have friends? Will he become a productive and welcomed member of a community?

The hope and the dream and the ideal of true inclusion is that by making kids who are different real members of diverse school communities, that when they reach adulthood each of these questions will be answered in the affirmative. To witness inclusion working; to see teachers, administrators, and fellow students enriched by my child and acknowledge the value in my child that I do as a parent, is what lets me begin to really believe that there truly is a place for my child.

—Jeffery Cohen

"Unique Week," which would teach students that all learners (not just those with disabilities) are different and that the community is more powerful because of this diversity. Parents in the school not only threw a lunch for the teachers but helped with the week's activities, created decorations (including signs that proclaimed "Great Minds Think Differently"), and celebrated the staff as well as the students.

Clear Structures for Information and Knowledge Sharing

Teachers use a variety of tools and strategies to reach, inform, and learn from families. Some send a newsletter. Others host a series of open house class meetings. Still others may use telephone calls or e-mail to stay in touch. These structures can be incredibly effective in helping all parties stay aware of a student's needs and progress.

Teachers may find, however, that some students and families need more information or more frequent or personal interactions than typical classroom communication tools and strategies allow. Outlined here are three ideas for enhancing school–home communication and giving and receiving critical information and knowledge.

Parent Reports

Harry (1992) suggested that parents be invited to participate in meetings in more meaningful and formal ways. One way to get information from parents and to let them know that their perspective matters is to ask them to present a report at the IEP or placement meeting:

> This report would constitute an official document, to be entered into the record and taken into account in decision making, along with the professional reports. This official parental role would not only increase the value that professionals place on parental input, but this role would signal to parents that their input is not only valued but needed. (pp. 128–129)

A parent report could be very formal or very informal. It might be 10 pages or a few paragraphs. Such a report might include information about the student's home life (e.g., new interests, changes in family routines), achievements he or she realized at home or in the community (e.g., played her first video game with brothers, was nominated to speak at church), skills taught in school that have been applied at home, and/or parent impressions of progress on IEP goals and objectives. Parents might also include any artifacts that would help the team better understand the learner (e.g., recent photographs, drawings, medical information).

Somehow, somewhere, an invisible barrier has been built between school and home. We all need to realize how much we both are an integral part of the child's education. What is done at home impacts what is done at school. What is done at school impacts what is done at home. Student progress would soar if we could all be on the same page.

As a parent, I feel that at times I've had to beg, borrow, and steal my way into the system, but I do believe we are beginning to make progress in this area. Through numerous conversations and stating the importance of collaboration, we are beginning to work together on techniques and assignments. If I would ever be granted one wish to come true, it would be that a school–home partnership be identified and developed on the IEP prior to any goals and/or objectives.

—Pat Wilson

Harry (1992) pointed out that in order for this suggestion to be effective, teachers and other educational team members will need to take seriously the charge of planning meetings that are family friendly. This may mean that teams consider holding meetings outside of traditional school hours so that parent work schedules can be supported, find places to meet where all stakeholders feel comfortable (e.g., school lounge, in the home of a family member), and make sure that all participants are encouraged to contribute ideas. One team ensured everyone's participation by setting a timer for 30 minutes; when the timer rang, members took inventory of who had already spoken and who still needed to have "the floor."

Audio/Video Exchange

Some ideas are difficult to express and share through the written word; in these situations teachers and families may share audio or video clips or recordings. Audio clips are especially helpful when the educational team and the family have a hard time connecting face to face or on the telephone. Audio clips are best used in situations in which a family member or educator needs to explain or ask something that is too complex or involved to write in a note. We know one family who communicated to their son's teacher through an audio recording every other week. The teacher listened to the clip as she drove home from work on Fridays and found that she got some of her best teaching ideas from this indirect exchange.

Video can be an incredibly powerful and convenient communication tool. With the dawn of cell phone cameras and digital clips that can be transferred electronically, parents and teachers can send and discuss video immediately after it is captured. We have most often used video to record "trouble spots" in the day by sending clips home to families and asking parents to review them and give feedback. For instance, a young woman, Shelley, was having a hard time in her high school physical education class and exhibiting self-injurious behaviors the team had not seen from her in years. For 3 consecutive days the teacher videotaped the class and sent it home to her family. His father watched the clips and gave this feedback:

- "She doesn't seem to understand the directions; maybe the teacher can write them down."

- "Kathy is in the class—maybe Shelley can be paired with her for some activities; she lives in our neighborhood and the two have known each other for years."

- "She got hurt playing volleyball in sixth grade so she might still be afraid of the game; she might need to take a more passive role during this unit."

When I consider how often I feel that people who describe my experience as the parent of a child with a significant disability "get it wrong," it humbles me. It helps me realize how imperfect are my poor attempts to understand my son's experience or the experiences of families other than my own.

One thing they never told me is that there would be fun parts: that the child is a child, engaged in life, frequently charming. Autism for us is like family language—certain words, actions, or juxtapositions take on inside meanings. Others wonder why we're laughing; but explaining a joke is hard, and often deflates the humor.

What saddens me most is how the rest of the world responds. It is so easy for any of us to ignore the things that really matter about someone if we are distracted by differences we think have to matter. We claim that a "need for sameness" is an autistic trait, but it is we who are unable to let go of difference, to become comfortable with others.

The real story about being anyone's parent is that they do not turn out to be who you expect them to be. This is as entirely true for my nonautistic children as for the guy with the label. Perhaps I was lucky enough to learn it sooner with the child who was "different." But things never turn out as anticipated: All of them outgrow us, disappoint us, surprise us, amaze us, and have the potential to delight us. And our children do all of this on their terms, not ours. If we're among the lucky ones, we might just learn to appreciate our offspring and remain friends with them as they leave us behind.

—David Smukler

All of Shelley's father's suggestions proved helpful, especially the information about volleyball being problematic. Sure enough, when the physical education teacher told Shelley she knew about the injury, she seemed to become more relaxed. The teacher stopped putting Shelley close to the net and instead let her rotate just through the back row for the rest of the unit. There would have been no way of knowing this critical bit of information without the input from Shelley's father.

Furthermore, Shelley's parents really appreciated seeing her in the classroom without having to constantly visit the school. It gave them a chance to review the day with her and view her progress. The video clips also had an unexpected and positive impact on Shelley; she began watching the clips frequently and seemed to grow calmer in the class as a result of visually rehearsing the classroom routines featured on the video.

Student Learning Logs

If the student can write or type, a daily learning log or reflection on the day's activities is both a valuable educational tool and a nice way for families to find out the answer to the question "What did you do in school today?" If written communication is not possible for the student with autism (or any student) to undertake at the end of each day, a classmate can easily provide some support for this task.

When chapter coauthor Eileen Yoshina taught fifth grade, all of the students were responsible for filling out a daily homework and reflection log before the final bell. Eileen and the students typically filled in the homework section together and then discussed as a class some possible entries for the reflection portion; this section could include personal achievements, new skills practiced, or anything interesting that happened during the day. Faith, a student with disabilities in the class, would dictate to her classmate, Trang, what she wanted to include on her reflection. If Eileen mentioned any reminders for families (e.g., pack a lunch for the picnic tomorrow), Trang would write that down too. Whenever possible, Faith would add a note of her own or embellish the day's entry with a drawing or with her choice of stickers.

The learning log is a nice replacement for the communication notebook that is often passed from the teacher to the parent of the student with a disability because it gives the family an opportunity to receive classroom news as well as information about their child. Furthermore, it gives the student an opportunity to participate in the interactions between teacher and family while also providing the learner an opportunity to practice both literacy and communication skills.

Summary

It is exciting to contemplate the possibilities of forming strong and productive partnerships between schools and families. We may not yet realize all of the ways in which we can improve on curriculum, instruction, communication, and social and behavioral supports until we commit ourselves to working closely with families and to creating new models of working in concert with them. Ro and Jo Vargo, the parents of a woman with Rett syndrome, share the importance of such a commitment:

> Our journey has taught us that we cannot work in isolation to accomplish Rosalind's inclusion. Rather, we must collaborate with others to make it work. It does not matter whether it is as simple as a discussion on the telephone about how to adapt arrangements for Rosalind to participate in a field trip (curriculum modifications) or convincing church officials to include her in a sacramental rite (intervention strategies) or as complex as advocating for more inclusive schools (e.g., collaboration, teamwork, normalizing environments). With little or no training, we still get the job done every day with the support of others. (2000, p. 243)

FOR MORE ANSWERS AND INFORMATION

Books

Ariel, C.N., & Naseef, R.A. (Eds.). (2006). *Voices from the spectrum: Parents, grandparents, siblings, people with autism, and professionals share their wisdom.* Philadelphia: Jessica Kingsley.

Collins, P. (2005). *Not even wrong: A father's journey into the lost history of autism.* New York: Bloomsbury.

Fling, E. (2000). *Eating an artichoke*: *A mother's perspective on Asperger syndrome.* Philadelphia: Jessica Kingsley.

Harry, B., Kalyanpur, M., & Day, M. (1999). *Building cultural reciprocity with families: Case studies in special education.* Baltimore: Paul H. Brookes Publishing Co.

Kephart, B. (1998). *A slant of sun*: *One child's courage.* New York: Norton.

Sakai, K. (2005). *Finding our way: Practical solutions for creating a supportive home and community for the Asperger syndrome family.* Shawnee Mission, KS: Autism Asperger Publishing Co.

Savarese, R. (2007). *Reasonable people: A memoir of autism and adoption.* New York: Other Press.

Waites, J., & Swinbourne, H. (2001). *Smiling at the shadows: A mother's journey through heartache and joy.* New York: HarperCollins.

Willey, L.H. (2001). *Asperger syndrome in the family: Redefining normal.* Philadelphia: Jessica Kingsley.

Zysk, V., & Notbohm, E. (2004). *1001 great ideas for teaching and raising children with autism spectrum disorders.* Arlington, TX: Future Horizons.

Web Sites

Alyson Beytien

http://www.alysonbeytien.com

Beytien is a nationally known, popular speaker as well as the mother of three children with autism.

Kristi Sakai

http://www.kristisakai.net/index.html

This mom, author, and speaker has three children on the spectrum. You can find her speaking schedule and many of her writings on her site.

Lianne Holliday Willey

http://www.aspie.com

Lianne is not only a gifted writer and speaker but an advocate for adults and young people on the spectrum. As a parent of an "Aspie" and an individual on the spectrum herself, Lianne's ideas come from literally a lifetime of experience.

NOTES: _____

_____

_____

_____

_____

_____

_____

_____

_____

_____

_____

_____

_____

_____

_____

_____

_____

_____

_____

_____

_____

_____

_____

5

Creating a
Comfortable Classroom

Why do you think I have so much trouble paying attention in the classroom?
I hear everything that goes on—every phone call that the principal makes in her office;
every single time an eighteen-wheeler truck gears down on the highway three blocks away.
I HEAR IT! I HEAR EVERYTHING! (Bober, 1995, pp. 114–115)

When I sit down to write, it takes me about 20 minutes to prepare. I can write without preparation, but I am most creative and productive when I have considered all aspects of my work environment. First, I brew some tea. Then I light candles (blueberry is my favorite), turn on the television, and tune into something only mildly interesting that can serve as pleasant background noise. For instance, a football game will not work because I am a fan and would be too engrossed. Cable news or even a somewhat engaging infomercial works fine.

I can sit in either my office chair or on a couch. I take my shoes off (but keep my socks on) and sit on my feet or cross my legs so I am not touching the floor (no, I don't know why this works—but it does).

Usually I write with all lights blaring; I even turn kitchen and bedroom lights on until the house looks like a runway or an interrogation room. Every 20–30 minutes I stop working and do the following things: browse favorite web sites, walk around my office, go into the kitchen to get a drink, or glance at another project. Then I return to writing until I finish around four or five pages. At that point, I usually need to print what I am writing and feel it in my hands.

Then comes editing, which involves another set of rituals. To edit successfully, I need to leave the writing environment. If I am at work, I usually go to a coffee shop. If I am at home, I will sit outside (depending on the weather) or simply switch rooms. Editing requires a big table and I need to mark changes using a special pen—preferably a green felt-tip marker. After I have finished editing, I return to the computer to work.

I use this extended example to highlight just how many elements of my environment I adapt or change in order to be productive. Although some may feel my writing process is eclectic or strange, most readers will identify with some part of it. In other words, I am not alone; *many* adults go to extremes to create an environment suited to their work or learning style, physical needs, and idiosyncrasies.

To be effective in my work, I need to make adjustments to my seating, the lighting, and the sights and sounds in the room. I even need the scent of blueberry! As I teacher, I always try to keep in mind all of the sensory-related and environment-related "gifts" I give myself when I am planning for my students.

In this chapter, I will discuss ideas for creating classrooms that bring out the best in all students. The first order of business is to answer arguments about support in the "real world"; some believe that changing the environment somehow isn't fair or that it hurts students with autism in the long run. I explore this challenge in the first section. Then, the bulk of the chapter—a section called "Creating Spaces Where Students Succeed"—is dedicated to creating supports. In this section, I have three objectives: 1) to examine the sensory needs of students on the spectrum and provide suggestions for making classrooms comfortable for students with mild, moderate, and even extreme sensitivities; 2) to discuss different types of seating options teachers can employ in K–12 classrooms; and 3) to share some ideas for using space and organizing materials in inclusive classrooms. Finally, I have provided ideas for working with the classroom community when the changes that need to be made call for cooperation from others. It is my hope that this very practical chapter will help teachers consider that differentiating does not always have to involve instruction and that some of the most effective supports for diverse learners are those involving furniture, fixtures, and a little flexibility.

What About the "Real World"?

Have you heard this argument? There are different versions, but it goes something like this: "If I let _____ have _____ (e.g., a beanbag chair, a baseball cap, headphones), he will never learn to function in the 'real world'!" This statement is built on at least two faulty premises: 1) that withholding needed sensory support from a student will somehow make him stronger and able to live without it, and 2) that a student will function in future settings (e.g., job site) that will not allow reasonable environmental supports.

You know the first premise is faulty if you have any sensory difficulties yourself. If you don't perform well under fluorescent lighting now, you probably won't perform any better under them in years to come just because you have been exposed to them and have had to tolerate them. Even though you may cope with the lights over the years, this is not the same as "getting used to them." In other words, it is important to remember that if a student has a serious environmental need that carries over into adulthood, he or she will need to choose a job, a home, and activities that are conducive to that need. The individual will need to negotiate how to get the supports he or she needs at that time. Not only will withholding adaptations during the school years fail to be helpful but providing effective, sensitive supports may give the student ideas for coping that can be implemented throughout the school years and beyond.

For instance, a colleague of mine noticed that Trent, a student with autism, had a hard time concentrating on school tasks on days when the Chicago Cubs played baseball. On these days, Trent spent the entire day asking, "When do the Cubs play? When do the Cubs play?" Although it was unclear whether he needed to know about the Cubs, he seemed to need to ask the question, or at least he was unable to stop asking it. The teacher, curious to see if a certain strategy would help him, taped the Cubs' schedule to the chalkboard. From that point on, whenever Trent asked about the Cubs' schedule, his teacher or classmates pointed to the chalkboard. Eventually, he was able to check the schedule himself. In middle school and high school he did not need the Cubs information posted in his classrooms, he simply placed the schedule in the see-through cover of one of his binders and brought it to all of his classes. Now that Trent works in an office, he simply keeps his Cubs schedule fridge magnet on a file cabinet in his work space.

The second "real world" premise—that work or community environments are inflexible—is more interesting to me and even a bit comical. Most of the people I know chose their job, workplace, and even their recreation activities based on what they can tolerate. My father worked in a factory until he realized he couldn't stand the rigid schedule and requirements. He then drove a butter truck but found that a poor match as well (too much sitting). Finally, he took a job on the railroad so he could move around more and work outside. When we claim that students "just need to adapt" to a classroom environment to be successful in the future, we ignore the fact that there are a variety of potential environments to live, work, and play in across our communities and that students will have opportunities to find a match for their sensory needs and learning style, just as the rest of us do.

With this second assumption we are also putting forward the idea that there are no opportunities to adapt "real world" environments for individual needs. Hmmm . . . What about the slinky on my sister's desk? Or the DO NOT DISTURB sign on my colleague's door? Or the desk lamp my friend uses instead of flipping on the light switch in her office? Or the iPod my uncle uses while he works on the assembly line? Or even the special booth the diner saves for my aunt so she can doesn't have to move her wheelchair too far into her favorite restaurant? Clearly, many adults have opportunities to get what they need "in the real world." For example, consider all of the things individuals do to alter or personalize the work environment: drink coffee at their desks, chew gum or eat candy, listen to music, place pictures of friends and loved ones in their cubicle, and talk to others whenever necessary or desired. Most adults even get to use the restrooms whenever they deem it necessary! Work environments, in other words, do often accommodate individual human differences, including sensory differences.

So, this means, the "real world" is not typically the problem when it comes to creating effective supports for students. In most cases, for most people, *school environments are more restrictive and less flexible than any other place where individuals will function as adults.* The real problem more commonly is attitudes about differences, understanding of student needs, and even a lack of ideas on how to meet all of the needs of a diverse group of students in one classroom. Solutions to these problems that can be implemented in any K–12 classroom are offered in the next section.

Creating Spaces Where Students Can Succeed

Sometimes, students are unsuccessful because they are uncomfortable or feel unsafe or even afraid in their educational environment. Providing an appropriate learning environment can be as central to a student's success as any teaching strategy or educational tool. Students with autism will be the most prepared to learn in places where they can relax, focus, and feel secure. In order to create environments that are most conducive to learning for students with autism and their peers without disabilities, teachers may need to examine how the classroom looks, feels, and functions. Specifically, teachers should evaluate learning atmosphere, seating options, and the utilization of space.

Creating an Optimal Atmosphere

When you walk into my favorite upscale restaurant, you can immediately smell fresh-baked bread. The lights are low and the music is soft and inviting. The waiting area is filled with huge comfortable couches, big glass bowls of fresh flowers, and an enormous tropical fish tank. The food is excellent, and they never let you leave until you have seen (and sampled from) the beautiful dessert cart. Clearly, this establishment is working hard to create a certain atmosphere. They have created a space that inspires patrons to act in certain ways; they want customers to relax, socialize, eat (and spend money), and come back again—so they create an environment that motivates people to do those things.

Teachers also spend a lot of time cultivating a classroom atmosphere that inspires certain behaviors. They want students to work hard, participate in activities, help each other, and pay attention to the lessons. In order to see these behaviors in all students, teachers may need to evaluate their classroom atmosphere and make adjustments to lighting, sounds, smells, or temperature.

Lighting

Restaurateurs, photographers, casino managers, and directors of Broadway productions understand the impact of lighting on emotions and behaviors. Lighting also can have a powerful influence on learning. The right lighting can soothe, calm, energize, or inspire students. The wrong lighting can be annoying, distracting, and even painful for students with autism (Crowther & Wellhousen, 2003).

Some individuals with autism have incredible sensitivity to light (Attwood, 2007; Reed, 1996; Willey, 1999; Williams, 1996). Liane Holliday Willey describes this sensitivity as "impossible to bear" at times:

> Bright lights, mid-day sun, reflected lights, strobe lights, flickering lights, fluorescent lights; each seemed to sear my eyes . . . my head would feel tight, my stomach would churn, and my pulse would run my heart ragged until I found a safety zone. (1999, p. 26)

Individuals with autism have reported problems with fluorescent lights in particular. Fluorescent lighting, the most common lighting used in classrooms, can affect learning, behavior, and the comfort level of your students. In order to determine whether fluorescent lights are problematic for one of your students, turn off the overhead lights for a few days to see if the change seems to benefit him or her. If the fluorescents do seem to be a concern, you may need to experiment with different ways of using light:

- *Try lower levels of light*. You might, perhaps, turn off one or two banks of lights instead of using them all.

- *Look up*. Use upward-projecting rather than downward-projecting lighting.

- *Experiment*. Turn on some overhead lighting but supplement with white holiday lights (Kinney & Fischer, 2001), nightlights, lamp lighting, or even a few colored (e.g., yellow or pink) bulbs around the room.

- *Mix it up*. Replace fluorescents with incandescent bulbs or simply have the student with autism sit near a lamp with an incandescent bulb while fluorescents are used elsewhere in the room.

If the fluorescent lighting cannot be changed, try the following strategies:

- *Replace*. Use the newest bulbs possible; fluorescents flicker more as they age.

- *Try sunglasses*. These can be worn during recess or even indoors (especially near bright lights). Wearing a baseball cap or visor may also be a solution for some.

- *Move the student's seat*. Sometimes the problem is not the lights themselves but the reflection of light on a wall or other surface.

- *Use colored overlays*. Some students find that the glare of white paper under fluorescents is bothersome.

- *Consider sound as well as sight.* Some students are most distracted by the sound of fluorescents. In these cases, the student may want to use earplugs or be moved away from the source of the noise.

Teachers might also experiment with using natural light in the classroom, especially in spaces with several windows. Not only is this a cost-saving measure, but also research has suggested that all students—not just those with disabilities—may perform better in classrooms with natural light (Kennedy, 2002). Do keep in mind, however, that even natural light can cause difficulties if it is too bright or too warm.

A final recommendation is to check the "tech" in your room as well as the lighting fixtures. Glare from computers can cause problems, too, so use flat-panel displays and laptops when possible, as they are often less distracting than standard monitors (Shore & Rastelli, 2006).

Sound

You know that horrible nails-on-a-chalkboard sound? Even thinking about such an unpleasant noise makes some people wince. For some individuals with autism, nails-on-a-chalkboard discomfort happens every day with even the most common of sounds (Grandin, 1995; Jackson, 2002; O'Neill, 1999; Prince-Hughes, 2004; Robinson, 2003; Shore, 2003; Stehli, 1991; Tammet, 2006; Waites & Swinbourne, 2002). Students with autism might be troubled by the sound an air conditioner makes, the shuffling of feet as another class passes by in the hallway, or the soft scratching of pencils moving across papers. Some of the unpleasant sounds most commonly reported by people on the spectrum include crying infants, vacuum cleaners, dishwashers, washing machines, lawnmowers, heavy equipment and sounds related to demolition and construction, alarms, sirens, repeating beeps (e.g., equipment backing up), the buzz of fluorescent lights, and large or particularly noisy crowds.

Some students with autism will not only struggle with sounds most of us view as annoying (e.g., car alarms, sandpaper on wood) but may also react negatively to sounds most of us would filter out or even find pleasing. At the same time, some may fail to react at all to the banging of a door or the scream of a siren. Wendy Robinson, the mother of a young man with autism, remembers how stunned she was at her son's uneven reactions to sounds:

One evening he was seated on my lap on the hall floor while [his brother] bounced and punched a very large balloon around him. Suddenly the balloon burst by Grant's side, which sent my heart into a flutter. However, Grant did not flinch or even turn his head to the noise. Later, when I had my electric whisk in operation, he ran screaming from the kitchen and I had to stop what I was doing to find and console him. He had the same reaction to the [vacuum cleaner] and other loud electrical equipment. (2003, p. 43)

Consider the following ways in which some individuals with autism and Asperger syndrome have described their sensitivities to sound:

The following are just some of the noises that still upset me enough to cover up my ears to avoid them: shouting; noisy, crowded places; polystyrene being touched; balloons and aeroplanes; noisy vehicles on building sites; hammering and banging; electric tools being used; the sound of the sea; the sound of felt-tip or marker pens being used to colour in and fireworks. (Jolliffe et al., cited in Attwood, 1998, p. 15)

It happens to me that I am very sensitive to voices. (Mukhopadhyay, 2000, p. 72)

I have always had a strong aversion to loud music or high volume on the TV set. As a result of this, I often find it awkward to ride with those who crave loud music in their cars, particularly heavy metal or rap. I have always loathed crunching and chewing sounds while other people are eating. Our family has meals in the family room with trays rather than the conventional dinner table gathering. I can tolerate restaurants and cafeterias because the background noise suppresses these bothersome sounds. (Hamrick, 2001)

The scratchy noise of teeth being brushed was physically painful to me, and when I walked past the bathroom, I would have to put my hands over my ears and wait for the noise to stop before I could do anything else. Because of this extreme sensitivity, I brushed my teeth for only short periods and then often only with the intervention of my parents. . . . Nowadays, I am able to brush my teeth twice each day without difficulty. I use an electric toothbrush, which doesn't produce the painful, scratchy noise that manual brushing does. (Tammet, 2006, p. 86)

When I was little loud noises [were] a problem, often feeling like a dentist's drill hitting a nerve. They actually caused pain. I was scared to death of balloons popping, because the sound was like an explosion in my ear. Minor noises that most people can tune out drove me to distraction. When I was in college, my roommate's hair dryer sounded like a jet plane taking off. (Grandin, 1995, p. 67)

One of the ways teachers can help students cope with sounds is to simply ask them or their families about which sounds tend to be the most problematic. If Grant Robinson's teachers knew about his fear of sounds from vacuum cleaners and electrical equipment, for example, they would think twice before signing him up for a woodworking course and could keep him away from things such as the electric pencil sharpener and stapler.

Consider these additional ideas for helping students deal with auditory discomfort:

- *Move the student.* Once a disturbing sound has been discovered, helping the student can be as simple as relocating her desk to another part of the room.

- *Whisper.* Use a soft voice, especially when the student seems upset or does not appear to understand what you are trying to communicate.

- *Reduce classroom noise.* Echoes and noise can be reduced by installing carpeting. Remnants can be obtained from a carpet or large home goods store. Some teachers also cut tennis balls in half and place them on the bottoms of chair or desk legs; this adaptation muffles the scraping sounds created when furniture is pushed or dragged (see Figure 5.1).

- *Change the sound.* For instance, if a student cringes when he hears clapping, students could develop another system of appreciation for presentations, birthday celebrations, and assemblies. In this instance, students might be introduced to the sign for clapping in American Sign Language—raising both hands in the air and wiggling the fingers on both hands.

- *Prepare the student for the sound.* If you know the school bell is about to ring, cue the student to "get ready," have her plug her ears, or simply have her move away from the sound source. Better yet, teach the student how to anticipate (and brace for) some loud noises (e.g., "If you see one emergency vehicle pass by the windows with sirens blaring, chances are, there could be a second or third one close behind").

- *Equip the person.* Allow the individual to wear earplugs or headphones for certain environments or activities (e.g., physical education). The person will still be able to hear the teacher's voice but will not hear as many distracters. If he or she does not tolerate headphones, don't give up until you have tried a few different types. Some students won't wear large head phones that completely cover their ears but will wear ear buds. Others

Figure 5.1. Tennis balls help soften the noise of chairs moving.

won't put anything in their ears but willingly use headsets with foam ear pieces. Noise canceling headphones (the type people wear on airplanes) also may be tried.

- *Turn on the tunes.* In noisy or chaotic environments, allow students to listen to soft music using their digital audio player or play soft music for all students.

- *Beware of the munchies.* It may be difficult for some students to tolerate the loud crunch of foods such as tortilla chips, rice cakes, or popcorn. Some students cannot eat these foods or endure listening to others eat them.

- *Prevent challenges.* Look for ways to avoid exposing the person to loud noises. A teacher, for instance, might have a student with autism leave the room during an experiment involving the popping of balloons.

- *Encourage self-advocacy.* Tell the student to let you know if he or she is experiencing auditory sensitivity.

   Also, be mindful of the fact that many students have effective ways of coping with problematic sounds. Some learners will concentrate on an object or scribble on paper when they are bothered by sounds, for example. Pay attention to these strategies and avoid interfering with them, if possible. Although a student's coping mechanisms may not be apparent to all, teachers should be open to the possibility that behaviors such as hand flapping and finger flicking may be *helpful* to the learner and that preventing the student from engaging in these behaviors may cause him or her more strife.

   Finally, as you consider auditory sensitivity in the classroom, it is important to know that students with autism may find some sounds very helpful or pleasant and may be able to use them for relaxation purposes. Dawn Prince-Hughes, a woman on the spectrum, recounts her favorite sounds in her autobiography, *Songs of the Gorilla Nation*:

A sound like the *thrum* of a tumbler full of milkshake when it was tapped by a spoon or the Westminster chime of the clock would fill me with rapture. I also loved the theme song of the local news program; wherever I was in the house, if I heard it come on, I would run in to listen to it. The theme song would play and the announcer would thank Gristo Feeds as a picture of a spinning globe provided a background. Something about the convergence of these things would fill me with deep happiness. Other sounds, though quiet, would be painful to me and make me see colors, after which I would fight a metallic taste in my mouth. (2004, pp. 23–24)

Wendy Lawson, a woman with Asperger syndrome, reports her relationship to sounds in this way:

Tunes and music or a gentle low-pitched voice can temporarily relieve moments of fear and anxiety. You'll still catch me humming, singing, whistling, and even talking out loud in an attempt to dispel confusion or unease due to change. The strategy enables me to think and calm down. (1998, p. 4)

As Lawson indicates, those on the spectrum often find solace and joy in music. For these learners, it should be used as both a teaching tool and as a curricular adaptation to support learning. Music even can be used as part of the curriculum. For instance, "When Johnny Comes Marching Home" or "John Brown's Body" might be played when the class studies the Civil War, or a unit on oceans might feature the complex song of humpback whales.

Teachers also might use music to inspire certain types of behavior. If an activity is calm or requires concentration, relaxing music might be used. For example, a teacher I once observed plays quiet instrumental music as students enter her classroom and begin individual math exercises. Another colleague plays classical music while students draw in their sketchbooks at the beginning of her art class. If an activity requires movement or high energy, music can be used to inspire this type of behavior, too. Hip hop music might be played as students exercise in physical education class or build sets for a school production, for instance.

To get started on incorporating music into the classroom, teachers might experiment with different types and styles of music such as instrumental, rap, classical, and popular to see how students respond. Tonal qualities in songs or instruments may upset students with autism more easily than they do others, so if the student on the spectrum responds negatively to some selections, the teacher may need to find other types to share. Playing different types of music can give the teacher an opportunity to expand the experiences of learners and to inspire and interest them, as well. For instance, in one classroom, Sally, a student with autism, was constantly singing the song "The Yellow Rose of Texas." Eventually the teacher and all the students learned that Sally's grandmother was from Texas and that the song was a family favorite. Sally seemed thrilled when all of the students in the class learned to sing "her" song. The teacher then asked all learners to bring in a song that meant something to each of their families.

A final piece of information that teachers may want to keep in mind about learners with auditory sensitivity is that often they can hear so well that they may inadvertently listen in on conversations meant "for teachers only." A colleague of mine found this out the hard way when her young student asked her how her divorce was progressing! He had overheard a whispered remark she had made to a colleague that morning on the playground. Mary Newport, a woman on the spectrum, recalls a similar incident from her own childhood. When she was sent to a clinic for hearing tests, the doctor patiently explained all of the procedures and then walked to the back of the room to speak to Mary's mother privately. During their conversation, he whispered, "Do you think she'd like a sucker when we're done with the tests?" Mary instantly turned and replied, "I'd love a sucker!" causing the doctor to call off the tests before they began (Newport, Newport, & Dodd, 2007).

Smells

Whereas we all associate a few smells—chalk dust, peanut butter, new crayon—with schools, some individuals with autism associate dozens of smells with K–12 environments. A student with a heightened sensory system may take in any number of odors in just a few moments—the wet shoes of a classmate, the icing on a cupcake, the stale odor of a musty locker, the dirty shavings in a hamster cage, the teacher's hair gel, and the rubber cement being opened across the classroom.

Echo Fling (2000), the mother of Jimmy, a young man with autism, reported that her son's sense of smell was so acute that he was able to use it as a tool for identifying his possessions! She recalled an incident that occurred when her son was just 7 years old. Jimmy was playing with his Star Wars action figures with neighborhood boys who had their own collection of the same toys. When the boys were done playing, they realized that their Luke Skywalker figures had gotten mixed up during the game. As Fling related,

> The boys paused, not knowing which Luke belonged to whom. To solve this dilemma . . . Jimmy held each one up to his nose, took a quick sniff, and immediately told the other boy, "This one is yours." (p. 146)

Although this example illustrates potential benefits of a heightened sense of smell, this sensitivity also can be a struggle. As one individual with autism describes, smells can often be overwhelming and cause extreme discomfort:

> I still have trouble with [animals]. . . . Dogs and cats and smells like deodorant and aftershave lotion, they smell so strong to me I can't stand it, and perfume drives me nuts. I can't understand why people wear perfume, and I can smell hand lotion from the next room. (Stehli, 1991, pp. 197–198)

Other classroom smells that may bother students include paint and other art products, school supplies (e.g., "smelly" stickers, markers, chalk), science chemicals and solutions, cleaning agents, class pets, and plants or flowers.

What can teachers do about smells, though? It can be a challenge to create olfactory provisions for students, especially when many of us may not even be able to detect those smells that might cause a student discomfort. The following precautions, when taken, can minimize some of the situations that are problematic for learners on the spectrum:

- *Restrict the use of perfumes, colognes, and other related products.* If a student seems to avoid a particular person or if she will only interact with that person occasionally, consider that the student may be reacting to the personal care items that person uses (e.g., lotion, hair gel, aftershave, shampoo). If a student is very sensitive to these types of smells, teachers and other professionals working in the classroom should avoid—as much as possible—the use of scented (or at least heavily scented) products.

- *Ban fashion magazines.* If you are a middle or high school teacher, ask students to share magazines such as *Seventeen* and *Teen Vogue* outside of class. The perfume and inserts can cause discomfort and even headaches in learners on the spectrum (Willey & Holliday Willey, 2003).

- *Cover or move food that may distract.* Cooking and food smells are incredibly distracting for some students. One of my former students could smell any treat two classrooms down from ours. Although he loved baked goods, once he smelled them he could not focus on his work. In order to support him, all teachers in our hallway decided to celebrate birthdays at the very end of the school day, parents agreed to bring all treats to the office, and the secretary offered to hold our sweets until 2:15 in the afternoon.

- *Find an opening.* In rooms that have strong odors (e.g., art room, cafeteria, science lab), students might be seated near the door or an open window. Or they might be able to use a personal fan to minimize the impact of the smell.

- *Let them learn.* If students seem to rely on their sense of smell to learn or to explore the environment, allow them to do so when it is possible and when the behavior does not hurt or disturb others. When Echo Fling's son, Jimmy (the previously mentioned identifier of the Luke Skywalker figures), was smelling her hair one day, she asked him, "What are you doing?" He replied, "I'm remembering you." Realizing her son's need to smell, she did not forbid or discourage this interesting behavior. She simply instituted a social rule for Jimmy at school: Don't sniff people without their permission (2000, p. 147).

- *Forgo that fresh pine smell.* Ask custodians and administrators to order and use unscented cleaning materials and products.

- *Teach mouth breathing.* Teach students to breathe out of their mouths in environments they find challenging (e.g., locker room) (Willey & Holliday Willey, 2003).

Finally, teachers should be mindful of the fact that students will likely not have a negative reaction to every strong or unusual odor. Many scents, aromas, or smells may, in fact, be pleasing and even comforting to students and, if these can be identified, they can be used as a tool for support. For instance, I knew a young man with autism who could be calmed by the smell of mint. His teacher, therefore, kept mint gum and candies in her desk in case he needed to relax.

Or cue students to do as Liane Holliday Willey (1999) does. This self-described "Aspie" brings her own olfactory adaptation with her wherever she goes. To keep her sensory needs in check, she simply puts a bit of a favorite scent (if such a thing can be found in a liquid or paste) on the end of a cotton ball or on the inside of her arm. This way, when she gets overwhelmed by certain smells, they can be minimized by sniffing the scent on the cotton or the arm. A pendant necklace can also hold a favorite scent (Willey & Holliday Willey, 2003).

Temperature

Some students struggle to concentrate or relax in rooms that feel too warm or too cold to them. Consider the words of Dave Hamrick:

> I often get uncomfortable when I go to other houses or businesses in the summer months where the temperature is above 75 degrees. Many people set their thermostats between 75 and 80 degrees during the summer and I'm comfortable in a 70-degree environment. As you might expect, I get really excited when the temperatures start falling in autumn. Blasts from an air conditioner or heater can feel painful to some and soothing to others. (2001)

Classroom temperature is difficult to adjust to individual student needs, so teachers will need to give each student ideas for keeping him- or herself comfortable. If the student is often cold, he or she might be asked to keep a sweater or sweatshirt in the classroom (hoodies are especially good choices as students tend to like the extra comfort and "mini sensory escape" they provide). If the student is often warm, he or she might be given opportunities to sit in a cooler part of the room (near a door or window), to keep a bottle of cold water or even ice water at his or her desk, or to use a personal fan to keep comfortable. These students (especially in schools without air conditioning) should be encouraged to dress in layers so they can easily adjust to the temperatures as they move from room to room or as the temperature changes throughout the day.

Providing Appropriate Seating

Providing appropriate seating in the classroom and around the school is another important part of classroom organization (Berkey, 2009). Consider your own needs as you plan for the learners in your classroom. Think how it feels to sit on a high stool when your feet don't touch the metal or wooden supports, to try to fit into a movie theater seat that is too small, or to fold yourself into an airplane seat that doesn't have sufficient leg room. You may physically squirm around and reposition your body. You may even be unable to keep track of a conversation as you focus on your discomfort.

Picking out the right chair may not be a teacher's first consideration when planning for a student with autism, but for some learners, it probably should be! One of my former students couldn't sit in a desk for more than a few minutes, but he could sit in a beanbag chair for 40 minutes at a time. We soon purchased several beanbag chairs for the school (a few for the library, two for the music room, a handful for hallways) so that this child could be at ease throughout the school and so that all students could enjoy a change in seating now and then.

Not every student with autism will need or like the feeling of a beanbag chair, however. In most cases, finding appropriate seating is a matter of trial and error. Another one of my former students, Kelly, seemed unable to settle into his desk; he did not seem comfortable in the beanbag chairs, in the rocking chair we kept in the room, or on the pillow pile we kept in the "living room" area of the classroom. After experimenting with many different seating options, materials, and strategies, we finally found that Kelly could sit for more than an hour at a time if we tied a cushion of woven wooden beads (the type you often see in taxicabs) to the back of his chair.

As these stories emphasize, having a few different seating choices in the classroom can potentially improve the educational experiences of all learners. Seating that may appeal to learners with and without autism include the following:

- Rocking chairs

- Beanbag chairs

- Lawn chairs

- Director's chairs

- Stadium chairs

- Couches, loveseats, armchairs, or large footstools

- Exercise balls

- Seat cushions (the type that can be tied on to the rungs of the chair)

- Reading pillows (large cushion with arms that props the user upright)

- Balance cushions

- Floor/exercise mats or large floor pillows

If these options do not meet all of your students' needs, keep experimenting. You might, for instance, cue students to use the floor, let them stand for parts of the day, create a new floor plan, offer study carrels, or set up a "home away from home."

Give Them the Floor

As you are brainstorming seating ideas, consider that some students (with and without autism) may prefer to sit on the floor for some part of the day (see Figure 5.2). To assess student response to this arrangement, teachers can design instruction that calls for such a seating arrangement. Students might sit on the floor when working with a partner, while tackling large-scale art projects, or when they need to spread out to manage materials.

In some cases, students might be given the option to sit on the floor *or* at their desks. Those who prefer to sit on the floor or in a chair without a desk can work on clipboards or use lap desks. Keep in mind that beanbag lap desks are inexpensive (and can serve as a sensory support if you cut them open, take out the beanbag material, and replace the beans with sand).

Let Them Stand

Other students may prefer to stand for some part of the day. This is an adaptation I have made for students with autism across grade levels and more recently in my college classroom for students who are pregnant or those with back problems. Students can be provided with a lectern and a desk at the back of the classroom and they can alternate between the two as needed.

Figure 5.2. A high school student listens to music in one of the stadium chairs available in her inclusive classroom.

Make a New Plan

Teachers should always consider how the placement of a student's desk or seat in the classroom can affect learning and behavior. One teaching team found that Becky, a student with autism in their classroom, had difficulty sitting at her desk until they let her sit in a different area of the room. Previously, Becky had sat in the back of the classroom. In this arrangement, Becky had few chances to interact with peers because she was positioned behind most of them. In order to get her more interested and involved in the classroom, the teacher changed all of the desks, moving the students so that there were two rows on the right side of the classroom and two rows on the left side. She then turned the rows so they would all be facing the center of the room; students on the left were now facing the students on the right and vice versa. This arrangement worked exceptionally well for Becky because she could easily see other students at work and learn from their actions and habits (Hedeen, Ayres, Meyer, & Waite, 1996).

These educators teach that classroom arrangement can be a powerful behavior support and that every response to student difficulties need not be one directed at the learner herself. In the spirit of creating new plans, other arrangements that teachers may want to consider include the following:

• Pushing desks together so that every student has a learning partner

• Grouping students into clusters of four

- Putting the desks into a horseshoe or semicircle so all of the students can see each other

- Seating students at tables instead of at desks

Offer Study Carrels

One of the challenges teachers in inclusive classes report is that students on the spectrum often get distracted during independent work. In some cases, a simple seating adaptation can help this type of student: desktop study carrels. A large piece of cardboard (about 2 feet tall) folded into thirds can be placed on the student's desk to shield her from other students, from classroom materials, and from visual information around the room. Because carrels are easy and inexpensive to construct, a teacher could make them available for any student in the classroom (see Figure 5.3 for an example of a study carrel used in an inclusive classroom). Another option is to purchase presentation boards (the type students use in science fairs) to use for this purpose or bring one or two study carrels (the type often found in college libraries) into the classroom and let any student work in the sheltered space when privacy or some focused study is needed. See Table 5.1 for a short list of study carrel vendors.

Help Them Feel at Home

Finally, consider a few "no place like home" seating adaptations. Some teachers find their students are more successful (behave better, work more productively) when they have a homey

Figure 5.3. A study carrel created for an individual student with autism.

Table 5.1.   Study Carrel Vendors
Classroomproducts.com
http://www.classroomproducts.com/study-carrels.html
These carrels are sold in packs of 20, 30, or 40.
Packaging & Design Co.
http://www.packaginganddesign.com/studycarrels/index.html
Corrugated study carrels—lightweight and highly portable.
School Outfitters
https://www.schooloutfitters.com/catalog/search_results.php?smSearch=Search&keywords=carrels&x=0&y=0
A variety of carrels and other classroom furniture.

retreat they can access right inside the classroom. A retreat might consist of nothing more than a carpet remnant in a corner with a few upholstered footstools. Or, take a cue from a kindergarten teacher I taught with who brought an old-fashioned, claw-foot bathtub into her classroom and filled it with colorful pillows. Another friend, a preschool teacher, had a loft built so students requiring privacy or comfort could find their respite inside the room. And still another colleague, a high school English teacher who was also the yearbook advisor, created a living room area in his classroom so that his club could meet comfortably after school. Because he found this arrangement so profitable for daily learning and because so many students were drawn to this space, however, he brought in a second couch and as many arm chairs as he could reasonably fit in his classroom. Other items that might be placed in a "comfort" area include

- Class pet(s)

- Water feature such as a desktop fountain

- Magazines and books

- Radio, CDs, and/or digital audio players

- Photo albums of the students and/or class projects

- Small games (e.g., Jenga, Etch-a-Sketch, Tic Tac Toe)

Teachers also may find that creating and using cozy learning spaces gives them opportunities to interact more personally with students. A teacher may be more relaxed or spontaneous or behave in a more unguarded fashion when he or she provides small-group instruction in this type of physical arrangement.

Organizing Learning Space

Although the classrooms of the past were characterized by students acting as passive learners in rows and columns facing the teacher at the front of the room, students today are often more active and more likely to be involved in collaborative work and, typically, will have more choices about where they work, how they work, and what materials they use. All of these changes require some thought and planning on the part of the teacher. Specifically, teachers will have to think about creating spaces for the students, materials, and activities.

Create Space for Students

Classrooms that best suit students with diverse learning needs have flexible learning spaces. This means that the way spaces are used and organized may change based on the needs of students. For example, as students in a particular school are increasingly included in general education classrooms, the resource room might be changed into a quiet "study hall," available to *any* student at any point in the day. When I was teaching second grade as a special educator, my colleagues and I revamped our resource room by giving it a new name—The Learning Lab—and a new identity. Any student needing a place to study or read quietly could use the room; and when we were co-teaching, we used the room to engage in project-based instruction. Three ways teachers can create space to maximize learning in the classroom are by designating low-congestion areas, quiet study areas, and active learning areas.

Designate Low-Congestion Areas   A student with autism may become frustrated if students are constantly walking past his desk or crossing in front of a chalkboard he is trying to read. Whenever possible, the pencil sharpener, classroom library, and supply cabinet should be kept in places least likely to interfere with the functioning of the class or at least away from the students who are the most easily distracted. In the same spirit, a learner on the spectrum might be seated in a low-congestion area, a spot in the classroom (much like the area near the cockpit of an airplane) where individuals are discouraged from congregating.

Designate Quiet Study Areas   Students with autism often need time away from the noise and chaos of the classroom to perform at their best. In most schools, spare classrooms do not exist; if they are available, however, an administrator might be willing to convert some of the space into a full-day quiet study area to which any student can have access. In crowded schools, teachers might work with the school librarian to create a quiet space just for studying or projects. Or a few chairs and even a small table might be set up in the hallway (depending on fire codes of the school) for any student who needs a break from the chaos of the classroom.

Designate Active Learning Areas   Although many students have the need for quiet, others need movement, activity, and interaction. A student who cannot sit in a desk or keep a low voice in a classroom can still participate by working on course material in a different part of the room or in a different environment with a few classmates. One student in a high school English classroom was unable to sit through long discussions and readings of *Romeo and Juliet*. Instead of making the young man fidget through the hour, the teacher asked him to assemble costumes for a class production of the play. Two students at a time (including the student with autism) were then allowed to work quietly in the back of the classroom while the rest of the class rehearsed the lines of the play and discussed the story.

A paraprofessional told me about a student with autism who could not sit in his desk during his science class. The teacher agreed to let the student pace during the lessons. Eventually, however, the pacing became distracting for some of the students because the young man was often crossing back and forth in front of the teacher and the chalkboard. The teacher's solution was to turn the back of the room into a pace-friendly zone. She taped off two areas with masking tape; one was named "sit and learn" and one was named "move and learn." The student was told he could pace anywhere in the area labeled "move and learn." He was instantly able to follow the simple rule; in fact, it was so successful that the student asked for designated "move and learn" spaces in other classrooms.

Create Space for Materials

Look around a typical classroom and you may find 20–35 desks (with sweatshirts or backpacks hanging off the backs of a few chairs); a few globes and a pull-down map; crates or cubbies full of student work; laptop and desktop computers; dozens or hundreds of books; bulletin boards filled with student work; a television and a DVD player; a chalkboard, whiteboard, or Smart Board; and maybe even a hamster in a habitat! Although all of these materials are central to teaching and learning, it is important that they are well organized, easily accessible, and visually manageable. Try these tricks for keeping your space orderly and your students calm and productive: give everything a place, avoid visual overload, section off your space, organize together, and keep key information at hand.

Give Everything a Place   Kindergarten teachers often have "a place for everything with everything in its place" so that students can easily find materials and learn how to participate in managing the classroom. Teachers in upper grades often abandon this type of organization, assuming that learners no longer need it. Most students, however, profit from being educated in an organized environment and from knowing how and where to get materials.

To add to the "place for everything" theme and to make sure that the system is easy for all of your students, label every box, bin, and bookshelf so that your students can assist in keeping the classroom tidy (see Figure 5.4 for an example of a labeled box of materials and Figure 5.5 for an example of labeled shelves). In addition, make sure that your storage solutions are accessible to students so they can help themselves to materials and clean up without teacher assistance.

Avoid Visual Overload   Another way to support learners with autism is to keep visual clutter to a minimum. One way to achieve this goal is to ask students to be especially conscientious about keeping the classroom neat and about storing their materials in their desks and lockers. To aid younger students on the spectrum, a desk map can be created to help them find and replace items independently (Goodman, 1995). To create such a map, the teacher or the student draws a diagram of all items in the desk on a small index card or a sheet of paper. The map is then taped to the top of the student's desk or attached to the inside "ceiling" of the desktop. Maps also can be created for the classroom in general or for a student's locker (see Figure 5.6 for a locker map created by a student on the spectrum).

Tarps or sheets also can help teachers avoid the look of chaos. If you have a slew of unfinished projects on a shelf or a table full of props for an upcoming production, you might simply drape these items with a cloth so the student on the spectrum is not visually distracted by them and, of course, so the items do not "walk away" or get lost or broken before they are needed.

Section off Your Space   One way to make the classroom extremely easy to navigate is to set up different areas for different activities. For instance, a high school teacher might have an area just for storage and teacher materials, a small library area, and an activity table. An elementary school teacher could have a puppet theater/drama center, a reading corner, and a whole-class gathering place. When possible, areas can be sectioned off (by using furniture or masking tape or even by painting the floor different colors) or labeled clearly to help all students understand how spaces are to be used.

Organize Together   Because many students struggle to organize materials, you might provide all students with explicit suggestions for keeping things orderly. For instance, instead of asking all students to clear their desks for a test, ask them to put their notebooks in their backpacks or to put their markers in their supply box. These types of direct and specific statements remind students that their supplies have a home and may help them learn organization skills over time. You might give some specific ideas on how to organize desk tops, lockers, cubbies, or backpacks (e.g., "Keep your protractor in your pencil bag and only in your pencil bag"). I know of one teacher who taught a student with Asperger syndrome to organ-

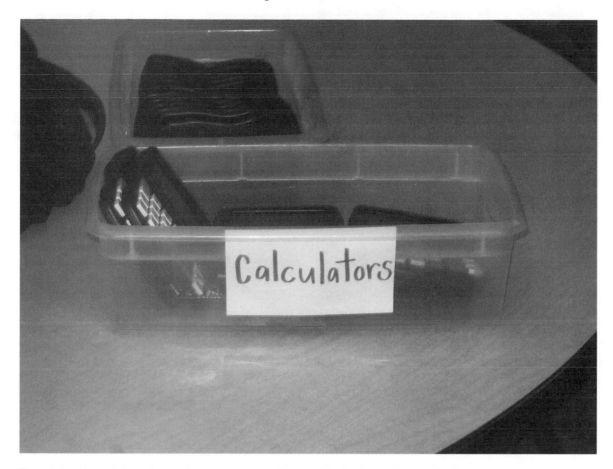

Figure 5.4. A labeled bin lets students find items easily and replace materials when they are finished using them.

ize his materials by color when he was in seventh grade (e.g., all math supplies are yellow, writing supplies are red). The student is now in community college and is still successfully using this system.

To make the maintenance of the classroom as easy as possible, you can give all students classroom jobs. For instance, a few students can be responsible for keeping bookcases orderly. Such an activity can even be parlayed into an academic learning experience. Younger students can practice alphabetizing and older students can learn the Dewey Decimal System or create their own categorical system. Students also can be responsible for caring for plants, organizing bulletin boards, and keeping desks orderly and floors neat. See Table 5.2 for a longer list of classroom jobs that will keep the classroom tidy.

Keep Key Information at Hand Finally, to keep the classroom working efficiently, keep important information posted clearly. A calendar, clock, and schedule can be kept in one area of the classroom (especially important for students with autism who seem to need these tools readily available). Students of any age can be held responsible for writing the date, changing the calendar, and even writing out the schedule each morning. Depending on the ages of the students and the content being covered, students also may be responsible for posting daily information such as stock quotes, a weather report, or vocabulary words.

Figure 5.5. Labeled shelves help students learn organizational skills.

Tap Into the Learning Community

Some environmental supports will involve compromise and conversation. For example, the teacher may need to poll students to find out if everyone can tolerate music during independent work time or if they like windows open or closed on warm days. Other supports are specific to one student and can be implemented easily without interfering with the learning experiences of other students. For example, if a student is uncomfortable at her desk, she can alternate between working at a classroom table, standing in the back of the room, and sitting in a rocking chair.

In other instances, the student with autism will need the help of his or her classmates to be successful in the environment. For example, George, a student with Asperger syndrome, was struggling to sit through Russian history class because of the strong perfume some of his classmates wore. When the teacher and the young man brought this problem to the class, the girls agreed to avoid wearing heavy perfume or to sit far across the room from George when they did. The teacher agreed to use a flexible seating chart so the girls could switch seats when needed. Interestingly, George reported that the girls stopped wearing perfume for the entire semester even though he had not asked them to do so in the meeting.

Similarly, Alice, a first grader with the label of pervasive developmental disorder, was having problems participating in physical education class because she could not tolerate the teacher's whistle. To solve the problem, students were asked to think of different ways the teacher could get their attention. Students suggested that the teacher could wave her hands, sing a song, ring a bell, play a trumpet, act like a monkey, wave a yellow flag, or squeeze a singing stuffed chicken. The teacher, in response, tried each one and gave students the option of picking the ones that worked best (the singing chicken, of course, came out on top). Everyone in the classroom benefited from the creative brainstorming process and from the act of building a community that was comfortable for all.

As these examples illustrate, student supports need not be "secrets" or known to teachers alone. In fact, students often make realizations about their own learning style and needs when they learn about the style and needs of others. After learning about his fifth-grade classmate's need to wear headphones to tune out noise, one young man (without an identified disability) claimed that he needed the same adaptation. When provided with the headphones, he did indeed work for longer periods of time and was less distracted.

It undoubtedly behooves individuals to learn about themselves and their learning needs from even the earliest years of school. Students who are given choices about their learning environment and are asked to express their preferences regarding factors such as lighting, sound, and furniture arrangement will come to better know themselves as learners. They are also likely to be more prepared to get the environmental supports they need in subsequent years and perhaps will be more capable of setting up an appropriate study area in their homes.

Cap (left)	Compass Collection (right)
Coat	
Floor Floor Floor Floor	
Gym Shoes (left)	Boots (right)

Figure 5.6. A locker map created for a student on the spectrum.

 Summary

I opened this chapter by detailing some of my own needs related to work environment. Although I can now see how central these supports are to my productivity, I fought implementing many of them for years. When I was in graduate school and learning how to write, I felt that serious academics would write at a desk in a professional environment. So I tried in vain to work in silence at the campus library. When I got my first university job, however, I began to see the diverse ways in which my colleagues tackled their work. Some only wrote at home

Table 5.2. Classroom jobs that will help keep the classroom tidy and running efficiently

Cleaning white boards and chalkboards

Emailing absent students

Hanging posters and classwork

Inspecting desks

Making sure lights are off when room is empty; cueing peers to turn off computers (green support)

Making sure technology is turned on and/or off and helping run presentations that involve technology (tech support)

Organizing art supplies (putting paint and brushes back in place)

Organizing craft area (putting construction paper, glue, and markers back in place)

Organizing lab area (putting glassware and instruments back in place)

Passing out mail, materials, or papers

Pushing in chairs and straightening furniture

Stocking and sharpening pencils

Taking care of and feeding pets

Updating bulletin boards/announcements

Watering plants (gardener)

Wiping tables

while others had to be in their offices with the door open and the radio buzzing in the background. One friend only wrote at coffee shops. Only after seeing this diversity did I give myself permission to craft my own work environment; as a result I soon became more relaxed and capable as a writer.

Making adaptations to the learning environment can help all of us work more effectively. It certainly takes time and thought to engineer many of these adaptations, but teachers often find that creating a good learning environment minimizes the need to provide other, more-restrictive supports. For instance, if the illumination of the classroom feels painful to a student and no adaptations are made related to the lights, the student may leave the classroom for long stretches of time and thus lose valuable learning time and opportunities.

Perhaps most important, educators also may learn about students, their needs, their abilities, and even their potential when they offer different types of supports related to learning environment. By assessing and, when necessary, changing the atmosphere and the learning spaces throughout the school to better meet student needs, teachers can help learners avoid behavior challenges and increase motivation and participation as well as set them up for school success, in general (see Figure 5.7 for a checklist that can be used for this purpose). In education, context matters, and teachers who attend to environment often see that with the addition of a cushion, the change of a bulb, or a shift of a desk, learners can look and feel differently and shine in new ways.

FOR MORE ANSWERS AND INFORMATION

Books

Berkey, S.M. (2009). *Teaching the moving child: OT insights that will transform your K–3 classroom.* Baltimore: Paul H. Brookes Publishing Co.

Gillingham, G. (1995). *Autism: Handle with care.* Edmonton, Alberta Canada: Tacit Publishing.

(continued)

(continued)

Heller, S. (2003). *Too loud, too bright, too fast, too tight: What to do if you are sensory defensive in an overstimulating world.* New York: Quill.

Kranowitz, C. (2006). *The out-of-sync child: Recognizing and coping with sensory processing disorder* (Rev. ed.). New York: Perigee Trade.

Kranowitz, C. (2006). *The out-of-sync child has fun: Activities for kids with sensory processing disorder* (Rev. ed.). New York: Perigee Trade.

Smith-Myles, B., Cook, K., Miller, N., Rinner, L., & Robbins, L. (2000). *Asperger syndrome and sensory issues: Practical solutions for making sense of the world.* Shawnee Mission, KS: Autism Asperger Publishing Co.

Yack, E., Aquilla, P., & Sulton, S. (2003). *Building bridges through sensory integration* (2nd ed.). Las Vegas, NV: Sensory Resources.

 Web Sites

BrainGym International
http://www.braingym.org
> BrainGym is a worldwide network dedicated to enhancing living and learning through movement.

MissKellyOT (Kelly Redd's web site)
http://www.misskellyot.com
> Visit Kelly Redd's web site for tips on hand strengthening, recommendations for appropriate toys and games, and ideas for addressing writing problems.

Sensory Fun
http://sensoryfun.com
> Learn about sensory issues from a mom's perspective. On this site, you will find a family's story of addressing sensory differences.

NOTES: _____

_____

_____

_____

_____

_____

_____

_____

_____

The Comfortable Classroom Checklist

Students with autism will be the most prepared to learn in places where they can relax, focus, and feel secure. In order to create environments most conducive to learning for students with autism and their peers without disabilities, teachers may need to consider the sounds, smells, lighting, temperature, and seating options in the classrooms.

Student's name: _____

Sounds

This student needs the following:

☐ A desk away from noisy spaces

☐ A classroom with "reduced noise adaptations" (e.g., tennis balls on bottoms of chairs): _____

☐ Adaptations for noisy classroom rituals and/or routines (e.g., needs peers to snap instead of clap): _____

☐ To be verbally warned about upcoming loud noises

☐ To be excused from particularly noisy lessons (e.g., certain science experiments)

☐ Use of earplugs or headphones at certain times of the day: _____

___ Independent work

___ Group work/active learning

___ Transitions

___ Other

☐ Music/iPod for some activities: _____

___ Independent work

___ Group work/active learning

___ Transitions

___ Other

Smells

This student needs the following:

☐ Staff to limit use of scented personal care products

☐ A desk away from any strong smells in the classroom (e.g., away from the class pet, away from chemicals in the science room)

☐ To sit near the door of certain classrooms (e.g., art, home economics): _____

☐ Access to a small personal fan

☐ Scent-related objects, materials, and/or items that help to calm, energize, or comfort the individual (e.g., scented oil or paper, lotion): _____

☐ Materials (e.g., markers, erasers) that are unscented

Figure 5.7. The Comfortable Classroom Checklist.   *(continued)*

"You're Going to Love This Kid!" Teaching Students with Autism in the Inclusive Classroom, Second Edition, by Paula Kluth
Copyright © 2010 by Paul H. Brookes Publishing Co. All rights reserved.

Lighting

This student needs the following:

☐ Opportunities to request seating in a dimmer part of the room

☐ A desk as far away from fluorescent lighting as possible

☐ A classroom that has incandescent instead of fluorescent bulbs or use of a lamp with an incandescent bulb

☐ A classroom that has and can use natural light as much as possible

☐ A classroom with upward-projecting rather than downward-projecting lighting

☐ Use of sunglasses at certain times of the day

☐ Use of a baseball cap or visor at certain times of the day

☐ Colored overlays or nonwhite paper (to avoid glare under fluorescent lights)

☐ Use of headphones or ear plugs (to avoid sound of fluorescent lights)

Temperature

This student needs the following:

☐ To keep a bottle of ice water at his desk

☐ To use a personal fan

☐ To sit near/away from the registers

☐ To sit near/away from the windows

☐ To keep a sweatshirt/hoodie at his desk

Seating

This student needs the following:

☐ Option to sit on the floor at times

☐ Option to stand at times (behind a lectern if needed)

☐ Option to pace in a designated part of the room at times

☐ Seat cushion or balance cushion on his desk chair

☐ Fidget objects in or on his or her desk (e.g., koosh ball, paper clips, drinking straw)

☐ Study carrel to sit behind

☐ Seating options that may include the following:

___ Rocking chair

___ Beanbag chair

___ Lawn chair

___ Reading pillow (cushions with arms that prop the user upright)

___ Floor/exercise mats

___ Floor pillows

___ Couch or loveseat or large upholstered footstool (if available)

___ Exercise ball

___ Other _____

Figure 5.7. (continued)

"You're Going to Love This Kid!" Teaching Students with Autism
in the Inclusive Classroom, Second Edition, by Paula Kluth
Copyright © 2010 by Paul H. Brookes Publishing Co. All rights reserved.

Friendships, Social Relationships, and Belonging

How peaceful it is to withdraw from the complicated world
of human relationships! I do however enjoy the presence of a
friend and feel so content in the company of one who is willing to take me
as I am. My friends have been willing to see me this way and I am so grateful to
have been given the opportunities to discover life in the real world. (Lawson, 1998 p. 100)

In *Listening to the Experts* (Keefe, Moore, & Duff, 2006), an inspiring book featuring voices of students with and without disabilities, a young man, Chad Schrimpf, details one of the many ways friends enhance life at school. In his essay "This is Me," Chad writes about meeting a new friend:

> I'm meeting new people all the time because of [my new peer collaboration class]. Now, meeting new people is easier for me. I met my friend Brittany this year. I went up to her and said, "Hi." We hang out a lot. Heather is also one of my friends. I met her at an art show. She came up to me and introduced me to all of her friends. That was cool. (p. 88)

Later in the essay, Chad shares how having friends can mean having support. He explains that music can make him very emotional ("the music got to the sensitive part of my heart") and that, at a certain concert, it all became too much to handle:

> The most important thing to know about me is that I'm very sensitive. That's just the way I am. That is my true self. A lot of things hit me hard, and tears pour down my face. That's where my friends help me. They help me a lot. Once, at a school concert in the performing arts center, the music got too loud. Things got out of hand, I was sitting alone at the top of the stairs when Brittany saw that I was upset. She asked me to sit with her. I was glad. (pp. 88–89)

As Chad illustrates, the best part about coming to school for many learners is seeing and spending time with classmates. And he is not a singular voice. Many students with autism who are being educated alongside their peers without identified disabilities are indicating that they need more than an inclusive classroom to feel successful; stu-

97

dents with autism are increasingly asking teachers to facilitate the development of friendships and provide them with access to social opportunities (Burke, 2002; Keefe et al., 2006; Kluth, 1998). In this chapter, I outline ways in which teachers can build classroom communities that encourage relationships and connection. I also provide suggestions for facilitating social interaction in the diverse classroom. Finally, I provide ideas for supporting the social lives of individual students with autism.

Building Community in the Classroom

Although no teacher can create friendships among students, every educator can create conditions in the classroom that will give students opportunities to strengthen social relationships, learn about and from each other, and get and give support. The hope is, of course, that these opportunities will eventually lead to the development of friendships.

Developing and sustaining a school community requires that educators use strategies and practices that purposefully encourage and teach sharing, learning, interdependence, and respect. For example, teachers might encourage community through cooperative learning experiences (Frank, 2004), conflict resolution opportunities, games (Glover & Anderson, 2003), class meetings, service learning, social-justice education, cross-age and same-age tutoring and mentoring, and school and classroom celebrations (Houston, Blankstein, & Cole, 2008; Shapon-Shevin, 2007).

Teachers also can cultivate community by working for whole-school change. By lobbying for smaller classes, challenging competitive school structures, and developing ways to connect students across classrooms, for example, teachers can not only strengthen the classroom community but also help the school as a whole become more responsive to a wider range of learners. A sense of community also can be developed and sustained through curriculum and the use of community-building activities.

Community Through Curriculum

One of the most effective ways to create a classroom community is to offer curriculum and instruction that is responsive and respectful. (Several examples are shown in Table 6.1.) Many teachers have effectively built community by framing lessons around issues of democracy and social justice, for example. When Erin Gruwell, a high school English teacher in a struggling urban community, confiscated a racist drawing from one of her students, she decided to reshape her curriculum to respond to the incident:

> I went ballistic. "This is the type of propaganda that the Nazis used during the Holocaust," I yelled. When a student timidly asked me, "What's the Holocaust?" I was shocked.
>   I asked, "How many of you have heard of the Holocaust?" Not a single person raised his hand. Then I asked, "How many of you have been shot at?" Nearly every hand went up.
>   I immediately decided to throw out my meticulously planned lessons and make tolerance the core of my curriculum. (Freedom Writers & Gruwell, 1999, pp. 2–3)

Gruwell built her entire curriculum around students, their experiences, their concerns, and their ideas. She supported their interrogation and critique of institutions and authorities in their communities. Gruwell's students thrived on the discourse of social justice that she cultivated in her classroom. Students in her classroom became involved in community service and political action as Gruwell helped them connect their own experiences to history. They raised money to bring Miep Gies, a friend of Anne Frank's, to visit their school; they held a peace demonstration; they co-taught a college class on diversity; they visited the Holocaust

Table 6.1. Ways to build community through curriculum

Ask students what they want to study, and integrate their ideas into standards-based lessons.

Have different students serve as experts in different units; be sure to find opportunities for every learner to serve in this role.

Integrate service learning projects into different subject areas.

Assign joint projects that capitalize on individual student strengths.

Have students write about themselves and share their writing formally or informally across the year.

Have the class create a play, a piece of music, or a piece of art together.

Have students learn about individual and group differences through the curriculum itself; talk about both Thomas Edison's and Temple Grandin's learning differences when you study inventions, for instance.

Museum in Washington, D.C.; they conducted a candlelight vigil honoring friends and family lost to violence; they mentored local elementary students; and they collectively wrote a book about their experiences.

In another school, Yolanda, a student with autism, was frightened of a mural hanging in the gymnasium. The mural—a picture of children walking in the woods that included the image of a snake coiled on the ground—scared Yolanda because she was afraid of reptiles. The mural had been painted years ago and the principal had often thought of replacing it because at least one student each year had expressed the same fear. Futhermore, the principal and teachers had, at different times, expressed irritation because all of the children depicted in the mural were Caucasian. They did not feel it represented the student body, which was comprised of many different racial and ethnic groups.

When Yolanda came into the school, the principal volunteered to have the custodian paint over the mural. Yolanda's art teacher had a better idea, however; students in the class were charged with creating a new mural that would be both appealing to the students and representative of the multicultural population of the school. Students worked with an art teacher to learn about mural painting. They studied colors, designs, and styles of murals. Yolanda was on the committee to choose a new design, and although she could not speak, her peers paged through books to find images that interested her. Students decided on a beach scene with images of children from racially and ethnically diverse groups. The mural also included a picture of a mermaid because *The Little Mermaid* was Yolanda's favorite book.

Painting the gymnasium inspired further study of murals—the students explored content ranging from the murals painted during Roosevelt's New Deal to the connections between mural painting and social revolution in Mexico—but the painting also brought students together as a community. The art gave students a voice and a forum for expressing themselves and the art teacher found that painting the mural not only helped students to learn more about Yolanda but also brought the whole class together as a group. For example, Armando, a student who was often teased for being quiet, became a leader for the first time as soon as his classmates saw his artistic talents.

Community-Building Activities

Another way to bring learners together is to regularly incorporate community-building exercises. Not only will students with autism need such opportunities to improve social skills and learn in nonthreatening ways but teachers will often have new students in the class who want the chance to get to know classmates. Students who already know each other will benefit from the opportunity to connect with classmates in more meaningful ways.

A variety of community-building exercises such as those listed here can be implemented to enhance relationships in the classroom, encourage friendships, and foster student-to-student learning opportunities. Although all of these activities can be used at the beginning of the year to help students become familiar with one another, they should not be abandoned thereafter. Community building and team building are not achieved by having students engage in a few games or icebreakers. True team building takes time and involves meaningful and continuous interaction over the course of the school year (and, it is hoped, over the course of the school career). Five community-building structures that K–12 teachers can use in diverse classrooms are The Story of My Life, Compliment Chair, Enrolling Questions, A Truth or a Lie?, and Paper Bag Interviews.

The Story of My Life

Although many celebrated figures have the unique (and probably transforming) opportunity to share their biography, ordinary folk typically do not have the chance to tell their story. The Story of My Life provides this opportunity and allows students to develop new connections with classmates.

One elementary school teacher used this structure as a getting-to-know-you exercise during a year when she was welcoming Beth, a student with multiple disabilities, into her classroom. When Beth's mother asked if she should come and explain her child's abilities, history, and special needs to the rest of the children, the teacher decided it would be nice for all students to learn this type of information about one another. Students spent a day collecting information for their books; this collection process involved interviewing family and friends, gathering artifacts from home, and filling in a questionnaire designed as a brainstorming tool. Then, students worked alone (or in pairs, if assistance was needed) to construct the books. The social worker visited the classroom to help students tell their stories and discuss their differences.

The speech-language therapist also visited during this time to teach Beth some new sign language vocabulary related to the book; she also helped Beth answer all the necessary questions by using both the new signs and some pictures other students tore from magazines. Students spent two mornings sharing their work. Their books were then displayed in the school library.

To use this structure, have students work individually at first. Ask each of them to take a piece of flipchart paper and fold it into quarters so it is shaped like a book.

Then, on the front cover, have students write a title. To add a bit of whimsy, you might instruct them to choose the title of a popular novel, song, movie, or television program to use as their title or part of their title (e.g., *Wendy's "Believe It or Not" Life Story*).

On the inside of the front cover (page 2), have them create an index of their lives, including the following:

- Date and place of birth

- Family information (number of siblings, names of pets)

- Favorite hobbies, sports, and/or interests

- Favorite quotes, phrases, and/or jokes

- Most exciting moment

- Thing that makes them unique

On page 3, ask students to draw a perfect day. Finally, on the back cover, students should draw a picture of their future (family, where they are living, their job).

When all of the books are complete, have each student tell their story using the book as a visual aid. Depending on the size of the class, you may want to have students share stories in small groups. If possible, leave the books in a central location for the day or for the week so classmates can learn more about one another.

Consider how well students know each other when designing prompts for the book; students who have worked together for years likely will be familiar with basic information about one another (e.g., name, family structure) and may be more interested in gathering information that is slightly more in depth, such as their most embarrassing moment, their family traditions, or their travel experiences.

Adaptations to this community builder include the following:

- *Sharing the story of your own life.* Show students a sample book featuring your own family, interests, and/or dreams. If you are working with younger children and you are using this structure to teach about diversity, individuality, or community, you may even want to invite other adults into the classroom to read their stories so that learners can see and hear about differences related to gender, sexual identity, family structure, and cultural and ethnic background.

- *Giving students a brainstorming worksheet before having them complete the activity.* Some learners will need time and some structure to generate answers to the prompts.

- *Using a wide range of materials to create books.* If there are learners in the classroom with fine motor problems, magazine pictures, rubber stamps, and clip-art images can be provided for students to use in the construction of their stories. Some students may even need to create their books using a writing software program such as Co:Writer or Write: OutLoud (both published by Don Johnston, Ltd.).

Compliment Chair

This easy-to-implement activity is appropriate for all ages and can be used throughout the year. First, arrange the classroom chairs in a semicircle with one chair at the front, facing the rest of the class. Then, one member of the group is selected to sit in the chair. As soon as this person is sitting, students take turns offering that individual compliments. You can give a set number of students time to share (e.g., five compliments per student), or you can have every student in the group offer a compliment before moving on to the next participant. When one student leaves the chair, have him or her pick another student to sit in the chair.

The Compliment Chair is ideal for use in classrooms where one or more students need to practice using augmentative or alternative communication. One reason some students with autism struggle socially is because they have limited ways to interact or connect with others. Giving students structured opportunities to communicate within the context of daily instruction, however, can help them hone skills such as staying on topic, expanding utterances, or spontaneously using a communication system.

Adaptations to this community builder include the following:

- *Allowing the student with autism to go first*—especially if he or she has worked hard on developing a comment, saying it, or using augmentative and alternative communication to express it.

- *Splitting students into two or three groups.* This way, more students can sit in the chair at one time and students get more opportunities to ask and answer questions.

- *Teaching students what a compliment is.* Some students on the spectrum and certainly some not on the spectrum will need assistance deciding on appropriate compliments.

- *Playing an express version.* Pick one or two students at the end or beginning of the day or week and have five classmates give those individuals compliments. Compliments can be general or specific to classroom content. For instance, a middle school teacher might show a student's science fair project and ask the class to provide five compliments related to it (e.g., "A unique idea," "You went above and beyond the requirements").

Enrolling Questions

"Raise your hand if you have blue eyes." "Stand up if you have ever been in a car accident." "Sit down if you have ever cried during a TV commercial." These are examples of what Jerry Evanski (2004), author of *Classroom Activators*, calls Enrolling Questions.

Enrolling Questions serve at least two purposes: They bring the group together as personal information is disclosed and connections are realized and they get students moving and interacting and can, therefore, help to punctuate or "shake up" a potentially dry lesson. Keep in mind that beyond community building, Enrolling Questions can serve as a quick introduction to content, too; a teacher kicking off a lesson on the U.S. Congress might use these Enrolling Questions: "Raise two hands if you have visited Washington, D.C." "Walk to the back of the room if you would like to run for Congress."

Adaptations to this community builder include the following:

- *Letting students create the prompts or questions and facilitate the game.* This is a less risky way to participate for some.

- *Adding in more movement.* This will be particularly helpful if students seem particularly restless (e.g., "Jump up and down if you like cheese pizza").

- *Show or write the questions as you speak.* Some students will be unable to process the commands quickly, especially in a noisy and somewhat chaotic environment.

A Truth or a Lie?

A Truth or a Lie? is fun and energizing and can be integrated into the classroom as a "get to know you" exercise or as a curriculum preview or review (Bennett, Rolheiser, & Stevahn, 1991). This may be an especially useful activity for some students with autism who need practice in understanding abstract concepts. For younger students, use of this activity will help them differentiate between the ideas of "truths" and "lies" and give them opportunities to engage in storytelling and verbal expression (Udvari-Solner & Kluth, 2008).

To begin, students simply write three statements about themselves. Two of them are truths, and one of them is a lie (see Figure 6.1 for an example of an A Truth or a Lie? worksheet that can be used for the game). Students then get into pairs or into small groups, read the statements aloud, and ask their classmates to guess which statements are lies and which are truths. Time is often provided for students to share short stories related to their truths and lies. Adaptations to this community builder include the following:

- *Asking students to focus on specific topics*—possibly even topics related to your curriculum—for the exercise; for instance, students can be asked to share two truths and a lie related to Africa, dinosaurs, or woodwind instruments

- *Asking students to share one truth, one lie, and one wish*

- *Having students perform.* Instead of writing ideas down, have students act them out.

Paper Bag Interviews

Paper Bag Interviews (Gibbs, 1995) are a great way to facilitate interactions between students and provide them with opportunities to ask and answer questions. Instead of one or two students having a chance to speak during a lesson, Paper Bag Interviews give all students time to share. This activity can be used to teach younger students turn taking or reading simple sentences. Older students can learn actual listening skills or ways to ask clarifying or follow-up questions.

To engineer the interviews, the teacher writes a series of questions related to classroom topics and places them in lunch bags. Students are then arranged into small groups of three

A TRUTH OR A LIE?

- Write down three statements.

- Two should be "truths" (things that are true) and one should be a lie (something that is not true). Try to fool other people into thinking that your "truth" statements are lies (in other words, choose "truths" that might surprise other people). You might also try to fool people into thinking your lie is a "truth" by choosing something that sounds true or sounds like it could be true.

- Examples of the types of statements you can use include the following:

I am _____. (e.g., I am a vegetarian.)

I like _____. (e.g., I like mayonnaise sandwiches.)

I have _____. (e.g., I have 19 white tank tops.)

I once _____. (e.g., I once ran a half marathon.)

I believe _____. (e.g., I believe the school year should be 11 months long.)

My mom or dad is _____. (e.g., My mom is 6 feet tall.)

#1 _____

_____

_____

_____

#2 _____

_____

_____

_____

#3 _____

_____

_____

_____

Figure 6.1. A Truth or Lie? worksheet.

*"You're Going to Love This Kid!" Teaching Students with Autism
in the Inclusive Classroom, Second Edition,* by Paula Kluth
Copyright © 2010 by Paul H. Brookes Publishing Co. All rights reserved.

to five and each group is given one bag. Learners then take turns drawing questions from the bag and answering them. At any point, a student may decide to pass on a question and draw a new one.

Paper Bag Interviews can be used regularly throughout the year. Teachers can either use this activity to give students opportunities to learn about one another or to comment on different topics of study in the classroom, or questions can give students a chance to do both. For example, the question "How are you most like Crazy Horse?" prompts students to disclose something about themselves while they consider information they have about this historical figure. Adaptations to this community builder include the following:

- *Having students generate the questions for the bags*

- *Asking students to use different types of expression.* Have them use gestures, drawings, and facial expressions (e.g., "Draw how you think Jesse feels when Leslie falls into the water").

- *Putting questions in the bags that relate to student interests* (e.g., if a student in the group has just become an uncle, include a question about families; if a student is really interested in the Beatles, include a question about 1960s rock and roll).

- *Collaborating with the speech-language pathologist.* If a student receives help in this area, Paper Bag Interviews might be an ideal time for that professional to work in the classroom. He can help all students improve skills related to maintaining conversations and asking or answering questions.

Facilitating Social Interactions and Relationships in the Classroom

Once teachers establish a classroom community, they can focus on developing and using specific strategies that will encourage social interaction and relationship building. Specifically, educators should create spaces for sharing, respect different ways of socializing, rely on students to support each other, support relationships through activities, and provide opportunities for connection beyond the classroom.

Spaces for Sharing

Teachers who seek information about students' experiences, dreams, interests, and needs can use what they learn to better educate their students and to facilitate relationships between them. Too often (especially in secondary schools), students are educated in the same classrooms day after day without developing personal relationships. When I was observing one middle school classroom, I asked a young man to tell me the name of one of his classmates. "I don't know his name," the student replied. "I've never talked to him." I later found out that these two students had been in the same classroom for 2 months and had never had a conversation.

Students' voices must be central to classroom work, and time must be carved out for communication and idea sharing. Teachers interested in incorporating students' voices might begin by increasing forums for student participation and leadership. For instance, students might be asked to lead weekly class meetings. Or, as in Kim Rombach's first-grade classroom, students may be in charge of managing conflicts. Rombach facilitates this process by providing two "talking chairs" that are available to students who are engaged in a disagreement. In the chairs, students discuss their issues and try to find a solution or explain their feelings. One boy explained the purpose of the chairs this way: "Sometimes it takes us a long time, but we try to get to be friends again" (Sapon-Shevin, 1999, p. 139).

Respect for Social Diversity

Some individuals with autism struggle to make friends and socialize in ways that are conventional and familiar to others. For example, some students with autism may be uncomfortable with touch and, therefore, unable to shake hands with others. Therefore, teachers must cultivate a classroom environment that encourages different types of social participation. As Wendy Lawson, a woman with autism, illustrates, asking a person with autism to socialize and behave like everyone else can be painstaking and frustrating:

> Over the years, I tried to contain my excitement and joy over life's happenings and watched to see what makes other people happy or sad. If they laughed or were unmoved, then this was my signal that it was alright for me to do likewise. This process was hard work and although it helped me to be more observant of others, it robbed me of spontaneity and enjoyment of the richness of my own experience. (1998, p. 116)

Teachers of students with autism will want to clearly communicate to students that there are many ways to engage in conversations, play and socialize, and participate in class. For instance, in a second-grade classroom, Cindy, a student with autism, liked to watch some games and play activities before or instead of joining in; students in the classroom grew accustomed to Cindy's participation and on occasion, Greg, a peer without a disability, joined her in quietly watching the classroom commotion.

Dan, a student with the label of autism who was nonverbal, often introduced himself to others using a photo album he had created. Whereas other students started their days by chatting in the cafeteria as they waited for the first bell to ring, Dan began his day by circulating around the cafeteria tables showing students the newest pictures in his album. Because Dan and his mother changed the pictures every Sunday, he had new "stories" to share every week. In Dan's school, students became so interested in this mode of socializing that they began bringing pocket-size photo albums to share with Dan and with each other.

Classroom Connections

Several years ago, I met Jason, a young man who struggled when it came to social interaction. In particular, he seemed uninterested in rituals such as greeting people or saying goodbye. For more than 3 years, his IEP featured goals about these rituals. Then Jason began attending second grade. Instead of going into his general education classroom for only a small "visit" each day as he had in the past, he started, ended, and spent every hour in between in his general education classroom. In this classroom, all of Jason's peers were verbal and, therefore, his mornings began with several boys surrounding him, slapping him on the back and wishing him a "good morning." In only a few weeks, Jason was looking up at his friends, initiating handshakes, and sometimes even sharing a "Hello" or "Hi, there."

As Jason's story illustrates, peer support is an essential part of inclusive schooling. In some cases, students succeed in supporting other students or helping them achieve when teachers cannot. Often, peers will learn quite naturally how to support a friend with autism. They will know how to calm, teach, and encourage a classmate without any direction or interference from adults. In addition, peers are valuable resources because they tend to under-stand each other in ways authority figures or adults do not. Students know each other's se-crets and fears. They often recognize each other's needs and gifts in ways not seen by teach-ers. This type of help and mutual support is great preparation for adult life for both or all participants.

In the popular and important book *The Dreamkeepers* (2009), Ladson-Billings writes about a teacher, Pauline Dupree, who keeps community issues at the center of her classroom prac-tice. Dupree fosters unity in her classroom and reports that she expects her classroom to be both a center of serious learning and a place of comfort and cooperation. Dupree teaches teamwork in her classroom and asks students to serve as resources for one another:

> From the day that they walk into my room they know they have to select a buddy. This is their learning partner for the year. A lot of times when a student is having a hard time I'll call the buddy to my desk and really give him or her an earful. "Why are you letting your buddy struggle like this? What kind of partner are you? You're supposed to be the helper." Within a couple of months I begin to see them looking out for one another. One student will hesitate before he turns in his paper and will go check to make sure the buddy is doing okay. Eventually, they begin to check very carefully and they may discover some errors that they themselves have made. (pp. 77–78)

The beauty of this example provided is that the students are engaged in a reciprocal partnership instead of in a helper–helpee relationship. It is critical that teachers seek such opportunities to give all students the chance to both give and receive help and support (Bishop, Jubala, Stainback, & Stainback, 1996; Broderick, Mehta-Parekh, & Reid, 2005; Strully & Strully, 1996; Van der Klift & Kunc, 2002). As Bishop and colleagues pointed out, students with and without identified needs profit from reciprocal relationships:

> In contemporary society, a healthy, well-rounded individual may be considered to be someone who is able to both give and receive help as necessary for continued growth and self-esteem. The ability to perceive oneself as both the helper and helpee in any friendship is valuable to the main-tenance and growth of that relationship. Too often, people with disabilities are presumed to be able to participate in relationships only as the helpee, which is detrimental to the depth and longevity of the relationship. (Bishop et al., 1996, pp. 163–164)

Students with autism must, then, be given opportunities to offer support to classmates. Relationships in which some individuals are always helped while others are always helping are neither natural nor particularly helpful in building a classroom community. It is a teacher's job, therefore, to cultivate a classroom culture that allows all students to give and get support. As Eugene Marcus, a man with autism, pointed out, the best relationships can only emerge when peers serve as supporters of each other, not as "bosses or role models":

> Peers are people who are in the same boat as we are, and who are our equals. That means people who must follow the same foul rules as we do. And who have ways of coping that we need to know about. Role models are expected to be perfect, but peers can fumble and make mistakes just like we do. Peers are fully human, and that welcomes us to be our fully human selves. Do not think you confuse us by telling us about your mistakes and fail-ures. Those things are what make us feel close to you. Good peer support is always from people who are eager to learn and that means people who don't mind being wrong a lot of the time. (2002, p. 1)

Classroom activities can be specifically structured to encourage reciprocity. For example, in one seventh-grade classroom, the teacher asked each student without an identified disability to serve as a "peer buddy" for Julie Ann, a young woman with Asperger syndrome. Within weeks of implementing the program, however, Julie Ann, who was a geography buff, was helping all of the students in the classroom with their social studies homework. When the students began asking to have Julie Ann serve as their "peer buddy," the teacher knew it was time to change the system. Instead of having class members sign up to be a helper for Julie Ann, every student had to develop an advertisement and a help-wanted poster to hang on a classroom bulletin board. On the advertisement, students had to list all of their strengths and specifically highlight the things they would be willing to teach others. On the "help wanted" poster, students had to list the things they needed or wanted to learn or things they needed help doing. With the new system in place, all students were able to see the gifts and abilities and the needs and struggles that they and their fellow students brought to the classroom.

Relationships Through Activities

Some students who find conversation and typical ways of socializing a challenge are amazingly adept at socializing when the interaction occurs in relation to a favorite activity or interest. Stephen Shore, a man with Asperger syndrome, has pointed out that one reason for this phenomenon is that basing relationships on a shared passion or task can reduce stress: "Having an activity as the focus of the interaction reduces the reliance on being able to detect, accurately encode, and respond appropriately to nonverbal social cues" (2003, p. 74).

For these reasons, perhaps, Dane Waites, a man with autism, created social connections through participation in sports. Waites, it seems, had few same-age friends until he took up weight lifting. After finding both athletic and social success in that sport, he began cycling and running for pleasure and again found he was able to develop relationships through these activities (Waites & Swinbourne, 2002). Jasmine Lee O' Neill, a woman with autism, has called activities such as those described by Waites "stepping stones" and suggests they be used to facilitate relationships:

Anything can be used as a stepping stone for forming a relationship. Art and music are superb for that. Use things the autistic individual enjoys to spark her interest. If she likes music and hums to herself, use music as an introduction to relating to other people. It is a falsehood that autistics do not relate. Rather, they relate in their own ways. (1999, p. 83)

A story from the work of Carol Tashie, Susan Shapiro-Barnard, and Zach Rossetti reinforces the idea of following a student's lead to create social opportunities. In their stirring book on friendship, *Seeing the Charade* (2006), these educators describe a young man named Samuel who loved fans. He often set them up to blow air across his face or to move things around in space. As teachers sought ways to get Samuel involved in extracurricular life, they were hard pressed to find a club of fan lovers. But as they searched for hobbies that might be related to fans in some way, they talked to a physics teacher who referred them to a few students who were building ultralight model planes. This group of youngsters was interested in having Samuel join them in their endeavor because he had some knowledge of and a lot of interest in wind currents; Samuel, for his part, had the opportunity to learn about aviation, engineering, and model building as a pastime and to form connections with students his own age who shared his passion.

Beyond the Classroom

To support the development of relationships in the classroom, teachers may need to scout for social opportunities outside of the classroom. Although schools often try to offer activities to meet the needs of all students, some need to develop a wider array of activities so that every student can find an extracurricular activity in which they feel at home. Some schools, for instance, have moved beyond the traditional sports-based and arts-based extracurricular options to offer clubs and activities related to academic content (e.g., chess club), political issues (e.g., conservation groups), and social support (e.g., antidrug groups).

All schools must be conscientious about offering options that will interest, engage, and be available to a range of students in the school. This means examining whether all students can afford certain clubs or activities, whether meeting times are convenient for students who may have after-school responsibilities, and whether students can get the appropriate supports they need to participate in after-school activities (Sapon-Shevin & Kluth, 2003). In a middle school, a student with autism wanted to join the track team but needed to have some individualized support to be able to attend practices and games. As the student's educational team was trying to develop a solution to the problem, two high school students volunteered to serve as junior coaches and give extra support to all of the students. This type of creativity is key.

In elementary schools in which typically there are few school-sponsored extracurricular opportunities offered, teachers and school administrators might work with families and community members to offer a few clubs or activities open to any student. Or, schools might investigate after-school options available in the surrounding area and help families connect to these activities. For instance, if the local recreation center offers after-school arts classes, the school might offer to do some staff training for the facility around issues of supporting diverse learners.

Specific Strategies to Help Students with Autism

Students in the most welcoming, social, comfortable, and accepting classrooms may still need extra support and guidance when navigating social relationships. Having a strong classroom community and using a range of approaches to facilitate relationships are prerequisites for building and sustaining relationships and supporting students' social worlds, but students on the spectrum will very often need or want help understanding and negotiating social situations. A few strategies that may be helpful to learners to this end are social narratives, role play, introduction of social secrets, video modeling, friendship-focused IEP goals, and acceptance and belonging.

Social Narratives

Many teachers, families, and students with autism have found social narratives (Baker, 2001; Ganz, Kaylor, Bourgeois, & Hadden, 2008; Gray, 1994, 2000, 2010; Gray & Attwood, 2010) to be useful tools in learning about relationships and personal interactions, coping with difficulties, getting information about novel situations, and knowing how to respond or act in under various circumstances. Three kinds of narratives that teachers may find helpful include social scripts (Ganz, Kaylor, Bourgeois, & Hadden, 2008; McClannahan & Krantz, 2005), social skills picture stories (Baker, 2001; 2006), and Social Stories™ (Gray, 1994, 2000, 2010).

Social Scripts

Social scripts provide students with specific language that they can employ in certain situations. They help learners with communication challenges to express themselves more effectively and engage more fully in social situations (Ganz et al., 2008; McClannahan & Krantz, 2005; Sarokoff, Taylor, & Poulson, 2001; Stevensen, Krantz, & McClannahan, 2000). Scripts may be written for any number of purposes and contexts, including helping students initiate a conversation, respond to common questions, or even to tell a joke.

To use this technique, the teacher typically creates a script and has the student practice reading it until they are fairly fluent in their delivery (making it more or less complex if necessary after a few readings). Then, the student should be given opportunities to use the script in an authentic context and to have several opportunities to practice and improve skills. Finally, when the student seems able to use the "script" without the paper copy, parts of it and eventually all of it can be faded out (Myles, Swanson, Holverstott, & Duncan, 2007). This is a social script example created for a student who was learning how to make small talk with peers on Monday mornings:

> If someone asks, "How was your weekend?" I can say, "My weekend was great! I spent a lot of time playing Wii with my brothers, as usual. Mostly I just hang out with my family on weekends." Then I can ask my conversation partner, "How was your weekend?"

Social Skills Picture Stories

Social skills picture stories, popularized by Jed Baker (2001, 2006), are visual teaching tools that help students learn new skills, behaviors, and competencies:

> Each skill is formatted sequentially, similar to a cartoon strip, with digital pictures of actual children combined with text and cartoon bubbles to denote what the children are saying—and sometimes thinking—as they engage in the skill. Included are the right (and sometimes the wrong) way to act with accompanying text that enhances the learning experience. (p. xvii)

Stories are taught in four stages: 1) teachers provide instruction, 2) students engage in role play, 3) the skill or competency is reviewed with corrective feedback provided, and 4) generalization is addressed, which involves opportunities to practice across environments (Baker, 2001). Once students are familiar with this teaching tool, they may enjoy creating their own stories by posing for pictures and writing captions.

Social Stories™

Social Stories™ give the student information about a situation and provide ideas or guidance on what to expect or how to respond to that situation. For instance, if a teacher was writing a story about going to the school play, he or she would want to include information about intermission and the clapping that is sure to occur at that time. The story would most likely also include information cueing the student to join in with the clapping when he or she hears it or—in the case of a student who is sensitive to loud noises—to plug and protect his or her ears as soon as the curtain goes down.

Dane Waites, a man with autism, uses the stories not only to learn about unfamiliar situations but also as a way to reduce anxiety. Dane's mother explains the process he uses to construct and use his stories:

> Before I discovered the Social Story technique, I used newspaper clippings, magazine cuttings and photographs to try to explain issues to Dane. Social Stories, however, can be devised to suit Dane's specific needs. If necessary, they can be illustrated with computer-generated photographic images of real people. (Waites & Swinbourne, 2001, p. 196)

Dane now has a folder of prepared stories covering various contingencies. The following extract is from a story that helps Dane overcome his difficulty in changing from weekend activities to work on Monday mornings, and it also helps him to follow his list. He has named it "A Time for Work and a Time for Interests."

I have an interesting life. Many people don't have a job. They don't get paid my wage each week. I don't get bored. I am paid to do all the work on my list. I am paid to finish my list and do a good job. When I finish work for the day I can do other things, like sport. Mum has to follow her list. If Mum did not follow her list, who would cook the meals, do the washing and keep the house nice for her family? When Mum finishes her list she can do other things, like reading. (Waites & Swinbourne, 2001, p. 196–197)

For Dane, social narratives convert his own words into reality. He creates and takes ownership of the narrative, and when he reads it again it gives him the motivation and reinforcement he needs. For months, Dane studied "A Time for Work and A Time for Interests" every Monday morning to remind him why he wanted to work and why he must follow his list. This story also reminds him that after work he can go the gym, go for a run, or ride his bike.

Although teachers and individuals on the spectrum like Dane Waites may create their stories without following specific guidelines, true Social Stories™ (Gray, 1995, 2000) involve the following steps:

1. *Think about and picture the goal of the Social Story.*™ The main goal of Social Stories™ is to teach social rules and cues directly. Therefore, accurate information and descriptions must be provided.

2. *Gather information about the topic.* Think carefully about the topic, including when and where it occurs, who is involved, what to do in the process or sequence, and so on.

3. *Tailor the text.* Write in three parts, introduction, body, and conclusion; provide accurate information about "wh" questions for the target behavior; write with a first-person perspective; use positive language; consider the Social Story™ ratio of two to five descriptive ("We have art class on Wednesdays"), perspective ("My brother loves video games"), and/or affirmative sentences ("This is important") for every directive or control sentence ("I will raise my hand when I have something to tell the teacher"); and use literally accurate words.

4. *Teach with the title.* A title addressing the main concept of the story should be included.

Stories should be reviewed often and can even be recorded with the student's teacher or the student him- or herself reading the story. If students can access audio and video on their cell phones, stories might be downloaded for easy access all day long.

Here is an example of a Social Story™ that can be used to teach sharing:

> *Sharing*
> I may try to share with people. Sometimes they will share with me.
> Usually sharing is a good idea.
> Sometimes if I share with someone, they may be my friend.
> Sharing with others makes them feel welcome.
> Sharing with others may make me feel good. (Gray, 2000, p.11)

See http://www.CarolGraySocialStories.com for the most current information.

Role Play

Role play is another strategy that many students find helpful when learning to socialize. Students may need only a quick verbal role play to get through a situation (e.g., rehearse steps involved in ordering lunch from the cafeteria), or a full dramatic role play can be used in which the teacher or other students take on different parts.

In a high school business class, the students engaged in role play to practice skills related to job interviews. William, a young man with Asperger syndrome, was taken with the exercise and asked his father to practice the role play with him several times at home. William's father even videotaped the role play so his son could watch it whenever he needed to be reminded of the language and behaviors associated with interviews. When William eventually landed an interview (with his teacher's help), he navigated the process with ease and was offered a job at a music store.

William found the role play so helpful and was so successful with it that his family and teachers began using it across environments and contexts. The business teacher, in the meantime, was so impressed with the effectiveness of the strategy for all students that he began using role play in other areas of his curriculum. Students in the business class engaged in role play to learn strategies for dealing with irate customers, for learning ways to share ideas in a business meeting, and for making small talk with new business contacts.

Role plays can be used to practice a specific situation (e.g., singing in a concert) or to improve certain skills (e.g., greeting people). One of my former students often asked his brother to role play "teenager conversations" with him. The student's brother would bring up a topic, and the young man with Asperger syndrome would practice entering and staying in the conversation.

Social Secrets

For many learners with autism, participating in a social interaction is like playing a game without knowing the rules or the objectives. Some individuals on the spectrum report that the social demands of making small talk or walking into a party can create stress, anxiety, and panic. Students report that they often feel as if everyone else knows the social secrets necessary for success and they do not (Grandin & Barron, 2005).

Jennifer McIlwee Myers (as quoted in Grandin & Barron, 2005) shares how confusing even "clear cut" rules can be:

> One set of hidden rules that make me nuts was the rules for gym clothes. Each year we got a handout that said all female students had to wear a solid colored t-shirt with no writing or logos or zippers. Each year almost all of the other girls wore logoed shirts, shorts with pockets, etc. The *real* rule was: you can wear any t-shirt and shorts in gym as long as they provide modest coverage and don't interfere with physical activities. (p. 138)

Similarly, Wendy Lawson, a woman with autism spectrum disorder, related just how puzzling the requirements of even the most common of social situations can be:

> "Can I buy dessert now?" I asked. We were at McDonald's, my favorite eating place, and my main meal was over.
>
> "Wendy, you don't have to ask my permission to buy dessert," my friend said. "You are an adult, you can do what you want."
>
> But that is how it is. Due to being constantly unsure of required behavior, I always ask my friends what needs to happen next. Some actions are routine and I understand what is required, but others are always changing. (1998, p. 100)

Clearly, it can be helpful, if not life-saving, to explicitly teach students social norms, unwritten rules, the hidden curriculum (Myles, 2004), or what I call "social secrets." Sharing secrets may involve systematically teaching social norms (see, for example, http://www.asperger.net/bookstore.htm for a "hidden curriculum" one-a-day calendar). Teachers can also give stu-

> **Table 6.2.** Examples of social secrets for Howard, a middle-school student with Asperger syndrome
>
> "When a teacher says, 'How are you Howard?' in the hallway, she doesn't expect a long or detailed answer. She just wants you to say, 'Fine. How are you?'"
>
> "When you are in the hallways and on the way to the office to get your meds, do not stop and talk to other students who are inside classrooms. Teachers in those classrooms are conducting class and do not want you to interact with their students."
>
> "Raise your hand to talk in Ms. G's class."
>
> "You can stand or pace in the room if you need a break, but do not stand or pace in front of Ms. G—especially when she is talking to the class. Stand or pace in the back of the room."

dents information about social secrets as situations arise. For instance, if a student is at a school dance and seems confused about what to do, the teacher might approach her and suggest that she get a snack, approach some friends to talk, or join other students on the dance floor. Some students may even want these options in writing.

It is important to remember that sharing social secrets is important even for students who do not speak or have reliable communication. Just because a student cannot express confusion related to social situations does not mean he or she is not confused. To err on the side of caution, teachers should provide information about social situations to every student. A list of social secrets can be found in Table 6.2.

Video Modeling

Sadie, a first grader with autism, needed help getting through her morning routine in the classroom. Her teacher videotaped one of Sadie's peers walking to her cubby, taking her home folder out of her bag, putting the folder in the cubby, and sitting down on the carpet. The clip was shown to Sadie several times. After just 2 days of viewing, Sadie was able to complete the routine without any adult support.

Video modeling, in which a video demonstration of a person performing a desired behavior is used as a teaching aid, and video self-modeling, in which students are videotaped successfully performing behaviors and then watch those videos as models for behavior, have both been used as ways to teach new behaviors to students on the autism spectrum. This strategy can be used with any learner (those with and without disabilities) and can help students develop and strengthen communication abilities (Wert & Neisworth, 2003), academic performance (O'Brien & Dieker, 2008), and social skills (Bellini, Akullian, & Hopf, 2007; D'Ateno, Mangiapanello, & Taylor, 2003). According to a study by Corbett and Abdullah (2005), video modeling works so well for students with autism because watching a video on screen (versus watching a role play or actual event) restricts a learner's field of focus, is visual, and does not require face-to-face interaction or the ability to process visual information more readily than verbal information.

To create your own movie, decide on which routine activity or task you want to record. Get your equipment ready, and wait to catch the student in a successful moment. For some behaviors, you may need to wait several minutes, an hour, or even a few days to get what you need. For instance, if you want a video of a student cleaning up her station after a cooking lesson, it may take some time and coaching to get a video of it actually happening. If the behavior you are targeting seems too challenging to capture or you simply don't have the time to wait for the right moment, you may need to film familiar peers instead of the learner him- or herself (as Sadie's teachers did with the morning routine). If students are willing and able, you can teach them how to behave or interact and film after letting them practice the "scene" a few times. Finally, if you are not able to get what you need from either the student or from familiar peers, you may film either adults or unfamiliar peers. Commercial videos are also available for certain behaviors and skills and both TeacherTube (http://www.TeacherTube .com) and YouTube (http://www.YouTube.com) have examples of video modeling that educators can access and use with their students.

Once you do get a clip, you can move to sharing it with the student. Let him or her watch the activity, sequence, or scene several times. Have them view it, in particular, before they will be asked to engage in the target activity again. For instance, if you are teaching a child to play catch, show him or her the video right before recess. It also can be very helpful to send the video home so parents can review the content several times with the student.

Friendship-Focused IEP Goals

Along with targeting social skills for students who need such support, friendships and social connection also can be focal points of the IEP. As Tashie, Shapiro-Barnard, and Rossetti pointed out in their seminal book, *Seeing the Charade: What We Need to Do and Undo to Make Friendships Happen* (2006), we can't exactly write a goal such as "Luis will have three good friends on 4 consecutive days with 80% accuracy"! Instead, we must write goals that create the necessary conditions for friendships to flourish while also making sure that the supports and services are geared toward relationship building as well as academic growth (see Table 6.3). Not only can both be achieved without sacrificing the other, but most of us would agree that human connection, socialization, and feelings of belonging help us learn and feel motivated, so focusing on friendships should never be seen as something extraneous to the "real work" of schools.

Acceptance and Belonging

Too often, individuals with autism are asked to make accommodations, to use "typical behavior," and to learn "appropriate social skills." Instead of asking students with autism to make all of the adjustments, teachers and students without identified disabilities can rethink their ideas about concepts such as "typical" and "appropriate" and question whether conforming is always the best way to support students with autism. For instance, instead of asking the student with autism to study all of the social norms of attending a basketball game (e.g., sitting on the bleachers, cheering when the team scores), all students and teachers in the school might expand their notions of what appropriate participation looks like. This exact issue arose when one of my former students, Tawanna, attended her first varsity game. Even though the teachers had talked to her about appropriate social behavior for the game, Tawanna appeared unable or unwilling to follow the social rules that had been outlined for her. Instead, she paced rapidly up and down the court during the game (perhaps in imitation of the schools' coach) and waved a colorful flyswatter (a favorite possession) when the home team had the ball. When a teacher tried to stop Tawanna from pacing, students intervened and pointed out how others were stomping on the bleachers; waving pompoms, foam fingers, and "rally" towels; and shouting at the players. A few students were even dressed as hornets (the school mascot), making the flyswatter a natural part of the scene! The teachers in Tawanna's school began to think more critically about what types of social supports they provided for her. Although Tawanna still wanted information about social situations and often did want to "fit in" to the life of the school, there were moments when she was relieved to be accepted with all of her differences and uniquenesses.

Table 6.3. Tips for writing friendship-focused IEP goals and objectives

Create an entire IEP that focuses on inclusion, belonging, support, and school membership.

Write friendship development into the services and supports section.

Create person-centered goals that focus on the individual's strengths and learning style.

Write objectives for participation in community-building activities.

Write objectives that focus on cooperative learning, active and collaborative structures, student teams, small groups, and peer tutoring.

Write objectives that start with phrases such as "working with a small group of classmates" or "working with a classmate of her choosing."

Write objectives that focus on peer support as much as possible (especially as a supplement to or replacement for adult support that might be needed).

From Tashie, C., Shapiro-Barnard, S., & Rossetti, Z. (2006). *Seeing the charade: What we need to do and undo to make friendships happen.* Nottingham, UK: Inclusive Solutions; adapted by permission.

Likewise, Jim Sinclair reported that part of forming true friendship is finding individuals who believe that relationships require "adaptation" and understanding on the part of *both* individuals:

> I had a friend—not a parent driven by love and obligation to want to reach me, not a professional who made a career of studying my condition, but just someone who thought I was interesting enough to want to get to know better—a friend who, with no formal background in psychology or special education, figured out for herself some guidelines for relating to me. She told me what they were: never to assume without asking that I thought, felt, or understood anything merely because she would have such thoughts, feelings, or understanding in connection with my circumstances or behavior; and never to assume without asking that I didn't think, feel, or understand anything merely because I was not acting the way [one] would act in connection with such thoughts, feelings, or understanding. In other words, she learned to ask instead of trying to guess. (1993, p. 296)

Summary

On my first day of teaching, one of my students with autism spent 6 hours running around the classroom. Every 30 minutes or so, he would get tired and collapse in my lap for a short rest. One of the paraprofessionals in the school walked in on this scene and remarked, "He can't be autistic. Kids with autism don't like to be near people." The paraprofessional was, of course, sharing one of the many myths related to the social lives of individuals with autism.

Certainly it is true that some people with autism need more time alone than others. Some even note that they are more comfortable alone or with animals than they are with people. Other individuals with autism crave social interaction and social situations, however. Of course this range of preferences parallels those of people without identified disabilities, so caution must be exercised when talking about a social preference or need as "autism-like."

What does seem true about learners with autism and socializing is that their needs and preferences are as varied and individual as the students themselves. For this reason, teachers will do well to support the student with autism and all other students by creating an inclusive and supportive classroom community and cultivating opportunities for connection and interaction within that classroom. It was within the social context of such an inclusive classroom that a young first-grade student, Ian Drummond, was inspired to write the first story of his life by typing on an augmentative communication device. His words should help teachers consider the ways in which inclusion and social interaction are enmeshed and how student stories and voices must drive the work we do and the ideas we have about autism:

THERE WAS A SBOYH WHO HAD AUTISM. HE HADF A HAFTD TIME DOING THINGS THAT OTHER KIDS DID BUT JHE HAD F5RIENDS. HE LIKED EDDIE AN TRISTAN AND ALL THE MKIDS. THEY WERDE HAPPY TOGETHERY. (Martin, 1994, p. 241)

FOR MORE ANSWERS & INFORMATION

Books

Baker, J. (2003). *The social skills picture book: Teaching play, emotion, and communication to children with autism.* Arlington, TX: Future Horizons, Inc.

Grandin, T., & Barron, S. (2005). *The unwritten rules of social relationships: Decoding social mysteries through the unique perspectives of autism.* Arlington, TX: Future Horizons, Inc.

Gray, C. (2010). *The new social story book: The 10th Anniversary Edition.* Arlington, TX: Future Horizons Inc.

Hughes, C., & Carter, E.W. (2008). *Peer buddy programs for successful secondary school inclusion.* Baltimore: Paul H. Brookes Publishing Co.

Sapon-Shevin, M. (2010). *Because we can change the world: A practical guide to building cooperative, inclusive classroom communities* (2nd ed.). Thousand Oaks, CA: Corwin Press.

Tashie, C., Shapiro-Barnard, S., & Rossetti, Z. (2006). *Seeing the charade: What we need to do and undo to make friendships happen.* Nottingham, UK: Inclusive Solutions.

Web Sites

Dennis Debbaudt's Autism Risk & Safety Management
http://autismriskmanagement.com/links.html
This unique web site should be in the "favorites" folder of every teacher, police officer, and parent. It has publications, links, and safety products to review.

Mara Sapon-Shevin's web site
http://www.marasaponshevin.org
A scholar focused on community building in inclusive schools, Sapon-Shevin has filled her site with resources related to her own research and consulting including great music downloads and printable articles.

Pacer Center's Kids Against Bullying
http://www.pacerkidsagainstbullying.org
A unique site that empowers kids to support one another and create safer school environments.

(continued)

(continued)

Peaceful Playgrounds

http://www.peacefulplaygrounds.com

   The purpose of Peaceful Playgrounds is to introduce teachers to the many choices of activities available on playgrounds. Articles, a blog, and an array of products (such as stencils for creating structured games) will help any school create better options for students with and without disabilities during recess.

Social Skills Training

http://www.socialskillstraining.org

   This site highlights strategies for teaching social skills to K–12 students.

NOTES: _____

_____

_____

_____

_____

_____

_____

_____

_____

_____

_____

_____

_____

_____

_____

_____

_____

_____

7

Building Communication Skills, Competencies, and Relationships

i love language more than anything
it links people
a language gives us dignity and individuality
(Sellin, 1995, p. 154)

Educators who are preparing to teach a student with autism for the first time often ask, "Where do I start?" I always suggest beginning with communication. If the student does not have a reliable way to express him- or herself, the educational team will need to experiment with strategies, systems, materials, or devices that might be effective. If the student does have reliable ways to communicate, the team should focus on building the student's communication skills and competencies and giving him or her opportunities to participate in class, engage in curriculum, and socialize using those skills and competencies. Supporting a student's communication is critical; if a teacher in an inclusive classroom wants to develop better curriculum and instruction for a student, find more effective and sensitive ways to support his or her behavior, or learn more about his or her social needs, that teacher needs to be able to gain access to that student's voice.

This chapter covers everything from types of augmentative and alternative communication (AAC) to echolalia to creating more communication opportunities in the classroom. The first section deals with methods of communication. This is followed by ideas teachers can use to create a context for communication. Finally, tips on being a good communication partner are shared.

Methods of Communication

Students with autism communicate in a variety of ways. One mother, for instance, shared how her son expressed his love to her through arts and crafts:

I recall a bad morning, when he had cut holes in the tips of his socks and squeezed a tube of toothpaste over several of his stuffed animals. We were upset with each other. I

117

did not understand his behavior that day, and he did not understand my rules. In the after-
math, he came to me as I was writing, with his head bowed. In his hands, he held a cutout
of two joined hearts colored with red magic marker. His hand drew near to mine and he
quietly pushed the joined hearts within my grasp. It was the best "I love you" I had ever
received. No words were necessary. (Bayer, 2008, p. 12)

Robert Hughes shares a similar "ah ha" moment with his son, Walker. As Hughes tells it,
the family was sitting around watching a favorite home movie; it featured Walker jumping
around while his parents tried to figure out how to work their camera. One day, as they were
watching the clip, Walker's mother noticed something she had never seen before: Walker
speaking. She shouted for Hughes to rewind the tape and, this time, both of them saw it;
Walker was talking but they couldn't make out what he was saying. In disbelief, they replayed
the tape and, as Hughes recalls, they were "astonished and mortified" at what they saw:

He's saying, very plainly now, "Look at me!" and "I love you!" but loud voices are so busy
with their video camera trying to get the boy to perform in the way they expect him to that
they don't even notice. In fact, until this viewing (the fourth? the fifth?) five years later, we
had never noticed him speaking, so caught up had we been in our preoccupied worrying.
     So there was a "non-speaking" boy who was actually speaking to us but we weren't
noticing. . . . And the awful thought hit us both at the same time: How often has this happened? How often have we, because of the buzzing in our heads, missed what he was
actually saying to us?. . . . [If we,] the goofball wishful-thinking parents, could miss something this obvious and basic and flat-out wonderful, how much more would others miss?
(2003, pp. 115–116)

Following the incident, the family created a rule that could keep them mindful of Walker's
potential: *Walker is always communicating more than even we—his ever-watchful parents—can
comprehend.*
     Teachers are charged with the complex task of learning about and trying to decode com-
munication efforts (such as those described in these two stories) so that they can respond and
use them as springboards for exploring new skills and seeing other abilities. As autism advocate Gail Gillingham shared, the role of the teacher is not to teach communication but to find
it, listen to it, and build sharing and understanding between the person with autism and others:

I do not take any credit from "teaching" them how to communicate. I believe that their desire and willingness to communicate with others is the same as that of any other person in
the world. They reach out to us in so many different ways, clearly communicating with
those in their presence at all times. They may not be using words. Their gestures may not
exactly match ours. Their behavior may appear "inappropriate." All of this is communication.
(2000, p. 111)

Educators can support students by seeking to understand all of the ways in which they
communicate and helping them to build on and enhance the strategies and approaches they
already employ successfully. Two ways in which students with autism often communicate are
explored here: 1) speech and 2) AAC.

Speech

Some students with autism use speech that is quite functional and appropriate. Others, however, use it in ways that are idiosyncratic and unreliable. For instance, some students can recite all of the words from a song but cannot ask for a drink of water. Another problem experi-

enced by some individuals is that they can use a few words functionally (e.g., "Hello," "My name is Ro") but have difficulties using speech for conversation.

Echolalia

Some students repeat phrases or expressions over and over again. They may repeat these words, phrases, or expressions immediately after hearing them. For example, if the teacher says, "Good morning, students," a student may also say, "Good morning, students." This phenomenon is called *echolalia*. If the student uses the words or phrase immediately after hearing it, the behavior is considered *instant* or *immediate echolalia*; if the student repeats something that has been said minutes, days, or even weeks after hearing it, it is called *delayed echolalia*. When a student repeats a phrase from a movie, a line from a song, or an utterance overheard days, weeks, or months earlier, that is considered delayed echolalia.

Uses and Purposes of Echolalia   Different people seem to experience echolalia in different ways at different times. This means that for some people with autism, the purpose of echolalia—when there is one—changes across the day and across contexts. Some people report, however, that their echolalia often serves no purpose; it "just happens." That is, they sometimes say things they don't want to say or speak when they do not mean to do so (Burke, 2002; Donnellan & Leary, 1995; Kasa-Hendrickson, Broderick, & Hanson, 2009; Kluth, 1998). For example, in Kasa-Hendrickson, Broderick, and Biklen (2002), Jamie Burke, a man who uses both speech and typed communication, explains that he often is burdened by what he calls "words of annoyance":

In class today I was anxious and I was typing out an English assignment and I kept saying, "Mickey turns into Frankenstein." But I was not typing that. I was typing about Edgar Allan Poe, but all of a sudden out leapt, "Mickey turns into Frankenstein."

Having shared some of the difficulties that those on the spectrum report, I turn to a discussion of how some individuals in some instances actually find echolalia helpful. Some use it because it can be pleasing or relaxing (Gillingham, 2000; Grandin, 1995; Webb, 1995). Jasmine Lee O'Neill, a woman with autism, reported that some words bring "a peaceful inner feeling":

In those who speak, they will often talk to themselves, chatting away about almost anything, and echoing tunes, phrases, or words that sound pleasing to them. The sounds of certain words can roll about deliciously and provide auditory stimulation. Even in completely non-verbal autistics there is a rare child who makes no sound at all. Each child picks and utters key noises to himself. (1999, p. 25)

Others may use echoed speech as a substitute of sorts for authentic speech. That is, students who cannot control or access all of the speech they need seem to "borrow" words or phrases that they *can* gain access to and control. Grandin (1995) explained that some individuals with autism often echo words or phrases that are associated with the words they do want. To illustrate this point, Grandin used the example of Jessy, a woman with autism who always uses the words "partly heard song" when she means "I don't know." Grandin hypothesized that at some point in Jessy's life, a partly heard song was associated with not knowing.

Individuals with autism may use echolalia to take a turn in a conversation, answer a question, or process information (Bayer, 2008; Prizant & Duchan, 1981; Vicker, 2009). Students may also use echolalia to make requests. A mother told me that her son often puts records on the stereo and subsequently will turn to anyone else in the room and ask, "Do you want me to leave you alone?" (something he hears from his mother), which the family has grown to understand means "Leave me alone, please."

Individuals may also use echoed speech to initiate conversations or otherwise socialize. Eric, a young Caucasian man with autism, shared a locker space with two young Latino men in the school. Every day when Eric came to the locker, his classmates would greet him by saying, "Qué pasa, man." Over time, Eric began to greet everyone he encountered with these same words. And Diane Bayer (2008) reported that her son, Jacob, uses the same phrases and words consistently to communicate several different messages. "Elephant" means Jacob is very angry. "Little blue engine, please help us" means he needs support. And "Birthday party! Toot! Toot!" is Jacob's way of communicating that he would rather be having fun at a party instead of doing what he is doing. Translating these phrases from "Jacobspeak" is one way Bayer helps her son (and his communication partners) interact and understand one another. Creating such a key is a helpful strategy for supporting someone with echolalia. See Table 7.1 for more suggestions on supporting people with echolalia.

Perceptions of Echolalia   Echolalic behaviors are sometimes seen as intentional or even as "interfering" or "challenging." Students who struggle with speech are sometimes reprimanded for saying things that are deemed silly, off topic, or inappropriate, but many on the spectrum report that they have little or no control over their words at times. Even those who sometimes use echolalia in functional ways may be unable to control how and when they access it. For instance, consider the potential problems caused for a student described by Susan Stokes, an autism consultant:

> A student with autism became upset with his teacher over completing a task. He then verbalized loudly, "Go to hell lieutenant!" His parents reported that he had been watching the movie, "A Few Good Men" quite frequently. This movie contains this exact same utterance in the emotional context of anger. This child with autism was unable to spontaneously generate language to communicate, "I'm upset and I don't want to complete this assignment," but could pull forth an echolalic utterance which he had processed in the context of the emotional state of anger. (Stokes, http://www.cesa7.k12.wi.us/sped/autism/verbal/verbal11.html)

Sue Rubin, a woman with autism who uses both speech and facilitated communication (FC) to communicate, shares that she runs into difficulties with her speech as well;

> When I use speech alone I sometimes mean what I say and other times I don't. My awful echolalia is . . . an example of movement of thought (problems). I say a word or sound and am unable to switch it off or change to a different sound. (Rubin et al., 2001, p. 421)

She also notes that her echolalia "disappears somewhat" when she is cognitively engaged.

Therese Joliffe, a woman with autism, also claims that she cannot use words reliably or easily:

> I sometimes know in my head what the words are but they do not always come out. Sometimes when they do come out they are incorrect, a fact that I am only sometimes aware of and often pointed out by other people. (Joliffe, Lansdown, & Robinson, as cited in Donnellan & Leary, 1995, p. 52)

Because of the types of "missteps" experienced by individuals like those described above, it is not uncommon for people who speak unusually to be seen as incompetent and even intellectually impaired. A teacher who hears a student repeat, "The sky is falling, the sky is falling," for weeks after the class reads *Chicken Little* (1904) might assume that the student is not aware enough to know that his speech is inappropriate. In mainstream American culture

Table 7.1.   Supporting students with echolalia

Reassure the speaker	Sometimes just assuring the person that you hear them and want to understand them can be a comfort. You might use one of the following phrases to communicate your support: • I can see that you are trying hard to tell me something; let me see if I can figure it out. • I think you are trying to tell me _____, and I apologize if I'm getting it wrong. • I know you sometimes say _____ when you feel/want/need _____. Is that what you feel/want/need now? • I can see that you want to tell me or ask me something. Let's see if we can figure out together what it is.
Go to the movies	If a student often uses phrases from a favorite movie or cartoon, help everyone on the staff become familiar with it. This is especially helpful if the student uses the phrases in functional ways. For instance, a student who watches *The Wizard of Oz* frequently might say, "Lions and tigers and bears" when he is frightened because the characters chant this phrase during a scary scene. A teacher would need to know the film to guess that the child might be afraid of something.
Make a key	Create a key to help others decipher a student's speech. Make a list of all of the phrases and words the student commonly uses. Then, work with the student's family to "translate" them. For example, a student I know often says, "the King of Rock and Roll"; this usually means that he wants to listen to music. All of his teachers have been informed of this translation. The key should contain every possible meaning of given words and phrases because educators and families will often be guessing at the meaning of the utterances. If a word or phrase is sometimes used in different ways across different situations, that information should be included as well.
Switch to writing	Stop talking and begin writing using a computer, paper and pen, chalkboard, or any other available materials. If a person is using echoed speech because he or she is confused, overwhelmed, or cannot understand a partner's speech, this strategy may be very helpful. Another way to use the written word is to ask the person with autism to communicate using typing, writing, or pointing. If the person is using echoed speech because he or she cannot get the right words out, this strategy can be helpful. One young woman I know communicates most effectively when the teaching staff writes questions to her and gives her opportunities to circle an answer (from a choice of three or four options).
Whisper	Try speaking more softly. For some students in certain situations, a quieter voice may actually be easier to process and respond to.
Teach a script	In certain situations, students will be able to move from echolalia to more functional speech if they are taught and have many opportunities to practice a related script (Kasa-Hendrickson et al., 2009). For example, the student can rehearse greetings or answering certain yes or no questions.

(as in many cultures), people often assume that atypical speech or a lack of speech or verbal communication translates to low cognition (Crossley, 1997; Donnellan & Leary, 1995; Rubin et al., 2001).

In fact, the *Diagnostic and Statistical Manual of Mental Disorders, Fourth Edition, Text Revision* (*DSM-IV-TR*) states that during the early childhood years, children with severe mental retardation acquire little, if any, communicative speech, and that they may learn to talk during the school-age years (American Psychiatric Association, 2000). Likewise, Winner (1996) cited exceptional oral language as one of five early indicators of the "globally gifted high-IQ child." She indicated specifically that "these children speak early, often progressing directly from one-word utterances to complex sentences. They have a large vocabulary and a large store of verbal knowledge" (p. 27). In other words, the story that guides professionals in fields from medicine to teaching is this: The more you talk, the smarter you are. Despite the existence of clear evidence that an inability to speak does not mean an inability to think, process, know, or learn (Bauby, 1997; Biever, 2009; Crossley, 1997; Giberson, 2007; Robillard, 1997; Rubin et al., 2001; Tavalaro & Tayson, 1997), this myth persists.

Augmentative and Alternative Communication

Of course, some students with autism do not use speech at all. Chammi Rajapatirana, a man with autism who uses typed communication, shared his frustration with not being able to speak:

Being mute is like having your brain gouged out. Autism/apraxia took away my voice, and a world that equates muteness with stupidity took everything else. Yes it really is as if my brain were gouged out. It hurts so much I want to scream. Pouring all my pain into my voice I want to scream till that searing sound fills my body, my soul and my world shattering us all into a million fiery shrieking pieces. (1998, p. 2)

Individuals like Rajapatirana must be supported through the use of AAC supports and strategies. *Augmentative and alternative communication* refers to communication that enhances, augments, or supplements speech and covers a broad range of methods and strategies, from sophisticated, computer-based systems with synthetic voices to teacher-created letter boards. Other examples of AAC include writing, drawing, gesturing, eye gaze, facial expressions, and sign language. (See Table 7.2 for more tips on using AAC in the classroom.)

All of us use various forms of AAC in our daily lives. We may, for instance, raise a hand to be recognized in a classroom or scribble a note to a friend during a quiet meeting. For a person with unique communication needs, however, AAC is more than a convenience. For those with disabilities or communication differences, AAC systems, devices, and techniques typically mean increased access to voice, control, freedom, and power. For some, in fact, AAC strategies and techniques are the only way to tell a joke, order a burger, sing to a child, or write a letter. Sharisa Kochmeister, a woman who uses AAC to communicate and to pursue her work as an author, poet, and activist, claimed that AAC has liberated her, given her opportunities for expression, and "shattered walls" in her life:

Almost as much as my various "disorders" disable me, typing enables me. It allows me to communicate with and exist within a world where I was and would otherwise still be a total stranger. It lets me show other people that I (and therefore, possibly other "non-verbals") am alive and smart, understand, think, feel, hope, plan, and dream just like verbal people. (1997, p. 1)

Even individuals who can use speech may prefer to use AAC to supplement it (Kasa-Hendrickson et al., in press; Williams, 2007). This preference should always be honored. Individuals with autism may need a variety of ways to express themselves, and those with reliable communication should be cautious about making judgments about the value of one mode over another. As Amanda Baggs, a woman on the spectrum explains, typing provides others access to her ideas, thoughts, and emotions that her spoken words cannot. Throughout her childhood, it seems, she struggled to use spoken words with accuracy but did so with little success, then she tried typing and was hooked:

It became more important to me to be able to say what I meant, not all these other people's words, when I became an adult. But speech was not working for that, even when I had speech. It was like grabbing a rusty lever and trying to hit a target across the room, often hitting another target altogether. Typing was more reliable. (Williams, 2007)

Five types of AAC commonly used with students on the spectrum are highlighted here. They are sign language and gestural systems, objects and pictures, communication devices, writing, and facilitated communication (FC).

Table 7.2.   Tips for using augmentative and alternative communication (AAC)

Augmentative communication systems should be available to the learner at all times. If a student who uses a device cannot easily do so in a particular situation (e.g., on the bus), it might help to use another system (e.g., a letter board) during that activity.

Students need to see other people using the system they themselves use. For example, if one student uses sign language, all of the students in the class can be taught several signs to model the use of the system and to expand their own communication skills. If one student uses a picture system to communicate, other students in the class should use these pictures for certain activities.

AAC is not just for choice making, communicating needs, and saying "good morning." These are important uses, but students in inclusive classrooms also need to use communication systems to access and learn standards-based content.

Students using pictures, signs, or typed communication may need to be taught how to properly engage a partner. Learners should be taught to get the attention of their communication partner before typing, pointing, or signing. Students using written words or picture communication systems should be taught to approach their partner and hand him or her the message.

Be sure to keep assessing the student and the system. Systems should change not just because students change, but because as students use their systems, their needs become clearer. For example, if a student using a new system learns it very quickly, it may be possible to give him a more complex system.

Show other students how to interact with someone using an AAC system. Model how to ask questions, greet the student, and have a conversation.

Sign Language and Gestural Systems

Some students have found communication success by using some type of sign language. The most common system is American Sign Language (ASL), which is the language system used by those who are deaf or hard of hearing. Students might also use Signed English or Signed Exact English. Still others may use "home" signs, which are gestures and signs created and used by an individual. For instance, I knew one student who could not go anywhere without his watch. When he couldn't find it, he signed for it by squeezing his right wrist.

Although some students with autism may use ASL because they are deaf or hard of hearing, most use signs because they cannot speak. The advantage, of course, to using sign language is that the individual does not need an aid or piece of equipment. The main drawback to using any sign system, however, is that many communication partners do not know sign language, especially if the student uses some signs or gestures that are unique to his or her communication.

A manual sign system for some individuals with autism may also be tricky because of problems some students experience with movement. Some may simply be unable to use signs accurately or predictably because of problems with initiation, volition, or modulation of movement. Some students, for instance, use ASL but move very quickly or use only approximations of the signs. These students can be quite successful with sign and gesture systems if those around them understand their movements as communication and work to understand the individual's unique system.

Of course, none of these cautions should prevent a teacher from using signs or gesture systems in the classroom; if a student seems able to imitate signs and learn new language this way, it should be pursued without question. Consider the case of my friend Rick, a single father, and his son Wyatt. For several months, Rick asked Wyatt's teachers to introduce sign language to his son; Rick had seen evidence at home that Wyatt could learn and functionally use different gestures and thought it was worth pursuing. School staff resisted the suggestion and cited the student's motor control problems and "low IQ score" as reasons he wouldn't be able to learn a complicated symbol system. Rick stopped pestering the school until the day Wyatt got a new babysitter. The teenager wanted to know why Wyatt couldn't talk. When Rick explained, she asked why he could not use sign language. Rick shared the explanation the

Table 7.3.   Gesture dictionary for Marv

What Marv does	What it means	How to respond
Makes an "uh-uh" sound	"I need some help."	Show him the manual sign for help and then provide help.
Grabs another student's hand or arm	"I like you."	Explain the meaning to the student's friend and help them work together, if possible.
Bangs or taps his desk	"I'm bored; I don't understand what's going on."	Quietly explain to him what is happening, using simple language and graphics if needed.

Mirenda, P. (2005). Augmentative and alternative communication techniques. In Downing, J. (Ed.), *Teaching communication skills to students with severe disabilities* (2nd ed., p. 91). Baltimore: Paul H. Brookes Publishing Co.; reprinted by permission.

school had given. The sitter, who was not a teacher (or even an adult), asked, "Well, do you mind if I try?" Rick encouraged her to do so, and using only a dictionary she bought at the bookstore, the young woman soon had Wyatt communicating using more than 30 words. Wyatt eventually was able to use hundreds of words—not only to make requests or label items but to hold conversations as well.

For students who do not use conventional signs, and even for students like Wyatt who use "real" signs that others may not know, teachers may want to assemble a gesture dictionary for use by all of the classroom staff and the student's peers (see Table 7.3). A gesture dictionary acts as a "translation guide by describing a student's gestures along with [his or her] meanings and suggestions for appropriate responses" (Mirenda, 2005, p. 91). If the dictionary is used consistently, the individual with autism may be less frustrated and more comfortable initiating communication with teachers and peers. In addition, educators may see a more complex profile of the student emerge as they begin to accumulate evidence of the various ways the learner gets his or her needs met and communicates information.

Objects and Pictures

A student may bring his teacher the chalk if he wants her to write on the board, or he may bring her his boots if he is ready to go outside. Although this type of communication is not sufficient in that it does not allow the learner to express complex thoughts and ideas, it should not be overlooked as an important supplement to other types of communication. In some situations, communicating through objects is enough. If a student can bring her teacher a cup to indicate that she wants water, she may be confused if the teacher asks her to show the same thing on her communication board in order to get a drink.

Students may also communicate by interacting with pictures, either by handing pictures to a communication partner or by pointing to pictures. Students may use different types of pictures to communicate, ranging from simple line drawings to complex and detailed photographs. These pictures and photographs may be used for a range of purposes including communicating quick requests, making choices, or starting conversations. A student may, for instance, point to items on a communication board to choose a snack.

Objects and pictures are commonly used to create communication boards. Boards can be used for choice-making, greetings, requests, and conversation starters. Teachers can also use the pictures from these boards to create daily schedules or stories for the student, thus giving him or her opportunities to better learn the pictures by using them across situations and environments.

One formal system of picture communication is the Picture Exchange Communication System (PECS) (Bondy & Frost, 2002). In this method, students present pictures to another person or form picture sentences on a board as a means of communication. Students typically keep pictures in a portable notebook so they can bring their "voice" with them across environments and situations.

The six phases of teaching PECS are as follows: In phase one, students are taught to initiate communication. The second phase expands the use of pictures. In the third phase, students make specific choices between available pictures. During the fourth phase, the student learns to build simple sentences. The fifth phase involves helping the student answer the question, "What do you want?" and in the sixth phase, students learn to comment about items and activities (Bondy & Frost, 2002).

Although many students have found success in learning the PECS approach, this method, like all others, should be part of a total communication system. The biggest drawback to using a system like PECS is that students are limited by the pictures available to them. Therefore, this method may need to be supplemented with others.

Communication Devices

Students with autism may come into the classroom with a variety of devices that can be used for everyday conversations and to engage in classroom lessons. Students may enjoy using communication devices (versus pictures or gestures) because many of them "talk." For students who do not speak, the device can serve as their voice. Some devices are very simple and carry only one or a handful of messages, whereas others have many "levels" and can carry thousands of phrases. Some are designed only to carry and deliver a message and others have a variety of functions and features including calculators, printers, and memory capacity for storing large amounts of text. See Figure 7.1 for photographs of a single-level, a multilevel, and a comprehensive device.

Although there are many drawbacks to using such devices to communicate (e.g., they can be cumbersome, they can break down), if a student is successful in using one, the benefits outweigh the drawbacks. Students using devices may not only gain access to a voice but may also hone additional academic skills and competencies as they become proficient with their particular device. One of my former students had the use of speech but could only express simple needs and wants. When he began supplementing his speech by using a communication device, he was able to compose more complex and detailed thoughts. In addition, he became incredibly adept at programming the device and was able to get extra credit from his computer teacher for learning that skill.

Some students are even making gains in literacy, in part through the use of communication devices (Kasa-Hendrickson et al., in press). Jamie Burke, a student with autism, learned to talk by reading the visual display on his communication device:

[Jamie's device] can be programmed to say each letter aloud as it is typed, read each word aloud when the space bar is pressed, and read whole sentences or paragraphs aloud when the speak bar is pressed. When the speak bar is pressed, the sentence scrolls by on the bright green visual display as the device reads it aloud. Jamie initially began incorporat-

1)   2)   3)

Figure 7.1. Examples of augmentative communication devices: 1) single-level device, 2) multilevel device, and 3) comprehensive device.

ing speech that seemed related to his typing by intermittently repeating aloud individual words after the [device]. Shortly thereafter, he began repeating aloud phrases and eventually whole sentences as they scrolled by, without the added support of repeating after the [device's] voice output. [Jamie's mother] describes Jamie's reading aloud as beginning "once he got the [device] and the use of the computer. . . . and all of a sudden [he] started reading back, and repeating after the machine had said it, that just opened the floodgates." (Broderick & Kasa-Hendrickson, 2001, p. 17)

Writing

Beginning in the 1960s, a woman named Rosalind Oppenheim (as cited in Crossley, 1997) taught a group of nonverbal students with autism to communicate through writing. The students, previously assumed to have mental retardation, were soon able to "talk" on paper (and, in doing so, show unexpected ability). Oppenheim noted that putting pressure on the student's hand seemed to be the key to writing success for those in her group:

We believe that the autistic child's difficulties stem from a definite apraxia . . . There seems to be a basic deficiency in certain areas of his motor expressive behaviour. So, in teaching writing, we find that it is usually necessary to continue to guide the child's hand for a considerable period of time. Gradually, however, we are able to fade this to a mere touch of a finger on the child's writing hand. We're uncertain about precisely what purpose this finger-touching serves. What we do know is that the quality of the writing deteriorates appreciably without it, despite the fact that the finger is in no way guiding the child's writing hand. "I can't remember how to write the letters without your finger touching my skin" one nonverbal child responded. (p. 40)

Although writing is not a common augmentative communication strategy used by those with autism, Oppenheim is not the only person to discover success with it. In *Communication Unbound*, Biklen reported on the work of Mary Bacon, an American special education teacher. Bacon described how she began using handwriting with one of her students:

I got a little perturbed with him when he wouldn't point to the ABC's for me. I slapped my hand on my side and said, "Garrett, you know the ABC's as well as I do. Now point to the W." That he did. He pointed to each one of them. I turned the page over and I said, "Now, we're going to write the ABCs and I'll help you." All I did, I put my hand on his and my god, he wrote them all. (1993, p. 96)

Tito Rajarshi Mukhopadhyay, a young man with autism who also uses writing as AAC, has been writing independently since age 6. His story is interesting because Tito does not have verbal communication that is well understood by others: "I can speak although many people cannot follow because it is not clear. Sometimes I need facilitation to begin my speech like opening a speech door in my throat. To facilitate me mother has to wave her hands" (2000, p. 76).

In the foreword of Tito's book, *Beyond the Silence*, Lorna Wing, a notable psychiatrist, describes her first impression of this young man:

[When he arrived] Tito's observable behaviour was exactly like that of a mute child with classic autism, ignoring people but exploring the objects that took his attention. [His mother] settled him down and wrote the alphabet on a piece of paper. We asked questions and Tito pointed to the letters to spell his replies. He did this independently, without any physical guidance from his mother. He replied to questions in full sentences, including long words used appropriately. He also spontaneously told us, in handwriting, that he wanted the book he had written to be published and demanded a promise that this would happen. (2000, p. 2)

Tito's story is also interesting because he shares thoughts and ideas that would be considered sophisticated for a person twice his age; he is a gifted and talented poet and writer. He describes his autism in many of his writings:

Men and women are puzzled by everything I do
Doctors use different terminologies to describe me
I just wonder
The thoughts are bigger than I can express
Every move that I make shows how trapped I feel
Under the continuous flow of happenings
The effect of a cause becomes the cause of another effect
And I wonder
I think about the times when I change the environment around me
With the help of my imagination
I can go places that do not exist
And they are like beautiful dreams
But it is a world full of improbabilities
Racing toward uncertainty (Mukhopadhyay, 2000, p. 99)

Facilitated Communication

Facilitated communication, commonly referred to as FC, is a communication strategy used by people with verbalization and motor skill difficulties. Specifically, FC is ". . . an alternative to speech that involves a communication partner who provides physical and emotional support to a person with a severe communication impairment as he or she types on a keyboard or points" (Biklen, 1990, p. 293). Facilitated communication is provided in several ways. It may entail a facilitator providing pressure to the speaker's shoulder or arm to support her as she types or points to a communication device, board, cards, or objects. It can also involve a facilitator providing physical counter pressure to the speaker's wrist, hand, or elbow; or it may take the form of the facilitator being physically present, observing the speaker's communication, or simply sitting next to him or her.

Through the use of FC, many students with autism and other disabilities who have limited use of words or who have never previously communicated with words were able to express their first thoughts, ideas, desires, needs, and feelings to family members, care providers, therapists, and educators (Biklen, 1990; Crossley, 1997; Martin, 1994; Savarese, 2007). FC is complex and involves more than physical contact. It requires emotional support and creative problem solving as well. Many practical considerations are related to the implementation of FC. Facilitators are responsible for ensuring that the student is comfortable, watching the FC user and communication board/device, giving feedback about the typing process (e.g., reading off individual letters as they are typed, reminding the individual to look at the target, making suggestions about the individual's posture), and providing prompts and cues that will help the FC user communicate his or her message (e.g., asking clarifying questions such as "I don't understand what you typed there. Can you try it again?") (Biklen, 1990; Shevin & Chadwick, 2000).

Questions About Facilitated Communication   Although people with movement differences and other disabilities have long communicated with a variety of physical supports, the dawn of FC drew unprecedented attention. The unique nature of the method and the physical touch, in particular, instantly raised questions and concerns, with some stakeholders questioning the validity of the words typed by FC users. Because of these concerns, many of the published studies about FC have focused on the validation of the strategy and authorship of written communications (Biklen & Schubert, 1991; Calculator & Singer, 1992; Cardinal, Hanson, & Wakeham, 1996; Simon, Toll, & Whitehair, 1994; Szempruch & Jacobson, 1993; Weiss, Wagner, & Bauman, 1996).

In authorship studies, many researchers have found that FC is a valid strategy and that individuals with disabilities produce original communications (Biklen, Saha, & Kliewer, 1995; Cardinal et al., 1996; Janzen-Wilde, Duchan, & Higginbotham, 1995; Marcus & Shevin, 1997; Simon et al., 1994; Weiss et al., 1996). Other researchers have reported that students could not produce original communication through FC (Calculator & Singer, 1992; Green & Shane, 1994; Hirshorn & James, 1995; Jacobson, Mulick, & Schwartz, 1995; Myles & Simpson, 1994; Regal, Rooney, & Wandas, 1994). Since these papers have been published, researchers, educators, and individuals with autism have studied the various reasons that individuals with autism might have "failed" tests of validity and have provided suggestions for studying the phenomenon more sensitively and effectively (see Biklen & Cardinal, 1997).

Some individuals with autism reportedly struggled with authorship/validity tasks and tests because the assessment conditions were uncomfortable or even threatening. Annie McDonald is a woman with cerebral palsy who once typed only with support and now types independently. Initially, she responded very badly to testing situations. When she first learned to communicate, school officials; government officials; and her teacher, Rosemary Crossley, constantly tested her. As a result of passing a series of tests and requesting to leave the institution, Annie was eventually allowed to move into the community and begin formal schooling. Even with the knowledge that testing could bring her these freedoms, Crossley remembers that Annie routinely rejected being tested before finally validating with all of the necessary authorities:

> I went through the list of questions with Annie, and she fooled around again. I was angry. The next day I tried again. I was feeling guilty about the day before. I rationalized that personal relationships were more important to Annie than test results, and that she was trying out the situation. I thought that she wondered how far I would go. Would I still like her if she did not perform? Was I only interested in her as a display object? (Crossley & McDonald, 1984, p. 127)

As noted earlier, FC requires emotional support such as treating the FC user with respect and reassuring the individual as he or she types. Biklen described why this type of support is so important:

> Not surprisingly, people who have had a history of difficulty with motor planning will lack confidence in their ability to carry out new tasks. Imagine what it must be like to have significant problems with motor planning and indeed any kind of voluntary action and to have this problem from a very early age. In effect, you will have never enjoyed success in getting your body to do what you want it to do when you want it and often have your body respond in ways that make you feel embarrassed! And imagine what it would be like to be evaluated on the basis of your nonresponsiveness or your impulsiveness. Hence the importance of being supportive to help the person develop confidence that he or she can develop the ability to be successful in communicating through typing. (1993, p. 11)

Sue Rubin, an FC user who not only can type independently but also has written her own Oscar-nominated documentary on the subject of her life and communication needs, has noted how the facilitator's encouragement and expressions of confidence have not only helped her to type but also to become independent in that typing:

> Confidence makes independence happen. I can now type independently with people I have just met because I am confident I can do it and they are confident it can happen

because they see me typing independently with others. I gained confidence over time by being successful with each level of fading; however, independence still eluded me for the first five years of typing. (1999, pp. 5–6)

Authorship   An issue that was overlooked by some during discussions of validity was the fact that many students had validated their communication through daily communication (Biklen et al., 1995; Kluth, 1998; Martin, 1994; Olney, 1997; Sellin, 1995; Weiss & Wagner, 1997). One study focused on how teachers confirmed the authorship of their students' typing (Biklen et al., 1995). Educators identified several different types of evidence they had collected on each student. This information was gathered beginning with each student's first FC experiences. The authors call this type of validation a portfolio approach because different types of evidence are collected over time instead of "testing" students on only one occasion or asking them to perform during formal assessment sessions (see Table 7.4).

In addition, some FC users have silenced doubts by learning to type independently. That is, many FC speakers who started "speaking" by being physically supported at the hand or wrist can now type without physical support (Biklen, 2005; Burke, 2002; Crossley, 1997; Gambel et al., 2002; Hussman, Kluth, Strong, & Tweedy, 2009; Kochmeister, 1997; Rubin et al., 2001), although some may need other types of support such as verbal or proximal cues to stay focused, sustain movement, and gain confidence (Kasa-Hendrickson et al., 2009). Rosemary Crossley (1997), who runs a communication clinic in Australia, reported that within several years of introducing FC to individuals with disabilities, 30 typed independently, although some of them required a light touch on the head or back.

Some of those who have learned to type independently have gone on to attend 4-year colleges, speak at national conferences, create documentary films of their experiences, and engage in research on their own typing (Biklen, 2005; Broderick & Kasa-Hendrickson, 2001; Burke, 2002; Harrison, 2000; Kasa-Hendrickson, Broderick, Biklen, & Gambell 2002; Kochmeister, 1997; Rubin et al., 2001). These successes, even if for a few, must receive their due attention. As Pat Mirenda, a leader in the field of augmentative and alternative communication and self-labeled skeptic, shares, we have to consider that, in part, we are surprised by these stories

Table 7.4.   Validating facilitated communication using the portfolio approach

Attention to typing	Students who previously could not sit for more than a few seconds were able to remain sitting and visually attend to a communication board or device. Due to the previous behavior of these students, this convinced some individuals in the students' lives that the communications produced were valid.
Relationship between typing and speaking	Some students typed words and letters that matched their verbalizations. Other times, students typed words or phrases related to their spoken words. One student typed out "CAN I GO" and verbally said "castle room" at the same time, indicating the place he wished to go.
Form, content, and style of communication	Some students used unique, idiosyncratic, or unusual phrases or spellings of words. For example, one student in the study often substituted the letter *y* for the letter *i* in a variety of different words. She used these same types of spellings across facilitators and contexts. Students also typed about the same topics over time and across facilitators.
Message passing	The conveying of accurate information previously unknown to a facilitator was also used by the teachers in the study. Students passed information from home to school or vice versa. Information was also passed across staff members. For instance, a student told his teacher that his father was getting married on a certain date. The student's mother confirmed that the father did marry on the date specified by the boy.

Source: Biklen, Saha, and Kliewer (1995).

because, in some cases, we were wrong; that is, we believed that individuals had intellectual disabilities and they did not. New stories about people and new ways of understanding them have created a sort of cognitive dissonance and has prevented some in the field from embracing or at least further investigating this phenomenon called FC. Mirenda shares that we need to pay attention to the success stories of FC and ask ourselves the question, "What's going on here and what can we learn from it?" (2008, p. 228).

Similarly, Hitzing indicated that arguments over FC itself as a viable method of communication should, at this point, be moot:

> Imagine, if you can, the following situation. You and I are arguing about whether people with autism can fly. I say that they can, at least some of them. . . . You argue strongly that they can't. Suddenly, in the middle of our debate a person with autism flies through the open window. The argument, as currently constructed, is over. Now, you could quite reasonably change the terms of the argument. You could, for example, argue that the person who just flew in the window is the only person in the world with autism who can fly. We could also argue about what it takes to teach a person with autism to fly, etc. But, unless you want to postulate that the person who flew through the window was misdiagnosed, or that the appearance of flying was the result of some sort of special effect, some slick illusion, you have to stop denying the validity of the "autistic" flying phenomenon. . . . Some of these folks are "flying!" It is indisputable that some studies have validated the communication abilities of people who are being physically assisted to communicate, whereas other people have progressed from physical dependence to independent communication. (1994, pp. 2–3)

Creating a Context for Communication

Whether a student talks nonstop or does not use spoken words at all, teachers can structure the classroom and engineer lessons to both recognize and inspire different types of communication. Teachers can be supportive by communicating with students, paying attention to student communication, teaching all students to use AAC, and creating communication opportunities.

Communicate with Students and Expect Them to Communicate with You

When teachers are working with students who do not have a reliable communication system, they sometimes ask me, "How can you tell how much she understands?" The truth is, teachers may not know how much a learner understands if he or she does not have a way to communicate. The rule should always be, when in doubt, assume that students can learn and do want to communicate.

Historically, "experts" have been tragically wrong about the learning potential and intellectual abilities of many different groups of people, including women, poor people, those from different racial and ethnic groups, people with physical disabilities, those with mental illness, those who are deaf and hard of hearing, and many others (Gould, 1981; Sacks, 1973; Selden, 1999). This history is important, as we will undoubtedly repeat our mistakes if we do not assume our students are capable, can communicate, and want to connect with us.

Some teachers may feel uncomfortable or unsure of how to interact with a student who does not speak or one who communicates in a way that is unfamiliar to him or her. This is understandable, but feeling uncomfortable is not an excuse for not learning new ways of inter-

---

Table 7.5. Guidelines for including a student who does not talk

Never talk about someone in front of them. Always acknowledge the person's presence. Some people may not be able to communicate through spoken words or body language that they understand what you are saying or that they are listening. Assume they are listening and interested in what you are talking about.

Talk in an *age-appropriate* manner, using age-appropriate content. Using a sing-song voice or a tone similar to that used with a young child should be reserved for babies and toddlers. Be sure to check your tone of voice and the content you are talking about.

While teaching, be sure to acknowledge the nonverbal student's presence often. You should not go an entire lesson without saying, "Sean I bet you'll like this part. I know you like to swim," or "Megan I see you smiling. I am sure you will like learning about volcanoes."

If students use a yes / no communication strategy, be sure to use this during a lesson. You can do this during a whole group lesson by saying, "Do you all think that 5 + 5 = 10?" If they answer incorrectly, then you can say, "Oh, I don't think that is quite right. Does anyone have other ideas?"

If the student uses an augmentative communication system, you need to be sure to have them utilize it across lessons.

Use partners during lesson activities. Model and encourage peers to talk about topics with each other.

Take every opportunity to talk with the student. Talk about current events, age-appropriate interests, things you like to do, places to go, and events around school. Also, let them use their communication strategy to make LOTS of choices throughout the day.

Be sure to include them in the academic curriculum in the classroom. Assume learning is possible.

From Kasa-Hendrickson (personal communication, 2008).

---

acting. A few simple guidelines for communicating with a student who does not talk are offered in Table 7.5. As Gillingham suggested, however, one of the most important ways to make a student feel included in the classroom is simply to communicate with him or her and expect the student to communicate with you:

> When I go into a home and say "hello" to an autistic person, they do not have to reply "hello" for me to feel that they are responding. Whether they approach me or withdraw to another room tells me something. I read an increase in repetitive behavior as an indication that they are excited to see me, and I verbally tell them that it feels good to see their excitement. I follow their lead if they take my hand to show me something. If they speak with garbled sounds, I acknowledge their efforts and openly admit that I don't quite understand what they are trying to say. As I spend time with them, I am continuously aware of what they are doing and how they are responding to me. (2000, pp. 111–112)

This way of interacting undoubtedly inspires trust in relationships and allows teachers and students to build communication opportunities and skills. As Gillingham goes on to share, "Concentration on acceptance of what is, instead of trying to fix what appears wrong, leads to improved communication" (2000, p. 112).

In communicating with students and expecting communication, it can also be helpful to reflect on one's assumptions. Shevin (1999) noted that in his role as a communication ally, he always begins with "default values" on which he acts until receiving specific information to the contrary. His own assumptions about individuals with communication differences are that they

- Are highly intelligent

- Have a deep interest in fostering relations with others

- Have stories they would like to tell, if the circumstances are right

- Have positive images of themselves that they wish to present as part of their communication

- Are paying attention to when others interact with them

Although every teacher will want to establish his or her own values and assumptions, those offered by Shevin (1999) should be carefully considered, as this particular way of thinking about people can inspire positive actions. For instance, a teacher who believes his or her student is intelligent will creatively include that student in lessons and respond to him when he seems particularly interested in an idea.

Pay Attention to the Communication Skills Students Do Have

Too often, professionals focus on what students cannot do instead of what they can do. All students with autism have some ways of communicating even if they do not use spoken words. Does the student point to objects she wants? Does she use facial expressions to indicate distress, pain, or happiness? Can she use an object or a picture to make a request (e.g., grab her lunchbox when she is ready to eat)? Can she accurately use a gesture to communicate a need, a want, or a feeling (e.g., clapping when she wants to hear music)?

Although teachers, therapists, and others who work with a student will certainly want to help him or her build on and enhance his or her communication strategies, support should begin by exploring and honoring the skills and abilities the student already has. Teachers may not be able to accurately identify ways in which learners are communicating after knowing them only a few days or weeks; therefore, families must be interviewed and consulted about their child's communication strategies. If the teachers and other team members are unable to generate a lot of useful information by simply meeting with the family, the group might sit together and view a few video clips of the student (at home and at school).

The purpose of such a viewing is to allow various members of the group to ask questions and share answers about how the student communicates across various activities. For instance, as the team watches a tape of the student getting ready for school, the student's mother might point out how he taps his head to ask for his hat or how he vocalizes "buh" to ask for his favorite book.

Teach All Students to Use Augmentative and Alternative Communication

Before any of us learned to speak, we had the advantage of observing and listening to thousands of people speaking, but before students are introduced to augmentative and alternative communication, they have likely not seen anyone else use it fluently, if at all. For this reason, researchers have become increasingly interested in promoting models of communication wherein students get to regularly observe others using their communication system (Cafiero, 2001; Jorgensen, McSheehan, & Sonnenmeier, 2009; Mirenda, 2008). For example, Cafiero (2001) described the use of what she termed a natural aided language intervention (NAL) with Timothy, an adolescent on the spectrum. Timothy was placed in a special education classroom that focused primarily on life skills instruction. Prior to the intervention, Timothy was provided with a 16-symbol display of Picture Communication Symbols (PCS); this was used primarily to make food choices. Timothy used 6 of the 16 symbols functionally.

During the intervention, Timothy was provided with context-specific PCS displays depicting relevant nouns, action words, descriptors, and yes/no symbols. His communication partners (staff members) pointed to symbols on these displays as they asked questions, re-

Figure 7.2. Three students typing on AlphaSmarts in an inclusive classroom.

sponded to his initiations, made comments, and expanded on his communicative attempts. Despite receiving no formal instruction on communicating with these materials, Timothy's functional lexicon increased from 6 to 29 words over a 3-month period. Over the next 19 months, his lexicon increased to 67 words, his challenging behaviors decreased significantly, and he began receiving a more academic education as his team's understanding of his ability began to change.

Cafiero illustrates the great benefit of giving students with autism opportunities to see their system in use. Any teacher can engineer opportunities to integrate AAC into classroom life. If a learner with autism uses a picture board to indicate choices, the teacher might ask all students to use pictures for choices at some point in the day. If one student uses a switch to "read" a repetitive line in a story, all students should get opportunities to do the same. And students in the inclusive classroom might learn to use some sign language if this is a communication system used by the student with autism. A teacher in this situation might even consider giving all students a spelling test using the sign language alphabet.

In teaching all students to use alternative modes of communication, teachers encourage expression and introduce learners to a wide range of choices they can make when communicating, creating, composing, and expressing. I worked with one young man without a disability who came alive as a poet when he started using another student's voice output augmentative communication device. And in a third-grade classroom, all students have started using AlphaSmart keyboarding devices because teachers found they helped everyone—those with and without autism—write more fluently (see Figure 7.2).

Create Communication Opportunities

Students with and without disabilities should have time to interact, share, and communicate with the teacher and peers throughout the day. In some classrooms, a handful of students dominate small-group conversations and whole-class discussions. Although it is important for these verbal and outgoing students to have a voice in the classroom, it is equally important for other students—including shy and quiet students, students using English as a second language, and students with disabilities—to have opportunities to share and challenge ideas, ask and answer questions, and exchange thoughts. To ensure that all students have opportunities to communicate, teachers need to put structures and activities in place that allow for interaction.

In one classroom, the teacher started every morning with a "whip" (Harmon, 1994). She pointed to each student in the class and asked him or her to give a three- to five-word phrase related to her prompt of the day. One morning, for instance, she asked students to report on something they learned on the previous day's fieldtrip to an art museum. Responses ranged from "Picasso was a sculptor" to "Dancing is art."

Another way to inspire communication is to ask students to "turn and talk" to each other at various points in the day. A high school history teacher used this strategy throughout the year to break up lectures and to give students time to teach the material to each other. After talking for about 15 minutes, he asked students to turn to a partner and answer a specific question or explain a concept he had taught. For instance, after giving a short lecture on the presidency, he asked students to discuss, "What qualities do Americans seem to want in a president?"

Teachers also can provide opportunities for communication by asking questions that require a physical response. For example, instead of asking, "Who can tell me what H2O is?" the teacher might say, "Stand up if you think you know the common name for H2O." This strategy not only gives all learners a chance to give an answer but also allows for some teacher-sanctioned movement, something often welcomed by students with autism and by any active learner in the inclusive classroom.

Another way to encourage communication is to prepare the student with autism for his or her participation. The teacher might give the student a question or prompt before the class starts so that he or she can formulate a cogent response and respond with confidence. Although preparing the student in this way is often helpful for any student with autism, it can be especially useful for individuals who use AAC and who will need to write or type it out or get it programmed by a teacher or therapist. See Figure 7.3 for a checklist that provides even more ideas for providing communication opportunities into the school day.

On Being a Supportive Communication Partner

Open any textbook on autism or disability and you will find several pages and perhaps several chapters dedicated to improving the communication skills or capacities of students with autism. Less common, however, are pages and chapters dedicated to the necessary skills, attitudes, beliefs, and abilities of the communication partner. This paradigm or view of seeing "communication improvement" as a task for only one person in the communicative act is puzzling because communicating is social. Therefore, both partners may need to make accommodations, at times. For instance, any teacher can become a better partner by respecting gaze avoidance, considering voice volume and tone, listening to AAC users, experimenting with indirect communication, and helping students understand language.

Respect Gaze Avoidance

When teachers want a learner's attention, many expect eye contact. Those who have taught students with autism, however, understand that eye contact can be irritating or even painful for these individuals. Wendy Lawson, who has Asperger syndrome, has claimed that for her, making eye contact with a speaker can result in a breakdown in communication:

How much easier it is to hear someone if you can't see his or her face. Then words are pure and not distorted by grimaces and gestures. I can listen better to the tone of someone's voice when I am not confused by the unwritten words of their facial expressions. (1998, p. 97)

Communication Opportunities
Across the School Day

In order for a student's individual communication goals to be adequately addressed, teachers may need to increase the communication opportunities given in the inclusive classroom.

Instructions: Review the options in the left-hand column and decide which ones will work in your classroom. Then decide how often you can commit to using each technique and provide any notes regarding adaptations you may need to make, how specifically you will use it, or into which lessons or units you might integrate it.

Subject area: _____

Techniques:	How often?	Notes:
News and Goods: Every student shares one new or good thing that has happened recently.	Daily ____ Weekly ____ Biweekly ____ Monthly ____ Occasionally ____ n/a ____	
Highs and Lows: Every student shares a high and a low of their day/summer/vacation break.	Daily ____ Weekly ____ Biweekly ____ Monthly ____ Occasionally ____ n/a ____	
_____ (e.g., vocabulary word, fun fact, joke) of the day: A different student each day shares one.	Daily ____ Weekly ____ Biweekly ____ Monthly ____ Occasionally ____ n/a ____	
Turn & Talk: Students turn to one another and share a comment or question.	Daily ____ Weekly ____ Biweekly ____ Monthly ____ Occasionally ____ n/a ____	
15+2: Teacher lectures or holds a discussion for 15 minutes, then lets all students talk with a partner for 2 minutes. This repeats a second or third time until the lesson is completed.	Daily ____ Weekly ____ Biweekly ____ Monthly ____ Occasionally ____ n/a ____	
Notes Share and Compare (Udvari-Solner & Kluth, 2007): Students take notes for a certain amount of time before turning to a partner or partners to compare and explain them.	Daily ____ Weekly ____ Biweekly ____ Monthly ____ Occasionally ____ n/a ____	
Whip (Harmin, 1994): Ask each student in the class, one by one, to answer a question or offer a comment (using no more than 5–7 words each).	Daily ____ Weekly ____ Biweekly ____ Monthly ____ Occasionally ____ n/a ____	
Physical whole-class responses: Have all students answer a prompt at once by responding physically in some way (e.g., stand if you agree, sit if you disagree; hold up one finger if you know one way to solve the problem, two fingers if you know two ways . . .)	Daily ____ Weekly ____ Biweekly ____ Monthly ____ Occasionally ____ n/a ____	

Figure 7.3. Checklist of Communication Opportunities Across the School Day.

"You're Going to Love This Kid!" Teaching Students with Autism in the Inclusive Classroom, Second Edition, by Paula Kluth
Copyright © 2010 by Paul H. Brookes Publishing Co. All rights reserved.

Similarly, John Elder Robison claims that if he makes eye contact with a communication partner, he risks losing focus on the conversation:

> To this day, when I speak, I find visual input to be distracting . . . I usually look somewhere neutral—at the ground or off into the distance—when I'm talking to someone. Because speaking while watching things has always been difficult for me, learning to drive a car and talk at the same time was a tough one, but I mastered it. (2007, p. 3)

Luke Jackson claims eye contact is more than ineffective. For him, it is physically uncomfortable:

> [When I look someone straight in the eye] I feel as if their eyes are burning me and I really feel as if I am looking into the face of an alien. I know this sounds rude but I am telling it how it is. If I get past that stage and don't look away, when whilst someone is talking I find myself staring really hard and looking at their features and completely forgetting to listen to what they are saying. (2002, p. 71)

And Jerry Newport explains that, for him, it is downright scary:

> Gazing into someone's eyes—even for a brief instant—was like standing on the ledge of a skyscraper and peering down into the emptiness below. It petrified me, thinking that I was going to tumble into the abyss. (Newport, Newport, & Dodd, 2007, p. 10)

From these accounts, it is clear that individuals on the spectrum are not just seeking their own comfort when they engage in gaze avoidance, they are likely doing their best to communicate efficiently and effectively. Stephen Shore, a university professor and individual on the spectrum, explains that eye contact, for many on the spectrum, disrupts quality communication:

> With most people, the nonverbal communication supplements or enhances the verbal communication. The two channels are processed together to give a deeper meaning to the communication. With people having autism and Asperger syndrome, however, the nonverbal component can be so difficult to decode that it interferes with getting meaning from the verbal channel. As a result, very little, if any communication occurs. (2003, p. 143)

Building on the words of these individuals, teachers would do well to proceed with caution in the area of eye contact. One way to learn what your student can tolerate is to ask him or her. If that isn't possible, you may need to gently assess how a student communicates best. This doesn't mean that eye contact cannot be addressed. Some students may not be bothered by making eye contact and may profit from learning how and when to use it. Others may appreciate learning tricks that will help them connect with people without feeling uneasy (e.g., making "forehead contact" or "nose bridge contact"). Few, if any, will likely respond well to commands (e.g., "look at me") that ignore inherent needs and fail to take individual differences into account.

Consider Voice Volume and Tone

Any teacher can attest to the powers of the voice. When I taught high school students, I often found that the best way to get the attention of a noisy room of teenagers was to whisper. Using this tone of voice seemed to unarm them in a way. When I taught kindergarten, I often gave directions in a sing-song voice. This, too, caught students off guard and appeared to capture their interest.

Playing with voice volume, quality, and tone can be a tool in connecting with any student, including those with autism. Gunilla Gerland, a woman with autism, indicates that whispers are extremely helpful as a communication tool:

> But whispers came rushing at me from a long way off, always straight into my head, easily passing through all the passages in my ears, sliding directly up into my mind and rousing it. I didn't have to be on guard for whispers. I didn't have to wait to let them in. Whispers had their own key. So if people whispered when I was cutting out my little bits of paper, I looked up. Then I heard them. (1996, pp. 31–32)

Gail Gillingham, who shares the "whispering strategy" with people in her workshops on autism, has received reports of success from attendees:

> A father tells his son "it's time to put on his pajamas" in a soft voice and the son turns off the television and heads to his room. A mother tells her child that he has to stay close beside her, as the store is so busy today, and the child sticks by her side. A mother tells her child that "the bus is coming" and he turns off his video game, puts it away and goes to find his backpack, things she did for him in the past. (2000, p. 118)

"Listen" to Augmentative and Alternative Communication System Users

The communication act requires visual and auditory attention when an AAC system is being used; therefore, the AAC user may have a difficult time interrupting, interjecting, or even initiating a conversation if the communication partner is not aware of this demand. For example, an AAC user may begin a conversation by pointing to a picture. Such an initiation will be missed if the communication partner does not attend visually to the AAC user and look for signs that he or she wants to join the conversation.

Jorgensen, McSheehan, and Sonnenmeier (2009) illustrated this need in a vignette about Jay, a fifth grader with autism. As the researchers reported, Jay's teacher led a discussion in which students shared events that happened in the book, *Maniac Magee* (e.g., "Maniac ran away"). After the students had offered several answers the teacher asked them to find just two more to finish the activity. As Jay's paraprofessional tried in vain to direct him to the events other students were sharing, Jay kept turning his adapted book back to a previous page of the story; once on the page he would tap on a particular passage. The paraprofessional, recognizing this as communication, raised her hand, and shared that Jay was pointing to a passage about Maniac living in a zoo. The teacher replied, "Good one, Jay," causing Jay to clap his hands and grin.

In addition to being open to the initiation of communication, partners should also be aware of and open to changes in the pace of conversation. Communication partners may cut AAC users off mid-sentence assuming they know what will be typed, pointed to, signed, or indicated next or they may grow impatient with the AAC users' attempts to communicate and prematurely end a conversation. These and other types of communication clashes are often reported by people using AAC (Bauby, 1997; Crossley, 1997; Robillard, 1997; Tavalaro & Tayson, 1997). Mayer Shevin, a disability activist and advocate, encountered such a challenge firsthand when he was hospitalized for a surgery related to his oral cancer. Shevin had to breathe through a tracheostomy and deal with a "seeming ocean of mucus in his mouth." The situation was made more challenging by the fact that he had to communicate by writing notes.

> I relied for my survival on the wall-mounted suction machine. . . . The hose and mouthpiece often clogged; I would clear them by dipping the mouthpiece in a glass of water. When

that didn't work, and the hose or mouthpiece needed to be replaced, I had only a few minutes "breathing space" before I would begin choking.

One afternoon, the hose and mouthpiece both clogged, and I waited an endless-seeming 15 minutes until the nurse responded to my buzzer. When she asked me why I had buzzed, I started to write, "My suction is clogged—the tube and mouthpiece need to be replaced." I wrote MY SUCTION IS . . . and the nurse started out the door, saying, "Oh, I see—you need a new mouthpiece—I'll get it for you." I knew that merely replacing the mouthpiece wouldn't work, and I was already gasping for air. I flung my notebook at her, and hit her in the back of the head. Startled and angry, she came back to yell at me; I kept pounding my pencil on the tabletop and gestured, until grudgingly she returned my notebook to me. I scrawled my panic-stricken message in its entirety, making sure she did not leave until I was done. "Oh," she snorted, and with ill-grace returned a few minutes later with my precious suction hose. I'm sure she went home that night to tell someone about the rude patient who had attacked her. (1999, p. 1)

Although Shevin's story holds lessons about the need to humanize the medical profession, it is also a powerful story about communication. When Shevin's nurse turned away from him, she did more than engage in poor nursing practices; she took his voice.

As this story illustrates, people using augmentative communication often have to struggle to be understood. Consider some of the problems of typed communication, for instance. Typed words do not always reflect tone, inflection, and emotion. It can be difficult to detect sarcasm, anger, joy, or surprise in the written word. Furthermore, body language may be of little help in interpreting messages when the physical movements of the participants are unpredictable or unintentional—as they often are in the case of individuals with autism. A careful communication partner is observant—allowing for the full and undisturbed expression of the AAC user. Attempts should always be made to minimize the dominance of the communication partner and maximize the involvement of the AAC user. Whereas some AAC users have equipment with voice output, an ability to store messages, and a digital screen, others work from simpler systems like paper communication boards. For this reason, some AAC users—especially those with simple systems—will need some feedback from their communication partner. For instance, a student using typed communication may need a communication partner to ask clarifying questions if he or she has a lot of misspellings or types only in sentence fragments.

Jean-Dominique Bauby (1997), in his book *The Diving Bell and the Butterfly*, shared just how challenging it can be to maintain the integrity of one's messages when augmentative and alternative methods are used to communicate. Bauby experienced a massive stroke and had to invent an AAC system. He shared a comical side of communicating in this unique way and explained how very dynamic the process is:

You read off the alphabet . . . until, with a blink of my eye, I stop you at the letter to be noted. The maneuver is repeated for the letters that follow, so that fairly soon you have a whole word, and then fragments of more or less intelligible sentences. That, at least, is the theory. In all reality, all does not go well for some visitors. Because of nervousness, impatience, or obtuseness, performances vary in the handling of the code (which is what we call this method of transcribing my thoughts). Crossword fans and Scrabble players have a head start. Girls manage better than boys. By dint of practice, some of them know the code by heart and no longer even turn to our special notebook—the one containing the order of the letters and which all my words are set down like the Delphic oracle's.

Indeed, I wonder what conclusions anthropologists of the year 3000 will reach if they ever chance to leaf through these notebooks, where haphazardly scribbled remarks such as "The physical therapist is pregnant," "Mainly on the legs," "Arthur Rimbaud," and "The French team played like pigs" are interspersed with unintelligible gibberish, misspelled words, lost letters, omitted syllables. (p. 21)

To minimize "gibberish, misspelled words, lost letters, omitted syllables" and the potential for miscommunication, the teacher should always work closely with the AAC user to decipher and confirm their communication when any augmentative and alternative methods are used.

Experiment with Indirect Communication

One night, as Echo Fling was tucking her son, Jimmy, in bed, she picked up a puppet and used it to ask him a question. Jimmy, who was not typically talkative, proceeded to participate in a long conversation with his mother. Fling described the experience as "shocking":

> What's your name?' I asked in a squeaky cartoon-type voice, and got the expected response. Jimmy had just recently requested that everyone call him 'Jim,' instead of Jimmy and began to lecture the puppet on his newfound preference. I asked the usual static questions about his family, and what he liked to do. Jimmy and I had a nice back-and-forth discussion about all the characters in the Ghostbusters movie. I was pleased with how well he was maintaining the conversation. I decided to push further to see what more I could learn.
>
> "Who are some of the kids in your class?" To my amazement, Jimmy began to rattle off some of the boys' names. Why would he be able to talk to the puppet and not me? (2000, p. 89)

Fling went on to share that the talks continued for weeks. The two conversed about everything from Jimmy's fears to school issues; eventually, Jimmy was able to have these conversations without the aid of the puppet.

Many individuals with autism feel uncomfortable engaging in direct conversations or direct interactions. Donna Williams, a woman with autism, shared that she prefers to interact and socialize in ways that are more indirect or detached:

> The best way I could have been given things would have been for them to be placed near me with no expectation of thanks and no waiting for a response. To expect a thank-you or a response was to alienate me from the item that prompted the response.
>
> The best way for me to have been able to listen to someone was for them to speak to themselves about me out loud or about someone like me, which would have inspired me to show I could relate to what was being said. In doing so, indirect contact, such as looking out of a window while talking, would have been best. (1992, p. 216)

In her compelling narrative, *The Boy Who Would Be a Helicopter*, Vivian Paley (1990) shared how she witnessed the power of using indirect communication with one of her students. Jason, a child enamored with helicopters, seldom talked to peers, and appeared to ignore typical types of play.

At one point in Paley's account, Jason was disrupting other children and the classroom community by running on to the stage that students used to perform plays. At first, Paley sat back, interested in why Jason seemed to need to "crash" the stage so often. After he repeated this behavior several times, Paley decided to problem-solve the situation with a few students:

> "Jason, sometimes you still run into the stage even if it's not your turn."
> "My blades are spinning."
> "But it seems as if your blades spin more in the story room than in the blocks."
> "Because he makes a airport there to land," Samantha [another student] points out.
> "Could that be the reason?" I wonder.
> "Yeah, it really is the reason," Joseph states with assurance.

"Aren't you sad because you don't have a airport in here to land? To stay landed?"

Jason is surprised by the question, but Joseph interprets his silence as agreement. "See, I told you. He's sad because there's no airport. His helicopter needs one." (1990, pp. 57–58)

The students went on to decide that Jason should build a small heliport near the stage so he could have a place to park that was not in the middle of the stage. The whole group managed to find a solution to a tricky problem without blaming or isolating anyone and, as important, they were able to communicate about something serious without involving Jason in a direct (and potentially stressful) interaction. The entire conversation that takes place is about finding a space for a helicopter, not about the behavior of a little boy.

Teachers can learn a lot from Paley and her students. Donna Williams (1998) suggested that teachers use costumes, foreign accents, rhymes, and puppets to cultivate interactions that "encourage expression in a way that allows some degree of personal distance." Williams suggested that these props and activities help students "develop self-awareness in a self-controlled and self-regulated way" (p. 306). Indeed, Junee Waites, a mother of a man with autism, shared in her book, *Smiling at Shadows*, that she couldn't get her son to engage in household routines until she sang to him:

I sang "We're sweeping the floor, sweeping the floor! We're making the bed, making the bed! Would you like . . . dah de dah . . . a drink of milk . . . la la la . . . ?"

[The] scheme worked. I sang merrily and Dane began to point to what he wanted—and he would look to me. (Waites & Swinbourne, 2002, p. 41)

If a student seems unable to answer direct questions, the teacher might take a cue from Waites and sing the question. Stephen Shore, a man on the spectrum and a music teacher, often uses singing to connect with his students: "All of my communications with one particular child with Asperger's are sung. If I mistakenly lapse into a typical conversational tone, he loses focus, engages in self-stimulatory activities, and drifts away" (2003, p. 69).

All of these ideas for making communication less direct can be used in K–12 classrooms. See Table 7.6 for even more ideas.

Help Students Understand and Decipher Language

Some people have trouble understanding certain aspects of speech. A student may not respond to his own name or may produce a fork when asked to get a spoon. In most cases, students who behave in these ways are not demonstrating hearing problems, they are experiencing processing difficulties. That is, they are having a hard time making sense of certain sounds, words, or sentences they hear. Because of these problems, the learner may seem inattentive, stubborn, or "noncompliant" at times.

Students with autism also have difficulty understanding some types of language. For instance, some students interpret language quite literally. I learned just how literal some students are when I took one of my students swimming. As Tom entered the pool area, he began walking straight for the deep end. I shouted at him to turn around, thinking that he would know to turn his back to the water in order to climb down the small hook ladder attached to the pool wall. I was puzzled at first but quickly understood my error when Tom began twirling in circles. He was "turning around" just as I had asked. Gunilla Gerland seems to be able to relate to Tom. She claims that she often gives literal answers to questions:

My attitude to questions was quite concrete. "Can you . . . ?" I answered with a "Yes" which meant, "Yes, I can . . . " But that it should also mean "I will" or "I shall . . . " was a totally alien concept to me. If I said "I can," then I meant just that and nothing else. So the

Table 7.6. Ideas for making communication less direct
Use props related to conversation such as toy microphones or megaphones.
Use costumes or pieces of costumes (e.g., storytelling cape).
Have the student "be" their favorite character or person and answer as him or her.
Incorporate gestures and signs (e.g., bump fists instead of saying, "What's up?").
Speak in/teach another language (e.g., allow student to apologize in Spanish or in sign language).
Bring in toys or puppets and have the toy give the information or ask the questions.
Have an exchange on paper, use text messaging, or email back and forth (even if you are in the same room as the student).
Speak on the phone (even if you are in the same room as the student).
Speak to the student while they are doing something else such as bouncing a ball or organizing materials.

effect of my "Yes" to the question "Can you tidy your room?" was not the required one. I didn't at all understand why they were so cross at me. (1996, p. 85)

Stephen Shore reported that slang can also be confusing:

During the third grade I remember a classmate telling me that he felt like a pizza. I couldn't figure out what made him feel that way. Besides he certainly didn't look like a pizza. Eventually I realized he meant that he felt like eating a pizza. (2003, p. 57)

Students with autism may need help interpreting figurative language such as idioms (e.g., "sitting on the fence," "hold your horses"), jokes or riddles, metaphors (e.g., "he was on fire"), phrases or slang expressions with double meaning, and sarcasm (e.g., saying "good work" to someone who has just spilled a glass of milk). Teachers might offer support in the following ways:

- Double-check with all students to make sure directions or questions are understood.

- Provide opportunities for students to learn about language (e.g., present a "metaphor of the week").

- Use visuals to help students remember the meanings of figurative language (e.g., draw a picture of an angry person literally "flying off" of a handle).

- Teach the student the origins of certain metaphors so he or she will be more likely to remember them (e.g., "the ball is in your court" refers to a tennis game; when the ball is in one's court, it is that person's turn to take action).

- Create a memory or Go Fish game featuring idioms (Notbohm & Zysk, 2004). Create two sets of cards with one set featuring idioms (e.g., "on cloud nine") and one set featuring the meanings of idioms (e.g., extremely happy). Many students—not just those on the spectrum—will profit from and enjoy these games.

- Encourage the student to keep a personal dictionary or encyclopedia of puzzling language. Every time the individual is confused by a word or the use of a phrase, explain it and have him add it to his dictionary.

 Summary

Communication affects everything else. Therefore, helping a student with communication can also serve to make other aspects of schooling easier. For instance, the more complex a student's communication becomes, the more meaningful the curricular adaptations will be and the less likely the student will be to share needs and wants through challenging behavior. Perhaps the most important reason for supporting a student's communication, however, is to help him or her direct his or her own schooling and life. I close by sharing the words of Richard Attfield, a man with autism and an AAC user, who stressed in this letter to a colleague just how important this kind of liberation is:

> I am now finally able to communicate and express my opinion. Recognize for myself communication with other people will also allow me to control my life. Decide for myself what the future will be. Give me a right to be heard. (1993, p. 11)

FOR MORE ANSWERS AND INFORMATION

Books

Downing, J. (2005). *Teaching communication skills to students with severe disabilities* (2nd ed.). Baltimore: Paul H. Brookes Publishing Co.

Flodin, M. (2004). *Signing illustrated: The complete learning guide* (Rev. ed.). New York: Perigee Trade.

Gray, C. (1994). *Comic strip conversations.* Arlington, TX: Future Horizons Inc.

Hundal, P., & Lukey, P. (2003). *"Now you know me think more": A journey with autism using facilitated communication techniques.* Philadelphia: Jessica Kingsley.

Mirenda, P., & Iacono, T. (2009). *Autism spectrum disorders and AAC.* Baltimore: Paul H. Brookes Publishing Co.

Mukhopadhyay, T. (2008). *How can I talk if my lips don't move: Inside my autistic mind.* New York: Arcade Publishing.

Welton, J. (2004). *What did you say? What do you mean?: An illustrated guide to understanding metaphors.* Philadelphia: Jessica Kingsley.

Web Sites

ASLPro.com
http://www.aslpro.com
ASLPro.com is a free resource for teachers. Four video dictionaries allow users to see and practice using thousands of words.

Closing the Gap: Changing Lives with Assistive Technology
http://www.closingthegap.com
Closing the Gap strives to provide parents and educators with the information and training necessary to locate, compare, and implement assistive technology. Through their annual conference, magazine, and web site, they provide some of the best information and training available on AAC.

Core Communication Partners
http://www.darlenehanson.com
This is a good web site with a great newsletter. Topics range from respecting your communication partner to learning about new technology.

(continued)

(continued)

The Facilitated Communication Institute
http://soeweb.syr.edu/thefci

This group conducts research, public education, training and scholarly seminars. The site contains dozens of short articles written by people with autism.

Simplified Technology
http://www.lburkhart.com

There are so many great make-it-yourself ideas on this web site. The site's creator provides clear directions on how to make your own talking switch, for instance.

NOTES: _____

_____

_____

_____

_____

_____

_____

_____

_____

_____

_____

_____

_____

_____

_____

_____

_____

_____

_____

Teaching Literacy
to Students with Autism

with Kelly Chandler-Olcott

> Books are my doorways into other worlds.
> (Jackson, 2002, p. 118)

In his memoir, Luke Jackson, a young man with Asperger syndrome, wrote, "[Books] cheer me when I am upset; they make me laugh, cry, and quake with fright. A good book should keep someone entranced right till the end" (2002, p. 118). By his own admission, however, Luke wasn't always so entranced with reading. During his first few years of school, he struggled mightily with this area of the curriculum. Then, when he was 8 ½ years old, he began to read as if "someone had switched a light on" in his head:

> I had an assessment by an educational psychologist when I was seven years and eight months old and my reading age was not assessable because I just couldn't read anything. The next day Mum got a phone call from the school asking her to come in and see them. She told me that she was very worried as that usually meant that I was having a massive tantrum, but when she got there the teacher had something that they just couldn't wait to tell. I had picked up a copy of *A Midsummer Night's Dream*, which the teacher was using to show how plays are written. It seems that I opened the book and began to read it fluently. How weird is that? (2002, p. 117)

Jackson has been an avid reader ever since, and his age-equivalent reading score, determined to be "not assessable" before this incident, was found to be 14 years and 10 months shortly afterward.

The same themes from Luke's story show up in accounts and observations of other learners with autism, including difficulties with phonics-based instruction, poor performance on standardized reading tests, and an unusual spike of progress not clearly at-

This chapter is condensed from Kluth, P., & Chandler-Olcott, K. (2008). *"A land we can share": Teaching literacy to students with autism.* Baltimore: Paul H. Brookes Publishing Co.; adapted by permission.

tributable to specific teaching methods. We share more about each of these ideas later in the chapter. It's important to remember as you move through this chapter, though, that individuals with autism differ widely in their skills, experience, and interest in reading. In contrast to Luke Jackson, some flourish with intensive phonics instruction. Some can decode text well orally but struggle with comprehension and engagement. Others' communication differences make it difficult for their teachers to know if they can read at all, and if so, how well. Because of this diversity, it is necessary to assess readers with autism carefully, using multiple sources of data over time, and to develop sensitive instructional plans tailored to their needs.

In this chapter, we hope to help our readers experience the type of light bulb moment that Jackson and his teacher did. To this end, we provide several ideas to help teachers craft appropriate lessons and to support the reading and writing skills and competencies of their students with autism. We begin the chapter by sharing the two perspectives we use to frame our work. Following that, we have included several strategies to use in the teaching of both reading and writing. Although some of these are more appropriate for young children, most of our suggestions will work across grade levels and age ranges with few adaptations.

Defining Literacy

Our definitions of literacy are grounded in two different theoretical perspectives. These include a disability studies–informed perspective on participation by people with disabilities in educational contexts known as *presumed competence* (Biklen, 1990, 2005; Biklen & Burke, 2006; Kliewer, Biklen, & Kasa-Hendrickson, 2006) and a sociocultural theory of literacy called *multiple literacies* (Alvermann, Hinchman, Phelps, Moore, & Waff, 1998; Gallego & Hollingsworth, 2000; O'Brien, 2001; Paul, 2006; Purcell-Gates, 2002). In the sections that follow, we lay out the key tenets of both of these perspectives.

Presuming Competence

In his decades-long work on inclusion, communication, self-determination, academic access, and literacy (Biklen, 1990, 2005; Kliewer & Biklen, 2001; Kliewer, Biklen, & Kasa-Hendrickson, 2006; Kluth, Straut, & Biklen, 2003), Doug Biklen has explored the concept of competence and the possibilities available to students when teachers and others working with learners reject deficit models of disability and, instead, look for student abilities. Biklen describes his philosophy in this way:

> In its simplest articulation, presuming competence means that the outsider regards the person labeled autistic as a thinking, feeling person. This is precisely the stance that every educator must take—failing to adopt this posture, the teacher would forever doubt whether to educate at all, and would likely be quick to give up the effort. Aside from the optimism it implies, another benefit of the presuming competence framework over a deficit orientation . . . is that when a student does not reveal the competence that a teacher expects, the teacher is required to turn inward and ask, "What other approach can I try?" (2005, p. 73)

Such a question, Biklen points out, "refuses to limit opportunity" and casts the person who asks it "in the role of finding ways to support the person to demonstrate his or her agency" (Biklen & Burke, 2006, p. 167). In his emphasis on agency and voice for the person with an autism label, Biklen and his collaborators remind us that the obligation of the individual who presumes competence "is not to project an ableist interpretation of something another person does but rather to presume there must be a rationale or sympathetic explanation for what someone does and then to try to discover it, always from the other person's perspective" (Biklen & Burke, 2006, p. 168).

One mother Paula knows shared a story of how her son was seen as illiterate even after she videotaped him identifying words on flashcards and interacting with books in his bedroom. Because he was largely nonverbal, had unusual ways of moving and behaving, and scored in the mental retardation range on a standardized test, educators told her he was unable to profit from literacy instruction (and documented this on his individualized education program). Those subscribing to a model of presuming competence resist both the ideology and the practices—exclusion and denial of educational opportunity—employed by these educators. Instead, as Biklen and Burke explain:

> Educators must assume students can and will change and, that through engagement with the world, will demonstrate complexities of thought and action that could not necessarily be anticipated. Within this frame, difficulties with performance are not presumed to be evidence of intellectual incapacity. (2006, p. 168)

Multiple Literacies

Literacy traditionally has been constructed as the ability to read and (more recently) to write print text (Graff, 2001). Narrow conceptualizations of these abilities, however, position those who struggle with conventional literacy tasks—despite any skill they may show with media texts or oral language—as illiterate, at risk, incompetent, or even lacking in intellect (O'Brien, 2001). Such models continue to be manifested in the standardized tools used to assess student ability and progress and in certain classroom practices such as ability grouping.

The theory known as *multiple literacies* asks educators to value a wide range of literacy skills and abilities that students may bring to the classroom and to acknowledge that individuals can demonstrate these skills and abilities in ways that might not be measurable or even easily observable. In this model, teachers understand literacy as a broad and complex set of behaviors. Consider this definition from Edwards, Heron, and Francis:

> An ideological model of literacy expands the definition of literacy from the ability to read and write to the practice of construing meaning using all available signs within a culture, including visual, auditory, and sensory signs. . . . To become literate, then, students must develop a critical awareness of multiple texts and contexts. . . . This involves an ability to understand how social and cultural ways of being and understanding affect how meaning is construed and conveyed. (2000, p. 1)

According to these authors, students demonstrate literacy when they act out a scene from a favorite movie, page through a book, have a conversation, listen to the teacher read a poem, illustrate an idea, tell a joke, or show a peer how to use their communication board or sign system. Students who are fantastic storytellers, who improvise their own rap songs, who can navigate a new online environment with ease, who communicate needs without words, and who understand the unwritten codes and policies of institutions are all demonstrating important literacies.

One example of honoring unique kinds of literate competencies comes from Paula's first year of teaching. One of the students in her school, Jay, was fascinated with Eric Carle's picture book *The Very Hungry Caterpillar* (1969). Every day, Jay, who did not speak, came into his classroom, grabbed the book from the classroom library, threw it on the floor, rotated it 360 degrees, flipped through the pages (often when the book was turned upside down), licked or pressed his cheek to the cover, and stared silently at each illustration. Although some of Jay's teachers found these behaviors bizarre and problematic, Jay's general education classroom teacher, Ms. Knight, saw Jay's actions as purposeful, complex, and literacy related. She therefore made efforts to enhance his skills and knowledge by asking the school librarian to bring other books by Eric Carle into the classroom and slowly introduced Jay to new pictures, plots, vocabulary, and characters. She then asked Jay's mother to identify literacy-related behaviors she saw at home. When Jay's mother told Ms. Knight that her son often sat in his red beanbag chair when he wanted a story, Ms. Knight bought a red beanbag chair for the classroom and shared this "story signal" with other teachers and students so that they could respond when Jay wanted to read. Ms. Knight also introduced Jay to the felt board and told him the caterpillar story using this tool. Jay was a kinesthetic and tactile learner, and he was instantly drawn to the board and began creating his own stories with the felt pieces.

Clearly, embracing multiple literacies means that embracing a notion such as reading readiness—the belief that "there is a set of cognitive, motivational, and intellectual skills that children must possess before they can benefit from instruction in reading" (Smith, 2002, p. 526)—must be rejected. Scribbles can then be seen as meaningful, stories can be "told" with gestures, and a computer-generated drawing can be viewed as no less important than a piece of writing. Students won't need to demonstrate certain kinds of literate competence before being invited to participate in curriculum and instruction in general education classrooms; learners won't be expected to develop, behave, and learn in the same ways; and individual differences in learning will be supported and appreciated.

One of the primary reasons we promote a multiple literacies framework is to address what we see as an overemphasis on functional literacy for students on the spectrum. Although we value practical uses of literacy and provide some suggestions in this book about how to foster them when appropriate, we feel that functional literacy has been grossly overemphasized for students with disabilities. Although this way of supporting learners dominated the literature in the 1980s and was viewed by most at that time as progressive, changes in technology, evolving understandings of disability, advancements in augmentative communication, and even insights from collaboration between general and special educators have resulted in a new set of best practices that ask educators to value academic curricula for students with disabilities and to consider the limitations of the functional curriculum as it has been implemented (Fisher & Frey, 2001; Jorgensen, 1998; Jorgensen et al.; Kluth, Straut, & Biklen, 2003; Pugach & Warger, 2001).

Next, we offer several ideas for teaching reading and writing to students with autism and Asperger syndrome. Although many can be used across lessons and contexts, all are best utilized in the inclusive classroom, with peers with and without disabilities, and in the context of standards-based lessons.

Expanding the Invitation: Reading

This section is organized around the key components of reading (phonemic awareness, phonics, and word recognition; fluency; comprehension; and vocabulary) that readers need to integrate in order to be successful. Each section that follows defines one of these components with reference to its research base, explains how each might be experienced by learners with autism, and recommends teaching practices designed to promote greater competence and confidence in that area for these students.

Phonemic Awareness, Phonics, and Word Recognition

Members of the National Reading Panel (NRP; National Institute of Child Health and Human Development [NICHD], 2000), devoted two sections of their final report to what they called *alphabetics,* a term used to cover two different aspects of literacy, phonemic awareness and phonics. The panel defined *phonemic awareness* as the ability to focus on and manipulate the smallest units of spoken language—for instance, the ability to recognize that the word *chat* is made up of three phonemes (/ch/, /a/, and /t/) that can be isolated from each other, blended together, or replaced to make new words (e.g., by changing the word's initial sound to make *chat* into *cat*). *Phonics* referred to knowledge of the correspondence between letters such as *c*, *h*, *a*, and *t* and the sounds they make, both on their own and in combination with each other (e.g., the letters *c* and *h* make a different sound when they appear together than they do when they appear with other letters). Phonics and phonemic awareness are not synonyms for each other—one refers to an oral competence and the other deals with skills applied to print—but they are related to each other; research suggests that children who develop good phonemic awareness often have an easier time cracking the code of print text than those children who do not (Blachman, 2000; NICHD, 2000).

Knowledge of phonics, in turn, is one of the resources that learners use for word recognition, defined by Fox as "the immediate, accurate, and effortless ability to read words in context or in isolation" (2003, p. 678). When readers encounter an unfamiliar word in print, they may sound it out letter by letter, the strategy most often associated with phonics instruction in school; use picture cues or logos to make informed guesses; or use structural analysis to identify "chunks" of the word that they know (e.g., suffixes such as *-tion* in the word *reaction* or parts of a compound word such as *ball* in *ballplayer*). However readers choose to attack a word, their goal should be efficiency, because quick and easy word recognition allows them to concentrate on other aspects of reading.

Considering Students with Autism

The NRP (NICHD, 2000) reviewed research suggesting that training in phonemic awareness helps children learn to read and spell better and that those who received systematic phonics instruction in the early grades comprehended what they read better than those who did not. Although there has been vigorous debate in the literacy community about the implications of these findings for organizing—or worse, mandating—particular kinds of instruction, few within the field question the NRP's basic claim that phonemic awareness and phonics play an important role in reading acquisition for most children. The evidence about the value of focused and explicit instruction in these areas is quite compelling, especially for learners who show early signs of reading problems, and we encourage all teachers with direct or indirect responsibility for literacy to be familiar with this body of research.

At the same time, we're mindful that the vast majority of the research cited by the NRP was conducted with "neurotypical" learners, not people with disabilities, and nowhere does this gap appear more important than in the areas of phonics and phonemic awareness. Considerable evidence from people with autism spectrum labels (Blackman, 1999; Jackson, 2002; Shore, 2003) and their teachers (Broun, 2004; Mirenda, 2003) suggested that these learners can have difficulties isolating sounds in verbal speech and associating those sounds with symbols. For example, Lucy Blackman reported in her memoir that she liked her phonics lessons because of the candy she received as a reward for successful responses (!) but that the learning didn't stick with her for long: "Somehow my speech memory could not contain the decoding messages for more than six or eight written words. If I learned more, some of the ones I had learnt previously went into limbo" (1999, p. 52). Pat Mirenda, a scholar in special education, shares something similar about problems learners with autism often have with phonics, though she frames her ideas with language that is more technical than Blackman's. Specifically, she critiques a "readiness" model on literacy—one requiring students to demonstrate certain "gatekeeper" skills before being introduced to others—that she argues continues to be employed in special education:

[T]he decontextualized nature of traditional phonics instruction makes it almost impossible for many [students with autism] to demonstrate mastery of the subskills in this area. Students without functional speech who require augmentative and alternative communication (AAC) are at especially high risk for failure in readiness-based literacy programs because of the supposition that reading is impossible in the absence of the ability to sound out words phonetically. For them, the readiness approach to literacy instruction "only serves to highlight [their] disabilities and emphasize differences in each student's performance from that of the mainstream population" (Ryndak, Morrison, & Sommerstein, 1999, p. 5). Those who prove themselves unable to master the "necessary" prerequisite skills are thus considered ineligible for further literacy instruction. (2003, p. 272)

In highlighting the potential issues with alphabetics-focused instruction that Blackman and Mirenda raise, we do not mean to suggest that all learners with autism will fail to benefit from thoughtfully planned instruction in phonics and phonemic awareness. This is simply not true. A good example of success in this area comes from Temple Grandin, who reported that her mother taught her to read with 30-minute daily lessons over several months:

I was still a poor reader at age eight, when my mother tried a new approach. Every afternoon after school, I sat with her in the kitchen and she had me sound out the words in a book. After I learned the phonetic rules and the sounds, she read a paragraph out loud to me. Then I sounded out one or two words. Gradually, she had me read longer and longer passages. We read from a real book that was interesting instead of a little kid's beginning book. I learned well with phonics, because I understood spoken language. It took me a long time to learn to read silently, though. (1995, p. 98)

From our perspective, several aspects of the approach used by Grandin's mother are worth highlighting. As Temple specifically notes, the two worked from age-appropriate texts, not from "a little kid's beginning book." This detail is crucial as it illustrates the importance of respecting students' life experiences (versus, for instance, their chronological age on a standardized test) and their need to learn in ways that are rich and motivating. Temple's mother also planned the instruction carefully and purposefully; their lessons took place for the same amount of time each day over a period of months, and she introduced Temple to the rules and sounds systematically, rather than haphazardly. Temple, who has shared information about her love of logic and order in other autobiographical writing, likely thrived on the structure provided both by the new content, which gave her some strategies to make sense of print, and by the lesson's predictable structure. Her mother apparently took care to embed the rule-governed phonics work in a broader context that included modeling and practice of fluent reading of meaningful, continuous texts. All of these factors likely contributed to the success of these interactions.

Like Mirenda (2003), we feel strongly that lack of demonstrated facility with phonemic awareness and phonics should not prevent students with autism from participating in instruction focused on fluency, comprehension, and vocabulary while they master or move beyond the smaller subprocesses of reading. Instead, attention to alphabetics and word recognition should be part of a balanced literacy program for these students, with their teachers keeping in mind that some of these approaches may work well for some students while having little or no impact on others. The section that follows includes our best recommendations for instructional approaches focused on these subprocesses of reading, given what we know about learners with autism.

Instructional Approaches

It is probably no surprise that it can be difficult for some learners with autism to develop and/or demonstrate phonemic awareness. Because many of these students neither produce nor hear speech in the same way that typical learners do, the oral activities meant to promote this competence often make little or no sense to them, especially at first. (This can be true of even those learners with autism whose speech is fairly reliable.) Consequently, the more phonemic awareness training can be incorporated into fun, relaxed classroom routines—preferably with peers without disabilities around to serve as literacy models and collaborative partners in instruction—the greater the chances that students with autism will experience success with such skills as recognizing and producing rhymes, hearing syllables, blending sounds together to create words, and segmenting words into their corresponding sounds.

Rhythm and Movement

Rhythm and Movement   Including some physical movement with sound work may be useful for all students, including those with autism. If you are working with young children, you might ask them to clap out the syllables in their own names and in the names of their classmates—first in unison as a class to model the process, and then perhaps with a partner to help reinforce the learning. Later, as they become more experienced at identifying syllables and coordinating their clapping, they can practice this skill on their own, using words that are less familiar than names. Similarly, we think that many students with autism will benefit from the multisensory approach of the Say-It-and-Move-It activity included in the *Road to the Code* program developed by Benita Blachman and her colleagues (Blachman, Ball, Black, & Tangel, 2000). This activity involves children in moving a disk or other high-interest object such as a tile or a block (or, in the case of Peter, a student who loves padlocks, a key) for each sound they hear in a word. Once all of the sounds have been isolated, the children blend them together to produce the whole word. Although the lessons were designed for students with functional speech, those who communicate in other ways can still participate by moving objects to indicate their understanding of the various sounds said by others or of sounds generated by augmentative communication devices or by observing as peers do so. Often, in these types of exercises, learners who cannot physically participate are excluded. But students who have fine motor problems can certainly observe, hold tokens, and hand tokens to peers as ways to participate in Say-It-and-Move-It.

Poems, chants, and songs are also recommended to help learners develop phonemic awareness (Adams, Foorman, Lundberg, & Beeler, 1997; Strickland & Schickendanz, 2004). These musical texts may be particularly good for helping students with autism learn, given that a number of authors on the spectrum—including those with significant communication impairments (Blackman, 1999; Shore, 2003)—reported that they can sing more easily than they can speak and that learning, in general, is easier when it is paired with music or a rhythm of some kind (Shore, 2003; Waites & Swinbourne, 2002). Musical texts are also meant to be performed multiple times, providing authentic repetition with the rhymes for students who need it, with less risk of boredom or embarrassment than would be associated with the rereading of conventional print texts.

Tactile Letter Recognition

Tactile Letter Recognition   Students' ability to use phonics—the relationships between letters and sounds—as a cueing system for reading depends, in no small part, on their ability to recognize those letters. To achieve this goal, teachers might allow students to feel letters cut from sandpaper or drawn with shaving cream or, depending on their fine motor skills, to form the letters themselves from clay or dough (of course, different substances will be appealing to different students, given the sensory differences described in Chapter 1). Alphabet stencils and stickers, especially those with pronounced textures, may also help some students attend to the differences in letters and words.

Alphabet Books

Alphabet Books   We also recommend providing students with a variety of alphabet books to browse—especially those tied to specialist subjects or fascinations such as trains, animals, or computers—because the combination of the letters and familiar objects they represent can aid with letter recognition as well as beginning phonics connections (see Table 8.1 for a list of alphabet books appropriate for both younger and older readers). If books don't exist

Table 8.1. Alphabet books for younger and older students

For Younger Students (Preschool–Grade 2)

Ehlert, L. (1989). *Eating the alphabet: Fruits and vegetables from A to Z*. Orlando, FL: Harcourt Brace & Company.

　Bright colors and bold lettering, trademarks of the work of this author and illustrator, are featured throughout this staple of the K–1 classroom.

Floca, B. (2003). *The racecar alphabet*. New York: Simon & Schuster.

　The alliterative, rhyming text features lively watercolor illustrations of a race that continues throughout the book. Many different models of cars are featured.

Hoena, B.A. (2005). *Farms ABC*. Mankato, MN: Capstone Press.

　The fun facts and large color photographs throughout make this a good choice to use in lessons about rural life, farming, or food.

Kellog, S. (1987). *Aster aardvark's alphabet adventures*. New York: Morrow Junior Books.

　Children are charmed by this alliterative text.

Kluth, P., & Kluth, V. (2009). *A is for "all aboard!"* Baltimore: Paul H. Brookes Publishing Co.

　The first alphabet book by Paula was co-written with her sister, Victoria, and was created originally for her friends on the autism spectrum.

Pallota, J. (2006). *The construction alphabet book*. Watertown, MA: Charlesbridge Publishing.

　Little ones will love this selection but, because of the realistic pictures, slightly older readers will, too.

Seuss, D. (1963). *Dr. Seuss's ABC*. New York: Random House.

　This classic combines rhythm, rhyme, classic illustrations, and plain old silliness to teach and reinforce the names of the letters, alphabetic order, and phonics.

For Older Students (All Ages)

Base, G. (1986). *Animalia*. New York: Harry N. Abrams.

　Base's fantasy world is complex, interesting, artistic, and for all ages.

Bryan, Ashley (1997). *Ashley Bryan's ABC of African American poetry*. New York: Simon & Schuster.

　Bryan's book captures the essence of 25 poems, making it ideal for a language arts poetry unit for students in any age group.

Chin-Lee, C. , Halsey, M., & Addy, S. (2005). *Amelia to Zora: Twenty-six women who changed the world*. Watertown, MA: Charlesbridge Publishing, Inc.

　A great introduction to notable women.

Mullins, P. (1993). *V is for vanishing: An alphabet of endangered animals*. New York: HarperCollins.

　This book would be a perfect compliment to a unit on ecology or animals.

Pallotta, J., Stillwell, F., & Bolster, R. (1999). *Airplane alphabet book*. Watertown, MA: Charlesbridge Publishing.

　Brightly colored pictures of mostly vintage airplanes will attract aviation enthusiasts as well as those who just love machines and transportation.

Schroeder, H. (2004). *The United States ABCs*. Minneapolis, MN: Picture Window Books.

　An alphabetical tour of the country that will be appreciated by geography and history buffs alike.

Smith, M., & Queener, C. (2006). *The alphabet and the automobile*. Phoenix, AZ: David Bull Publishing.

　A great choice for fans of racers, roadsters, sports cars, or sedans. Even adults with a passion for cars will find this beautifully illustrated text appealing.

From Kluth, P., & Chandler-Olcott, K. (2008). "*A land we can share*": *Teaching literacy to students with autism* (pp. 137–139). Baltimore: Paul H. Brookes Publishing Co.; adapted by permission.

on topics of interest, a teacher or parent can create them using words and images of significance to—perhaps even selected by—the learner. As with phonemic awareness, a combination of experiences requiring the use of more than one sense will help many students develop skills with letter identification.

Word and Letter Sorts   Word and letter sorts are another way to promote students' letter identification skills, as well as knowledge of letter–sound correspondences crucial to both reading and spelling. These activities involve students in creating categories, recognizing patterns, and making decisions about certain features of letters or words. Sorting may appeal to learners with autism for a variety of reasons. Some will like the active, physical work of creating piles or categories. Others will enjoy the cognitive challenge of creating groups with something in common. Gunilla Gerland, a woman with autism, reported that she often sorted letters as a child, not as an academic chore but as a chosen play activity:

> I often used to sit on the floor somewhere in our house arranging the alphabet cards I kept in a white plastic bucket. Father had made the cards for Kerstin, cutting them out of cardboard and drawing the letters on them. He was good at this kind of thing, and now I had taken them over from my sister. I used to lay out the cards in patterns or arrange them in various ways, perhaps putting all the Es in one pile and the As in another. I loved those alphabet cards. They were so clean and clear, on white cardboard with red edges. But it disturbed me that there weren't equal numbers of each kind. I thought there ought to be as many Xs as Ss, so that all the heaps became equally large. And just as many Ys as Es. I didn't know why the letters were in such unequal numbers. (1996, p. 47)

One of the best-known sorting activities is Pat and Jim Cunningham's (1992) *Making Words,* the phonics-focused component of their popular *Four Blocks* literacy program. During a *Making Words* session, students are given a number of cards with letters on them. They are then instructed to use the cards to create as many words of two letters, three letters, four letters, and so forth as they can, recording the words on the chalkboard if the activity is done as a whole class or on a sheet of paper if it is done individually or in small groups. The "challenge word" is one that can be created by using all of the designated letters (see Figure 8.1 for a sample set of words with the challenge word *hibernate*). Challenge words are selected on the basis of the opportunities for learning that they will offer particular groups or classes of students. Young or inexperienced readers are thus asked to work with shorter words (e.g., those with one or two vowels only) or words that yield more-familiar patterns and word families (e.g., *-an, -ell, -it*). More proficient readers might work with words yielding blends (e.g., *bl-, fr-, str-*) or vowel teams (e.g., *ay, ea, ou*) when rearranged. In either case, choosing content-area vocabulary such as *hibernate* can give students the chance to review previously learned material or to explore a word from a current area of study.

After students have created all of the possible words from their cards, either on their own or with guidance from the teacher, they are then instructed to sort those words into categories using criteria that focus them on particular features—for example, "words that begin with *b* and words that don't"; "words with a short *a* sound and words that don't have one"; or "words with one, two, and three syllables." This kind of sorting gives them valuable experience in thinking through how written language works and provides many practice opportunities for developing phonemic awareness and phonics skills.

Fluency

Fluency is the ability to read with speed, accuracy, and expression (NICHD, 2000). Although fluency can refer to either silent or oral reading, it tends to be associated with—and assessed most often in the context of—oral reading. Research suggests that fluency is related to comprehension, as readers who don't have to use so much cognitive energy figuring out how to pronounce individual words can devote more energy to monitoring the meaning of what they've read (Pinnell et al., 1995; Rasinski, 2003). It's important to note, however, that this relationship is a complex one: It's possible to read fluently without understanding what is read, as many students with and without autism have demonstrated, especially when reading their secondary textbooks. It's also possible, though less common, for learners to understand the meaning of a passage even if it is read in a halting fashion with many errors.

Challenge word: HIBERNATE
Vowels: *A, E, E, I*
Consonants: *B, H, N, T, R*

Two-letter words	Three-letter words	Four-letter words
AT AN IN IT	ATE EAT BET BAT BIT HAT RAT TAR HIT EAR TIE THE	RATE BEET NEAT HEAT BEAT BEAR TEAR HEAR NEAR BRAT BATH THAN THEN THIN RAIN TREE TIER BITE

Five-letter words	Six-letter words	Seven-letter words
HEART BATHE TRAIN TREAT	HEATER BEATER BATHER	NEITHER BREATHE

Figure 8.1. A sampling of sorted words from a Making Words activity. (*Source:* Cunningham & Cunningham [1992]. From Kluth, P., & Chandler-Olcott, K. (2008). *"A land we can share": Teaching literacy to students with autism* [p. 112]. Baltimore: Paul H. Brookes Publishing Co.; reprinted by permission.)

Considering Students with Autism

For students with autism, achieving fluency as a reader can be complicated by a variety of factors. Like all learners, they need to develop automaticity with word recognition and decoding. Where oral reading is concerned, many people on the spectrum also need to overcome problems related to *prosody*—the patterns of stress and intonation in a language—that typical learners do not face. As we discussed previously, their speech may be flat, stilted, or unusual in its pacing, and these peculiarities can manifest themselves in the context of oral reading.

Dysfluency by people with autism may suggest that they are having difficulties recognizing particular words, but it also can indicate something completely different. For example, Liane Holliday Willey's memoir includes this description of her early experiences with reading:

I loved the way most words played on my tongue. I loved the way they caused different parts of my mouth to move. But if I did come across a word that hurt my ears, typically words with too many hyper-nasal sounds, I would not say them aloud. Similarly, I would refuse words that looked ugly by virtue of being too lopsided or too cumbersome or too unusual in their phonetics. (1999, p. 25)

A teacher with a conception of reading fluency focused primarily on its cognitive components and not its affective ones might easily have misinterpreted Willey's refusal to pronounce certain words as an indication of a lack of knowledge about certain letter–sound correspondences. Such an inference might have led that teacher to plan repeated experiences with words containing the same kinds of features—an instructional decision that might have unintentionally created stress for a child like Willey. If examined using a different lens, however, Willey's balking at pronouncing these words can indicate proficiency rather than a weakness related to decoding. Her hyperawareness of the sounds that letters produce in particular combinations was uncomfortable for her because of how she experienced them bodily. Without probing these data from Willey's perspective, however, it would be difficult for any teacher to reach this conclusion.

These examples illustrate why teachers must be very cautious in how they interpret a learner's skills, abilities, and behaviors. These individuals help us as teachers to understand that we must seek the perspective of the learner as we assess our students and, further, we must take into consideration the sensory, communication, and movement differences that might create fluency and other reading performance problems for students with autism labels.

Instructional Approaches

A number of instructional approaches can be used to promote students' fluency development. Among our favorites are the following: read-alouds, collaborative oral reading, and repeated reading.

Read-Alouds   Almost every teacher, elementary or secondary, shares a book or some passage from a text aloud with students during the school week. Including students with autism in this simple activity with both fiction and nonfiction texts can be powerful because it exposes them to a model of fluent reading they might otherwise not have access to (Koppenhaver, Coleman, Kalman, & Yoder, 1991). Because many learners with autism struggle to read bodies and emotions (Blachman, 2000; Lawson, 1998; Shore, 2003), listening to the teacher read with expression may help them in understanding postures and facial expressions as well as appropriate uses of volume, tone, and inflections in speech. When the teacher reads about a child fighting with his brother, the student has an opportunity to review the language that is associated with anger and, if the teacher reads with feeling, the facial expressions and body language that an angry person might use. Of course, there are more than a few students with autism that find the passive nature of the read-aloud a challenge. Table 8.2 lists a variety of ways that the read-aloud can be adapted to meet such learners' diverse needs.

Collaborative Oral Reading   During read-alouds, the teacher is the only one to view the printed text. Shared reading, choral reading, and echo reading are all variations of what we call *collaborative oral reading*—activities meant to increase fluency because they engage more skilled readers in navigating a shared text—one that everyone can see—in some way with less skilled readers.

Shared reading (Allen, 2002) involves the teacher or another fluent reader in voicing the text while the learner tracks the print at the same time. In the elementary grades, this activity often takes place with a Big Book (a commercially produced version of a picture book that is enlarged so that a group of children can see it from their seats) or a chart on an easel. Teach-

Table 8.2.   Ideas for adapting the read-aloud

Give the student (or students) the same book or an adapted version of the book (e.g., a version with communication symbols added) so they can follow along.

Give the student a copy of the text to highlight words or phrases of interest.

Give the student cards to hold up during key passages (e.g., every time the teacher says "respiratory system," the student holds up a photo of the lungs).

Give the student something text-related to fidget with as the story is read (e.g., a small toy airplane as the teacher reads about transportation).

Give the student a job during the read-aloud (e.g., turn the pages of a big book, click a PowerPoint slide with the pages of the text displayed on it).

Have the student read the book (if possible) to the class, alone or with a partner, instead of listening to the teacher read it.

Have the student co-teach the book by asking key questions (prepared on cards or programmed into a communication device) throughout the read-aloud (e.g., "What do you think will happen next?").

Have the student participate by reading the first sentence of each page (verbally or via a communication device) or by repeating important passages.

Give the student a notebook to draw images that come to mind as they listen to the story or passage (this may also help to boost comprehension).

Give the student a special "book listening space" to use during the read-aloud (e.g., sitting in a special chair, standing at a lectern).

See http://www.paulakluth.com/articles/readingaloud.html for more ideas on adapting the read-aloud in K–12 classrooms.
From Kluth, P., & Chandler-Olcott, K. (2008). "*A land we can share*": *Teaching literacy to students with autism* (p. 117). Baltimore: Paul H. Brookes Publishing Co.; adapted by permission.

ers of older learners are more likely to project the shared text for the class on an overhead transparency or computer screen. Either way, the benefits are the same: Students get to see the print as it is voiced by another person, a process that helps them learn how to pronounce unfamiliar words, how to deal with conventions of print such as punctuation, and how to pace their reading differently for different purposes or while reading texts in different genres.

Choral reading is an approach that includes some of the same features as shared reading, such as a proficient reader's modeling and a common text, but that introduces a new variable: supported oral reading by the learner. One of the best examples we know of choral reading comes from an autobiography by Tito Rajarshi Mukhopadhyay, a young man with autism, whose teacher required him to follow along in a text as she read to him, with the voice–print connection helping him to stay focused:

> When she read, I had to naturally follow the words in order to keep pace with her speed. Slowly my concentration improved and I could keep my eyes fixed on a page without getting distracted. Mother practiced it at home and within a month I read a two hundred page book, reading about seven pages a day, reading in chorus with my mother. (2000, p. 75)

In the classroom, choral reading is more likely to take place in a whole-group setting, with the teacher and all students reading the text in unison. Such a strategy not only promotes fluency but also encourages participation by all students because individuals may feel less self-conscious about their reading performance when acting as a group.

Echo reading positions learners a bit more independently than shared reading or choral reading and, consequently, is often employed after students have developed familiarity with those other methods first. With echo reading, the teacher or another expert reader reads a portion of the text fluently while the learner follows along, tracking the print and paying attention to how it is voiced by the model. After completing a meaningful chunk of text—a few sentences for a beginning reader or a paragraph or section for a more experienced one—the expert turns the reading over to the learner, who rereads the same material while trying to use similar pacing and inflection. As students become more proficient, they might alternate passages with the more proficient reader rather than repeating what the expert had previously read.

Repeated Reading   According to the NRP (NICHD, 2000), the method of promoting fluency with the most unambiguous research support is repeated reading, associated most closely with work by S. Jay Samuels (1979). The approach works like this: After reading the text along with a teacher, a parent, a more competent peer, or even an audio recording to ensure comprehension, the learner is challenged to read the designated passage in the same length of time it would take a fluent reader to do so at a moderate pace (generally estimated at between 200 and 350 words per minute). The student then reads the passage as many times as necessary to achieve that goal, timing himself with a stopwatch and recording how much time elapses for each reading. Some versions of the activity also require students to keep track of their errors and to reread the passage until they can do so with accuracy as well as at an appropriate pace.

Repeated-reading activities will appeal to some students with autism because they set clear, unambiguous targets for performance such as a 100-word passage read in 40 seconds. They also involve students in charting data about their progress in an organized fashion (a Google search with "repeated reading" and "chart" as your search terms should yield a number of options students might use for this purpose), which some students on the spectrum will likely enjoy.

At the same time, we have a few cautions to share about this approach. First of all, many students with autism balk at participating in instructional activities that they perceive as "pointless," to borrow a word from Kenneth Hall (2001), a young author with Asperger syndrome. Unless their teachers are clear about the purpose for and benefits of repeated reading (e.g., focused practice with fluency, increased comprehension), it's likely that some students might greet a request to reread with a response like this: "Why do you want me to do that? I already read it once." Students with autism may also become too "stuck" on their immediate goals for a passage rather than the bigger picture of developing fluency. To keep individuals from worrying or focusing on reaching 100% accuracy in their reading—a focus that might lead them, for example, to unnecessary correction of small substitutions that don't interfere with the meaning of the passage and actually reflect their comprehension of the text—some learners may need their teachers to set a limit on the number of repeated readings they can do. Rashotte and Torgesen (1985), for example, recommend that students with learning disabilities read a given text no more than four times.

Finally, students with autism might be coaxed into repeated readings if their teachers can find authentic opportunities for them to do so. For instance, a reading specialist we know encouraged several fifth-grade students to plan and develop a poetry slam. This activity required the students to write their own poems and to practice them several times before performing them in the school library. See Table 8.3 for additional ideas.

Comprehension

Since the 1970s, a number of components in the comprehension process (i.e., comprehension strategies) have been identified, and it is generally understood that proficient readers use these flexibly, in concert with each other, as needed to understand a particular text for a particular reason. Although different lists of these component strategies exist, strategies such as the following are all recognized in the field as some of the most crucial for learners to master: making connections between what they're reading and their own lives, other texts, and the world around them; asking themselves questions and creating mental images as they

---

Table 8.3.   Finding opportunities for repeated readings

Have the student practice and perform skits, plays, or monologues; or, better yet, encourage him or her to try out for the school play.

Create a buddy program in which older students read to younger students. At each meeting, the older students should read the same book to several different children.

Introduce music into the curriculum so that students can read the lyrics during each class "perform-ance." For instance, fourth-grade students in Rochester, New York, sang the Erie Canal song fre-quently throughout the year as they studied New York State.

Teach a poem or chant that links to your curriculum. For instance, students in a ninth-grade English class read the same Langston Hughes poem every day for 10 days until they could recite it by heart.

After students write something, have them move around the classroom and read it to other students. For example, a seventh-grade teacher had her students write dialogue. Then, in pairs, students walked around the classroom performing their piece for at least three other teams. An ecology teacher had students write environmental pledges on index cards and tour the classroom to read them to at least five other students.

---

read; making inferences that go beyond the information stated explicitly in the text; determin-ing what information is most important in a text (given a particular purpose for reading); and monitoring when their understanding breaks down and taking steps to repair it (Dole, Duffy, Roehler, & Pearson,1991; Harvey & Goudvis, 2007).

Considering Students with Autism

Many people with autism spectrum labels report that reading comprehension is a problem for them, sometimes because of the content of the text and other times because of its structure, syntax, or vocabulary. It is not uncommon for learners with autism to decode at or above grade-level expectations while performing substantially less well on tests of comprehension (O'Connor & Klein, 2004).

One of the most common difficulties reported is difficulty in separating main ideas from details, as one mother learned while assisting her child with a homework assignment:

> In fifth grade my son was assigned to write a paper on Benedict Arnold. When I looked at his rough draft, I noticed that he had included all of the important facts about Arnold's life ex-cept for one—the fact that he had betrayed the Revolutionary Army to the British for 10,000 pounds and a commission in the Royal Navy! I asked him whether he hadn't left out some-thing important, to which he replied, "But all of it is important!" (Rosinski, 2002, p. 1)

Other learners with autism labels find it difficult to make inferences—to read "between the lines," as some people say—because they tend to interpret language very literally. This can be difficult with texts such as novels, poetry, or folklore whose power depends on literary devices such as metaphor.

Luke Jackson (2002) included an illustrated dictionary of idioms in his "user guide to adolescence" for people with Asperger syndrome. He shared that figurative uses of language were initially difficult for him to understand and encouraged those who interact with people on the autism spectrum to make themselves as explicit as possible. Others (Broun, 2004) have reported that understanding character motivation can be difficult for students with autism, especially if the dimensions of the characters are revealed through subtle details of gesture, tone, or behavior rather than spelled out clearly in the narration.

Although these examples demonstrate that many learners with autism face challenges with comprehension related to dimensions of their disability, we want to make it clear that many learners who are neurotypical find it difficult to comprehend at high levels as well, es-pecially when faced with discipline-specific reading such as textbooks, reports, and journal articles. In fact, one of the strongest recommendations arising from comprehension-focused research in the past two decades is the importance of explicit strategy-focused instruction for all learners across the curriculum and across the grade-level span (Biancarosa & Snow, 2004). For this reason, the instructional approaches to promote comprehension profiled in the next section will be useful for most, if not all, learners in a classroom, not just those with autism labels.

Instructional Approaches

Although students' reading comprehension can be supported with some of the instructional ideas we've already described—read-alouds, for example—the following approaches have comprehension instruction as their primary goal: boosting background knowledge, think-alouds, reciprocal teaching, and retellings.

Boosting Background Knowledge   Research has shown that good comprehenders draw on relevant prior knowledge to make sense of texts they are reading (Pressley, 2000). Students' comprehension can be increased when their teachers help them to activate, and sometimes even build, background knowledge about the topic in question. Many students with disabilities need this type of support because they are more likely than learners who are neurotypical or physically able to be excluded from in-school and out-of-school activities that lead to the development of extensive background knowledge.

A range of approaches can be used to assist students in calling up what they know about a topic and/or learning new information that can enhance their comprehension. For example, you might tell students a story from your own experience on a topic related to the text (students are so often intrigued by narratives from their teachers' lives) or ask them questions about experiences they might have had or media texts they may know (often, students don't realize that knowledge from television, film, and computer games can be valuable in understanding school-based topics). To help students create mental images as they read, you might show them a movie clip, slides of artwork, or illustrations related to the topic. You might also help students create connections between their experiences and the topic by using a graphic organizer such as a Know–Want-to-Know–Learned (KWL) chart used by learners to record what they _know_ about a topic and _want to know_ before reading as well as what they _learned_ after navigating the text (see Figure 8.2 for an example).

Perhaps the most significant support that can be offered in this area is to include all students in the typical routines and activities of school life. Students will build background knowledge daily when they are included in the social (e.g., recess, art class) and academic (e.g., math class, orchestra, academic clubs) life of the school. Oftentimes, teachers make the erroneous assumption that reading skills are honed only during the literacy block when, in fact, students learn these skills and acquire these competencies all day long. If the class is reading a story about mummies, for example, and the learner with autism was not in his general education classroom when Egypt was studied, he will most likely have a harder time comprehending the story than his peers.

Think-Alouds   The think-aloud (Baumann, Jones, & Seifert-Kessell, 1993; Harvey & Goudvis, 2007; Oczkus, 2009; Tovani, 2000) is one of the best ways for teachers to help students learn to control reading strategies as well as monitor their overall comprehension. This approach requires readers "to stop periodically, reflect on how a text is being processed and understood, and relate orally what reading strategies are being employed" (Baumann et al., 1993, p. 192). Teachers who model the process offer students a helpful look at how a proficient reader deals with challenges associated with a particular text. For instance, they might model the strategy of prediction—a crucial one when beginning a novel—by saying, "The title is

What I <u>K</u>now	What I <u>W</u>ant to Know	What I <u>L</u>earned
Lacrosse was invented by the six nations in the Iroquois Confederacy. It used to be played by whole villages at one time. Lacrosse has some elements in common with soccer.	How has the game changed over time? How long does it take to make a wooden lacrosse stick? When did European Americans begin playing the sport?	Most players use metal and plastic sticks now, but during traditional games, handmade wooden sticks were always used. It takes at least 8 months to make a wooden stick. People started playing box lacrosse in the 1930s. In the Territory, the Onondagas play in a box now rather than on a field. The name lacrosse was given to the game by French settlers. Lacrosse was made the national game of Canada in 1867, so white people must have been playing it by the mid-19th century. The Iroquois National team was not accepted into the International Federation until 1987.

Figure 8.2. Sample KWL chart completed before and after reading *Lacrosse: The National Game of the Iroquois* (Hoyt-Goldsmith, 1998). (From Kluth, P., & Chandler-Olcott, K. (2008). *"A land we can share": Teaching literacy to students with autism* [p. 125]. Baltimore: Paul H. Brookes Publishing Co.; adapted by permission.)

Tales of a Fourth Grade Nothing [Blume, 1972], so I think it will be about a kid in the fourth grade. When I look at the picture on the cover, I think maybe the main character will be a boy. The cover has a picture of a classroom, so I think a lot of this book will take place in a school."

According to Tovani, a professional development specialist who works with secondary teachers from all disciplines, preparing for and performing a think-aloud has four steps:

- Select a short piece of text that will allow you to model the desired strategy.
- Foresee difficulty, anticipating what aspects of the text might serve as obstacles to student comprehension. (You may want to make notes for yourself about what these obstacles are and how you solve them as a competent adult reader.)
- Read the text out loud in front of students (using an overhead projector or computer or distributing copies to students) and stop often to share your thinking.
- Point out the words in the text that trigger your thinking. (2000, pp. 27–28)

Most teachers who use this approach write their thoughts on chart paper or on a transparency as they share them with the class, so that students can see and hear the process. Tovani also recommends using body language to cue students when she is thinking aloud:

"Looking at the transparency when I read and looking at the students when I share thinking helps them distinguish the difference between reading and thinking aloud" (2000, p. 28). This last idea should be helpful for students with autism because it adds a visual cue to a largely auditory experience.

Reciprocal Teaching   In the 2000s, reciprocal teaching (Palincsar & Brown, 1984) experienced a renaissance in schools because it was cited in the NRP report as a method for promoting comprehension with a good deal of research support. Combining the explicitness of a teacher think-aloud with the power of cooperative learning, reciprocal teaching is essentially a dialogue between teachers and students. The dialogue is structured by the use of four high-utility comprehension strategies: summarizing, question generating, clarifying, and predicting.

Once students are comfortable with the four strategies and the reciprocal teaching procedures, they are invited to become "the teacher" and conduct reciprocal teaching dialogues with new material. At this point, the teacher's role shifts from providing direct instruction to facilitating student interaction, monitoring progress, and providing feedback. As students become more skilled with the strategy, they can work in pairs or small groups to coach one another's strategy use in the context of many different reading tasks, from textbook chapters to poems.

Reciprocal teaching can be useful for learners with autism because its specific procedures create a clear set of expectations about students' roles and because it permits teachers to make decisions about group sizes and partnerships that will maximize student comfort. It also positions learners, during the time they play the "teacher," as experts rather than novices, which may give them confidence as well as the opportunity to shine in front of their peers. Whalon (2004), in fact, found that when she taught three students with autism reciprocal questioning techniques to use in the context of their inclusive classroom, all of the students increased their frequency of question generation and responding. In addition, two of the three participants increased their performance on standardized comprehension measures, and the parents of all of the participants reported improvement in their child's language, reading fluency and reading comprehension skills. Undoubtedly, one of the reasons these learners achieved the level of success they did was due to the inclusion of several visual supports in the intervention. For instance, students had a checklist complete with icons illustrating key words and/or phrases to monitor their own reading and their interactions with peers (e.g., "Before reading: Ask each other, 'Why is it important to ask questions when we read?'"). They also had a series of illustrated question cards (e.g., WHEN, WHO, WHERE) to help keep their discussions on track as well as to map their stories while and after they read (see Figure 8.3 for an example of cards that might be created).

Retelling   As we explained already, some learners may fail comprehension assessments because they are uncomfortable with the direct nature of question/answer interactions. For this reason, some students may respond well to being asked instead to tell about their reading. Retelling (Hoyt, 1999; Shaw, 2005) is an instructional approach that is also used as a tool for assessment. A retelling is done by the reader after he has read or heard a text. The student is asked to "tell everything" he can about what has been read after having the approach modeled by the teacher. (Do not assume that this behavior comes naturally, as students need to be taught explicitly how to sequence their retellings as well as how to include essential information in them.) As students talk, you can record the key features of their retellings using a form such as the one in Figure 8.4, reproduced from Chandler-Olcott and Hinchman (2005). With fictional texts, retelling reinforces story structure and the language and imagery used by the author; with informational texts, it helps students determine what material is most important.

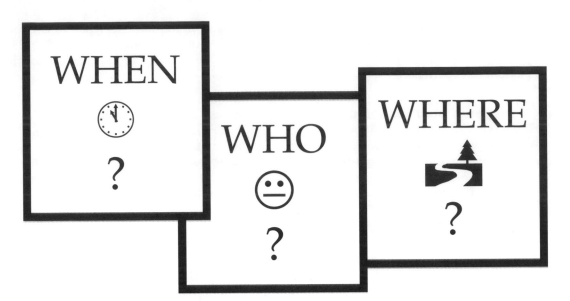

Figure 8.3. Reciprocal teaching visual supports (From Whalon, K. [2004]. *The effects of a reciprocal questioning intervention on the reading comprehension of children with autism.* Unpublished manuscript, Florida State University, Tallahassee; adapted by permission.)

Putting the text into their own words helps students organize new information, connect it to what they already know about the topic, and remember it.

For those who communicate better visually (or for those who have unreliable speech) a graphic retelling might work better. Students can be taught a story-mapping strategy (Boulineau, Fore, Hagan-Burke, & Burke, 2004; Sorrell, 1990) to help them capture information as they read or immediately after they finish a piece of text. Students can be taught to map out the events in an artistic and symbolic way by literally drawing a path or trail and inserting images as they move through the story. Or they can map by taking visual notes in chronological order in a notebook or in consecutive boxes on a page. For example, a third-grade teacher had her students map out *Mystery in the Night Woods* (Peterson, 1969) using an exercise we call collaborative 4-Corners Comprehension (see Figure 8.5). This involves having students read sections of text (in this case, chapters) and then pause to draw or map what they read at the end of each section. Cora, a young woman with autism, could not draw pictures or use a pencil easily, so she worked on a collaborative map with a peer. Cora's classmate drew the pictures and then, together, the two found pieces of dialogue to fit each quadrant (e.g., "Where is FS?"). Cora was responsible for creating a sticker of each, using a handheld label maker, and positioning it on the correct quadrant. (See Table 8.4 for more ideas for adapting the retelling strategy.)

Vocabulary

Wide reading of a rich range of texts is one of the best ways to increase word knowledge (Nagy, Herman, & Anderson, 1985); indeed, we learn many of the words we know from reading without consciously realizing that we've learned them. But wide reading on its own is generally insufficient for developing a strong vocabulary (Beck, McKeown, & Kucan, 2002). For most learners, it must be supplemented by 1) the teaching of specific words, especially those of particular utility in the various academic disciplines; 2) the teaching of specific word-learning strategies, such as the use of context clues; and 3) the deliberate promotion of word

Retelling Checklists

Expository Retelling

Student name: _____ Date: _____

Text title: _____ Text author: _____

Text structure elements	Unprompted	Prompted
Main ideas		
Details		
Structure (e.g., main idea/detail, cause/effect, compare/contrast)		

Comments:

Narrative Retelling

Student name: _____ Date: _____

Text title: _____ Text author: _____

Story elements	Unprompted	Prompted
Setting (time, place)		
Characters		
Problem		
Events leading to solution		
Solution		

Comments:

Figure 8.4. Retelling checklists for expository or narrative retelling.

From Chandler-Olcott, K., & Hinchman, K.A. (2005). *Tutoring adolescent literacy learners* (p. 47). New York: Guilford Press; reprinted by permission. Copyright © 2005 by Guilford Press.

In *"You're Going to Love This Kid!" Teaching Students with Autism in the Inclusive Classroom, Second Edition,* by Paula Kluth (2010, Paul H. Brookes Publishing Co.)

Figure 8.5. Collaborative 4-Corners Comprehension for *Mystery in the Night Woods* (Peterson, 1969). (From Kluth, P., & Chandler-Olcott, K. (2008). *"A land we can share": Teaching literacy to students with autism* [p. 130]. Baltimore: Paul H. Brookes Publishing Co.; reprinted by permission.)

consciousness, defined by Ryder and Graves as the "disposition to notice words, to value them, and use them in precise and effective ways" (1998, p. 32). Attention to all three of these aspects of vocabulary learning can and should be incorporated into literacy instruction for students with disabilities.

This means that if students cannot read on their own, teachers will need to read to them "a rich range of texts" as they will need this background not only to make their lives more in-

---

Table 8.4. Ideas for helping students with autism with the retelling process

Have peers model the strategy in order to provide multiple models of the process (models that are often more accessible than those provided by adults).

Encourage students to type or write part or all of the retelling rather than saying it orally (some might prefer to read their retelling aloud after they have written it [Biklen, 2005]).

Give students illustrations, photographs, or sequencing cards to use in the retelling.

Identify key information that should be included in the retelling (e.g., "Make sure that you talk about all three challenges faced by the protagonist").

Have students retell the story by completing a graphic organizer that will cue them about some of the key elements (e.g., a box to discuss the story's setting and another to discuss its conflict).

Let students engage in the retelling in a dramatic way by acting it out.

Allow small groups of students to retell a story together.

From Kluth, P., & Chandler-Olcott, K. (2008). *"A land we can share": Teaching literacy to students with autism* (p. 126). Baltimore: Paul H. Brookes Publishing Co.; adapted by permission.

teresting but also to help them acquire literacy skill. We'll discuss more specific approaches to vocabulary instruction that meet these criteria in a subsequent section of this chapter; first, however, let us share some information about how vocabulary learning might play out for students with autism spectrum labels.

Considering Students with Autism

As a number of authors have shared (Barron & Barron, 1992; Gerland, 1996; Prince-Hughes, 2004), words can be a source of comfort and fascination for people with autism. In some of the earliest autobiographical writing by a person with autism, Sean Barron shared his own quest to learn new words by reading the dictionary in sequence:

> That day, after school, I started reading with the first definition. Every day I read as much as I could, concentrating as hard as possible. Nearly eight weeks later I finished the dictionary. I felt a sense of power, and I was eager to have people hear me use those words! I didn't know how to use them in context, I realized later. But when I was fifteen I thought I could substitute a big word for a small one and everyone would say, "Boy is he smart!" (Barron & Barron, 1992, p. 198)

Not every student on the autism spectrum will revel in the opportunity to learn new vocabulary words as Barron did. But even for students who like to discover new words, the teacher may struggle to turn this fascination into a lesson. We suggest that educators look for ways to bring new vocabulary into daily work so that students with autism (and any others needing extra support) do not see the learning of new words as an auxiliary activity but as a part of the work readers, writers, and communicators do every day.

Instructional Approaches

Students develop vocabulary knowledge from many sources, including incidentally from their membership in a print-rich community. We like the following instructional approaches, however, with vocabulary development as an explicit goal: fascination-focused books, word walls, and skits and pantomime.

Fascination-Focused Books   One promising way to engage students with autism in improving their vocabularies is the use of what we have dubbed fascination books. Any of the interests students bring to the classroom might be used to develop materials that will help them learn new vocabulary and develop what Ryder and Graves (1998) call "word consciousness." For instance, one student with autism, Joe, initially struggled with vocabulary-focused lessons, often retreating from them by paging through picture-book adaptations of the Harry Potter series by J.K. Rowling. In response to his interest, his teachers developed a learning tool—a Harry Potter dictionary—intended to push Joe to learn new words while honoring his main area of expertise and interest. New concepts and words were connected to material he had already mastered from watching Harry Potter movies and enjoying the books. For instance, the entry for the word *aloft* included a drawing of Harry Potter playing Quidditch and flying through the air on his stick. The entry for *terrified* showed Harry encountering ghouls in the hallways of his wizard school.

Word Walls   A classroom word wall is "an interactive, ongoing display . . . of words and/or parts of words" pulled from meaningful contexts such as class discussions, group viewing of films, and independent reading (Wagstaff, 1999, p. 32). These words may be related to a subject such as science or tied to a discrete unit of study such as colonial America.

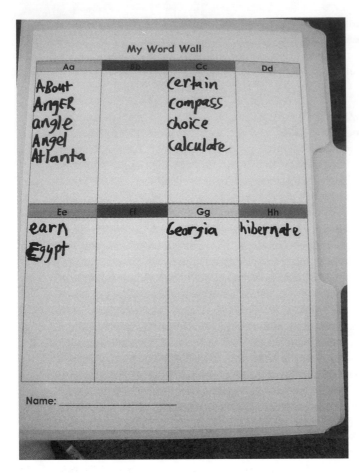

Figure 8.6. Example of a personal word wall.

Some teachers even choose to have more than one word wall so that each can address specific needs or purposes—for instance, to accompany a word study of adjectives or to highlight all of the vocabulary associated with a new math concept such as statistics. Words walls can be used to support vocabulary development in various ways. Students can invent cheers and chants for words, suggest new additions to the wall as they read and write, group words for a new purpose, and use the words as a resource when spelling.

A word wall also can be used to inspire learning games appropriate for a wide range of learners' needs. For instance, one teacher used her word wall as an inspiration for bingo. Each student had a bingo card with nine blank spaces. The students wrote one word of their choice from the wall in each space. Then the words were removed from the wall, put into a hat, and called out one by one by the teacher while students listened for the words they chose. One student with autism in this classroom told the teacher that he "lived" for the weekly bingo review as he had a passion for game shows and the teacher always let him be the caller so he could practice his "Bob Barker" voice (and get extra practice with the words on the wall at the same time). Activities such as these will ensure that students are constantly interacting with the words on the wall rather than allowing them to fade into the background.

One way to make the word wall more accessible to students with disabilities is to create a portable version of the wall that learners can study and manipulate at their own desks and take home at the end of the day. Karen Erickson and David Koppenhaver describe such an adaptation in their book *Children with Disabilities: Reading and Writing the Four-Blocks Way* (2007). They create these supports primarily for learners with visual impairments or for those who have a hard time looking back and forth from the wall to their papers. The wall is simply recreated inside a manila folder, and the student or a teacher adds new words to the portable wall when the classroom version is updated (see Figure 8.6). A benefit of the portable wall is that it can be personalized for the learner with disabilities. If there are words on the classroom wall not seen as high priority for the student with disabilities, these can be omitted. Similarly, if there are words the class is not learning (e.g., vocabulary for the learner's augmentative communication device) but the student with disability is, these can be added.

Skits and Pantomime   Movement, drama, skits, pantomime, and similar types of activities can be used to introduce new vocabulary to students and to help them remember word definitions and uses. In a book Paula wrote with her colleague Alice Udvari-Solner, they describe a game called Act Like It, in which students work in small teams to "become" words, concepts, ideas, or things. Teachers can either assign all groups the same word or concept or give different groups different (but related) words or concepts. Depending on the students' needs, the teacher may choose to offer options that are very concrete such as *pyramid* or *microscope* or ones that are more abstract and complex such as *community, element, cosine,* or *imagery.* The vocabulary words might be known to everyone in the room, or each group might have a secret identity that must be guessed by observing groups. The prompt is given to each group either verbally or in writing. For instance, a group might get this assignment: "You are *propel*. Act like it!" Give groups a short period of time to generate ideas for a performance; this version sometimes can be fun as students need to think on their feet and react based on the most salient points in their mind.

Another way to engineer the activity is to give learners time to plan and treat the performances more like a formal review. In this version, you can give specific criteria. For example, you might require that the performances last at least a minute and that students use at least two props as they perform. For instance, in a language arts lesson, the teacher asked students to "act like" the following vocabulary words: *evocative, nefarious, pithy, onerous, precocious, sordid,* and *restitution.* Each group had to act out each one of the words while the audience guessed which "skit" represented which word from the list. This exercise was especially useful for Renee, a student with Asperger syndrome. Renee found the visuals helpful in learning new words (especially those with abstract meanings). The lighthearted atmosphere of the activity helped her feel relaxed, which was a contrast to the feeling of stress she experienced in other language-laden academic experiences.

Extending the Invitation: Writing

This section begins with an overview of purposes and contexts for writing, then turns to several key components—fluency, planning and organization, and revision and editing—that recent scholarship (Farnan & Dahl, 2003; Graham & Perin, 2007; MacArthur, Graham, & Fitzgerald, 2006; Smagorinsky, 2006) leads us to suggest may be foundational to success with composition for students with autism. Each section begins with reference to its research base, explains how each topic might be experienced by learners with autism, and recommends some teaching practices designed to promote greater competence and confidence in that area for these students.

Fluency

We discussed fluency in the teaching of reading, but the concept also applies to writing, so we consider it here as well. Fluent writers are able to encode their messages comfortably and smoothly, with few interruptions or difficulties. According to cognitive scientists, fluency is important to writers because "more fluent text-production processes free working memory resources, allowing the writer to move beyond knowledge telling and engage in higher level processes, such as planning and reviewing" (McCutcheon, 2006, p. 126).

Recent research shows that students' fluency can be increased with targeted instruction (Eckert et al., 2006; Graham, Harris, & Larsen, 2001; Quinlan, 2004). What's striking to us is how simple some of these effective interventions are. For example, Eckert and colleagues (2006) studied the effects of a writing fluency intervention in which, once a week for 8 weeks, third graders were asked to write in response to a story stem like the following: "I never dreamed that the door in my bedroom would lead to. . . . " Before they began drafting, they received individual feedback sheets listing the following: 1) the number of words they produced during the previous week's writing session, 2) the number of sentences they wrote during the previous session, and 3) the number of correctly spelled words from the previous session. Each of the three numbers was accompanied by an arrow symbol to represent visually whether the numbers had gone up or down from the previous week. Students who received the individual feedback achieved statistically significant gains in both fluency and spelling when compared with the performance of students who received a similar writing task but no instructor feedback. The results from Eckert and colleagues suggest to us that setting fluency goals explicitly for students and involving them in tracking their own progress can go a long way toward supporting improvement in these areas. Students with autism who love numbers (and there are many) will be especially interested in this exercise that allows them to use their quantifying skills.

Other researchers have shown that writing fluency increases for many students, including some with disabilities, when they are provided with access to assistive and augmentative technologies. Quinlan (2004), for example, reported gains for less fluent writers, ages 11–14, when they used speech recognition technology rather than handwrote four narratives. The length of their pieces increased when they used the software, and the number of surface-feature errors decreased. Graham and colleagues (2001) found that technologies such as word processing, semantic mapping software, word prediction programs, and speech synthesizers aided students with learning disabilities in writing more easily. In addition, Bedrosian, Lasker, Speidel, and Politsch (2003) reported that written output for a nonverbal middle school student with autism increased over time during an intervention that involved him and his writing partner, a same-age peer with a cognitive disability label, in using a story-writing software program in conjunction with an AlphaTalker communication device. Although students still need responsive instruction in how to employ various technologies for composing purposes—the technologies themselves are not enough—these researchers suggest that such tools are making fluency a more attainable goal for a wide range of learners than it has ever been before.

Considering Students with Autism

The communication and movement differences often associated with autism can make it difficult for many individuals with this label to achieve writing fluency. Even writers who eventually learn to create significant amounts of text may approach fluency using different perspectives and different strategies than learners who are neurotypical. For example, when Lucy Blackman, an Australian woman with autism who is largely nonverbal, began to generate written language by typing, she reported that her mother, who served as her most frequent communication partner, believed the following:

> [She] thought I was using it like other teenagers do. She did not realise that I typed more fluently if I imagined I was sitting above my own body, watching, as another Lucy would, a new character, also called Lucy, going through the motions that all other literate people did. It was as if I were role playing. (1999, p. 105)

At the same time, some learners on the autism spectrum report little difficulty with writing fluency (Grandin, 1995; Williams, 1992, 1994). Some of them appear to process and produce written text more easily than speech. For example, consider the words of Gunilla Gerland, a woman with autism, in her autobiography:

> First of all, I learned to write, which was easier, and then I learnt to read. I liked words, and needed new challenges for it to be fun. I wanted to learn more and more complicated words. When I heard a new one, I always grabbed at it, and even if I had seen a word in writing only once, I usually knew how it was spelt. I enjoyed writing and being good at it.

Expressing words in writing was much easier for me than taking the long way round, as I experienced it, via speech. (1996, p. 53)

Likewise, Daniel Tammet, a man with Asperger syndrome and a self-proclaimed "savant," shares that as a child, fluent writing was one of his many academic gifts. He recalls that, around age 8, he wrote compulsively (often for hours at a time), using up endless reams of computer paper and covering all of the paper's surface with "tightly knit words" so tiny that a teacher complained about having to change the prescription on her glasses just to read the text:

> The stories I wrote, from what I can remember of them, were descriptively dense—a whole page might be taken up in describing the various details of a single place or location, its colors, shapes, and textures. There was no dialogue, no emotions. Instead I wrote of long, weaving tunnels far underneath vast, shimmering oceans, of cragged rock caves and towers climbing into the sky. I didn't have to think about what I was writing; the words just seemed to flow out of my head. Even without any conscious planning, the stories were always comprehensible. When I showed one to my teacher, she liked it enough to read parts of it out loud to the rest of the class. (2006, p. 44)

Given the heterogeneity of experiences with fluency that Blackman, Gerland, and Tammet describe, you will need to observe student writers with autism closely in multiple composing contexts to see whether they struggle with fluency and, correspondingly, whether they might benefit from the kinds of fluency-focused instructional approaches we present in the next section.

Instructional Approaches

According to many composition experts, students need ample amounts of practice in low-anxiety contexts to develop fluency as writers (Kirby, Liner, & Vinz, 1988; McCutcheon, 2006; Strong, 2006). Ungraded daily journal writing of one kind or another is frequently cited as one way to provide that practice (Fulwiler, 1987; Kirby et al., 1988), and we support that approach whole-heartedly for learners with and without disabilities. (Table 8.5 includes brief descriptions of different kinds of journals that might be implemented in inclusive classrooms.) We also advocate the following approaches, each of which is discussed in this section, that may be less familiar to you: using the language experience approach (LEA), scribing, having silent discussions, differentiating writing materials, and offering handwriting alternatives.

Language Experience Approach Like Copeland and Keefe (2007), we see LEA, originally conceived by Stauffer (1970), as a method of developing writing fluency that is appropriate for students with wide-ranging needs, including those with significant disabilities. The steps of this approach are fairly simple:

- Engage the students in a shared experience such as a teacher read-aloud of a picture book, a field trip, a cooperative activity, or a classroom visit from a community member that will give them something meaningful and interesting about which to write.

- Record individual students' contributions to the text on the board or on a projected screen as the ideas are dictated, rereading them for each contributor to make sure you transcribe them accurately.

- Reread the text periodically from the beginning to help students see how it is progressing, editing and revising as necessary.

Table 8.5.   Variations on journal writing appropriate for inclusive classrooms

Dialogue journal. Students write entries in the form of a friendly letter about their reading and/or their lives, and their partners, who may be peers (Kirby, Liner, & Vinz, 1988) or a teacher (Atwell, 1998), write back.

Double-entry journal. Students divide the page into two columns, noting information from the text—quotations or paraphrases—in one column and their own responses (e.g., questions they have, connections they make) in the other column (Daniels & Zemelman, 2005).

Family literacy journal. Students and their families read literature or tell stories together and then record their responses with writing, drawings, photographs, and/or captions (Parker, 1997).

Sketch journal. Students sketch, draw, or include images in their journals, sometimes using the visual material alone to capture an idea but often using it as a springboard for writing such as captions or labels (Ernst, 1994).

Writer's notebook. Students make entries about all aspects of their thinking about writing, including observational notes, lists of potential topics, questions they have, interview notes, favorite quotations, and so forth; they often review these entries for ideas or drafts that they can add to, polish, and share (Hindley, 1996).

From Kluth, P., & Chandler-Olcott, K. (2008). "*A land we can share*": *Teaching literacy to students with autism* (p. 149). Baltimore: Paul H. Brookes Publishing Co.; adapted by permission.

- Continue taking individual contributions and rereading the draft of the text until the students are satisfied it is complete.

- Read the text aloud in its entirety so that students can hear what it sounds like, then ask them to reread it chorally with you.

- Invite students to engage in follow-up activities such as illustrating the text, rereading it in class, and/or taking it home to share with families.

LEA is often used by teachers in inclusive classrooms because it is typically collaborative and students can add a contribution in any number of ways including by choosing a picture to represent an idea, by pointing to a choice of a few words or sentences, or by verbally sharing a word or short utterance that can be weaved into the group story. Downing (2005) suggests that for students with the most significant disabilities, objects related to the story might be used to draw students into the activity and to help them express ideas.

Recently, Labbo, Eakle, and Montero (2002) adapted LEA to tap the potential of digital photography and computer software to promote student learning, even for the youngest writers. In the kindergarten classroom this team studied, the Digital Language Experience Approach (or D-LEA) still began with a stimulus experience, but that experience was photographed with digital cameras as students participated. Students then used the photographs to prepare for their compositions by 1) importing them into creativity software such as Kidpix (available from Learning Company, www.learningcompany.com), which allowed them to add text to the images; 2) discussing which images to select that best represented the experience; and 3) sequencing those images, sometimes with a storyboard. Next, teachers typed students' contributions into the digital document (or helped students to do so, if they had enough facility with writing and the software). In addition to editing the print aspects of the text, students had the option of adding multimedia effects such as music, sound effects, or animation. The final phase of the approach was also enhanced by the features of the technology, as students could read the text on screen, with or without the voice synthesizer.

We think that this adapted LEA has even more potential to support students with autism than the traditional version because it allows for multimodal representation that can build on the visual strengths many learners with autism possess as well as tie in to the fascination with computers that some of these same learners report. It also allows students with fewer verbal skills to participate meaningfully, as they can select and sequence images even if they cannot produce written text to caption them.

Scribing The LEA we've described is implemented in a small- or large-group setting, as students benefit from the opportunity to hear others' perspectives on a shared experience and see how that experience is represented in print. Students who are more skilled oral communicators or who know more about how print works serve as models for peers who need additional support in those areas (this is, in our view, yet another academic benefit of students' participation in inclusive classrooms). It can sometimes be beneficial to an individual student's writing fluency, however, for a teacher, parent, or peer to serve as his scribe while he plans and drafts a piece of writing aloud. For students with autism who have relatively reliable speech but who find the physical act of writing to be difficult because of their lack of experience or problems with fine motor control, scribing can free them to compose more quickly and, in some cases, in more complex ways. The scribe may simply invite the author of the text to begin talking and then record the words as they are said; or the two may engage in a multistep process together in which the author brainstorms possibilities recorded by the scribe in list form or on a graphic organizer, then tells the scribe what to include in the actual draft while using the brainstormed notes as a reference. The approach to select depends on the purpose, length, and complexity of the text: A student's quick response to a poem read by a peer may not require advance planning, but a research paper in science most likely will.

One specific adaptation we have used often in inclusive classrooms is collaborative journaling or "writing buddies" support in which the student with a disability chooses photos or pictures from magazines to use as writing prompts and glues them into a spiral notebook. He or she then invites peers to "write" with him or her during workshop or free writing time. To be sure that the students talk about ideas together and that they remember key components (e.g., generating a title), we place simple age-appropriate directions right into the front cover of the notebook (see Figure 8.7 for an example) so that partners are reminded of the exact steps to take to support their classmates. For instance, a notebook created for a fifth-grade student contained the following directions:

- Pick a picture and talk about it with your buddy. Think about a story you can write about the picture. You can also make up a story on your own without using a picture.

- One person should write the story in the journal.

- Think of a name for the story together.

- Write the title at the top of the page.

- Write your names at the top of the page.

We should note that some educators resist scribing because they fear it does not provide students with enough independent practice with writing or that teachers, especially those working with students with severe disabilities, may come to depend on the practice too much. We believe that there are plenty of learning situations in which the most important concern is using writing to participate; in those cases, scribing is vastly preferable to silencing a student who has something valuable to say. At the same time, we're aware that some writers lack comfort with the physical act of writing simply because they have had too few opportunities to develop that comfort.

Because our goal is always to help literacy learners do as much on their own as possible, we recommend that teachers who scribe for students try to fade their level of support over time as they observe students gaining more control as writers. When Kelly used this approach, she began by scribing complete texts for students that they can then use for reading practice (their own language structures are so familiar to them that this helps them to develop reading fluency). When students' texts got longer and they appeared to compose them orally with greater comfort, she began to scribe only the topic sentences for each paragraph, leaving blank spaces between the paragraphs to cue students about how much text they might in-

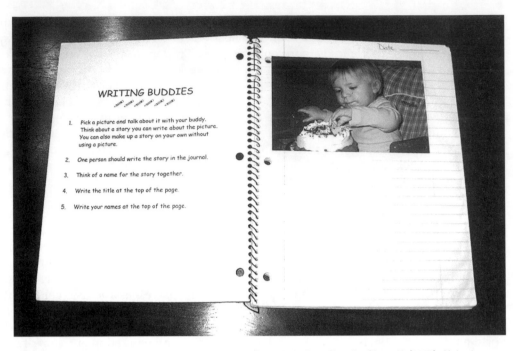

Figure 8.7. Example of a collaborative writing notebook. (From Kluth, P., & Chandler-Olcott, K. (2008). *"A land we can share": Teaching literacy to students with autism* [p. 151]. Baltimore: Paul H. Brookes Publishing Co.; reprinted by permission.)

clude to support those topic sentences. Eventually, she would scribe only an outline or just a few key words to serve as a reminder to students as they wrote independently.

Silent Discussions   Sometimes, students struggle with writing not because they can't organize their thinking but because they're not sure what to say. One way to help them practice generating written text in a social context is the "silent discussion," an instructional activity developed by Kelly's friend Tanya Baker, an English and literacy teacher. As Tanya organized it, each student in the class received a blank piece of paper on which he or she wrote a question about a shared reading. After students passed their papers to the right, they answered the question they were passed and then added a question of their own before passing the paper again. Tanya usually ended the passing after five or six turns, at which time she invited students to "report one interesting thing from the paper they have in their hands" (Wilhelm, Baker, & Dube, 2001, p. 141). In Tanya's classroom, students typically generated their own questions, but the basic structure of the activity could be retained with a teacher-designed prompt or question to begin the conversation, followed by students' responding to that question in turn.

We speculate that this activity has the potential to promote fluency because students are cued by their peers' questions and previous answers about what to write. Except for during the first turn, they are not expected to compose from scratch. However, a silent discussion doesn't need to be a group task. It can take place with only two participants, and one of them can even be the teacher. Michael, a student with autism whom Paula taught, often asked her to converse with him on paper. During even the shortest exchanges, he preferred to write rather than talk. He would type short answers and Paula would respond in longhand. Although they could not engage in conversations in this way every time he requested it (it was time-consuming, and she had other students to tend to), she tried to dialogue this way with him whenever time allowed. He found these exchanges on paper to be more calming, comforting, and easier to comprehend than those he participated in verbally.

Differentiated Writing Materials

Still another way to encourage fluency is to use a wide range of materials and provide choice in how the learner will complete writing tasks. Teddy, a young man with Asperger syndrome, for instance, was often much more willing to write longer passages when he used markers or when he could use colorful paper. Another student we know did higher quality work when he wrote on the chalkboard instead of on note paper or the computer. Still another learner was motivated to write when his teacher honored his passion for kitchen utensils by attaching his pencils to small cooking ladles and allowing him to, in essence, write with a spoon (see Table 8.6 for more ideas on differentiating writing materials).

June Downing described her student Joannie, who profited from both choice activities and from using different materials during writing exercise. This learner, who, previous to being included in a first-grade classroom had been in a room for students labeled as "trainable mentally retarded," made gains when she was given materials that allowed her to construct text and participate in typical classroom activities:

> When asked to write in her journal, she was given choices of pictures from which to select. She tended to select topics around her classmates, in particular, her friend, Monica. Initially starting with pictures and then fading to word cards alone, Joannie was able to complete sentences by using index cards placed sequentially in separate boxes following the sentence pattern of "Monica is _____." Joannie seemed to take great delight in choosing the adjectives (a choice of three) to complete the sentence, which were then read to her and written in her journal. She held a pencil but used the word cards to put in the sequential boxes to form her sentences about her friend. (2005, p. 68)

Assistive technology also should be considered for each learner with autism. Students may need low-tech options such as a slant board or pencil grip or high-tech options such as

---

Table 8.6.   Differentiated writing materials

Implements	Surfaces	Related tools
Pencils	Paper	Magazines
Markers	Computer screen	Glue sticks
Rubber stamps	Chalkboard	Stickers
Crayons	Dry-erase board	Sticky notes
Paintbrushes	Magnetic board	Etch-a-Sketch
Chalk	Sidewalk	Language Master
Vibrating, novelty, or textured pens	Chart paper	Correction fluid
Stylus	Paper with raised lines	Stencils
Label maker	Index cards	
Computer mouse or touch screen	Cardboard	
Letter or word magnets	Note pad	
Typewriter	Overhead projector	
	Interactive whiteboard/SMART board	
	Carbon paper	

From Kluth, P., & Chandler-Olcott, K. (2008). *"A land we can share": Teaching literacy to students with autism* (p. 154). Baltimore: Paul H. Brookes Publishing Co.; adapted by permission.

software programs and augmentative communication devices. Common writing supports for students with autism include word predication software, voice recognition software, "talking" dictionaries, letter or picture boards, alternative keyboards (with larger keys that can be arranged to suit the learner's needs), and even typewriters (a favorite for students who are sensory learners and like to "feel" what they are writing).

Sometimes, students will need a combination of assistive technology supports. For instance, Erickson and Koppenhaver (2007) shared an example of a student with significant physical disabilities who typed slowly on a keyboard equipped with a keyguard. He often typed letters of words out of order (CTA for *cat*), causing his teacher to question whether he had spelling difficulties or was simply fatigued from typing. Working with her special education colleague, the teacher replaced the learner's keyboard with a joystick, an onscreen keyboard, and Co:Writer 4000, a software program (Don Johnston, Inc.) that assists the user with both writing and spelling. These authors report that after implementing these adaptations, the student was able to type more easily and spell more accurately. (See Figure 8.8 for an example of one student's collection of differentiated writing materials.)

Handwriting Alternatives   We can't conclude our discussion of promoting students' fluency as writers without some attention to handwriting. Even Hans Asperger, the man responsible for characterizing students with the disability that now bears his name, noted that the individuals he saw had great struggles with penmanship. In a description of a student he called Fritz, he wrote:

> In his tense fist, the pencil could not run smoothly. A whole page would suddenly be covered with big swirls, the exercise book would be drilled full of holes, if not torn up. In the end it was possible to teach him to write only by making him trace letters and words which were written in red pencil. (Asperger, 1944, p. 49)

This characteristic is one that is oftentimes very frustrating for learners on the spectrum, especially when teachers are not aware of or sensitive to it. In fact, this was one of the most striking commonalities we discovered in our research on autobiographies written by people with autism (Grandin, 1995; Hall, 2001; Mukhopadhyay, 2000; Prince-Hughes, 2004; Shore, 2003; Tammet, 2006). Author after author lamented their difficulties with neatness and legibility, even in those situations where they were highly motivated to achieve those goals (Grandin, 1995).

We urge you to allow students with autism to compose on the keyboard as much as possible, as many of them will achieve fluency with this piece of adaptive technology that they simply could not while using a pen or pencil. For example, numerous K–12 teachers with whom we work find the AlphaSmart 3000 (Renaissance Learning), a word processor that is relatively inexpensive, to be a terrific tool for encouraging writing fluency for a wide range of learners, both with and without disabilities.

Planning and Organization

A considerable body of research suggests significant differences in the planning processes of experienced writers compared to novices (Bereiter & Scardamalia, 1987; Langer, 1986; McCutcheon, 2006). Although many children jump immediately to drafting upon being invited to write, some do rehearse their ideas orally first, speaking either to themselves or to others around them (Dahl & Farnan, 1998). Artifacts of their planning are often indistinguishable from their drafts. Older writers appear to delineate their planning from their drafting more easily than younger children, expanding upon their notes and discussing how their decisions related to the overall purpose of their pieces (Bereiter & Scardamalia, 1987).

These broad developmental trends notwithstanding, the research also indicates that writers with varying degrees of experience can learn to plan better if they are taught explicit strategies for doing so (Chapman, 2006; Graham, 2006; Graham & Perin, 2006). Collaborative talk among teachers and students may play a key role in supporting this sort of strategy acquisition. For example, in a frequently-cited study, Bereiter and Scardamalia (1987) found evidence that group interactions can promote a higher level of planning, even in very young children. The researchers found that when a variety of alternative ideas were presented in a collaborative setting, children were forced to weigh and analyze ideas before writing. In these cases, planning was much more conceptual and did not represent simply a mirror image of the composition itself (Dahl & Farnan, 1998, p. 55).

This body of scholarship suggests that teachers need to incorporate deliberate attention to planning and organizing into their writing instruction, and that they would do well to embed that instruction in meaningful social interaction. This will be especially vital for students with autism, who may have less experience with writing for a variety of reasons than their age peers, and who may, due to their communication and movement differences, be less able to facilitate informal social interaction around their writing for themselves without a teacher's careful assistance.

Planning and Organizing Texts: Considering Students with Autism

Very little empirical research has been conducted on composing processes used by students with autism, but our personal experiences and reading of the autobiographical literature suggests that some individuals on the spectrum struggle to plan and organize their writing. Some authors with autism report taking a stream-of-consciousness approach to their writing that makes it difficult for them to predict or control where the text will take them (Blackman, 1999; Williams, 1992). Conversely, others have experienced difficulty veering from a writing plan when the act of composing suggests a new direction that might be fruitful but that was not laid out in their original scheme.

Despite these trends, several authors have reported that assistance from other people has helped them in approaching their writing planfully, rather than too spontaneously or rigidly. For example, when 10-year-old Kenneth Hall, of Northern Ireland, decided that he wanted to write a book explaining Asperger syndrome to people working in schools, the Education Department where he lived sent a student to work with him weekly on planning and structuring the text. In the book, Kenneth reports with noticeable self-satisfaction:

> Michelle helped me by using index cards. First I had to decide all my section headings and have an index card for each one. This meant that all the proper information and ideas could be sorted into their proper sections. Later on I opened folders on the laptop for them all instead. (2001, p. 85)

With clear headings and subheadings for its various topics, Hall's finished text manifests the organizational help he received, suggesting that teachers who model and scaffold the use of such strategies explicitly can have a significant impact on the quality of students' composing.

Planning and Organizing Texts: Instructional Approaches

Most people, including those without disabilities, need explicit instruction from more experienced writers to develop a repertoire of strategies for planning and organizing their compositions that works best for them (Dahl & Farnan, 1998; Graham, 2006; Graham & Perin, 2006). A few instructional approaches that we have used to help students with autism acquire and refine these strategies include the following: Speak and Write, framed paragraphs, and story kits.

Figure 8.8. An example of a student's differentiated writing materials.

Speak and Write Because some students may find the initiation of or the idea generation aspect of writing difficult, teachers may want to seek strategies that simply get students to put something on paper (or on the computer screen). One such strategy that we call *Speak and Write* involves listening to student conversation or engaging in conversation with learners and suggesting which pieces of the discussion might be starting points for an essay, story, or other written product. Whereas many learners plan better on paper and with visuals in front of them, others may find this method too restricting in the early stages of organization. Some learners may want to do initial idea generation aloud and then move to traditional planning on paper for the next steps.

The Speak and Write strategy (or at least an unintentional form of it) is illustrated in Debra Ginsberg's (2002) memoir, *Raising Blaze*, about her adolescent son and her life's journey with him. The author tells of how Blaze came home from school and, as usual, began sharing stories of the day. Like many busy mothers, Ginsberg was distracted by another task and was only half listening to her persistent son; however, he finally caught her attention with his lyrical description of a classmate:

"Breanna was crying yesterday, Mom," he told me. "She was really upset."

"Oh, uh-huh?" I said, distractedly editing a poem about the color red.

"Mom, really," Blaze went on. "She cried and it was like a storm. Her face was all dark and light and quiet. She didn't make any sound but there were all these clouds and rain in her face."

This I paid attention to. "Blaze," I told him, "why don't you write that down? Write down what happened to Breanna yesterday. Just like you told me."

"Oh, okay," he said, as if this was a good idea that hadn't occurred to him. Blaze's difficulty with the physical act of writing inclined him toward brevity, so he was finished very soon after he started. He handed me his paper and when I read it, I had the same surge of joy that I felt whenever I had read anything particularly good.

When Breanna cried it looked like a storm
She didn't make any sound
but there was rain
and clouds
and sun
and darkness in her face

Blaze hadn't used any punctuation, so I added a couple of commas and periods. That was the extent of my edit.

"That's a really great poem, Blaze," I told him. "I love it."

"Really?" he said, disbelieving. (pp. 185–186)

Ginsberg then told her bewildered son that he needed a title and provided several suggestions such as "The Quiet Storm" and "Raining Tears," but Blaze, once again, surprised his mother with his well-chosen words: "'Breanna Crying,' Blaze said simply. 'That's what it's called.' Yes, I thought. Yes, indeed" (2002, pp. 185–186).

Framed Paragraphs   The term *framed paragraph* is used to refer to a paragraph with sentences that include carefully chosen blanks for students to fill in. Some instructors use framed paragraphs to help inexperienced readers understand how expository text structures such as description, comparison/contrast, or problem/solution are organized (Olson & Gee, 1991). Others use them to help scaffold students' writing by modeling what a successful paragraph in a genre or on a topic should include. Although framed paragraphs are most often used in language arts classrooms, they have applicability across the curriculum (see Figure 8.9 for a sample framed paragraph that a student used for a book circle discussion).

Framed paragraphs are a common way for teachers to engage students for whom the production of much text would be difficult in writing. For example, in their book on teaching literacy to students with significant disabilities, Copeland and Keefe described an approach to framed paragraphs that has the potential to build home–school connections, especially for students who lack reliable communication. The teacher they profile sent home a weekly questionnaire for families to complete that included check-off items such as the following:

This weekend I went to:
_____ mall
_____ toy store
_____ grandparents
_____ the lake. . . . (2007, p. 117)

This teacher then used the families' responses to construct framed paragraphs for journal writing for those writers needing the most intensive support. Some learners filled in the blanks independently, others used a model to write or trace the words, and still others selected pictures to complete the sentences. This approach allowed all students to produce some text about their lives that could be shared with others in the group.

Story Kits   Another way to help students plan their writing is to engage them with a *story kit*, a term we use to describe a bag or box of items related to a particular text, concept, genre, theme, or even author. A story kit for the popular intermediate-grade novel, *Island of the Blue Dolphins* (O'Dell, 1960), for instance, might contain a stuffed dog, a small toy canoe, a rock, some sand or water in a vial, and a dolphin figurine. Such a kit has multiple uses; it can be used to introduce, enrich, or save as a review for student readers and/or listeners.

Students also can participate in creating such kits. One teacher we know asked her first graders to help construct kits that could be used by all learners in the classroom, especially one child with Down syndrome who needed help understanding abstract concepts. A kit that the class spent weeks assembling was the one representing fairy tales, a theme they thoroughly explored. The kit contained finger puppets of a princess, a frog, three bears, a wolf, and a grandma; a "magic" wand; and a red cape. Students then used the kit as the catalyst for writing their own fairytales. Each child chose an item from the kit and wrote a story that was in some way related to that item. One student who chose the red cape developed a story about a flying princess who only had her special powers when she remembered to accessorize her cape with matching shoes or bag! See Figure 8.10 for an example of a story kit for *Curious George Goes to the Hospital* (Rey & Rey, 1973).

Revision and Editing

Since the 1980s, the terms *revision* and *editing* have entered literacy teachers' everyday lexicons to such a degree that many classrooms have posters on the wall listing them as discrete steps of the writing process, with revision usually preceding editing in the numbered sequence. We like that these terms are not used interchangeably because we think that they reflect different

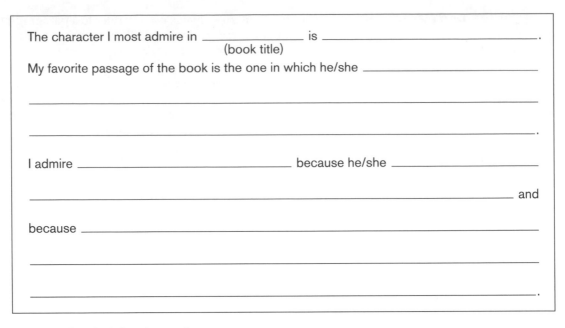

The character I most admire in _____ is _____.
(book title)

My favorite passage of the book is the one in which he/she _____

_____

_____.

I admire _____ because he/she _____

_____ and

because _____

_____

_____.

Figure 8.9. Example of a framed paragraph.

ways of thinking about text and they require different strategic processes. For us, Gere, Christenbury, and Sassi's distinctions are very useful: Revision is "best thought of as re-vision, re-looking, re-working of a piece of writing," while editing is "a look at a revised piece of writing to review and change word order and sentence structure and to check usage issues" (2005, p. 45). We think it's beneficial for teachers to talk with students about how revision and editing differ from each other, and we think that writers need explicit instruction about how to do both. The latter may be especially important with revision, because writing instruction—or perhaps more accurately, writing assessment—has historically paid more attention to correcting errors than it did to addressing structure or content (Russell, 2006).

Early proponents of process-oriented writing instruction suggested that students be freed to compose without expending too much energy on the niceties of conventions related to spelling, punctuation, and so forth until late in the process (Calkins, 1986; Graves, 1983). To do otherwise, in the view of these advocates, risked impeding the flow of students' ideas and focusing their attention on small details rather than the big picture. To a certain degree, this makes sense to us, especially given the research we reviewed earlier on writing fluency. A student writer who spends 3 minutes trying to figure out how to spell a word in the middle of a paragraph may forget what that paragraph was supposed to be about. It may indeed be a waste of time to edit a paragraph perfectly that might be cut from the piece entirely if it gets rearranged with a new opening and a different sequence—decisions that would fall under the category of revision for us, not editing. For these reasons, we subscribe to the general idea that it is more productive for most students to draft first, revise next, and edit later.

That said, we want to point out that our own writing, as well as the writing we've observed students doing in school, has led us to theorize that these processes are not always distinct from each other as they are carried out and that revision need not always precede editing. Therefore, we encourage you to think flexibly about revision and editing and to acknowledge how these processes are often recursive, rather than linear (Dahl & Farnan, 1998; Routman, 1994; Strong, 2006).

Considering Students with Autism

Students with autism spectrum labels vary greatly in their profiles where revising and editing are concerned. In our experience, those students who struggle to produce written text using conventional methods tend to have few experiences with revision and editing and receive little instruction in these areas. Some students with autism who draft with a fair degree of fluency report difficulties with revising and editing their compositions that are similar to those they experience with planning and organizing. Lucy Blackman, for instance, wrote about her problems as a teenager with envisioning how a reader would make sense of her text:

Figure 8.10. Story kit for *Curious George Goes to the Hospital.*

As a rule writing came in response to visual stimuli which had stirred up my internal language enough to link words spontaneously with what I had seen, rather than typing obliquely about what I had felt. Really, it never occurred to me, in spite of what I heard from teachers and friends, that the prime purpose of poetry was not to make word-pictures of my linked vocabulary, but to rework this so as to let someone else have the illusion they were sharing whatever it was I composed. (1999, p. 176)

Blackman tied growth in this area to general education literature classes requiring her to participate in a variety of peer-response activities, including one where she went over her poems line by line with a partner, explaining what she wanted to change about each one. As she recalled, "This conversation was kept, printed out, and included with the drafts in the completed project when it was handed in" (1999, p. 209). Although Blackman resisted making changes in some of the poems she considered to be most appealing in their current form (and what writer, with or without autism, doesn't engage in that sort of resistance from time to time?), she reported that these lessons made an impact on her thinking about her compositions:

This was the first time that I had corrected finer details in my own creative writing, as opposed to correcting factual or grammatical errors I had made. I could now start to see that it was the path to other people getting more pleasure and therefore more impact from my stories. (1999, p. 210)

Other individuals with autism report paying too much attention to what Blackman calls the "finer details" of their writing. Daniel Tammet reported getting stuck not on word choice but on the mechanics and surface features of writing itself:

I poured over every letter and word and period. If I noticed a smudge or error I would erase everything and start over. This stream of perfectionism meant that I sometimes worked at a snail's pace, finishing a lesson in a state of near exhaustion, yet with little to show for it. (2006, p. 50)

Jerry Newport points out that this tendency toward perfectionism can stymie writers with autism. In his book *Your Life Is Not a Label*, he speaks directly to people with autism about this characteristic:

The best writers misspell words. People make mistakes on national TV on quiz shows. Mistakes are an important part of life, so relax and stop trying to control your world because you are sick and tired of always being corrected and don't want to ever make a mistake again. (2001, p. 36)

This direct way of addressing the problem, and the person with autism, may be one effective strategy for supporting that individual.

At the same time, some individuals with autism demonstrate unusual prowess with conventions of writing, making them natural editors of their own work and perhaps of others' work as well. Spelling, for example, came prodigiously easily to Gunilla Gerland—so easily, in fact, that one of her teachers questioned the validity of her skill:

In that teacher's world, you simply couldn't be as good at spelling as I was. The way she saw it, I was afraid to make mistakes, so I looked things up in the book when we had spelling tests. But the fact was that I would never even have dreamt of cheating. . . . (1996, pp. 93–94)

Gerland's experiences remind us of the importance of teacher expectations in framing what can be seen about a particular learner in the classroom. They also point out that students with autism may be blessed with gifts related to writing as well as, or instead of, hurdles and obstacles.

In their valuable and teacher-friendly text *Children with Disabilities: Reading and Writing the Four-Blocks Way*, Erickson and Koppenhaver (2007) emphasized how critical the revision process is for students who do not communicate in conventional ways. When students write or type slowly or express themselves in incomplete phrases or thoughts, revision, they explain, can accomplish a number of instructional goals. Revision and editing of writing can help students, among other things, expand on their ideas, consider their word choices, and practice using any of their assistive technology supports or devices. These researchers share the story of a boy with autism named Eric, who views an image of a wounded bird and proceeds to write a story about it:

At first the child wrote "BIRDS OWIE HERTS." The following day a classroom aide worked with Eric to revise his text, asking questions such as: "How did the bird get hurt?" and "What do you think will happen next?" Eric's revision read as follows:

BIRDS OWIE HERTS
ARROW IN THE BIRD
BOY IS SADE
XSNDINT
AMBULINS

Eric then continued to add to his story with the aide supporting him in this work. Eric wrote another text for a subsequent picture that was very confusing to readers:

BIRD DINNER EATING BOY.
His teacher, aide, and mother could not determine if he meant the boy and the bird were eating together, the boy was eating the bird's dinner, or the boy was the bird's dinner. After revision, his text read:

BIRD DINNER EATING BOY
BIRDS EATING WERMS

Although this didn't clarify all the questions entirely, it suggested that he was writing about the boy eating dinner with the bird, who was eating worms. (Erickson & Koppenhaver, 2007, p. 91)

The researchers share that the aide's support during this activity was critical and that she was able to move Eric along in his writing because she understood key principles about beginning writing. She knew, for instance, to avoid putting words in Eric's mouth and to help him share his own message. She also asked several open-ended questions and gave Eric time to answer them. Finally, she understood that revision for many emerging writers involves adding new ideas and she, therefore, did not ask Eric to reorder and organize his text before he was ready to do so. This savvy educator also took notes on what kind of instruction Eric would need to be more successful as a writer (e.g., help with sentence expansion). In sum, she understood the purposes of and knew the tools associated with the successful revision and editing of student work.

Instructional Approaches

A number of approaches can help students learn to revise and edit their writing. Instructional approaches that can be specifically advantageous with these dimensions of writing that we have not previously profiled include the following: authentic audiences, teacher think-alouds, and editing checklists.

Authentic Audiences   One of the most important suggestions we have for helping students with revising and editing is to make sure that they have authentic audiences for their texts. Revising and editing are difficult processes for all writers, regardless of their experience level or dis/ability status. If the teacher is the sole audience for classroom writing (as is most often the case), it's a rare student writer indeed who can accept critical feedback and settle down to solving the problems in her text simply because those are skills that will earn her a good grade or translate into success in some distant work or college setting. In our experience, students work the hardest—and for the most sustained periods of time—when the piece in question has an audience whom they want to impress or convince. See Table 8.7 for ideas for authentic writing opportunities.

Teacher Think-Alouds   Just as teacher think-alouds are a useful way to demonstrate to students how to use comprehension strategies, they also can be a good instructional tool for teachers to model various approaches to revising and editing one's writing (Anderson, 2005; Atwell, 1998; Robb, 2004). Think-alouds are flexible because they can be done with nearly any size group, ranging from a whole-class modeling session to an individual conference, and with learners of any age. What's important is that the teacher makes her own composing processes both audible and visible to students by explaining her decision making in language they can understand while simultaneously demonstrating with an overhead transparency or a projected computer the changes she makes in her text. Successful revision and editing depend on such decisions, but learners (both with and without disabilities) typically receive very little explicit modeling about how to make them.

You might consider using a think-aloud with a text of your own to model any of the following aspects of revision and/or editing, including how to do the following:

- Reread a text aloud to yourself to see if any necessary words have been left out.

- Insert a caret (^) or asterisk (*) into a text to indicate that a word or sentence should be added in that spot

Table 8.7.   Creating authentic opportunities for student writing

Here are some scenarios you might consider, some of which require advance planning but some of which are fairly simple to facilitate:

- Invite students to create picture books on a theme or within a content area with younger children as their audience. Many young people feel a special responsibility to "get it right" when placed in a tutoring or mentoring role, and the opportunity to share the text personally with the younger children also can create authentic motivation for developing reading fluency through multiple practice sessions.

- Exchange a batch of student writing on the same topic or in the same genre with another class at your school, or invite each group to write pen pal letters about what they liked about each other's writing as well as what questions they have.

- Assign students to write a text in a particular genre—we've found that poetry and memoir work well—as a gift for a friend or loved one, possibly around a holiday or celebration (e.g., Mother's Day, a birthday). Some students write about an aspect of their relationship with the recipient; others simply want to produce their best work for someone who is important in their lives.

- Post samples of student work on a class or district web site. This option is appealing to many students because it allows students to use links, graphics, images, and sound effects in addition to print text. Encourage your students to submit their writing to local newspapers that often publish texts authored by young people on their editorial pages, neighborhood sections, or school beats. You also can be on the watch for contests that students can enter or calls for online publications to which they might submit.

From Kluth, P., & Chandler-Olcott, K. (2008). "*A land we can share*": *Teaching literacy to students with autism* (p. 170). Baltimore: Paul H. Brookes Publishing Co.; reprinted by permission.

- Choose a different image or symbol than was originally selected from a communication overlay to convey a change in your thinking.

- Decide on a spelling for a word from a set of choices generated by a word-completion software tool (e.g., the kind used in personal digital assistants such as a Palm Pilot or in other kinds of assistive technologies).

- Reread a text, looking for one kind of error (e.g., to make sure that all sentences end with a punctuation mark or that the right form of *their/they're/there* is used).

- Use the "find" function within a word-processing program to locate all of the instances of words that you habitually misspell.

- Highlight and copy/cut text within a word processing program to move it to another location in the text.

As we hope you can see from our list, these possibilities include skills that are appropriate for beginning writers as well as skills that require students to have more experience and sophistication.

Editing Checklists   Editing checklists are a useful scaffolding tool for student writers as they review their own work. When they are made public in the classroom, checklists serve as a concrete reminder of teacher-directed lessons, among other benefits. Jeff Anderson, a teacher in San Antonio, Texas, has written extensively about his use of the editor's checklist in his middle school English classroom. He posts a large piece of butcher paper on the wall, and he adds items to it such as "Check homophones: *there, their, they're*" or "Capitalization rules!" as he teaches them. He often enlists students' help in wording the items before they are posted, and he and his students occasionally decide to create additional posters with more specific information about a particular rule. For instance, he teaches the seven rules for capitalization before hanging them in the classroom to serve as a permanent reference. Once a rule has been discussed enough that students understand it, Anderson explains that students should now be accountable for checking it:

From now on, every time you finish a piece of writing, instead of saying, "I'm finished," I want you to look at this list and reread your work," correcting it for whatever area of focus has been added to the checklist. (2005, p. 46)

In some classrooms, especially at the elementary level, teachers help students to develop personal editing checklists in addition to or instead of classwide tools. We see these as useful tools for students with autism because they can be tailored to the peculiarities that these students sometimes exhibit in their writing. A writer such as Dawn Prince-Hughes (2004), a woman with Asperger syndrome who capitalized all nouns in her poetry, might be taught to isolate these words in her writing as she edits, adding Anderson's seven capitalization rules to her checklist. A student with less sophisticated writing skills than Dawn's could have a checklist with questions such as "Do all of my words have a vowel (*AEIOU*, sometimes *Y*) in them?" and "Do all my sentences start with capital letters?" As students learn to control new conventions, some questions can be deleted to keep the process manageable, and others can be added. The key consideration here, as with most aspects of teaching writing and other forms of representation to diverse populations, is to be willing to adapt the editing expectations to reflect students' current level of competence while stretching them toward new levels.

Consider that some learners may need desktop versions of these checklists. One student we supported liked to have certain editing rules stuck to his desk with hook and loop tape. Whatever rule he was focusing on at the moment would be secured to his desktop. He rotated several rules throughout the year, making new cards as needed.

Literacy and Students with Significant Disabilities

Think of a student with significant disabilities you know. Maybe he's the one who flaps his fingers in front of his face or dances alone in a corner or spends hours on end gazing out the window at passing trains. We want to be clear that, *yes, we mean that learner, too,* when we implore teachers to have higher expectations, to include, and to provide meaningful and varied literacy experiences.

In his landmark book *Schooling Without Labels*, Biklen (1992) described a boy, Melvin, who lived in an institution during some of his childhood years. Melvin, who did not have reliable speech, was seen by many at the institution as a "hellion" and as "having severe mental retardation." When he was adopted at age 8, however, his new mother saw a different person than the one described in his records. According to his mother, he emerged as a "bright little kid" (p. 24) after gaining membership in a home, school, and community. One of the most striking aspects of Melvin's story is how he was viewed as incapable of learning although he demonstrated complex, literate behaviors from an early age. For instance, while he was still living in the institution, Melvin (who at the time knew only five sign language words) managed to escape from his ward and order lunch from a neighborhood restaurant:

When he was still only 5 years old, he left his unit at the institution, went down to the ground level on the elevator, got past the receptionist at the admin desk and out the door. An hour later the receptionist took a call from the local McDonald's, two blocks away but across two busy streets. "There is a little boy here demanding a hamburger and I think he is one of the kids that has come down here with your folks," the caller announced. When the institution staff went to retrieve him, they found him making the sign for "eat." Obviously he knew where he was going. He knew what he wanted. (1992, p. 21)

After Melvin was adopted and moved from the institution to his home, his literacy development continued and his mother marveled at how quickly he developed new skills. One way Melvin was able to show his competency was through his acquisition of communication skills. Despite coming into his home with just a handful of signs, he soon knew two hundred. His mother attributed this growth in part to Melvin's attendance at their church where the service was signed.

Another story Melvin's mother told about his literate behavior was about his interest in a certain book. It seems she came upon him one day and his engagement with it was so apparent, it stunned her. Once again, Melvin was demonstrating literate behavior, and more importantly, confirming his mother's suspicions that he was a complicated, aware, and intelligent person:

> He was sitting on the couch quietly with a book open, just crying. I couldn't imagine what was happening. He had never had quiet moments like that at that point or at least very rarely. I just looked and didn't say anything. He was looking at *Christmas in Purgatory* [1966, an exposé of abuse in mental retardation institutions by Burton Blatt and Fred Kaplan]. He looked up and said "big house." It was like he recognized that this was about where he had been. I sat down and we went through the book together. He just cried. At this point he had very little language. It was just amazing to me. . . . He has shown me time and time again, "Don't underestimate me and don't judge me by your outside perceptions." (Biklen, 1992, p. 28)

This story is noteworthy for so many reasons. As Biklen pointed out, it is an important story about having an inclusive philosophy; it is also a story of seeing student strengths, questioning what we *think* we know about learners, and following the lead of students who have limited ways to show us what they know (Kliewer & Biklen, 2001). This story illustrates how vital it is to support the literacy development of students without reliable communication no matter how slow, challenging, or tentative the process may be.

Perhaps the most critical piece of supporting the literacy development of learners without reliable communication is inclusion in the classroom community. Consider the example of Rebecca, a "primarily nonspeaking" fifth-grade student with autism considered "preliterate" by professionals who had evaluated her (Kliewer & Biklen, 2001). The classroom teachers, determined to include their new student in classroom life, asked students to brainstorm ways to include Rebecca throughout the day. Some of the girls in the class thought of notes (the type that students typically pass to each other during class to socialize). The teacher recalls that students started passing notes to Rebecca, unfolding them, and then reading them to her. Over time, the teachers noted how interested Rebecca became when notes were read to her. Sometimes the notes would include questions such as, "Do you like James? Yes? No?" and the students would ask Rebecca to answer. After Rebecca started nodding her head at some of the questions, the teaching team constructed a yes/no board and built a range of literacy experiences around the note-passing experiences.

> Within the course of a single school year, Rebecca had gone from being perceived as nonsymbolic to constructing symbolic interactions with her classroom friends. Rather than requiring proof of symbolic competence prior to the development of relationships, Foster [the teacher] had turned the traditional equation on its head. Entrance into interaction constituted the terrain on which symbol literacy was recognized. In this sense, social engagement in specific, localized situations preceded demonstrations of intellectual competence and a more abstract definition of Rebecca as a thoughtful, engaged, and engaging human being. (p. 6)

Stories such as this remind us to question our assumptions, to look for student ability, and to provide the richest experiences possible for learners who may not always be able to show us—in the most conventional way—what they know and what they can do.

Table 8.8.   Supporting the literacy development of students with significant disabilities

Put students in situations where they can profit from hearing multipartner dialogue, eavesdrop on and participate in student-to-student conversations, and learn from the communication habits and abilities of others.

Use the closed-captioning function when showing students videos or educational television shows.

Include words and/or labels on picture schedules and communication systems. Often, students with significant disabilities work with pictures, icons, or symbols for years without having the opportunity to learn the words represented by the images.

Talk to students even if they cannot reliably communicate with you. Do more than ask questions or give directions; share ideas, give information, read, show, demonstrate, and communicate respect for the learner.

Teach and use augmentative and alternative communication with all students. Incorporate a few American Sign Language words into your teaching, have all students hold up communication cards (versus shouting out answers) for some lessons, or have all students occasionally dialogue on paper with a partner.

Always use age-appropriate materials and activities. If an older student cannot demonstrate literacy ability, resist using books intended for a primary audience. Instead try magazines, coffee table books, or comic books appropriate for all ages.

Look for alternative opportunities to hone literacy skills, especially for older students who may not have many opportunities to receive literacy instruction across the school day in their inclusive classes. For instance, consider extracurricular opportunities that allow for reading, writing, speaking, and listening opportunities.

Have students read to each other. Have students needing practice with fluency read to those who cannot read aloud. In older grades, look for opportunities to encourage reading in natural ways. For example, a high school drama teacher might have students read monologues to one another in pairs and then switch pairs several times so they can practice their "performance" repeatedly. The student with significant disabilities can listen to the work of peers while possibly being asked to respond to or critique the performance by using a yes/no board or picture board.

Create opportunities for students to constantly share information, socialize, and connect via reading, writing, speaking, or listening. For instance, have students share a joke of the day or keep a classroom newsletter going throughout the year.

Keep students involved in all aspects of classroom life (e.g., sharing secrets, being the "student of the week," voting for Prom Queen). Evaluate the structures and routines of the school (especially those that might have a literacy learning link), and consider how you might increase the participation of students with significant disabilities.

Encourage students to support each other, talk to each other, and share ideas with each other. Liberally use think-pair-share structures (Kagan, 1992), cooperative learning, class meetings, and small-group structures. These allow all students to practice communication and social skills and allow students with autism to interact, move, share, and practice new skills (e.g., initiating communication).

It is our belief that the next several decades of research on autism will illuminate just how much students with significant autism know, can understand, and have been trying to show us. For this reason, we hope that we have offered encouragement in this chapter to try something new and to be creative as we approach an area of curriculum and instruction that is largely unexplored. See Table 8.8 for a few ways teachers can support students with significant disabilities in inclusive literacy instruction.

Summary

As Luke Jackson (2002) points out in this chapter's introduction, students can surprise us at any time. Because of his own situation, Jackson reminds teachers that they should "never give up on a student who seems unable to read" (p. 117). We could not agree more with this statement and hope that, in this chapter, we have provided teachers with both a framework for thinking about their practice as well as many strategies to use in inclusive K–12 classrooms. It is also our desire that teachers take seriously our plea to create literate lives for their students with significant disabilities, as this population, for too long, has struggled to gain access to appropriate and challenging opportunities to read and compose.

Our last wish is for educators to see the research and stories shared in this chapter as a beginning. At this point, too little exists in the professional literature on teaching literacy to students with autism; therefore, we implore teachers to study their own practice; talk to others who are committed to teaching reading, writing, communicating, and listening to students on the spectrum; and, when possible, share what they know and have learned with others. In addition, teachers may want to learn what they can from their students, who, like Luke Jackson, may not only use literacy to "find doorways into other worlds" but to write so that teachers may learn.

FOR MORE ANSWERS AND INFORMATION

Books

Copeland, S.R., & Keefe, E.B. (2007). *Effective literacy instruction for students with moderate or severe disabilities.* Baltimore: Paul H. Brookes Publishing Co.

Downing, J. (2005). *Teaching literacy to students with significant disabilities: Strategies for the K–12 inclusive classroom.* Thousand Oaks, CA: Corwin Press.

Erickson, K., & Koppenhaver, D. (2007). *Children with disabilities: Reading and writing the Four-Blocks™ way.* Greensboro, NC: Carson-Dellosa Publishing Company, Inc.

Kliewer, C. (2008). *Seeing all kids as readers: A new vision for literacy in the inclusive early childhood classroom.* Baltimore: Paul H. Brookes Publishing Co.

Kluth, P., & Chandler-Olcott, K. (2008). *"A land we can share": Teaching literacy to students with autism.* Baltimore: Paul H. Brookes Publishing Co.

Web Sites

The Center for Literacy and Disability Studies
http://www.med.unc.edu/ahs/clds
> Visit this web site created to learn about the important work of Karen Erickson, David Yoder, and their colleagues.

Currents in Literacy
http://www.lesley.edu/academic_centers/hood/currentshome.html
> "Currents in Literacy" is an electronic journal published by Lesley University dedicated to exploring literacy issues from the perspectives of teachers, students, parents, and others.

Disability, Literacy, & Inclusive Education for Young Children
http://www.uni.edu/inclusion
> This web site, created by Dr. Chris Kliewer and his colleagues, contains articles, web links, and resources (e.g., photographs, stories) that can be used to create literacy opportunities for children with disabilities in inclusive classrooms.

(continued)

(continued)

Paula Kluth's web site

http://www.paulakluth.com/literacy.html

> This link will bring you to the literacy tab of my web site. Here, you will find several short articles on teaching literacy to students with disabilities.

Tar Heel Reader

http://www.tarheelreader.org

> The Tar Heel Reader is a collection of free, accessible books. Each book can be speech enabled and accessed using multiple interfaces.

NOTES: _____

_____

_____

_____

_____

_____

_____

_____

_____

_____

_____

_____

_____

_____

_____

_____

_____

_____

Rethinking Behavior

Until you stop trying to make us normal
and work on acceptance and understanding about us
individually, your attempts will be impossible. (Cutler, 1998)

On his first day of third grade, one of my former students, Todd, ran through the building, crawled under tables, banged his head against the floor of the locker room, walked away from peers who approached to assist him, and screamed throughout an entire unplanned fire drill. Teachers in the building were more than apprehensive about educating this student in our school. Todd, who came from a special school attended only by students with disabilities, seemed scared and confused in his new setting. At least two colleagues approached me to ask if I thought our school was the right place for Todd.

I was certainly nervous about working with Todd; I desperately wanted him to be successful and was unsure of where to begin in supporting him. At the same time, I was certain that our school was the best community for him. When my colleagues challenged Todd's placement, suggesting that he needed a more restrictive environment, I pointed out that he was new—not only to our building but to many of the routines, norms, and expectations of a typical elementary school classroom. It seemed that what Todd really needed was a chance to succeed as a member of the school community.

Prior to coming to our school, Todd had been educated with several students with significant disabilities (all of whom were largely nonverbal) for years and was, therefore, unaccustomed to socializing via games, humor, and school-age chit-chat. In addition, he was educated with two students who banged their heads when frustrated and—presumably from observing this behavior over time—had unfortunately also adopted this behavior. Further, he was seldom given instructional materials to handle on his own; therefore, he was not particularly careful with them or even potentially aware that he needed to share them with his 30 other classmates. Finally, he had been educated all day in one room, so changing environments during the day and navigating such a big school were initially very confusing for him.

Changes came slowly but consistently for Todd. Our staff watched and waited for success and it came. After spending a lot of time observing other students and engaging in typical school routines, Todd was able to use some speech and sign language to request a drink of water, a trip to the bathroom, or a favorite book. Students gradually learned his communication system and began socializing with him. Very slowly, his head-banging behavior (and all episodes of crawling) went away.

Within a few weeks, Todd learned where to put his belongings and materials in the classroom and began using a picture schedule to learn about daily activities. In time, he learned where he was supposed to be at different points in the day and stopped running around the building. His teacher then acquired a few small rocking chairs and some floor pillows and Todd stopped ducking under desks, opting instead to sit in his desk, on the chairs, or propped up against the pillows.

One of the most drastic changes we witnessed was Todd's reaction to fire drills. After seeing his panic on the first day, the school community worked together to help Todd prepare for future incidents. Teachers talked to the class about Todd's sensitivity and worked out a plan. During the next drill, two students flanked Todd the moment the alarm sounded and modeled how he could put his hands on his ears as he walked out of the building. Although he never grew accustomed to the noise, Todd's screaming ceased and he was able to tolerate the sporadic drills.

It took several months for Todd to acclimate, but after 2 months had passed, the staff marveled at how different this young man looked and acted. He continued to make impressive gains, and by his fifth-grade year, Todd was participating in all aspects of classroom life, engaging in the general education curriculum, and working collaboratively with peers. He even became a member of the track team and performed in a school musical. Although he once had a paraprofessional sitting next to him at all times, Todd now could work in his classroom with regular spot checks by his paraprofessional or special education teacher and help from peers.

The results, though impressive, were *far* from instant. And, many of the ideas tried were eventually rejected. In the end, we attributed the changes in Todd to persistence (his *and* ours). When one thing didn't work, we tried another. Perhaps most important, the team didn't try to "manage" or deal with behaviors; we worked on making Todd's day more comfortable, fun, productive, and successful.

It wasn't until the school hosted a team of visitors from another district that we all understood how important the commitment to inclusion (and to Todd) had been. The visitors, who were hoping to learn more about inclusive schooling, peered into Todd's classroom and watched him working for the better part of a morning. As the group gathered in the principal's office later that day, however, they lamented that "our model" of inclusion simply would not work for their teachers and their school. When our principal pushed them to elaborate, they explained, "Well, you are doing a great job here, but you have to admit that it is easy to include kids like Todd." Curious, the principal pressed on, "Kids like Todd?" One of their group clarified, "You know, kids that are so capable . . . without behavior problems."

Luckily, most of Todd's teachers did not have the same set of beliefs our visitor had. We did not believe, for instance, that inclusion was only possible for certain learners (those who came to us without behavior challenges). And, we did not believe that only students needed to make changes in order to create success. In fact, if Todd had been seen as "the problem," then teachers would not have created so many adaptations for him, they would not have given him so much time to learn about his surroundings, and they would not have made such significant adjustments to their own expectations or practices. Todd's teachers did not see him as "the problem," though. Instead, they viewed *the situation* as challenging and collaborated with Todd to make life at school better.

In this chapter, I attempt to help teachers create supports such as those developed for Todd—those that take the person's quality of life into account and help him or her learn and succeed in school in general. To this end, I will share some guidelines for assessing behavior challenges and creating solutions. To begin the chapter, however, I ask readers to consider their beliefs and assumptions. For this reason, the first section of the chapter is titled "What Is 'Behavior'?" and is about seeing and understanding behavior as personal and contextual. Following this discussion, I offer my top three considerations and cautions for teachers and teams who are in the position of solving behavior problems. It is my hope that the six ideas in this section will help teachers ask better questions as they address behavior concerns and, ultimately, make decisions that are both more generous and more effective. Then, I explore two questions that must be addressed before attempting to face any challenge: "Is the behavior really a problem?" and "Where is the problem?" Following that, I offer 10 ideas for supporting students on the spectrum. Each idea has been used across grade levels and is appropriate to consider for any learner in the classroom, including students without disabilities. Finally, the chapter ends with advice for dealing with crisis situations.

What Is "Behavior"?

Because the concept of "supporting behaviors" is so tricky, conceptualizing this chapter was difficult. In the special education literature, in teacher preparation courses, and in daily language, words and phrases are used that seem to suggest that behaviors such as screaming, hand flapping, and "noncompliance" occur in a vacuum, or worse—that they are located *inside* students. In reality, behavior cannot be set apart from curriculum, instruction, teaching and learning, relationships, school culture, classroom community, and many other factors and issues.

For these reasons, I attempt to discuss behavior as a phenomenon that is personal; no two individuals react in the same way to the same experience; even the same person on a different day or in a different moment may react differently to the exact same situation. I also treat behavior as contextual in this chapter; all behavior occurs under circumstances, in settings, and with people. An example that may help to illustrate the importance of understanding behavior as both personal and contextual comes from the autobiography of Lucy Blackman, titled *Lucy's Story*. Blackman describes how her behaviors can be confusing and even frightening to others if they are framed without an understanding of her life, her explanation, and information about the given situation. In this passage, she described how she would behave as a small child if someone tried to treat her as a friend:

The strange thing was that I could see the ridiculous and comic scenario in my mind's eye, but I could not alter the behavior. As the other person got more and more embarrassed, I became more and more "autistic." Once when I was 18 I was walking home from school. An elderly lady stood next to me at the pedestrian crossing. I assume she was concerned at my odd movements. She asked me if I were all right. Confused by the fact that she expected me to respond, I started running in a little circle.

My would-be benefactor was standing aghast, with the attitude of an affable bird mesmerized by a newly hatched snake.

So my weird social overtures (for that is what that behavior was) created inappropriate responses in others. This made it even more difficult for me to respond appropriately in return. I still do not turn and speak or sign when someone speaks to me.

I know that I should say, "Goodbye!" to the speaker after these one-sided conversations, but cannot spontaneously look at someone and speak. Instead I glance sideways and walk off, or wait for someone else to tell me that this is the moment to say farewell.

Occasionally when I am very relaxed and pleased to see someone in a place where I am comfortable, a wonderful flash of enchantment takes over. (2001, pp. 41–42)

Behavior as Personal

As Blackman (2001) rightly pointed out, her own perspective is critical if outsiders are to understand her behaviors in social situations. Without reading about the bus stop incident from her perspective, for instance, we might assume Blackman is not interested in other people or that she is incapable of understanding how to socialize with new people. Observers might even conclude that she is dangerous or violent. Such assumptions are often made because we are thinking about behavior from our own vantage point, assuming that everyone reacts as we do or even that every person with autism will behave in the same way for the same reasons.

Here, Blackman's story is key; she helps us understand more about her body, her reactions, her thoughts, and her *individual* needs. She also helps us see how complex human behavior is. Perhaps the most striking aspect of Blackman's story, though, is *just how wrong* most onlookers would be about the intent and function of her behavior (especially those not on the spectrum!). Keep the bus stop story in mind, and let it serve as a cautionary tale as you observe behavior, make observations, and create supports.

Behavior as Contextual

As Blackman stated, sometimes when she is very relaxed and pleased to see someone in a place where she is comfortable, a sort of magical feeling occurs. With this statement, she illustrated how much context matters; her behavior improves when the setting feels right. Of course, all of us experience fairly significant differences in behavior across environments. Our behaviors may also be influenced by the presence or absence of certain individuals, the time of day, the ways in which others are reacting to and interacting with us, and dozens (or perhaps hundreds) of other factors.

Considering context is critical; when a student is held responsible for "exhibiting a behavior," he may actually be communicating in the only way he can, responding to pain, asserting himself, escaping from an unpleasant or intolerable situation, or resisting the way he is being treated. It is critical, therefore, that practitioners solve all behavior challenges in context, with as much information as possible. When I am giving a seminar and am asked a question about behavior such as "How do you get a student to stay on task?" I commonly refuse to give a response. Without seeing the student and learning a lot more about the situation, I don't know if he can't stay on task because he is physically uncomfortable, because he doesn't understand the directions, because he is unable to do the work, because the room he learns in is too hot, or even if the task is appropriate for the person. Without this information at hand, even attempting to solve the "behavior problem" is not possible.

Behavior Support: Considerations and Cautions

Before diving into any assessment of behavior needs, it can be helpful to think about the tendencies, habits of mind, and beliefs we bring to our problem solving. When I work with teams, I like to take time to discuss how we think and examine current practices before diving into the creation of new ones. To this end, I offer three considerations and three cautions that may be helpful for teachers and teams to review prior to any formal analysis of students or their behaviors.

Considerations

The three thoughts offered here are simply too important to leave out of a chapter on behavior. In my opinion, the most comprehensive and carefully designed plan will fall apart if these morsels of advice are ignored or forgotten. Therefore, I try to remind teams of these three recommendations before any goals are written or plans are created: remember that language matters, focus on strengths, and put your own oxygen mask on first.

Remember that Language Matters

Attending to issues of perception and language are central to providing effective supports for learners with disabilities primarily because our beliefs about students affect the way we teach. Brophy and Evertson (1981) found, not surprisingly, that teacher expectations were tied closely to student achievement. Specifically, they learned that teachers' expectations that students will learn curriculum are positively related to student achievement. Therefore, educators must engage in constant reflection and interrogation of their words and their thoughts.

In his powerful poem "The Language of Us and Them," Mayer Shevin, a disability rights activist, highlighted the ways in which language has been used to stigmatize, ostracize, and—in some cases—dehumanize individuals with disabilities:

The Language of Us and Them

We like things.
They fixate on objects.
We try to make friends.
They display attention-seeking behavior.
We take breaks.
They display off-task behavior.
We stand up for ourselves.
They are noncompliant.
We have hobbies.
They self-stim.
We choose our friends wisely.
They display poor peer socialization.
We persevere.
They perseverate.
We like people.
They have dependencies on people.
We go for a walk.
They run away.
We insist.
They tantrum.
We change our minds.
They are disoriented and have short attention spans.
We have talents.
They have splinter skills.
We are human.
They are?
(Personal communication, March 20, 2002)

Why do we use language in these ways that privilege some and label or hurt others? Why is it that students with autism who have extraordinary talent are called "savants" whereas students without identified disabilities are called "gifted," "talented," or "geniuses"? Why is the label *at risk* used primarily for poor students (usually poor students of color), whereas wealthier students who struggle are thought to have learning disabilities or academic needs (Coles, 1987; Sleeter, 1986)? Perhaps it is the same reason we call young, socially disadvantaged

Table 9.1. Revising the language used to describe students on the spectrum

A student described as . . .	Might also be described as . . .
Stimming	Regulating
Having obsessions	Having interests, passions, or areas of expertise
Perseverating	Hyperfocusing
Hyperactive	Active, energetic
Using escaping or avoiding behaviors	Requiring breaks or frequent changes in activities
Being self-involved	Intrapersonal, introspective
Stubborn	Independent, steadfast, confident
Unable to _____ (e.g., sit for 10 consecutive minutes)	Able to _____ (e.g., engage for 8 consecutive minutes)
A "screamer," a "runner," a "biter," a "kicker," a "head banger"	One who communicates by _____ when he feels/experiences/is _____ (e.g., one who communicates by biting when he is scared or feels threatened; one who screams when he experiences sensory overload)
Social deficits	Social differences
Communication deficits	Communication differences

women "unwed mothers" but would never use this term to describe the single Hollywood star who gives birth. She, of course, is a single mother!

The importance of examining these labels is realizing that language does matter. It has an impact on the way we see a student, and it can facilitate or prevent us from offering meaningful support to learners. One way to think about perception is to use the Lead to Gold framework developed by Thomas Armstrong (1987), which encourages individuals to consider the negative language used to describe a particular learner and think about how the language, and therefore, the perception of the learner might be changed. For instance, a student who is described as "lazy" might also be seen as "relaxed," and one seen as "irritable" could be viewed as "sensitive." Keeping this framework in mind, teachers could review the language often used to describe students with autism (see Table 9.1 for some of my suggestions).

Questioning the discourse used in schools (Ayers, 2001; Broderick, Mehta-Parekh, & Reid, 2005; Henderson, 1992; Udvari-Solner, 1995) is critical to the work of a caring educator. The point of this exercise is not to hide important information but to closely examine the perceptions that educators bring to teaching. When I ask teachers to consider the Lead to Gold framework, some suggest that I am asking them to "sugarcoat" the description of the student or that I am ignoring real problems. I explain to them that I don't mean to suggest that difficulties they encounter in the classroom are not real or that teaching is easy if you just have the right attitude. I do think this reframing is helpful, however, because behaviors or characteristics of learners can often be perceived in many different ways, and, in many cases, the revisions are more respectful *and* more useful. To make this point, I often ask teachers to compare their two descriptions and then I ask them, "Is the new version as true or more true than the initial version?"

To see how one preservice teacher used the Lead to Gold framework to shift her perceptions of one learner, Ron, see Figure 9.1. As you can see, the same individual and characteristics are presented in each report. In the revised account, however, Ron's gifts and abilities are highlighted. As important, his needs are accurately described but not characterized in a negative way. From a practical perspective, the revised profile is also more useful. A teacher reading the first profile will likely feel discouraged about teaching a student with so many prob-

---

Who Is Ron? Two Profiles

When asked to describe a student who challenges her, a student wrote this profile of Ron, a middle school student with the label of Asperger syndrome:

* Unmotivated by academic work, hates math
* Bothers other students
* Disturbs others constantly by asking questions
* Obsessed with Michael Jordan
* Resists transitions, won't leave class when the bell rings

When I asked this student to assess the language she used in her profile, she realized that she used a lot of negative descriptions. We also discussed her feelings about Ron. She was feeling frustrated by not knowing how to help him, and this feeling of inadequacy was seeping into her perception of him. When she rewrote her description of Ron, I asked her to think about other ways Ron might be described. I asked her to concentrate specifically on things Ron could do and on his strengths but not to hide his struggles or needs. This is the revised profile she wrote:

* Very motivated by working with peers; learning about basketball and car racing; and reading books about magic, wizards and warlocks, and time travel
* Very social; enjoys working with others
* Inquisitive; will initiate conversations
* Likes to work collaboratively
* May need support to focus on individual work, needs to be reminded to raise his hand to ask questions
* Is an expert on basketball—especially knowledgeable about Michael Jordan
* Very interested in lessons related to sports (e.g., calculating shooting percentages in math) and is willing to teach others about sports
* Transitions are a challenge for Ron. He requires support before and during most transitions; it is helpful if a peer reminds him that it is "almost time to go" a few minutes before class ends.

Figure 9.1.   A revised student profile.

lems and will have absolutely no ideas about how to reach the student. A teacher reading the second profile, however, likely won't have negative feelings about the learner and will also have a variety of ideas for engaging, supporting, helping, and educating him.

Teachers interested in using language as a tool for change will also be interested in the work of educator Becky Bailey (2001). Bailey also suggests creating language makeovers but focuses on not just the language but the intent assigned by the teacher. For instance, the statement, "He keeps others from learning," assumes that the learner's intent is negative. The statement, "He needs work he can be successful at," however, does not. This second statement assumes that the intention of the child is not necessarily to be disruptive, and it also helps the educator to generate solutions. Bailey suggests that teachers work at moving from statements of negative intent to those that suggest positive intent. Engaging in this work, suggests Bailey, strengthens student self-esteem, helps students see the teacher as an ally, sets the learner up for a teachable moment, and serves as a positive model for students.

Still another tool that teachers can use to be mindful of their language and descriptions is the "birthday present rule." This rule—created by educator Cathy Apfel (as cited in Tashie, Shapiro-Barnard, and Rossetti, 2006, p. 121)—suggests that when you read a description of a learner, examine a report about him, or listen to his team discuss his profile, you should be able to generate an idea for a birthday gift for him. If you can come up with a great gift idea, you should well be able to come up with good ideas for teaching materials, positive behavioral supports, and lesson formats too.

Focus on Strengths

The way that we talk, think, and write about our students affects our practice. In addition, our perceptions of learners and the ways in which we communicate about them can serve to strengthen or damage our relationships with families. Consider the experience of Sheila Webster-Heard, the mother of a child on the spectrum:

> Shifting uncomfortably, I sat in my son's individualized education plan meeting trying hard to conquer fatigue. I was near tears and trying desperately to project an appearance of strength. My very first question was, "What are Darius' strengths?"
>
> In complete silence sat the principal, the psychologist, the speech therapist and her assistant, along with Darius' teacher, the case worker and the occupational therapist. My 7-year-old son had been in their presence six hours a day for a little over a month and none of them was able to think of anything good to say about him. Their obvious displeasure showed on their faces. . . . (2008, p. 61)

Certainly, collecting and monitoring the good news of our practice can help teachers gain and keep the trust of families; it also has the added benefit of making teaching easier and more effective. In the beginning of any school year, teachers can be seen scrambling to find strategies for responding to behavior problems of new students. This scramble often results in the generation of a whole new menu of ideas that may or may not have been tried previously. Instead of this reinvention of the wheel, teachers will feel more empowered and students will likely experience more success when the brainstorming process begins with everything that is *already* working!

For these reasons, I began using a simple document titled the Strengths and Strategies Profile (Kluth & Chandler-Olcott, 2007) when I plan with teachers, families, and students. This document, developed with my colleague, Michele Dimon-Borowski, can help educators focus on the abilities and strengths of learners instead of only on their difficulties and areas of need. As important, this tool also helps teachers pay attention to what is already working in the individual's program. The Strength and Strategies Profile consists simply of two lists that provide positive and useful information about a single learner. One list contains a student's strengths, interests, gifts, and talents. The other list answers the question "What works for this student?" This list should contain strategies for motivating, supporting, encouraging, helping, teaching, and connecting with the learner.

The Strengths and Strategies Profile can be used anytime for any purpose. I often use it to begin IEP meetings, but it also can be used as an attachment to a positive behavior plan or as a communication tool for teams who are transitioning a student from teacher to teacher or school to school. Although this tool is not complex and does not necessarily provide a team with new information, it can help teachers organize the information they have and understand it in a new way. The focus on positive language and abilities can prompt educators to think and talk about students in a more proactive way. It can also help teachers make changes in their planning and in their daily practice. Specifically, educators may be able to use these forms to do the following:

- Plan curriculum and instruction.

- Create curricular adaptations.

- Develop student goals and objectives.

- Design supports for challenging situations.

- Work more collaboratively with and elicit concrete ideas from families.

- Collaborate and communicate with each other.

See http://www.paulakluth.com/articles/strengthstrateg.pdf for a blank form that can be copied and used to create your own profile and for a completed example of a Strengths and Strategies Profile.

Put Your Own Oxygen Mask on First

Before takeoff on an airplane, as the flight attendants explain safety procedures, they always warn parents to put their own oxygen masks on first before assisting their children to do the same. This is a good metaphor for support in general. Before you can help others, you must have your own oxygen!

When I was student teaching, I discovered this need for "resuscitation." I had formed a close relationship with a high school student in my class. Typically, Patrick was an easy going and personable young man. One day, however, he had a falling out with friends and came into the classroom muttering, frowning, and kicking furniture. After I asked him to calm down, he picked up a chair and threw it in my direction. Although it missed me by more than a foot, the incident was upsetting, and I went home shaken.

When I got home, my host teacher called to check up on me. We talked for an hour; she shared some of her worst teaching moments and told me funny stories about her own student-teaching experience. This talk turned into a regular Thursday afternoon social engagement. We sometimes went to dinner or had coffee at a local bookstore. Other teachers and paraprofessionals in the department sometimes joined us. Although we typically talked about our lives outside of the classroom, these outings were also used as a time to process events from the work week.

These Thursday get-togethers became a way for me to get teaching ideas from my more seasoned colleagues, but they also served as a model for how to cope with stress and stay fresh and focused as a teacher. Teaching can be a very exciting job but an exhausting one as well. When the educational team is coping with a behavior problem, the work can be even more tiring. Noddings wrote, "An ethic of caring is a tough ethic. It does not separate self and other in caring. . . . If caring is to be maintained, clearly, the one caring must be maintained" (1984, pp. 99–100). Those who are engaged in a profession as intimate and dynamic as teaching need to pay attention to their personal needs and hone their coping skills.

Cautions

Although it is typically most useful to consider practices that may be helpful versus those that are potentially problematic, a few cautions must be issued in order to adequately address the topic of supporting behavior. In my work as a teacher educator and as a consultant, I try to help teachers form solutions to behavior based on the 10 ideas outlined throughout this chapter, but I typically begin problem-solving sessions by outlining at least three cautions: Realize the limitations of behaviorism, avoid removing students from the classroom, and do not focus on compliance as a goal. Although I could share a range of other cautions in addition to these, I choose to share these consistently because these approaches are so common across schools; and when teachers do not heed these three cautions, it becomes difficult to create behavior supports that are both sensitive and effective.

Realize the Limitations of Behaviorism

Behaviorism is the philosophical position that says that psychology, to be a science, must focus its attention on what is observable; it is a theory of learning that focuses on objectively observable behaviors (Skinner, 1976). Some have challenged the usefulness of behaviorist technologies, but Lovett reminded us that it is the *application* of behaviorism that is often reprehensible and not behaviorism itself:

> There is no reason we cannot pay attention both to research and to social realities. In working with persons [with cognitive disabilities], for example, we can use task analysis to make what is com-

plex simpler. But my experience is that many persons using behavioral interventions reduce complex social situations too simply. (1985, p. 64)

Even when the person designs his or her own behavior plan, the technology may backfire. Sue Rubin, a woman with autism, explained why rewards and consequences do not always work for her:

> Often [aggression and self-abusive behavior] are triggered by specific events, but sometimes they just happen. Maybe it is some kind of chemical imbalance. So if you are looking for an antecedent and plan on giving a consequence, [it] might be unfair. A negative consequence will change the behavior, but it will just be replaced by a different awful behavior. I actually asked for lost privileges to help control my behavior, but always understood that they were only bandaids and would be good for a short time. (Rubin, 1998)

Another reason to be cautious about behaviorism is related to its history and misuse. Behaviorist technology has too often been used to hurt, humiliate, or manipulate (Harris, Handleman, Gill, & Fong, 1991; Lovaas, Schaeffer, & Simons, 1965; Powell & Azrin, 1968; Tanner & Zeiler, 1975). For example, those who misuse behaviorist methods might reinforce "desire-able" behavior (e.g., making eye contact) without considering whether or not the person finds that behavior useful or try to change behavior by taking away materials or activities that the student needs in order to feel calm or safe (e.g., making a student earn computer time instead of building it into the daily schedule). And Gareth Nelson (as cited in Trivedi, 2005) a founder of the group, Aspies For Freedom, shares that successful behavior change is in the eye of the beholder. He points out, for instance, that although it is possible for many people on the autistic spectrum to force themselves to stop stimming, to do so requires such constant self-vigilance that it actually limits one's ability to take in and process information. Nelson says, "Any behavior can be stopped with enough willpower, but sitting in a classroom focusing on 'don't stim' rather than focusing on the work is obviously harmful" (p. 37). And Jane Meyerding, another adult on the spectrum, points out that "behavior" cannot be addressed in a vacuum; it is nuanced and may have important meaning to the person engaged in it: "Behaviors are so often attempts to communicate. When you snuff out the behaviors you snuff out the attempts to communicate" (as cited in Harmon, 2004).

Two approaches that are often used in behaviorist programs are 1) rewards and reinforcement and 2) punishment. I will examine both of these techniques and outline ways in which each can be misused.

Using Rewards and Reinforcement
Many of us use rewards and reinforcements in our own lives to alter our behaviors. We may buy tickets to a concert if we manage to stay within our budget for 2 months in a row or treat ourselves to dessert on Saturday night if we eat well during the week. These types of rewards are quite different from those used in school in that we design them, we are in control of monitoring our progress and we determine when and how we should follow through on the rewards.

When an outsider is involved in reinforcing and rewarding us, we may be less motivated and, therefore, less effective in meeting our goals. If my sister decided how much healthy food I needed to eat in order to get my dessert or if my mother determined how strict I had to be with my budget or my husband decided how much I could spend on concert tickets, I might well lose my urge to "behave." As Lovett explained, we need to pay attention to our own lives when supporting people with disabilities:

> Think of some chore around your house that you do not much like. Suppose you can cope with house chores except for making the bed, doing the laundry, or shopping for groceries—

something basically trivial but eventually unavoidable. Do you think you would do it more often if others around you automatically said, "Good bed making Karen!" (1985, p. 65)

In general, putting a great deal of focus on rewards and reinforcement to change a student's behavior results in frustrated teachers and students and, often, quite a bit of lost time and energy. Further, even when rewards do "work," the problem at hand may not be solved. A student who is rewarded when he doesn't pinch for 10 minutes might learn to quit pinching but begin hitting if the purpose of his pinching behavior was to initiate a conversation with others and his opportunities to interact remain unchanged. Consider the case of Joan, a young music lover:

> Each day when [Joan] returned home from school she would sit quietly for awhile listening to her favorite tapes. Her parents met with a psychologist to design a behavior program for Joan's behavior of destroying property. He started by asking her parents to list those things Joan found reinforcing. Music was at the top of the list. It was decided that her parents would hold Joan's cassettes. When Joan did not destroy anything all day she would be offered her choice of a cassette to listen to for a half-hour before bed. Joan's psychologist was shocked when the program was criticized—"but it's all based on positive reinforcement!" he insisted. (Weiss, 1999, p. 22)

In Joan's case, the program was anything but reinforcing and positive. The ways in which the psychologist used behaviorism failed to help Joan and her family understand her tendency to destroy things; it certainly did not provide Joan with any new skills or strategies; and it served to potentially eliminate one part of her day that already was calm, quiet, and relaxing. Instead of being helpful, this plan was both disrespectful and counterproductive.

Dan Reed (1996) shared a similar story about a man named Ted and his understanding of the fine line between rewards and punishments. As Reed recalls, Ted's program was being discussed by the staff of his group home. As they talked about his weekend schedule, one of the staff members suggested changing Ted's Friday activity from his longstanding pizza dinner to something new. At this point, Ted—who communicated with an augmentative communication system—grabbed his letterboard and typed, "DON'T TAKE MY PIZZA AWAY, I LOVE PIZZA." When the staff responded with surprise and commented that Ted didn't act like he cared much about the menu, Ted retorted, "IF YOU KNEW I LOVED IT, YOU WOULD HAVE MADE ME EARN IT" (p. 96). Ted's clear critique of the program illustrates how some learners may view our attempts at controlling them and shows how—in the name of management —we may put our relationships with people at risk.

Using Punishment   *Punishment,* in behavioral terms, is defined as the application of an unpleasant or aversive consequence immediately following an undesirable behavior. Common punishments include making students stay after school or assigning them extra work. Punishment follows a behavior and is intended to decrease the likelihood that the behavior will occur again. Therefore, if a student who is sent to the principal's office for talking during a lesson continues both the talking behavior and the visits to the principal's office, the consequence is not serving as a punishment.

Many common criticisms are given regarding using punishment in classrooms. One of the main objections to punishment is that it doesn't teach students what to do; it only teaches them what *not* to do. Spanking, for example, can be very effective in stopping a toddler from fighting with his sister, but it will not teach him anything about sharing toys or using words to communicate. In addition, the spanking may result in the child fearing the parent and, ironically, learning that it is sometimes okay to hit other people to solve a problem. Likewise, a student who is punished for getting out of his seat repeatedly may be able to stay in his chair after a punishment, but if he was getting out of his chair because he craved movement, he may feel anxious, restless, and unable to concentrate on the rest of the day's lessons.

Punishment is also criticized because it can cause students to distrust or fear adults. It may cause students to feel disconnected from the teacher and hurt the teacher–student relationship. This may be especially true for students with autism who have experienced physical punishment in the past.

Despite criticisms of punishment, teachers often use it because it is familiar. Sometimes behavior plans are developed because of the belief that students "have to learn" to behave. One of my former students often bit and kicked staff members; and as the days passed without much change in these behaviors, so did the frustration of the teachers and paraprofessionals supporting him. Even teachers who did not support him directly felt angry and approached me to suggest proper ways to discipline him. One teacher told me that I shouldn't let him "get away" with the behavior.

It became apparent after some time that the school community wanted this student to be punished—not necessarily for his benefit—but perhaps to "do something." Perhaps they wanted a punishment in order to cope with their own stress. Because staff members were being hit and kicked, they may have—consciously or unconsciously—wanted this student to be punished so that they could respond in some way to being hurt. Although it *is* certainly upsetting to be injured, punishing students (*especially* for behaviors that may be related to sensory or movement problems) typically does *not* make teachers feel better in the long run and does little to inspire new learning and build classrooms in which all students can feel secure.

Avoid Removing Students from the Classroom

I was visiting a school when I passed a child sitting in the hallway crying and sucking on his wrist. When I asked another teacher about the child she told me, "Oh that's Peter. He's out there more than he's in the classroom. He can't handle it."

I fear there are a lot of Peters out there waiting for opportunities to re-enter the inclusive classroom. Many students who are included in general education environments are only allowed in for a portion of the school day. Others are allowed in on a contingency plan; they can stay as long as they can behave.

During my first week of teaching, I was in a fifth-grade classroom co-teaching with a veteran teacher. Although she had never been a teacher in an inclusive classroom before, Ms. Goldman had been teaching for more than 25 years and had experience with students with a wide range of abilities, needs, skills, and gifts. During the first 10 minutes of the day, George, a student with autism, began to show signs of anxiety; he threw his notebook on the floor and then stood up and spilled the wastebasket. I was so anxious for Ms. Goldman and others to see how well inclusive schooling could work and was mortified by the situation. I walked over to George and began to guide him out of the classroom. At this point Ms. Goldman began chattering away, "Well, things get spilled in the classroom. George, can you sit down again please and we will get started." She got the students started on an activity and then walked over to him and helped him put the garbage back into the basket. While they worked she gave him information about activities the students would be engaged in that morning. Without hesitation, he helped her to clean up and took his seat.

I was surprised by George's reaction, but Ms. Goldman, the more experienced teacher, was not. She had been teaching long enough to understand that students are often anxious during the first week of school. Furthermore, by handling the situation *in* the classroom, she showed George that she valued him and wanted him to be a part of the community. Over time, Ms. Goldman was able to teach George ways to calm himself in stressful situations; she looked for signals that he was becoming agitated or overwhelmed by noise and taught him to self-manage by taking deep breaths or by pacing in the back of the room.

Any student may need to leave the classroom for a variety of reasons throughout the day, and it is important for students to have this option when they feel upset, sick, or angry. Furthermore, students may need to leave the classroom at times so that their dignity may be preserved; if a student needs privacy or wants a break, it should be provided. There is absolutely nothing wrong with having a place of harbor where any student can go to relax, calm down, or have a few minutes alone. In fact, all students should be given this option; and when a situation escalates, a student can be calmly reminded that he or she can use this space.

Students should not, however, be escorted out of the classroom every time they struggle or every time a teacher struggles *with* them. Too often, students with autism are asked to leave the classroom or are pulled out of educational environments without their permission. Faber and Mazlish asked people to put themselves in the place of a student who is isolated. "As an adult you can imagine how resentful and humiliated you would feel if someone forced you into isolation for something you said or did" (1995, p. 115). For a young person, however, this type of rejection can be even more serious because she may come to believe "that there is something so wrong with her that she has to be removed from society" (pp. 115–116). Vivian Paley reminded us that teachers send messages of exclusion and rejection when they isolate learners. These messages, in turn, affect the classroom community:

> Thinking about unkindness always reminds me of the time-out chair. It made children sad and lonely to be removed from the group, which in turn made me feel inadequate and mean and—I became convinced—made everyone feel tentative and unsafe. These emotions show up in a variety of unwholesome ways depending on whether one is a teacher or child. (1992, p. 95)

Perhaps the primary reason students should not be removed is related to the definition of inclusion; students should feel without question that they are members of their classroom community and they should not have this membership constantly threatened. Asking or forcing students to leave an educational environment may even cause new problems—both for them and for teachers; students removed from the classroom may feel rejected, hurt, or confused and, in response, may struggle academically, socially, or emotionally. Students who are removed also lose valuable content when they are away; they miss instruction, lose work time, and have fewer opportunities to interact and learn from peers.

Furthermore, students need to learn to negotiate behaviors in the most natural ways possible. They cannot learn social skills without opportunities to make friends. They cannot learn communication skills without interacting and working with classmates, and they cannot learn competencies related to behavior if they are not allowed to solve problems and work through difficulties with others in natural and authentic environments.

Finally, removing students from the inclusive classroom frames the behavior as the *student's* problem and prevents students and teachers from understanding behaviors as complex and socially situated. If a student is removed from the classroom, teachers are unable to see how the classroom community, the environment, the behaviors of others, and the curriculum and instruction might be affecting a student's actions, feelings, movements, and moods.

Do Not Focus on Compliance

The word *compliance* is often found in the school records of a student with disabilities. It is not as common in the records or reports of students *without* disabilities, however. Although general educators might assess the engagement, citizenship, or listening skills of a learner without disabilities, they typically do not talk about or report on how "compliant" students are. At some point, this term became part of the discourse and values system of human services and special education and, over the years, has driven many a behavior plan and educational program.

Weiss (1999) addressed problems with compliance by detailing the story of a student with disabilities named Laura. Laura was in a typical fourth-grade classroom, but instead of participating in the same activities and lessons as her peers, her teachers had developed a largely separate curriculum for her that consisted in part of engaging in sorting activities, playing matching games, and completing jigsaw puzzles. Laura showed little interest in this curriculum and seemed far more interested in the activities of the other fourth graders. For this reason, Laura would often wander around the classroom disrupting the work of her peers. When she was redirected back to her seat and her activities, Laura would often become upset, throwing her materials on the floor and occasionally even pushing the teacher. Weiss recalls that Laura's teacher labeled her as "noncompliant" and called in a behavior specialist to solve the problem. The teacher wanted to create a behavior program that would encourage Laura to stay in her seat, and attend to her work:

> The behavior specialist was happy to begin designing a careful system of reinforcement to assist Laura to achieve these behavioral goals. The ethical questions are clear. Simply because the technology exists to train Laura to be compliant in an inappropriate environment doesn't make it ethically acceptable. An astute teacher or behavior specialist would recognize Laura's behavior as one of the most objective critiques of service quality that they are ever likely to receive. (Weiss, 1999, p. 27)

The story of Laura shows how a focus on compliance can shift attention away from what really matters and prevent teachers from forming solutions that are creative, meaningful, and related to enhanced teaching and learning.

Another problem with compliance is that it teaches students the wrong things. Compliance can teach students to obey without question and to listen to adults at all costs. Students who learn to be compliant not only may be confused about why they are to do what they are asked to do but may also learn to comply with requests that are inappropriate or even dangerous. For instance, a student who is taught to be compliant might fail to question a fellow student who tells him to pull the fire alarm; or worse, a student who is taught to blindly follow any adult's command might follow a stranger's directions as willingly as those of a teacher.

Instead of compliance, students should be taught the same things students without disabilities are taught—to be good citizens, to cooperate, and to collaborate effectively with peers. A curriculum of self-determination should also be a focus for learners on the spectrum. Students who are taught self-determination will be able to protect and advocate for themselves. Furthermore, students who learn choice-making, decision-making, problem-solving, and goal-setting skills will be better able to help themselves around issues of behavior and may be able to help others offer the most appropriate supports.

Getting Started: Is There a Problem Here?

Now that the concept of behavior itself has been explored and key cautions and considerations have been outlined, attention can be focused on problem solving. To begin any discussion of behavior challenges, two key questions must be addressed: 1) Is this behavior a problem; and 2) if a problem exists, where is it? Each question is examined in the following section.

Is This Behavior a Problem?

A longstanding tradition exists in special education of eliminating or changing behaviors deemed challenging without fully exploring their function or message. Many people with autism are contesting this paradigm and suggesting new ways of coping with behaviors and bodies that work in atypical ways. Often, when a student exhibits an unusual behavior (e.g., hand flapping, verbalizing loudly), professionals move toward "extinguishing" it. Although it might be appropriate to help the student minimize some or even most interfering behaviors (especially those that may hurt the student with autism or others), in some cases, it may be more appropriate to focus on acceptance of the movement, quirk, or tendency or to work to understand it better.

For example, Marcus, a high school student, played drums in the school band. He was a skilled musician and could easily follow along as the teacher conducted, but he often parroted the teacher's directions. The teacher might say, "Okay, get your instruments ready," and Marcus would bellow the same command. This quirk didn't appear to bother the band members, but it upset the teacher a great deal. Although Marcus seemed somewhat embarrassed about his outbursts, he appeared to have little control over them. Over time, the instructor became increasingly frustrated with Marcus; after only 3 months in the band, Marcus finally quit rather than deal with the stress of his teacher's frustration.

What solutions might have been generated in order to support Marcus?

- The band teacher might have ignored the utterances.

- The band teacher might have asked Marcus to occasionally give directions.

- The band teacher might have asked all students to shout out the directions.

- The band teacher might have asked Marcus or his family about the utterances.

- Students might have tried giving Marcus different cues to speak more softly.

Dozens of other possible solutions to these types of perceived problems are possible if stakeholders are creative and open-minded. The following questions should always be considered: Is this behavior really a problem? What makes us believe it is a problem? Is it a problem for everyone involved or just for one person or a few individuals?

If educators fail to study behaviors in this way, they will offer "support" that is not supportive. Furthermore, they may attempt to change some behaviors that are problematic for teachers but helpful to the student with autism. For instance, a student who flicks his fingers may be using this behavior to tune out outside noise. A student who continuously spins or drops his pencil may be using the activity to relax or calm down after a difficult moment. A student who "refuses" to look at the teacher may be doing so in order to *listen* to the teacher's words more carefully. A student who rocks back and forth when asked to sit for long periods of time might find this behavior necessary for staying alert. A student who mumbles throughout the day might be doing so to process new information.

Furthermore, teachers should consider that they may be focusing on the behaviors of students with disabilities more so than those of other students. Reid and Maag (1998) found that in some cases, teachers expected students with disabilities to behave *better* than students who were not labeled or seen or as having behavior challenges. For example teachers expected students with attention-deficit/hyperactivity disorder (ADHD) to sit quietly and pay attention longer than students without this label.

One of my former students, Amir, experienced such discrimination when a few educators requested that he not ride the school bus with other students. These well-meaning teachers felt that Amir needed more supervision than the driver could provide. Most of us who knew Amir well felt that because he always seemed to relax when riding in vehicles he would be very successful on the bus. We felt that he might need some additional supervision and had considered assigning a paraprofessional to the bus, but given this extra support, Amir's family and his classroom teacher felt he should ride the regular school bus. To calm the nerves of all involved, a district administrator offered to ride the bus and observe Amir in order to put everyone at ease. The results were quite interesting; the administrator reported that the bus ride was chaotic but that Amir was one of the only students sitting quietly and following the driver's directions!

By sharing this story, I do not mean to imply that Amir did not perhaps need more supervision than the bus driver could provide; I do mean to point out, however, that our ideas about problem behavior are often as influenced by our students' labels as they are by their actual actions.

If a Problem Exists, Where Is It?

I was asked to consult with a school district about Phinney, a young man with autism. I went to visit Phinney in his high school. He was being supported by two paraprofessionals for most of his school day because of his "severe behavior problems." He sometimes hit staff members; he often slapped himself; and on more than one occasion he had thrown another student into a locker. This young man struggled as much with his schooling as he did with his body, however. After observing him and meeting with his family, it became clear that his educational supports were not well matched to his individual needs. For example, Phinney thrived when he was allowed to interact with other students, but he spent most of his day separated from his peers. Whereas many teachers and administrators saw Phinney as a student with challenging behaviors, a few teachers saw him as a struggling student who was working hard to cope under difficult circumstances.

When I told the building principal of my concerns about Phinney's education, he answered, "I brought you here to deal with the problem. First you need to tell us what to do about Phinney, then we can look at his program." I didn't know how to respond—Phinney was seen as *the* problem, so the approach to the problem had to be some treatment *of* him. I was stunned and felt I could offer little to this team in the way of support or suggestions. It was, in my opinion, impossible to do anything *to* Phinney that Phinney or his team would find useful. Clearly, many aspects of the situation would need to be examined. The problem was not only *in* Phinney and did not belong to him.

Phinney's behaviors, as I saw it, would not be reduced by creating a simple behavior plan. In this situation, changes in environment, curriculum, and educational program were necessary. The team may have started brainstorming solutions to their struggles by locating the problem. Was the staff frustrated? Did they feel prepared? Were they well trained? Was the school ready for inclusion? Were team members collaborating? Were Phinney's primary needs met? All of these issues needed addressing and as long as this team viewed Phinney as owning the problem, they were blocked from making changes that would help him and make their work with him more productive, successful, and enjoyable.

Ten Positive Ways to Assess and Support Students with Behavior Challenges

If a student with autism and his or her team decide that a particular behavior is problematic and needs to be addressed, there are several different ways to support the student and help the team. Here, I offer 10 ways to understand, cope with, and learn about behaviors. By considering some of these suggestions, a teacher may be able to appreciate a student's behavior in a new way or help him or her to make changes to it. These ideas are not offered as a recipe or as part of a linear problem-solving model. Rather, they are presented as a set of reminders that individual teachers or educational teams may want to review before a behavior plan is constructed or individualized education program (IEP) goals are drafted. These ideas may help teams as they reconsider their own attitudes and values related to behavior and help the student with autism become more successful in their classrooms.

1. Focus on Connection and Relationships

Perhaps the best way to better understand behaviors is to seek ways to connect with students and build relationships with them. This is especially important when students do not have a reliable way to communicate; these students cannot easily express themselves, so teachers must form relationships with them and their families in order to provide meaningful support. Pitonyak pointed out how making connections is central to the work of those who wish to provide effective support:

> The first step in supporting a person with difficult behaviors almost seems too obvious to state: *get to know the person*! It is too often the case that people who develop interventions to eliminate unwanted behavior do not know the person in any meaningful sense. They know the person as the sum total of his or her labels, but know little about the person as a "whole" human being. (2005)

Connecting with students can be accomplished in a number of ways. Some teachers make it a habit to explicitly convey caring. Expressing care can be especially important for students who are struggling academically or socially or for those being ridiculed or teased because they are "different."

Listening is another important part of relationship building. For students who can speak, listening will involve giving students time to share of themselves; eliciting stories from them; encouraging them to express themselves through drama, art, or writing; and getting to know them across contexts (e.g., in school, at home). For students who do not communicate reliably, listening may involve some of these same practices, but teachers will also need to pay special attention to a student's body language and behaviors. For example, if a student vocalizes, the teacher might "listen" by giving the student attention, showing concern, trying to interpret her distress, or simply letting her know she is being heard.

In my 2008 book *"Just Give Him the Whale!" 20 Ways to Use Fascinations, Areas of Expertise, and Strengths to Support Students with Autism*, my co-author, Patrick Schwarz, and I shared a story about Mr. Rye, a teacher who tapped into his student's interest in order to develop a relationship with him. Kip, who loves tractors, was shocked when Mr. Rye invited him to lunch and proceeded to ask him all about John Deere, Case, and other companies that the student revered. This was a turning point in Kip's education, as no teacher had ever treated his love of farm equipment as anything more than a tolerable quirk:

> [After being interviewed by Mr. Rye,] he became excited to go to school and his mother reported that he worked harder for Mr. Rye than he had for any other teacher. When Mr. Rye asked Kip to take risks or to challenge himself, the young man would take the charge seriously and work to impress his teacher. When asked the reason for his turn around, Kip replied, "I work well with Mr. Rye. We both love tractors. We understand each other." (p. 3)

2. If Possible, Get the Student's Perspective

Ryan was a high school student who spent time at the YMCA swimming and exercising as part of his school program. Although he seemed to enjoy his time at the Y, his teacher, Mr. Steib, could not get him to use the showers in the locker room. As Mr. Steib, explained, this aversion became a barrier:

> He loved the hot tub. That was like this huge thing to him—pie in the sky—sitting in the hot tub, but in order to get into the hot tub or pool you have to shower first. It's a Y rule, and it had been brought to our attention that Ryan needed to also follow those rules. So how were we going to get through the whole shower thing, because he fought the shower? I

had turned it on to what I thought was an appropriate, comfortable temperature or whatever and he wouldn't even get in there. (Kluth, 1998, p. 108)

When Ryan gained access to reliable communication, he gave his teachers an explanation for his behavior. Ryan's insight not only solved the immediate problem but also gave Mr. Steib and other teachers enough information to prevent difficulties in the future. Mr. Steib explained as follows:

 One of the days when Ryan was really "on" and able to communicate, I was able to ask him about why he didn't like to shower. [Using his communication board], he typed that it was too cold, that the shower was too cold and he said that he likes it extremely hot, so it's almost, not scalding, but extremely hot and now I don't even have an issue of going in the shower . . . because we turned that shower to hot. Now he goes in and he just grins ear to ear when he's in there. (Kluth, 1998, p. 108)

In this instance, Ryan was using behavior to communicate his discomfort in the best way he could. Ryan's story is an important reminder to examine every behavior from the perspective of the student, if possible. How does the student see the behavior? Is it hard or easy to control? Is it purposeful? Is it painful? Is it useful? Does the student want to stop engaging in the behavior? Does he or she view it as problematic? Is it something he uses to cope? Is it something he needs to stay calm? Often, individuals with autism engage in behaviors that look strange to others but serve an important purpose. Consider some of the ways in which people with autism explain their behaviors:

Sometimes I had to knock my head or slap it to feel it. (Mukhopadhyay, 2000, p. 73)

My failure to modulate or express emotions appropriately also makes me appear retarded. When someone comes to see me and I am happy, I sometimes run through the house or else I go to my room. I am happy, but the emotions overwhelm me.

   Appearances also contribute to the assumption of retardation. Many people with autism look quite normal, but some of us look goofy. We are also not well coordinated so we move inelegantly. (Rubin, 1998, p. 2)

[Asking house guests questions about the United States was] a form of escape for me. When I asked about Montana, for example, I would picture myself there instead of where I really was. I may not have had a very accurate picture of Montana in my mind, but I did know that it was far away from Ohio, and consequently, from me. So, in a way I was at least temporarily removing myself from the pain of my present situation. (Barron & Barron, 1992, p. 106)

[As a child], it was inconceivable to me that there could be more than one way to play in the dirt, but there it was. [My friend, Doug] couldn't get it right. And that's why I whacked him . . . being three years old was no excuse for disorderly play habits . . . I would use my mother's kitchen spoon to scoop out a ditch. Then, I would carefully lay out a line of blue blocks. I never mixed my food, and I never mixed my blocks. Blue blocks went with blue blocks, and red blocks with red ones. But Doug would lean over and put a red block on top of the blue ones . . . after I had whacked him, I sat down and played. Correctly. (Robison, 2007, p. 7)

I would move my hands a few inches from my eyes for hours on end, and feel at one with the leaves fluttering against the white pergola. In time the movement became a form of self-expression, so that even as an adult woman, when I feel very content, my fingers twitch in a formalisation of that movement. However, originally the finger movement gave me a means of analysing near and far, and could lend coherence to light and shade, much as a spinning peep-show did in a nineteenth-century fair booth. (Blackman, 2001, p. 11)

 [Rocking, hand-shaking, and chin-tapping] provide security and release, and thereby decrease built-up inner anxiety and tension, thereby decreasing fear. (Williams, 1992, p. 213)

 Screaming was my only way of telling Mother that I didn't want to wear the hat. It hurt. It smothered my hair. I hated it. (Grandin & Scariano, 1986, p. 17)

Ronny, who would raise women's skirts over their heads, said he did so to keep people from getting too close to him. Close touching, he claimed, made him feel as if he were being smothered. He knew if he took the offensive, people would avoid him. His actions helped by keeping them away, but he also hurt because he was alone. (Reed, 1996, p. 94)

These descriptions are insightful and even surprising. Few would assume that someone who lifts women's skirts is communicating a need to be left alone or that rocking and hand shaking can provide security. These accounts can help practitioners learn more about life on the spectrum, realize misconceptions, and craft supports that individuals will truly view as supportive.

3. Prioritize Prevention

Andrew, a fifth-grade boy on the spectrum, constantly had difficulties during recess. The recess monitor often had Andrew stand against the wall of the building as a punishment for chasing girls or running through the kickball game. For some time, Andrew's team spent time trying to generate new consequences for this behavior. The principal had another idea: Why not look for ways to make the playground experience more successful and interesting instead of inventing ever more powerful responses to his behavior? Using the principal's idea, the team came up with a list of illustrated activities Andrew enjoyed on the playground. They gave Andrew this list to take outside so he always had ideas for spending his time. In addition, the group asked a few of Andrew's classmates to spend a week of time teaching him rules to common games such as tetherball, kickball, and four square. These students even spent two recess periods indoors researching rules on line (as many students played by invented rules) and provided copies to each classroom so everyone playing would have the same set of guidelines. Finally, they allowed Andrew to pick another student with whom to have indoor recess on Fridays. During this time period, the two were given a pass to play chess in the library.

With all three of these adaptations in place, Andrew's negative behaviors decreased dramatically, and for the first time, he showed an interest in joining in structured games. Andrew's situation illustrates that many of the problems we see in schools can be prevented. Some take just a bit of creativity. Others, in truth, may take creativity and willingness to brainstorm, troubleshoot, and keep trying when the first, second, and third ideas don't work!

Prevention is paramount when addressing behavior challenges (Baker, 2008). To engineer preventative strategies, teachers must consider the potential difficulties students may have and—one by one—strategize ways to sidestep those difficulties. For example, if the student always seems to have problems during transitions, brainstorm specific strategies that can be used to ease the process. If the student gets upset when he hears loud noises, put a plan in place for these instances. If the individual resists certain kinds of work and escalates when pushed to finish tasks, create a list of all of the effective strategies that family and staff members have used to help him take risks or complete work. See Table 9.2 for a list of additional ideas related to prevention of behavior problems.

> **Table 9.2.** Ideas to use in the prevention of behavior problems
>
> Look for competence in students and see the best in them.
>
> Be respectful. Speak about students using positive language and never speak about students in front of them.
>
> Look for sensory offenders. This might be something that those without autism do not even notice, such as a flickering light or a sound in the distance.
>
> Make sure the person experiences joy, novelty, and fun at school. Lessons should be appropriately varied, favorite topics and activities should be included in the curriculum, and students should have plenty of opportunities to shine.
>
> Make sure the person has opportunities for social connection and relationship building (e.g., games, free time to talk) throughout the day.
>
> Always be sure the learner has a way (or many ways) to communicate. If the person is nonverbal or does not have reliable speech, he or she will need augmentative and alternative communication for socializing with peers, responding to the teacher, and engaging in lessons.
>
> Provide plenty of opportunities for movement throughout the day. Build walking or sensory breaks into the day for the purpose of regulating and releasing tension. When an individual seems especially frustrated or "off," look for opportunities for vigorous exercise (e.g., taking laps with a friend on the playground).
>
> Teach by the numbers. Help the student to recognize and interpret feelings that lead to a breakdown. Use a number scale or similar tool to have the student describe and visualize his emotional state. Then teach about different scenarios. For example, if the teacher starts class 5 minutes late, he might put himself at 2/10 on the scale; if his piano teacher is sick and misses a lesson, it might rate a 6/10. Teaching and discussing this process during calm moments makes it more likely the student will be able to draw on the language and descriptions when he needs it.
>
> Be explicit about rules, norms, procedures, and expectations. Students' behaviors may be their response to a confusing world. Provide a list of school and classroom rules in a student's notebook or desk as well as a list of ideas he or she can use to relax and deal with difficult moments.
>
> Think beyond smiles and frowns. Avoid categorizing each hour or segment of the day as "good" or "bad," as in, "How did you do in math?" and, "Were you good during first period?" Many behavioral programs put students in a position of being evaluated and assessed day in and out (e.g., a smiley face for a segment of good behavior and a frown for a segment of bad behavior). This constant scrutiny can be very stressful.
>
> Break it down. Chunking big tasks down into more manageable parts can prevent some difficulties. A child will probably respond better to a request to "pick up ten blocks" than to "clean up the play area."
>
> Adapt if possible. Assess the student's environment to see which tasks or activities cause problems and whether these can be avoided or adapted in some way. For instance, if the child gets into trouble on the bus when he sits near older students, assign him a seat mate, allow him to play a video game during the trip, or offer him extra credit for observations he makes during the ride (e.g., how long the bus takes to get to his house on average).

4. Talk to the Student's Family

I am always amazed at how family resources are underused. Parents offer expert advice and teachers must take advantage of it. When I taught kindergarten I became really stuck on how to support a little boy who did have speech but wouldn't or couldn't talk at school. He also seemed confused when we gave him directions or asked him questions. I called his mother and asked, "Could you come and work with me for an afternoon?" She agreed and this collaboration led to powerful problem solving. She initially seemed reluctant to provide suggestions, but after I asked her to watch me and take notes, she came up with several ideas that I was able to draw on throughout the year. Among other things, this parent told me to use a louder voice with the student. She told me, "I don't use such a low voice; you could try speaking a little louder or even singing your questions a bit—he likes that." She also suggested that if I wanted him to talk more, I should ask him about his dog or show him pictures of my pet. This feedback was as helpful as a key opening a lock. Although this parent's suggestions may not seem especially earth shattering, the information was exactly the type of feedback I was seeking.

In another instance, I called on a parent to help me with a student's spitting behavior. Every day during lunch, Mike would take a big gulp of his milk and then spit it out, sometimes on the table and other times on his classmates. I was confused; the parent survey I collected at the beginning of the school year reported that Mike often drank milk and that he wasn't allergic to it.

At first, Mike's classmates were understanding and tried talking to him about the incidents. Over the next few days, however, students began to avoid sitting near him. Because Mike was new to the school, I was desperate to find a solution quickly; I felt that every day I failed to help him, I was jeopardizing his chances for social success.

Mike did not have much reliable speech, so it was difficult to get information from him about the spitting, but I did explain *to* him that he was upsetting other students. That didn't work either. Then I hypothesized that the cafeteria was too loud for him. I removed him and, instead, invited a few students to join him for lunch in the classroom each day. Mike didn't seem to mind eating in the classroom; however, the spitting continued.

Finally, I decided to call Mike's mother. I invited her to school to simply proactively "review Mike's program." She agreed to visit the school, but I was still too insecure to ask for her advice directly. Instead, I asked her to sit in on some of Mike's classes and give me general feedback. Mike had never been educated in an inclusive setting before, so I felt she would appreciate an opportunity to observe. Mike's mother was pleased with the morning and agreed to follow me to the lunchroom at noon. We arrived as Mike was about to open his milk. At this point, I mentioned the spitting to his mom in a nonchalant manner: "Oh—I almost forgot—does Mike ever spit out his milk at home, because he has done that once or twice here." As I spoke, we both turned to Mike at the moment he spit a mouthful all over the young woman sitting next to him. His mother turned to me and said, "Oh that's easy. He hates chocolate milk."

I love this story because there are so many lessons in it. This is a story about learning to be an effective teacher and approaching problems from different angles. It is also a story about asking, "Where is the problem?"; we may assume that a student has a problem when in reality, it is the situation that is problematic. Finally and most important, it is a story about listening to families.

Families often can tell us a great deal about autism, but more important, they can tell us about *their child*. In the case of the chocolate milk described above, Mike's mother knew that her son automatically drank whatever was put in front of him (in the past he had gulped his grandmother's hot coffee, his father's beer, and even his baby sister's bottles) and we had been giving him chocolate milk every day because we assumed that most kids preferred it. She also knew that he spit when he didn't like what he had ingested. In this situation, *only* the mother had the information we needed and only the mother could help us provide the proper support. The "consultation" provided by Mike's mother was free of charge, completely effective, and helped us to see our student in a completely different light.

5. Use the School Community

I once worked with a first-grade student who was tormented by the sound of crying. If a parent brought a wailing baby into the school or if a peer started whimpering or shouting, Gino came unglued. He would scream and drop to the floor in agony. Although these episodes decreased gradually, they were difficult for Gino and heartbreaking for his teachers. During the episodes, nothing seemed to calm Gino—even his parents were at a loss for solutions.

In one instance, Gino was walking down the hallway with his classmates when a child from the preschool class came running in from the playground with a bloody lip. The child was sobbing, and soon Gino was, too. Two teachers rushed to calm Gino, but nothing seemed to relax him. At that moment, Jerry, the school custodian, was walking by and stopped to help. We told him Gino would be fine and waved him away. Jerry made no move to leave and we became flustered by his attempts to help. Three of us were now surrounding a little 6-year-old boy and, gauging from Gino's reaction, none of us were offering any comfort. Suddenly, Jerry began singing to Gino in Italian. Before we had time to tell Jerry that singing wouldn't work, Gino had stopped screaming and was staring at Jerry with his huge brown eyes. Jerry finished one song and sang another while helping Gino to his feet and walking him back to his classroom. My colleague and I looked at each other with amazement.

If Jerry taught me anything, it was that students with autism can and should be supported by all members of the school community. It certainly "takes a village" to educate students (both those with and without autism) and every member of the school community should be considered a potential collaborative partner. Support might come from a secretary, the librarian, a volunteer, a PTA member, the school nurse, or the campus security officer.

Students also can be great supports for each other. Many insightful teachers I know use peers as resources and help all students understand that they have a responsibility to support one another. Although students are not often viewed as collaborative partners, they often thrive in this role. Sometimes students see and understand things that adults do not.

I once worked with a little girl named Yee who loved to go to physical education class but hated to leave. When it was time for students to line up at the door, Yee would screech and run into the supply closet. She told us that she "loved the gym" and wanted to stay all day. In order to make Yee more comfortable, we had the physical education teacher visit her kindergarten classroom to give suggestions about how we might give Yee more opportunities for movement during daily lessons. The physical education teacher also let Yee lead some of the clean-up activities so she would have a concrete way of transitioning from one classroom to the next. Both of these supports seemed effective, but the most powerful support came from a little girl named Jillian. Jillian noticed that Yee was getting distressed after physical education class and offered to buddy up with her during that time. Without being asked, Jillian started approaching Yee after class and whispering in her ear, "Okay, Yee . . . we need to leave pretty soon. Okay, Yee?" We wouldn't have predicted that this gentle warning would be effective; yet these simple interactions worked wonders. The girls began pairing up for clean-up activities and then leading students out of the gymnasium as a team.

How did a child provide something an adult could not? Maybe Yee was comforted by those specific calming words or by Jillian's small, caring voice. Maybe Yee was confused about the routine and Jillian helped—in just the right way—to ease her through the sequence of events leading up to leaving the room. Maybe Jillian provided understanding or compassion in a way others could not or did not. Pinpointing why this peer support works so well is certainly difficult, but assessing its benefit is not. Peers are a rich, underused, and plentiful resource that should be used liberally across grade levels.

6. Assess and Adapt the Environment

A mother recently approached me to ask about her son's dangerous behavior in her minivan. Her teenager had recently started behaving in an agitated manner when she drove him to school. He would sometimes thrust his upper body so far out the window it frightened her, occasionally grabbed at the steering column or the rearview mirror, and once tried to open his door and jump out of the van. She asked if I had any ideas for dealing with a child who refuses to stay seated. I always struggle to answer questions such as this one, as it is almost impossible to brainstorm when I can't see the behavior or consider all of the possible causes.

Together, we began to pick the situation apart piece by piece. I asked her when the problem started and she said the behavior had been escalating since the beginning of the school year. We talked a bit about problems at school, and I asked if he might he be trying to avoid the destination. She didn't think so because he was engaging in the same behaviors after school and at other times, as well. She hypothesized that it was about a recent move and that, potentially, he didn't like the new routes or location and was disoriented. We both thought that was plausible but wondered why he didn't seem upset when his father drove him to swimming lessons or when his grandmother took him to his religious education. We turned our attention back to the van and, after a series of questions that yielded little information, I asked if the van was new or if it had recently been cleaned. "No," the mother replied sheepishly, "That thing is a mess! I never clean it; I just keep hanging new air fresheners!" We looked at each other with the same thought and her mouth dropped open. She then explained that at the beginning of the school year she had also spruced up her van with a new garbage can, new carry-alls for the kids' materials, and an air freshener with a new scent! Suddenly, the attempts to get the windows open, to grab the mirror (where the freshener was hanging), and to escape made sense. To solve this problem, we didn't need to do anything "to" the young man; the intervention was needed for the van itself!

This story is a cautionary tale and should serve as a reminder to always assess the environment when behaviors erupt. Students may require adaptations to classroom lighting or seating. Or, they may need some tips on how to stay comfortable in places that are not "friendly" to their needs.

Keep in mind that whereas some examples of environment change are large and schoolwide, other effective changes can be very minor. For example, a teacher who had a student with auditory sensitivity asked all of his fourth graders to cut holes in four tennis balls and stick the balls on the feet of their chairs. This adaptation cut down on the noise created by 30 students moving their chairs all day and greatly reduced the stress (and related behaviors) of the student with sensory problems.

Helpful questions that can help us evaluate learning space for individual students include the following:

- How does the noise level in the classroom affect the student?

- How, if ever, is music used?

- What materials are in the environment? Are they adapted for the learner? Age appropriate? Varied?

- What types of visual inputs or cues (e.g., picture schedule) are in the room?

- Is the lighting appropriate? Is it too bright or too dim for some learners?

- What seating options does the student have?

7. Teach New Skills

Vicki loved to play with the dollhouse in her classroom, but she had a hard time sharing the toy if others approached to play with her. Her response to peers who approached her was to gather up as many dolls as possible and put them in her pockets so other children couldn't use them. This, of course, caused a lot of frustration for other students and almost always ended with one or more children in tears.

In this situation, the teacher could have warned Vicki that she would be removed from the doll corner if she continued behaving in this way, or she might have asked other students to give Vicki time to play in the dollhouse on her own each day. Instead, she taught her young student some new skills that helped her share toys and play more cooperatively.

The first skill the teacher addressed was sharing. All students were taught a quick strategy to divide up the dolls; anyone who wanted to play with the dollhouse got to choose one doll from the shoebox in the doll corner. If there were still dolls in the box after everyone chose one, students took turns choosing again and so on until all of the dolls had been selected.

Then, the teacher taught the girls to take turns as the "head of the house." Using a timer to keep the intervals equal, students get a set amount of time to be the head narrator of the game and to, therefore, direct the play. She also taught the girls to say, "Your turn!" when they switched roles.

It took Vicki months to feel comfortable with the new skills, but by year's end, the students no longer needed such rigid parameters and were able to shift the "head of the house" on their own and without a timer.

This is just one example of how teachers can deal with challenges by teaching new skills. Sometimes we go for a "shortcut" response to behavior that will solve it temporarily, but teaching new skills, when possible, is likely to provide more long-term success. Many different types of skills might be taught, including communication, social, academic, and functional or self-help.

You may also want to teach skills specifically to help students feel calm and gain control of themselves during challenging moments (Baker, 2005; Schwarz & Kluth, 2007). *Progressive relaxation* is one such skill. This technique involves a protocol of tensing and releasing various muscles of the body from the head to the toes (Cautela & Groden, 1978). The beauty of this technique is that once students are taught the steps, they can employ them at any time, without adult support. When teaching this exercise to students with learning difficulties, it may be useful to share either an audio recording of the steps or a visual representation of the technique (such as photographs of the different steps).

Role play is a technique that helps students try new behaviors, language, and experiences in a low-risk situation with teacher support. For instance, if it is hard for a student to take turns on the classroom computers, you could role play how to request a turn, wait without interrupting peers, and play games or navigate web sites cooperatively. Teachers can create or write the mini-dramas for students, or learners themselves can take the lead in setting the scenes and acting out the various parts.

Visualization is the art of creating a mental model of a situation. It is controlled, directed, and purposeful; and it can be useful to any student in the inclusive classroom. "Seeing" oneself achieving a goal (or behaving in a certain way) has a way of making the brain believe that attaining that goal is possible. Students might use visualization for dealing with a bully, calming down during an altercation, or even managing anxiety before a test. When teaching the exercise to students, suggest that they add details (e.g., have them imagine words they will speak and clothes they will be wearing), embellish it (e.g., tell them to add background music), and create a vibrant image that they can "view" over and over again.

8. Evaluate Curriculum and Instruction

Although most conversations about behavior are centered on the learner and his or her needs and challenges, teams seeking lasting change must look at how and what the student learns and how he is being taught. One problem I see in working with teams across grade levels is a mismatch between the curriculum and the student's interests and abilities. When a student is struggling, especially when he or she is struggling in one environment or subject area more than others, teachers should consider whether the content or the instruction needs to change. For instance, in one "inclusive school" I visited with my colleague (Kluth & Straut, 2001), all of the students in the classroom were engaged in a social studies stations-teaching lesson and were using computers, sorting fossils, and answering teacher questions. Reese, the student we came to observe, was not only uninvolved in the lesson but was in a corner coloring a worksheet when we arrived. He was evidently not thrilled about this task as he repeatedly told the paraprofessional at his side that he was finished and tried to escape to the bank of computers more than once. My colleague and I were confused as to why Reese was not involved in the lesson, especially because it was so appropriate for students with various abilities.

When we asked about Reese's participation, we were told that the teachers felt he needed to work on his IEP objective of following three-step directions, so they gave him a worksheet that required him to 1) find shapes, 2) color them, and 3) share information about the finished picture. The irony, of course, was that nearly every station in the classroom asked students to follow multistep directions and, had he participated in that lesson, he also would have had the opportunity to learn about fossils and archeology while honing both his communication skills (answering teacher questions), his social skills (such as his IEP objective targeting appropriate interactions with peers), and his computer skills.

In my classroom visits, this type of scenario is seen too often. Some of the most common causes of challenging behavior in students with autism include the following:

- Curriculum that is dull and lacks variety (e.g., same flashcards or worksheets are used repeatedly)

- Curriculum that is not age-appropriate (e.g., a 9-year-old still working on number, letter, or color identification)

- Instruction that is a poor match for the individual's learning style (e.g., a very active student who is required to sit for long periods of time)

- Instruction that is incompatible with the learner's challenges (e.g., asking a student with fine motor problems to write all assignments longhand instead of allowing typing; assigning work with directions that are too complex)

- Not enough opportunities for communication, conversation, and choice making (e.g., a nonverbal student participates in lessons without augmentative and alternative communication)

- Not enough social interaction (e.g., too much learning in one-to-one settings)

- Not enough fun or joy in the day (e.g., not enough of the student's interests embedded in activities, few novel or exciting elements in lessons)

Students who experience these challenges in curriculum and instruction may respond with negative behavior. Although teachers may not be trying to make the day difficult (or even be aware that they are), it is certain that some behaviors are "inspired" by curriculum and instruction. Teachers can alleviate this problem by gathering information about student learning style in the beginning of the year and acting on the information they receive. Challenges also can be averted if the teacher differentiates instruction and offers a wide range of lesson formats, teaching strategies, instructional groupings, and assessments throughout the year.

9. Be Willing to Adapt

Years ago, I was asked to observe a middle school student named Micky. The principal told me that Micky was disturbing other students because he often chewed on his notebooks. I asked if the staff had tried asking Mickey about the situation. The principal told me that they *had* asked Mickey and he said having gum would help him stop chewing on the notebook. This sounded reasonable to me and I told the principal as much. She told me that while it did seem to be an appropriate response, it could not be implemented because the school did not allow students to have candy.

Consider also the story of Guy, a young man who needed some simple adaptations to make it through the school day. Guy constantly disrupted lessons because he arrived late to his classes, struggled to find a place to sit, and often did not have the necessary course materials. Although some of his team members had ideas for adaptations, seeing them implemented would not be so simple:

> After discussions between his mother and [a special education administrator], it was suggested that he should be allowed to have a fixed desk at which to sit in every lesson—preferably at the

back of the class where he would be less of a distraction to other pupils. In each classroom the desk would also contain the minimum equipment necessary for him to cope with the lesson (paper, pens, ruler, etc.). Some teachers were happy to implement these suggestions and in their classes Guy's behavior improved rapidly. Others refused to change long-established teaching practices and in these classes his behavior remained highly disruptive and erratic. (Howlin, 1998, p. 244)

Both of these stories illuminate how behaviors are facilitated or even created when students are not allowed access to the adaptations and supports that they need. In the beginning of this chapter, I noted the importance of seeing behavior as personal and contextual. Guy's situation is a perfect illustration of how behaviors are *not* fixed realities; when teachers work to understand students and their needs, undesirable behaviors can be minimized or eliminated. Guy's "behaviors" disappeared or were facilitated by each teacher's willingness to provide him with the seating he needed.

A meeting I had with a student's family and my building administrator helped me to understand the potential power of creating adaptations and working toward solutions instead of focusing on problems. The team was concerned about Matt, a young man who would frequently run out of his classroom and into the schoolyard. Once there, he would jump on the swing, at which point he would burst into tears if his pursuer refused to push him on the swing. Matt repeated this behavior approximately five times each day. When we tried to lock the doors near his classroom (terrified he would run into the street at some point), he would make a break for the library and jump on the hammock hanging in the corner.

Everyone felt that Matt must need the input the swing could provide, but none of us wanted him to continually miss out on the activities, interactions, and opportunities provided in his general education classroom. My boss, a district administrator, piped up during the meeting, "Matt shouldn't have to go to the swing, the swing should go to Matt," and proceeded to draw out plans for installing a hanging basket swing in the back of the first-grade classroom. All of us—the first-grade teacher, Matt's mother, my boss, the school principal— got excited about the idea and began planning ways in which we would naturally integrate this piece of equipment into the classroom. We decided that the swing would become part of a reading corner and that all children would have opportunities to use it when Matt was taking a break from it.

I left that meeting upbeat and with a new understanding of how teachers could think about adaptations. It was the first time I had seen a team of professionals treat "inclusive schooling" as an action (versus as a phenomenon that was or was not appropriate for a given student). That is, the stakeholders in Matt's education—especially the administrators— challenged themselves to make inclusion happen for him; they worked toward including him until it happened instead of declaring that inclusive schooling wasn't for Matt because he needed too many adaptations.

10. Do Something Else

Supporting behaviors is often trying work. I have driven home from work in tears on more than one occasion, frustrated by behaviors I didn't understand, terrified that I was hurting a student by not being able to respond to his or her needs appropriately, and frightened that those around me would see that I didn't know what I was doing after all. During one of these low periods in my teaching career, a friend read me an attitude-altering story about observing a desperate creature:

There's a small fly burning out the last of its short life's energies in a futile attempt to fly through the glass of the windowpane. The whining wings tell the poignant strategy: Try harder.
But it's not working.

Table 9.3.   Ideas for "doing something else"

Do nothing. Think: Is action required? Is it okay not to act?

Ask a different question. Instead of asking how to stop the behavior, you might ask, "Is there any other way to understand this behavior?" or, "Is this behavior necessarily negative? Is it ok in any context at all?"

Talk with people who care about the person; discuss the behavior from different angles and, instead of trying to solve it, just try to ask better questions.

Consult with someone new (e.g., the student's grandmother, an adult with autism, the crossing guard, the student's best friend).

Try to understand the behavior another way, from a completely different perspective (e.g, how would an artist, an athlete, a CEO see this behavior?).

Capture the student on video to see if you can get more information by watching the same situation many times.

Quietly observe the situation for a few days instead of intervening.

Journal or write about the concern to see if an answer emerges, or have the student journal or write about the concern.

Consider making a home visit to get more information about the student's life beyond school.

Confide in the student, telling him or her how you are feeling about the situation.

Schedule a series of lunch meetings or soda breaks with the student or with a student and a friend to learn more about him or her.

The frenzied effort offers no hope for survival. Ironically, the struggle is part of the trap. It is impossible for the fly to try hard enough to succeed at breaking through the glass. Nevertheless, this little insect has staked its life on reaching its goal through raw effort and determination.

This fly is doomed. It will die there on the windowsill.

Across the room, ten steps away, the door is open. Ten seconds of flying time and this small creature could reach the outside world it seeks. With only a fraction of the effort now being wasted, it could be free of this self-imposed trap. The breakthrough possibility is there. It would be so easy. (Pritchett, 1993, p. 222)

This simple metaphor helped me to understand the need to continuously approach problems from different angles, to step back and view the difficulty in another way, and to occasionally resist the urge to "do something" when a struggle arises. Sometimes thinking outside of the box can help individuals and teams find solutions that they could not uncover by doing more or working harder. See Table 9.3 for a list of "something else" ideas you might try with your students.

Dealing with Crisis

This chapter would not be complete without providing some guidance for crisis situations. The supports teachers use in crises are sometimes different from those they use in other situations; therefore, special treatment of this topic is needed. Here, I offer advice for remaining calm and for getting out of crisis.

Remaining Calm During a Crisis

Reflect on the last time you lost *your* temper. Did you yell? Scream? Did you say things you would later regret? How did you feel when you were engaged in these behaviors? Embarrassed? Furious? Lonely? When most people are in this type of crisis, they need gentle support to calm down. They may need to take a walk, curl up with a favorite book, find a place to be alone, or call someone who will listen to their problems. When we are coping with our own crises, we realize that gentle approaches are the only way to decompress. This same philosophy is critical to use in our schools.

Recently, I was visiting a preschool and I saw a teacher use this gentle approach with a child. As I walked in the front door, I immediately heard a piercing cry. I couldn't yet see the child, but any teacher or parent hearing this wailing would recognize it as "the real thing." In other words, these screams did not belong to a child who was merely tired or cranky. They belonged to a frightened, angry, or otherwise wounded child. I listened for the teacher's voice. Was the child being punished? Was someone scolding him? Was he even with a teacher? I began to walk faster.

As I rounded the corner, I relaxed as I saw the child sitting on the floor in the arms of a teacher. I immediately understood why I didn't hear her voice amidst the screams; she was talking to him but she was whispering. I stood watching them from a distance, touched by this gifted teacher's poise and grace. The boy's sobs subsided as she stroked his back and continued whispering to him. She had a compassionate look on her face and her body communicated acceptance. After 3 or 4 minutes, the child was calm and the two stood and walked back into a classroom. For the rest of the day I thought about how gently she had treated his crisis.

To be gentle during a crisis, a teacher need not hug or hold a student, although this is sometimes quite appropriate. It may be enough to touch the student's hand, arm, or back in a reassuring way; ask how he or she wants to be helped; sing a favorite song or repeat a calming phrase; or simply to keep one's own body relaxed. An individual experiencing stress will most likely *not* be helped by the following:

- Loud voices

- Punitive statements (e.g., "You had your chance," "You just lost your reward")

- Confiscation of preferred or comforting materials or activities

- Physical redirection

- Angry tone or body language

Although a student experiencing challenging behaviors might need to know how the behavior is being interpreted or might benefit from information related to the behavior, it is seldom, if ever, appropriate or useful to intervene in these ways while the behavior is taking place. One of the most critical skills a teacher can have is the ability to be calm and comforting in a crisis situation. When a student is kicking, biting, or screaming, he or she is most likely miserable and scared. The most effective and humane response at this point is to offer support, relax, and help the person feel safe. For more ideas on dealing with crises, see Table 9.4.

Getting Out of a Crisis

When I was working with teachers at one high school, they found that communicating a common protocol to all staff members—including general education teachers, paraprofessionals, and therapists—was nearly impossible. To make staff responses to crisis more uniform and to be sure that everyone was "on the same page" philosophically, I worked with them to create the CALM (Comfort, Avoid contact, Lower voice, Manage) protocol (see Figure 9.2 for a description of each step of the protocol).

The CALM protocol reminded everyone, first of all, to *comfort*—to be as gentle as possible and to keep in mind the most important rule of crisis management, which is to *get out of crisis*. The second step of the protocol—*avoid contact*— is a reminder of the team's commitment to keep their hands off of students unless it is absolutely necessary to do otherwise. Not only is contact at this point likely to escalate the situation, but the risk of injury becomes higher for

Table 9.4. Ideas for dealing with a crisis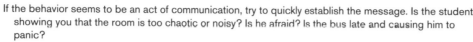

If the behavior seems to be an act of communication, try to quickly establish the message. Is the student showing you that the room is too chaotic or noisy? Is he afraid? Is the bus late and causing him to panic?

Consider any medical or physical cause of the behavior. Is the person in pain or experiencing discomfort? Some outbursts (especially those that seem to come out of the blue) may actually be seizure activity. Epilepsy is not uncommon in people with autism and can be difficult to diagnose due to both the communication and sensory differences of those on the spectrum.

Do not try to teach. When a student appears to be losing control or is already out of control, it is not an appropriate time to make threats, review what the consequences will be, remind the learner of the upcoming punishment, or even teach about what the individual needs to do to avoid such a crisis in the future. The goal during crisis is to get out of the crisis situation.

Keep a low and calm voice. If you raise your voice or use threatening words, the student will, most likely, pick up on this, and the crisis may escalate.

Try walking without talking. Do this not in a punitive way (i.e., cold shoulder) but rather to communicate solidarity, peace, and calm.

Remember that inappropriate and difficult behavior often can be linked to high levels of anxiety. Consider how you might help the person to relax in these situations. Meditation, self-talk, and taking deep breaths can be helpful to some.

Bring the demands down. If the individual is struggling because the task is too difficult or because there is too much going on at once, move the person to a calmer environment, reduce the requirements of the task, or redirect them to an activity or task that is less stressful.

Find a favorite. In some cases it may be necessary and appropriate to let the student have access to preferred materials or activities (e.g., a comfort object).

Do something unusual that the person might not expect and may find soothing. Try singing softly, counting to one hundred, or grabbing a notebook and drawing a comforting "message"; any of these may serve as a distraction and help the person shift attention away from his or her discomfort.

the student and the staff member alike. The third step—*lower voice*—helps the teacher or other staff member check their body language and communication. As students escalate, we as teachers need to de-escalate, drop our voices, and keep a calm exterior. There is a chance the student will be able to follow our lead. In addition, we preserve the person's integrity when we use this step. *Manage*, the final step, refers to keeping the area and the situation under control by 1) checking to be sure each step is being followed, 2) keeping other people away unless they are needed (a hand signal or code word can be used to get help if necessary), and

Comfort

    Keep in mind that your goal is to get out of crisis; be as soothing as you can to the person to help him or her calm down.

Avoid contact

    Do not touch, hold, or restrain the person unless absolutely necessary.

Lower voice

    Drop your voice to a whisper as you assist the person; others in the environment should not be able to hear your words.

Manage

    Keep extra adults away unless absolutely necessary; as much as possible, avoid having others look on or offer comments.

Figure 9.2. Team protocol for supporting students in crisis—CALM.

3) providing any supports the person needs to get out of crisis. This may involve getting preferred materials, giving the person information, or just waiting with the individual until the situation is over and he or she regains control. When the crisis is over—and only when it is over—evaluating, discussing, and teaching about the situation can commence.

Summary

As I have attempted to convey in this chapter, we will not be able to support students effectively until we begin to treat behavior as something that is personal and contextual. Too many students are excluded because they are thought to "own" their behaviors and because these behaviors are assumed to be problematic and unchangeable. Teachers seriously need to question these beliefs and this tradition of exclusion. Although behavior can certainly pose a challenge to individuals with autism, their peers, and their educators, it should not serve as a barrier to inclusive schooling. In fact, inclusive schooling may be exactly what students with challenging behavior need most. The story of Todd in the beginning of this chapter teaches us that, ultimately, we need to face challenges with both ideology and practical solutions and develop ways of supporting students that resonate with the beliefs and values we want to promote in our inclusive classrooms and schools.

FOR MORE ANSWERS AND INFORMATION

Books

Bailey, B. (2001). *Conscious discipline: 7 basic skills for brain smart classroom management.* Oviedo, FL: Loving Guidance, Inc.

Davis, K., & Dixon, S.D. (2010). *When actions speak louder than words: Understanding the challenging behaviors of young children and students with disabilities.* Bloomington, IN: Solution Tree.

Dunn, K., & Curtis, M. (2004). *The incredible 5-point scale: Assisting students with autism spectrum disorders in understanding social interactions and controlling their emotional responses.* Shawnee Mission, KS: Autism Asperger Publishing Company.

Lovett, H. (1996). *Learning to listen: Positive approaches and people with difficult behavior.* Baltimore: Paul H. Brookes Publishing Co.

Mahaffey, H., & Newton, C. (2008). *Restorative solutions: Making it work.* Nottingham: Inclusive Solutions UK Ltd.

Schab, L. (2008). *The anxiety workbook for teens: Activities to help you deal with anxiety & worry.* Manassas Park, VA: Impact Publications.

Web Sites

The Alliance to Prevent Restraint, Aversive Interventions and Seclusion
http://aprais.tash.org
The Alliance is a group that has formed to end aversives. If you know a child who is in danger of being injured at school, you need this site.

(continued)

(continued)

Crafting Gentleness
http://www.craftinggentleness.org

> This web site invites visitors to "consider the practice of gentleness."

Gentle Teaching
http://www.gentleteaching.nl

> This site focuses on fostering gentle support in our schools, especially for students with significant behavioral needs.

Imagine Consulting (David Pitonyak's Web Site)
http://www.dimagine.com

> David Pitonyak's site offers many useful and thought-provoking articles on behavior (including a few in Spanish). This is a great site in particular for those supporting teenagers and adults.

The Incredible 5-Point Scale
http://www.5pointscale.com

> Two teachers, Kari Dunn Buron and Mitzi Curtis, developed this site to share ideas for reducing student stress and anxiety.

NOTES: _____

_____

_____

_____

_____

_____

_____

_____

_____

_____

_____

_____

_____

_____

_____

_____

Inclusive Pedagogy

Before I came to an inclusive school,
I never got a chance to learn in a classroom that taught
academics but I was all ready to learn. It made me feel so sad and angry.
(F. Wilson, personal communication, May 2, 2000)

Amy, a colleague of mine, once asked me to observe a lesson in her second-grade classroom. Jalen, a student with autism, had just joined her class and Amy was concerned about providing an appropriate education for him. I agreed to observe a lesson on prisms and light. Amy began by outlining instructions for an activity in which students were going to create kaleidoscopes and make observations about light and color. The lesson was clearly explained before students began their work. Amy circulated around the room and provided both verbal and written directions (complete with simple diagrams). She then set paper, markers, and other supplies out on a table and sent the students up in pairs to retrieve materials. Jalen and his partner, Ty, were sent to the table first. During the activity, Amy rotated from student to student, answering questions and giving assistance. Jalen and two other students in the classroom seemed to need a lot of help assembling the small parts of the kaleidoscope, so Amy asked all of the students to work on the assignment with their partners. Each pair had to answer questions about the activity and fill in a worksheet. Because Jalen had a difficult time with the worksheet, Ty filled in the answers while Amy asked Jalen a few questions verbally to give him an opportunity to show his understanding of the material in a different way.

After the lesson, Amy asked me what I thought. She was sure that I would be able to tell her some way to enhance her lesson, and she was equally sure she had done something wrong. With this particular lesson and this particular student, however, I did not think any changes were necessary. Although any teacher can find some way to improve any lesson, I found the kaleidoscope activity to be extremely appropriate and engaging for Jalen, Ty, and all of the other students in the classroom. The teacher created an active and interesting lesson that incorporated the needs of all students and provided individualization for Jalen when he needed it. In other words, Amy was using what I am calling *inclusive pedagogy*. In this chapter, I will define that term as well as describe how, in a step-by-step fashion, teachers can plan lessons in K–12 classrooms that meet the needs of all of their students.

What Is "Inclusive Pedagogy"?

Since the inception of inclusive schooling, scholars and practitioners have used many different terms to describe curriculum, instruction, and assessment that meet the needs of diverse learners. Udvari-Solner (1996) proposed a reflective decision-making model for creating curricular adaptations and responding to all students. Tomlinson developed a model of "differentiating instruction" to illustrate ways in which teachers can "shake up" what goes on in the classroom and give students "options for taking in information, making sense of ideas, and expressing what they learn" (1995, p. 3). Oyler (2001) used the term "accessible instruction" to describe the use of democratic practices and the development of learning experiences that challenge and support all students. In this book, I use the term *inclusive pedagogy,* which incorporates tenets drawn from all of these models to describe a process of meeting the needs of all learners in diverse classrooms.

The first time a general education teacher finds a student with an identified disability on his or her class list, he or she may feel unprepared to support a learner with such a label. I have often heard teachers say that they are "not trained in special education" and, therefore, cannot be effective with students with disabilities. Although it can be beneficial to know about autism before teaching students with that label, teachers are most effective when they show acceptance, look for strengths in learners, provide personal attention when necessary, and allow for differences in the ways students approach tasks and complete classroom work. That is, teachers are often practicing inclusive pedagogy when they are simply engaged in good teaching. Consider the following examples:

- When a teacher allows students different ways to express their understanding of a novel (e.g., taking a test, designing a piece of art related to the book, giving a speech comparing the novel to other works), she is using inclusive pedagogy.

- When a teacher uses cooperative learning approaches and assigns students roles that will challenge them as individuals, he is using inclusive pedagogy.

- When a teacher provides students with a range of materials to teach photosynthesis (e.g., real plants, plastic models of plants, encyclopedias, interactive software), she is using inclusive pedagogy.

- When a teacher makes informed decisions when grouping students for instruction, he is using inclusive pedagogy.

- When a teacher allows some students to stand, stay in their chairs, or sit on the floor during whole-group instruction, she is using inclusive pedagogy.

- When a teacher gives students opportunities to support and teach each other, he is using inclusive pedagogy.

- When a teacher shows students how to complete an assignment by demonstrating it and by providing the directions in writing, she is using inclusive pedagogy.

- When a teacher designs lessons around the interests and experiences of students, he is using inclusive pedagogy.

Table 10.1 provides more information on what inclusive pedagogy is and is not.

Table 10.1. What inclusive pedagogy is not and what it is

What inclusive pedagogy *is not*:	What inclusive pedagogy *is*:
An approach designed primarily to meet the needs of students with disabilities	An approach that benefits all learners, including those who are racially, culturally, and linguistically diverse as well as those with a range of skills, gifts, strengths, needs, abilities and disabilities
Adaptations that are "tacked on" to predeveloped lessons	Curriculum, instruction, and assessment that is carefully designed to incorporate the needs of all learners *up front*
Another disconnected model and/or approach for teachers to implement and fit into the school day	A reform that intersects with and ideologically fits with dozens of other current reforms and approaches including response to intervention, differentiated instruction, cooperative learning, authentic assessment, co-teaching, constructivist teaching, project-based instruction, active learning, culturally relevant teaching, community-based instruction, and multicultural education
Changing pieces of the lesson for one or two students	Continuously assessing and creating lesson formats, materials, groupings, teaching strategies, and personal support for all learners
A new and unfamiliar approach to teaching and learning	Something that most teachers are doing already, perhaps without realizing it; teachers who offer a range of assessment choices, assign diverse roles to students in cooperative groups, or offer enhancement to learners who need extra challenge are using differentiated instruction. For most teachers, using an inclusive pedagogy will simply involve expanding strategies and approaches already used in the classroom.

Using Inclusive Pedagogy to Plan Lessons

A step-by-step guide to lesson planning for inclusive classrooms is outlined in this section. Lessons planned using this framework will support the needs of students with and without autism and other disabilities; students with a range of gifts, talents, and interests; and students who are ethnically, linguistically, and culturally diverse.

Step 1: Choose Content that Matters

A teacher writes the question, "Were the ancient Egyptians black?" on the chalkboard. Students begin a discussion. They wrestle with the relevance of the question and talk about how race is treated, hidden, or highlighted in history. The teacher breaks the students into groups to begin a month-long investigation of the question, with different teams taking on different pieces of the research. The students raise questions about Egypt and learn why it was regarded as a great civilization. In doing so, they explore contradictory information and learn that even the experts disagree sometimes in matters of science and history (Ladson-Billings, 2009).

Students in Boston take a ride on the subway (the "T"), construct models and draw pictures of the trip, and discuss and write about the experience. (This part of the lesson includes personal stories.) Teachers then teach mathematics during the trip by asking students about directionality and distance (e.g., "In what direction and how many stops is Park Street Station from Central Square?") (Moses & Cobb, 2001).

When two students find a field contaminated with "ooze" near their school, it leads to an intensive investigation of the health hazards found in their own backyard. Students videotape toxic sites, collect soil samples, and engage in discussions with the Moore Oil Company (the group responsible for the pollution). Eventually, students inspire the company to clean up the mess (Miller & Opland-Dobs, 2001).

What do all of these lessons have in common?

- They engage students in real-world problem solving or connect them to authentic work.

- They ask students to participate actively in their own education.

- They allow students to arrive at answers, gain understanding, and participate in many different ways.

- They are challenging, interesting, meaningful, and relevant to students' lives.

- They are multidimensional.

- They offer opportunities for students to address individual goals.

When planning for a diverse, inclusive classroom, the first and perhaps the most important aspect is choosing curriculum that is motivating and available to all. Lesson content that appeals to many and is accessible to all often minimizes or eliminates the need for other types of adaptations or special supports.

When I was a student teacher, I supported students in a general education remedial math class. When I walked into the classroom, almost every student was slumped in his chair; one was sleeping, two students were not working at all, and two others were being "shushed." The teacher sat at her desk and encouraged students to approach her if they had a problem. Although the teacher seemed caring, the content did nothing to communicate a belief that the students were capable and skilled. Students were completing worksheets related to money skills. These high school boys were solving problems such as "If you buy a hat and a pair of cowboy boots, how much will you need to spend? How much could you save by buying tennis shoes instead of cowboy boots?"

I couldn't help thinking how differently students might have responded to the same types of math problems had they been in charge of purchasing for the school store, investigating the wages local businesses pay to subgroups of teenagers (e.g., comparing by gender, race, or ethnicity), or helping a local nonprofit organization analyze the types of donations they received in the past year. This type of content communicates respect for learners. It demonstrates caring through challenge and shows students that teachers expect and trust them to work hard and demonstrate creativity. It also shows them that teachers care about their ideas and want to learn from them.

Consider Authenticity

Learning about the three branches of government can put some learners to sleep, but learning it as you petition for a new state law—especially one that profits young people—can grab the attention of even the most reluctant student. Measuring lines and assessing area can be dull, but measuring real materials and assembling tires, boards, and bars to create a new playground is exciting. Likewise, writing an essay can seem less than inspiring, but creating a screenplay for a movie the class will film can be quite motivating.

Students understand from an early age the difference between real work and tasks that are manufactured. Authentic work is more engaging, interesting, and worthwhile because students who work for a real audience can also get real-world feedback. For instance, a teacher needing some audiobooks for his middle school classroom asked a handful of girls to record Sandra Cisneros's novel *The House on Mango Street* (1991), the story of a young Mexican American girl growing up in Chicago. The students became completely spellbound by the project and learned about issues of culture and identity through their storytelling experiences.

Their teacher was so impressed with their reading that he took them to a professional sound studio to create the final version of the drama. The girls were so enthusiastic about the work that they wrote to Cisneros to invite her to the school. The girls were both surprised and delighted when Cisneros accepted their invitation and came to give a special lecture at their school (Michie, 1999).

As this story illustrates, there is much to be done in the world and so many authentic audiences and experiences to tap into, teachers need not manufacture work. To keep students inspired, educators need only be open to the many ways students might be involved in exploring issues, solving problems, and completing necessary tasks. Consider the story of 11-year-old Hunter Scott and how his attention to an existing problem stirred the awareness of thousands and brought peace to dozens of brave World War II veterans. In 1996, Scott watched the movie *Jaws* and heard one of the characters talk about how he had survived the sinking of the USS *Indianapolis*. (The *Indianapolis* was torpedoed in the South Pacific in 1945, shortly after delivering part of the atomic bomb that would be dropped on Hiroshima.)

Scott became curious about the event and soon found himself interviewing nearly 150 survivors of the *Indianapolis* and reviewing hundreds of documents related to the incident. As part of his research, Scott surveyed all of the survivors about the court-martial of the captain of the ship. He quickly learned that the survivors did not feel that their captain, Charles B. McVay, should have been court-martialed. After conducting his initial research, Hunter dedicated himself to clearing McVay's name.

What began as Hunter Scott's history project turned into a national crusade. Since Hunter Scott began his research, he has attended the survivors' reunions in Indianapolis; joined a group of survivors in Hawaii for a trip on the nuclear submarine the USS *Indianapolis*; traveled to Washington to meet with politicians; and testified in a Senate hearing. As a result, in part, of Hunter Scott's work, Congress eventually decided that McVay's record should reflect that he was exonerated for the loss of the *Indianapolis*, representing acknowledgment at last by the federal government that he was not guilty for the tragedy that led to his conviction.

Although most teachers will not be able to facilitate a project as grand as Scott's, this young man's adventure might inspire teachers to connect learners with problems that matter and people who need them. Authentic problems often inspire students in ways typical classwork does not. Even the most "unmotivated" learners often "show up" as competent when teachers invite them to address real issues, contemplate and solve real problems, create real products, or educate a real audience.

Plan with Students

To ensure that curriculum resonates with students, include them formally or informally in the planning process. Even students in preschool and kindergarten can participate in curriculum design by making choices about what they want to learn and bringing questions into the classroom. They may want to further develop their gifts and strengths (e.g., fishing, making tamales, dancing, drumming). They may want to tackle curriculum that gives them answers or makes them feel useful (e.g., researching neighborhood homeless problems or the nutritional value of school lunches). They may want to pursue topics that they view as central to their lives. Students in rural areas might want to investigate new farming technologies, a Native American student may want to study the storytelling traditions of a local tribe, a group of girls in the class may want to examine how gender affects their own educational experiences, and students with autism may want to learn more about their own disability or study human and civil rights issues related to disability.

Many individuals with autism suggest using personal interests or hobbies as a teaching tool (Grandin, 1996a; O' Neill, 1999; Shore, 2003). Students with autism may be fascinated by anything from the 50 states to whales to power tools (Kluth & Schwarz, 2008), and any of these can be brought into lessons. A student who knows a lot about using tools, for instance, may excel when some lessons focus on building things.

I once worked with a young man who struggled constantly in his English class until his teacher encouraged him to use the class to pursue one of his primary interests: Asperger syndrome. Inspired, the student constructed his own web site on autism. He wrote a few essays for his site, and when the class began the poetry unit, he wrote a sonnet about his experiences as a person with Asperger syndrome.

As in these examples, teachers can plan with students in informal ways by incorporating their interests and concerns into curriculum and instruction, but teachers also can plan with students formally by working with them to explicitly design units of study. Teachers might share planning by asking students to generate content ideas or to choose ways in which the class will approach topics of study.

Develop a Central Question or Problem

Perhaps the easiest way to differentiate for all learners is to frame lessons and units as questions, issues, or problems (Bigelow, 1994; Onosko & Jorgensen, 1998; Simon, 2002). Lessons posed as problems often pique student interest, can accommodate the needs and skills of many learners, and tend to be more interesting than those that are structured as topics (Wiggins & McTighe, 2005).

Think of the typical fifth-grade unit of study. In one classroom, the teacher introduces the topic of "poetry." In another classroom, the teacher tells students they will be thinking about ways in which poetry has influenced American politics. Which group will be more intrigued and, perhaps, more likely to engage in higher order thinking? Onosko and Jorgensen pointed out that using problems, questions, or critical issues as the base of a lesson or unit helps the teacher to narrow the topic and reduce the likelihood of "fragmented and superficial treatment of subject matter" (1998, p. 76).

Simon (2002) suggested that good central questions address an essential element of the subject matter, are provocative, and can be addressed over time and explored and reexplored as students continue to learn. Therefore, "What are the unsolved mysteries of the oceans?" is a better question than "What type of life can be found in the ocean?" Likewise, "Is a democracy always democratic?" is a better question than "What elements make up a democracy?" The two former questions are clearly more thought-provoking and open-ended. Furthermore, students with a range of skills, abilities, and needs can answer both of these questions in a multitude of ways.

One high school teacher shared how she came to view the use of a central problem as a way of differentiating instruction in her classroom:

> When I did a unit on slavery and the Civil War, we used the question, "Can you be free if you aren't treated equally?" Some students in my class could answer that question using information from their Civil War reading and by thinking about the progress of civil rights in the United States. One or two students in my class had to approach this question first from their own personal perspectives. Amro knew that he was treated differently from his brothers because of his disability, and he has a strong opinion about that. If we start with his personal experience, it's a little bit easier for him to make a connection with the Civil War. (Onosko & Jorgensen, 1998, pp. 77–78)

Step 2: Use Flexible Groupings

Throughout the unit, a wide range of groupings should be used. Groupings should change throughout the day and year so that students have opportunities to work with all classmates and learn from all peers regularly (Broderick, Mehta-Parekh, & Reid, 2005; Ferguson et al., 2001; Kasa-Hendrickson, 2002; Oyler, 2001). *Flexible grouping* means that at different times and for different lessons, students might be grouped or paired based on goals, interests, needs, or skills (Diller, 2007). During some lessons the teacher may group students with *similar* goals, interests, needs, or skills. During other lessons, the teacher may group students with *different* goals, interests, needs, or skills in order to give students a chance to share and teach each other.

One of the most important reasons to shuffle groupings is to give all learners opportunities to learn from all of their peers. In Kasa-Hendrickson's study of students with autism in inclusive classrooms, she found that the teachers mixed up groups, in part, to "work against the static labels that often came when groups were created according to perceived ability" (2002, p. 121). Consider the perspective of a teacher who does not believe ability labels are productive:

> We always change the groups so no kid is stigmatized as being in the low group. Because I don't believe that any kid is low, medium, and high. Kids aren't that simple; you know they all have things they are great at and things to work on. We just group them to work on certain skills at the learning clubs, they're very diverse. There's no, "You're smarter than I am." It helps to not build that. (p. 121)

Students might work in pairs, in small groups of three or four students, or in larger teams of five or six. Students with autism will profit from working with a range of peers, but for new tasks, some will feel most comfortable with a trusted friend or classmate.

Some teachers allow learners to choose partners or team members. Although this practice gives students opportunities to work with familiar peers, it can also cause isolation and frustration in the classroom for those students who are not asked to be a partner or team member. Furthermore, students who choose partners and team members for every activity may constantly select from the same peer group. When this happens, students fail to become acquainted with and learn from all class members, and the community of the classroom is threatened.

One way to honor student preferences while engineering groupings that benefit all learners is to ask students to give input on group formation. Teachers might ask students to provide this information informally through a short interview or by listing a few names on a sheet of paper. Or, students might be asked to fill out a worksheet that provides more detailed information about grouping preferences. Of course, this tool should be used to give students opportunities to learn about their learning, so instead of asking students to name those that they want in their group, ask them to list "a few students with whom you feel you can do your best work." Even if the teacher does not ask every student for input in forming the groups, the learner with autism should be given this opportunity because unexpected changes or unfamiliar situations can cause undue—and, in some cases, extreme—stress and frustration.

Finally, the teacher should always let the student with autism know in advance when groups will be changing. If the student will be working in different groups throughout the day, he or she might be given a schedule with this information included. One of my former students needed not only a schedule of which groups she would work with and when but also photographs of each group so she could study the images and prepare herself to be with each different team.

Step 3: Use a Wide Range of Materials

One of my colleagues teaches longitude and latitude by slicing up an orange in front of her students (sections are longitude, slices show latitude). A science teacher tosses a rubber chicken around his classroom to keep students interested and alert (if you catch the chicken, you answer a question!). Students in a math class read newspapers to learn about the stock

Table 10.2.   Adapting materials to meet the needs of all learners

In addition to . . .	Try . . .
Books	Adapted books (e.g., laminating favorite pages for easy gripping, rewriting text to make vocabulary more or less complex, replacing illustrations with personal photos); electronic book readers (e.g., Amazon Kindle, iPhone), computers (e.g., PowerPoint books), audio books, movies and filmstrips; and other reading materials (e.g., magazines, pamphlets, technical manuals, comic books, advertisements, flipbooks)
Pencils and/or pens	Computer (word processing programs), speech recognition software, communication devices, typewriters, label makers, rubber stamps (e.g., pictures, letters, words), magnetic letters or words, pencil grips, letter guide
Calculators	Adapted calculators (e.g., large buttons, large display), adding machine, keyboard/computer, manipulatives (e.g., unifex cubes, seeds, pick-up sticks, number tiles), number line or ruler, abacus, multiplication table, money, dominoes, number cubes, math games, flash cards
Paint and/or crayons	Colored pencils, paint pens, drawing and/or painting software programs, "sensory" art supplies (e.g., shaving cream, pudding), markers, stickers, charcoal, tools for print making (e.g., potatoes, blocks)
Papers and/or worksheets	Adapted worksheets (important information highlighted or written in bold letters), laminated sheets and grease pencil, mini-chalkboard or wipe board, overhead projector, colored overlays, a Smart Board, touchscreen

market. Using a range of materials such as these can sometimes make the difference between students' mere presence and their participation (Kluth & Danaher, 2010; Onosko & Jorgensen, 1998; Udvari-Solner, 1996). Students who are studying United States geography and culture might be introduced to brochures from different state landmarks, tour books, and travel literature. This offering of materials is important because it gives every student a chance to be successful and learn in a way that best suits him or her. One student may be unable to effectively interact with an atlas or globe but may be able to learn concepts easily by creating and studying a salt and flour map of the continents.

Another reason to differentiate materials is to provide students with autism more access to certain lessons, activities, or experiences. For instance, many students find writing with pencils and pens difficult and prefer to use an AlphaSmart, typewriter, or computer instead. Likewise, a student I know has a hard time turning pages, so his teacher adapted his reading material by copying the text and placing as much of it as possible on small, laminated poster boards. She also purchased several different poetry posters for the classroom so her student could "read the walls." More recently, she has loaded books and literacy games on his iPhone so that he can move from page to page with just a tap of his finger. See Table 10.2 for several ways teachers can adapt materials to meet the needs of all learners.

Step 4: Mix Up Lesson Formats

Sometimes I hear teachers say that they do not have time for "bells and whistles" in the classroom. Some say that they cannot fit simulations, role plays, skits, group work, debates, cooperative learning, project-based instruction, games, drama, workshops, station teaching, centers, or labs into the school day. In reality, teachers cannot afford to *not* use a range of formats across subject areas and throughout the day. Students with and without disabilities will be more engaged, retain more, learn in a deeper way, and use higher order thinking skills when they can learn in a variety of ways (Jensen, 2008; Patterson, 1997; Silberman, 1996). According to Holt (1967), learning is enhanced when students can state information in their own words, make use of it in various ways, and recognize it in various guises and circumstances.

When teachers use a wide variety of formats and decrease their reliance on whole-class discussions and lecture, many students, but especially those with autism, will benefit. Many students with autism report that they need "hands-on" opportunities to learn. Temple Grandin, a woman with autism who eventually earned a doctorate in animal science, recalled that she learned most when teachers allowed her to actively participate in lessons:

> I vividly remember learning about the solar system by drawing it on the bulletin board and taking field trips to the science museum. Going to the science museum and doing experiments in my third- and fourth-grade classrooms made science real to me. The concept of barometric pressure was easy to understand after we made barometers out of milk bottles, rubber sheeting, and drinking straws. (1995, p. 97)

Udvari-Solner (1996) defined *lesson format* as the "infrastructure of architecture on which the learning experience is built." She explained that "the organizational framework, methods to impart information to the students, and ways in which students interact with that information are all elements of lesson format" (p. 248). In this section, I outline several lesson formats that can be used to meet the needs and bring out the talents of every learner in the inclusive classroom.

Cooperative Learning

With cooperative learning, students interact with each other and work together to achieve optimal learning. Typically, this work is done in small groups, with students sharing information, working toward common goals, and individually participating for the good of the team, product, or learning outcome (Gilles, 2007; Kagan, 1992; Putnam, 1997).

Cooperative learning is advocated by those invested in inclusive schooling due to the demands of cooperative structures. These demands include sharing, learning about differences, working together, and achieving common goals. Cooperative learning also provides opportunities for students to work outside of the "rows and columns," listening-and-taking-notes formation of traditional classrooms. It, therefore, addresses a broader range of learning styles and individual performance characteristics of students. Cooperative learning also gives students the power to organize and operate in groups, to give each other feedback, and to collaborate on problem solving (Dyson & Grineski, 2001; Putnam, 1997).

Cooperative learning is a powerful teaching and learning tool (Gillies, 2007; Johnson & Johnson, 1989; Jolliffe, 2007; Sapon-Shevin, 1999), especially for students with autism, because it creates opportunities to learn new and improve existing social and communication skills. Specifically, cooperative lessons provide natural opportunities to learn new language, initiate conversations, respond to verbal directions and requests, practice turn taking, and possibly develop social relationships. Specific goals can even be targeted during cooperative learning. For instance, a student learning a new augmentative and alternative communication (AAC) device might practice communicating MY TURN, GOOD IDEA, or READ IT AGAIN during a lesson.

Cooperative learning also seems to benefit students with autism academically (Dugan et al., 1995; Kamps, 1995; Whalon & Hanline, 2008). One study conducted in a fourth-grade classroom showed that when students worked cooperatively, both learners with autism and their peers without disabilities demonstrated learning gains (Dugan et al., 1995). The researchers documented that more learning occurred during cooperative groups than during traditional teacher-led, whole-class instruction.

Many teachers realize intuitively that this type of active, student-centered instruction boosts student learning and understanding, but few may realize how helpful this type of interaction can be for learners with autism who may have an increased need to move, manipulate materials, and interact with others in order to learn. Three cooperative learning structures that I have found particularly helpful in inclusive classrooms are outlined in the following sections.

Roundtable Recording   Roundtable Recording is a technique used for brainstorming or reviewing. Groups are seated around a table with one pencil and one piece of paper. A question is posed, and students take turns recording answers on the paper as it is passed around the table. The question should be carefully chosen. It must have multiple answers, and all students should be capable of answering it in some way.

When the time is up, teams count the responses they have written on the paper. The entire class then shares answers. Variations of this technique include asking groups to read and evaluate their lists for the most creative or "on target" responses or asking groups to summarize lists in a few sentences. This technique also can be used during a movie or lecture. For example, as students watch a documentary on endangered species, a page titled "What I Know About Endangered Species" could be passed around. As they are listening to a lecture on the human body, they can record responses to the prompt: "One fact I now know about the circulatory system is _____."

Roundtable Recording is especially effective when a teacher has one or more students who tend to "drift off" during lectures, movies, or whole-class lessons. Gunilla Gerland, a woman with autism, reported that she often needed to take notes or doodle in order to maintain attention to a lesson:

> At [my] junior high school the teacher had let me sit and draw on rough paper during lesson and this had helped me stop sinking in to myself. With paper and pen, I could keep my nervous system awake. I didn't know that advantages of this kind were suddenly to be withdrawn, and that now that we had a new teacher . . . all special treatment had come to an end. I had to understand that it was not permitted to sit drawing during lesson times.
>
> But as the teacher was talking, a monotonous heaving ocean would well up in my ears, a sea with surging waves of rustling and coughing. It would make me slowly sink into myself and stay there. (1996, p. 122)

Roundtable Recording is one way to give students like Gerland teacher-sanctioned opportunities to move and interact during even the most traditional of classroom situations.

Adaptations that can be made to Roundtable Recording include the following:

- Allow a student who cannot write or talk to point to an existing response with which he agrees. A tally mark can then be placed by that response.

- Give students labels containing two or three possible responses to the question; when they get the page, they are responsible for attaching one of the stickers to the roundtable paper to answer the question.

- Give students the option of either adding graphics *or* writing a phrase.

- Have students work in pairs to produce a single response.

Numbered Heads Together   In the strategy Numbered Heads Together (Kagan, 1992), students are arranged in teams of three or four, and each individual is assigned a number (e.g., Dave is a 1, Cy is a 2, Ashanti is a 3, Allison is a 4). Groups are assigned a question to answer, an idea to brainstorm, or a task to complete. For example, a teacher might ask students to name everything they know about the food pyramid or to generate a list of simple machines. Everyone is encouraged to participate and contribute, and groups are given a set time to brainstorm and to make sure that everyone in the group can answer the question.

Therefore, Dave is not only responsible for providing an answer to the question, but he also needs to make sure that Cy, Ashanti, and Allison can answer the question. Depending on the task, students are given a few minutes or even an entire class period to work.

The teacher then poses the question to the group of students represented by a particular number (e.g., "Tell me what you already know about healthy a diet. I want to hear answers from the 4s in each group"). The student with that particular number in each group is responsible for reporting to peers and the teacher.

When teachers use a structure such as Numbered Heads Together, all students have an opportunity to participate and learners get input and ideas from several classmates, not just one or two. Contrast this structure with a traditional whole-class lesson in which only one person at a time may talk and students need to "wait their turn" to share. During this wait time, many students become bored and restless.

This structure also gives students opportunities to support each other. If a student is struggling to understand a concept, listening to his or her peers explain it in several different ways can boost understanding. Students also can receive social support when they engage in this structure as they can ask and answer one another's questions related to content or the lesson structure. For instance, Luke Jackson, a young man with Asperger syndrome, reported that he is often confused when engaged in individual work at his desk:

> Everything is so busy at school and everyone else, all the kids and all the teachers, seems to have a purpose and I never have quite fathomed out what that purpose is. I know we are there to learn, but there seems to be so much more going on than that. It is like beginning a game without knowing any of the rules or passwords. (2002, p. 114)

Allowing learners to work together in structures such as Numbered Heads Together can help students such as Luke Jackson learn the "rules and passwords" of each lesson.

Adaptations that can be made to Numbered Heads Together include the following:

- Ask all students who are called on to give an answer without using words; students can use sign language or gestures or act out an answer.

- Call on two groups of students to answer (e.g., "2s and 4s give a response together").

- Have students write a collective response or responses on paper and give it to the student whose number has been called to hold up or hand to the teacher.

Jigsaw   To begin Jigsaw (Aronson & Patnoe, 1997; Hertz-Lazarowitz, Kagan, Sharan, Slavin, & Webb, 1985), students in small base groups are assigned material or a multifaceted problem. Each member of the group selects or is assigned some piece of the material or aspect of the problem on which to focus. For example, in a classroom in which students are studying the 20th century in America, one base group of five students might split responsibilities this way: Tom is responsible for learning about transportation; Mike wants to learn about wars and conflict; Evie opts to study human and civil rights issues; Scott chooses politics and leaders; and Lisa examines entertainment (Barb Saxon-Schaffer, personal communication, June 2, 1995). In each of the other base groups in the classroom, students will split responsibilities in the same way. That is, every group of five would have one student responsible for transportation, one responsible for wars and conflict, and so forth.

At this point, each student is responsible for learning enough about his or her topic to be able to teach that content to the rest of the base group. Students do not need to do this work alone, however. Students engage in research with their expert groups. The expert group consists of a team of students who have the identical assignment. For example, all students assigned to the topic of transportation advances meet, engage in research, gather information, become experts on the topic, and rehearse their presentations together. This expert group is particularly useful for students who have problems gathering or organizing information on their own.

When students in the expert groups feel that they have thoroughly learned their portion of the material, they plan a few strategies and perhaps even create materials for teaching it to their original base group. Students then return to their original base groups and each student teaches his or her material to the others. In this way, all students in the classroom learn all of the material.

Adaptations that can be made to Jigsaw include the following:

- Have students break out into expert groups with a partner (be sure to adjust the number of expert groups accordingly).

- Give all or some of the students the materials necessary to present their ideas to the base group.

- Allow students to present their learnings in a variety of ways (e.g., role plays, drawings, gestures).

Games

Using games is another way teachers can involve all learners, teach new skills, and give students opportunities to participate in a variety of ways. Games tend to be fun and nonthreatening. When teachers use games, they provide students with "opportunities to treat each other in prosocial, desirable ways," say nice things to one another, and work actively to include each other (Sapon-Shevin, 1999, p. 27).

Although teachers in the elementary classroom often use games, educators in secondary school classrooms often abandon these approaches in place of more didactic and traditional strategies. Secondary teachers may be apprehensive about using games because they believe that this type of activity will squander important classroom time and diminish curriculum and instruction. In contrast, the creative and effective use of games can boost the participation and interest of students, help teachers make curriculum relevant and more comprehensible, and make abstract concepts concrete (Marzano, 2010). All of the games outlined here are appropriate for students of any age.

Walk It to Know It   Walk It to Know It (Udvari-Solner & Kluth, 2007) is a useful tool for enhancing understanding for students who are visual and kinesthetic learners. To prepare for this game, teachers or students design flow charts on paper and then transfer each square to a separate piece of poster board or butcher paper. Then the squares are laid out on the classroom floor and all students walk through the sequence. Teachers might have students explain each step as they walk over it or simply have them read the information on the board or paper aloud. Students might trod over the charts one time or move through them several times over the period of a week or month. Teachers might make charts to teach any number of concepts including the scientific method, steps to solving a binomial equation, or the parts of a business plan. Students also can walk through a timeline or a sequence of events chain (see Figure 10.1 for an example).

Students tend to enjoy Walk It to Know It because it gives them an opportunity to get out of their seats. A lack of movement during the school day can cause some learners to be restless or anxious. It also can be detrimental to learning. Patterson (1997) pointed out that many kinesthetic activities allow students to see a more complete picture of the subject matter and free them from learning inhibitions. These activities also often produce long-term rather than short-term recall (Patterson, 1997). Students with autism who need a lot of movement, especially those who need occasional "walking breaks," may be especially attracted to this game.

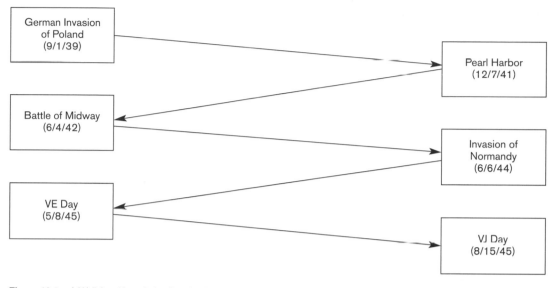

Figure 10.1. A Walk It to Know It timeline of major events of World War II.

Adaptations to Walk It to Know It include the following:

- Ask students to chant the words on each square as they step on them. This will help some learners retain the information more effectively.

- Show students how to add movements to each square so they are not only "traveling" through the content but acting it out as well.

- Let students hop (or skip or gallop) through the sequence. Adding this extra bit of movement can give some students an opportunity to release energy in a constructive way.

Match Game   Match Game allows students to teach each other. To play, the teacher distributes a card to each student. The teacher needs two groups of cards (A and B); each card in one group (A) must have a matching card in the other group (B). For instance, the teacher might create one group of questions (A) and one group of answers (B); one group of words (A) and one group of definitions (B); or one group of incomplete sentences (A) and one group of words that complete the sentences (B). See Figure 10.2 to view sample cards used to teach students new math vocabulary words.

Every student is given one index card and told to walk around the room, talking to other students and comparing cards. Students are directed to help each other find their matches. Once students have found the individual whose card is a match for theirs, they should sit down next to that person and wait for others to find their matches. Then, pairs can simply read their cards to the others or quiz the rest of the class using the match information.

One teacher used Match Game to showcase the talents of one of her students, Marn, a young woman with autism who was interested in trains. During a unit on transportation, Marn created one set of cards that contained words and phrases related to trains. On the other set of cards she wrote the corresponding definitions. One card, for instance, had the term "run-through" written on it. The definition of run-through, "a train that generally is not scheduled to pick up or reduce cars en route," was written on another card. Students had to find matches for terms and phrases that were, in most cases, completely new to them. Students had fun leaning the new lingo and were impressed with Marn's expertise in this area. According to the teacher, Match Game provided the first opportunity that students in Marn's

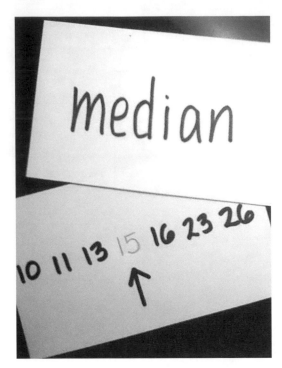

Figure 10.2. Match Game cards for a math lesson.

classroom had to go to her to get help and information. This experience changed students' perceptions of their classmate and gave Marn the courage to share more of her knowledge with others. In addition, all students became interested in Match Game and were anxious to take turns designing their own set of cards for the group.

Adaptations to Match Game include the following:

• Have some students participate in creating the cards; this will be especially rewarding for a student who has particular expertise on a subject.

• Encourage students to support each other during the game; remind them that they can help classmates find matches.

• Add pictures or icons to the cards if some students learn better this way.

The Company You Keep The Company You Keep, a fast-paced and entertaining game created by Mel Silberman (1996), is appropriate as an ice breaker, an introduction to new material, or a review. To prepare for this activity, the teacher makes a list of categories helpful for teaching or reviewing certain content. Each category should include at least two (if not more) "sides," opinions, or items so that in choosing to affiliate themselves with certain choices, students can form themselves in subgroups. Content areas and categories might include the following:

• Social studies: Agree or disagree with capital punishment

• Math: Do or do not understand how to measure angles

• English: Favorite character from the young-adult novel *An Audience for Einstein* (Wakely, 2005)

• Geography: Spanish-speaking nation you would most like to visit

• Science: Chemistry experiment from which you have learned the most

The teacher clears some space in the classroom or moves students to a hallway. Then the teacher or a student leader calls out a category and students mill around the classroom looking for others in their same category. Therefore, in the first example, students who agree with capital punishment would cluster together and those who disagree would do the same. If the prompt contains multiple responses, the teacher should tell students to cluster together with their small group and make sure they move away from other groups so all discrete groups can be identified.

Once students have formed their groups, instruct them to shake hands with the "company they keep." Then do some debriefing with the class. Students can be asked to teach each other about the category they chose or to explain their choice. For example, if students were asked to choose their favorite character from a book, call on them to defend their choice and ask students in other groups to ask clarifying questions. This discussion among participants can last for as much as 30 minutes (if used to teach a lesson) or during the last 5 minutes of a class period as a recap.

The Company You Keep is ideal for the diverse classroom in that it offers movement and action for students who need to get away from their desks. It gives quiet students structured opportunities to interact and social students time to talk with their classmates. Social skills also can be taught during this activity. Students with autism might be able to practice greeting people or asking or answering verbal questions.

Adaptations to The Company You Keep include the following:

- Give students different roles during the activity; some might lead the activity while others walk around facilitating the forming of groups.

- Write the prompts on the board so that students can hear and see choices.

- Ask students to sit down together or to link arms once groups have formed so that all participants can clearly see where the different groups are. Groups might even be asked to hold up a sign indicating the name of their cluster.

What Is It?   What Is It? is a perfect game for injecting laughter into a lesson and for encouraging students to take small risks in front of the group. This game begins with the teacher placing an object in front of the room and asking the group, "What is it?" He or she then encourages students to come forward and transform the object into something related to class content. One student can approach at a time and act out a short scene. He or she can tell the others what they are doing and how they are using the object or students can yell out guesses. For example, a high school English teacher might present a roll of paper towels to the class and challenge students to act out idioms and colloquialisms. One student might grab on to the end of the roll to illustrate "out on a limb" or pass a towel around the classroom to act out "passing the buck." Typically, the more ridiculous the skits are, the better, and the only rule is that students must wait for one student to set the object down before standing up to take a turn. You can have students get up to participate on their own; you can have them raise hands to take turns; or you can have learners pass the object to each other randomly, giving individuals an opportunity to pass if they do not have an idea. After the game, the teacher might give additional information about the performances or even act a few out him or herself.

Students with a flair for the dramatic will really enjoy What Is It? This activity can be particularly helpful for students with autism who need help understanding different types of humor, especially if the teacher or a peer takes a moment after each transformation to explain "what is funny" about each of the transformations.

Adaptations to What Is It? include the following:

- Give some students time to rehearse their "transformations."

- Invite students to come to act out their scenes in pairs or in small groups.

- Show the object and have students brainstorm ideas for transforming the object on paper before attempting to act out a scene.

Human Treasure Hunt   Human Treasure Hunt requires every student to gather information by interacting with several different classmates. Each student receives a worksheet with a list of prompts (e.g., "Find a person who knows how to draw the carbon cycle and ask him or her to demonstrate this skill for you"). The objective is for students to find an answer to every prompt on their form (see Figure 10.3 for a sample Human Treasure Hunt). Those who finish early should circulate and offer support to those still working or go back to their desks and design new prompts to be answered.

There are only two rules for this game: 1) Students can only get one answer from each peer and/or participant; and 2) if a student gets an answer from another student, he or she needs to give an answer to that other student. Teachers may also want to insist that students answer each question only a certain number of times.

Human Treasure Hunts can include simple (e.g., label, list) and complex (e.g., compare/contrast) questions, personal questions, questions related to content, or questions that are

Human Treasure Hunt

Instructions: The goal of this activity is to learn as much as you can from the experts in this classroom. You may only get one answer from each person you approach and that person may only get one answer from you.

1. Find a person who can draw a picture of "a force acting through a distance."

   Have this artist sign here: _____

2. Find someone who can name a use of radioactivity.

   Answer: _____

   Have this science expert sign here: _____

3. Find someone who will act out, explain, or draw the Doppler effect.

   Have this creative individual sign here: _____

4. Find someone who can explain the sinking of the Titanic in terms of density. After the short lesson, have your instructor sign here:

   _____

After you are finished, walk around the room and help your classmates finish their treasure hunts.

Figure 10.3. Human Treasure Hunt: Physical science example.

"You're Going to Love This Kid!" Teaching Students with Autism in the Inclusive Classroom, Second Edition, by Paula Kluth
Copyright © 2010 by Paul H. Brookes Publishing Co. All rights reserved.

both personal and content related (e.g., "Find a person who will write you a haiku about his or her family"). It is fairly easy to create hunts that allow students to discuss curriculum while sharing something personal at the same time.

Sapon-Shevin (1999) suggested that teachers include items that many students will find relevant and be able to answer. This activity is a perfect opportunity to highlight the expertise, specific gifts, or strengths of individual learners. For example, if a student has just moved from Saudi Arabia, the teacher might include an item related to the Middle East. If a student with autism has a particular interest in U.S. presidents, the hunt might prompt students to write a three-sentence biography of President Barack Obama.

Adaptations to Human Treasure Hunt include the following:

- Allow students to travel.

- Have a few students serve as "hunt helpers"—their job is to walk around and offer assistance to students who are struggling to complete their forms.

- Let students generate their own items. If a peer cannot answer a question verbally, his or her classmate can invent one that can be answered with a gesture, for example.

Service Learning

Service learning blends thoughtfully planned service or volunteer work with critical reflection and opportunities to meet educational goals (Gent, 2009). Having students collect canned goods for the local food pantry is not service learning, it is a nice deed. If, however, students in an Food Science class study hunger in America, examine the problem locally by talking to people at the pantry, engage in research related to specific areas of need, create healthful and tasty recipes and a recipe book based on the foods most often available at the pantry, publish and distribute the book, elicit feedback on it, reflect on the process, and discuss how grassroots work can affect a community, that would qualify as service learning.

Service learning opportunities such as the one described here are valuable for so many reasons; they allow students to participate in projects with tangible outcomes, make decisions, speak and be heard, inspire and create change, and achieve recognition (Gent, 2009; Schine & Halsted, 1997). In addition, service learning provides many opportunities for differentiating instruction because there are typically various tasks to complete, angles to study, and ideas to explore in a single project.

Because students with disabilities, linguistically diverse backgrounds, and "at-risk" labels often *receive* services within schools and communities (Grassi et al., 2004; Morris, 1992), educators are especially interested in introducing service learning to these populations. These students not only often thrive given opportunities to provide services but can develop positive identities as a result (Gent & Gurecka, 2001; Klein, 2000). Yoder, Retish, and Wade (1996), for example, found that students with disabilities who participated in service learning acquired increased self-knowledge and improved communication, problem solving, and social skills.

Service projects may also motivate students to learn new skills including many that may be lifelong and quite relevant to students' lives. Koliba and colleagues (2006), for instance, found that learners acquired skills such as managing time, planning projects, budgeting, gardening, and scheduling. And Krystal reported that she saw students develop stronger community ties, enhance feelings of self-worth, and challenge themselves to learn more in order to help others:

Justin, a special education youngster [sic], gawky and uncomfortable with his body, was involved in a Learning Helper Model, in which older youth read to young children. He and his peers had prepared diligently for the week's tutoring lesson because, as his teacher explained, "They don't want the 5th graders to know a word that they don't." With their guided reading books and exercises in hand, Justin and the noisy group of adolescents entered the cafeteria of the public school and metamorphosed into young adults. Suddenly, they became thoughtful and caring, smiling gently as the 5th graders ran into the cafeteria.

Little Colin jumped into Justin's arms, exclaiming, "I couldn't wait to see you!" Another tutor, Shawanna, was having a different experience. "Lucinda isn't here, and this is the only reason I came to school today," she announced, hands on hips, upset that her young tutee was not among the 5th graders. (1998/1999, p. 60)

Krystal indicated that these students moved from being "unruly adolescents" to caring and thoughtful young adults by simply being needed, engaging in a meaningful curriculum, and uncovering talents they didn't know they had.

When I was working as a second-grade teacher, I planned several service learning units with my colleagues that successfully met the needs of all of our students—including two learners with the label of autism, Luis and Katie. One such unit we implemented was designed with the needs of all students in mind. We knew that Luis and Katie would need lessons that incorporated movement. We also wanted both students to have a lot of opportunities to interact with peers because both seemed to learn best in social situations. We were cognizant of the students' individual goals when planning this unit; both students were learning new communication systems and needed opportunities to practice using these systems.

We combined two traditional second-grade units (animals and communities) and designed a new unit titled "How can we support wildlife in our community?" We talked to students about the question and, as a group, decided we would build bird feeders and donate them to places in our neighborhood. The bird feeder building was the highlight and culminating activity of the unit. In the weeks leading up to the building, students also had opportunities to

- Create "bird facts" pamphlets using a new software program; pamphlets also became a service project and were distributed to libraries and animal supply stores in our area.

- Write letters to local businesses asking for materials or funding for bird feeder building.

- Engage in authentic mathematics exercises related to the bird feeders (e.g., How many nails will we need? How much will it cost to make each bird feeder?).

- Listen to bird calls and create paintings inspired by this "music."

- Hear a lecture from a bird expert from a local specialty shop. She treated the students to a slide show and introduced them to the wildlife in their own backyards.

On the building day, we invited parents, teachers (e.g., the art teacher who gave up her planning hour), and other community members (e.g., college students, senior citizens) to contribute to the project. The response was wonderful. We had so much help that students were able to work in pairs with one adult assisting each pair! Students needed assistance with tools but were able to do a lot of the work independently. For many learners, this experience was their first time using a hammer or screwdriver. They learned new skills and gained confidence as well.

After the feeders were built and painted, students voted as a class on where we would deliver our gifts. After a long discussion about helping our community and what types of businesses and services exist in our area, students decided to donate the feeders to an area hospital, a senior center, a local library, the town's domestic violence center, the YMCA, and a community center. My colleagues and I then took turns bringing small groups of students into the community to deliver the bird feeders. Students were required to use maps to find buildings and were asked to give a short dedication speech when presenting the feeders to the organizations.

Both students with autism were able to participate fully in this unit with a few adaptations, including the following:

- Whereas every student with a signed permission slip got to visit at least one community site, Luis and Katie each went on several trips. The outings gave both learners opportunities to practice communication and social skills and to learn new skills related to the community (e.g., using a map, riding the bus).

- For the building of the bird feeders, Luis and Katie were paired with familiar and trusted peers.

- Katie was allowed to work on a cooperative art project while others did individual pictures of birds. Instead of spending class time listening to the bird calls and developing a picture, Katie drew a small bird (with the help of a friend) and then moved around the room, handing her picture to classmates and getting them to add something to her collective picture.

- Luis's occupational therapist worked with his group during the building of the feeders and showed the students the best way to use the screwdriver.

- When students wrote letters to local businesses, Katie worked on the computer with a friend to compose a letter and Luis participated by stamping the school's address on the top left-hand corner of every envelope.

One caution teachers should note when using service learning is that some learners may find some projects overwhelming, especially if they require socializing with new people or spending a lot of time in new environments. Gent offered that in these cases, teachers may want to use video self-modeling to prepare learners for upcoming situations:

> For instance, teachers videotape the student role playing a conversation with a senior citizen and also a senior citizen conversing with another person. Using computer video editing software, teachers superimpose the two so that it appears that the student is conversing with the senior citizen. Teachers play the tape for students and say, "Let's watch how you act at the long-term care facility." (2009, p. 81)

Of course, not every learner will need this much preparation, but keep in mind that some may. (For a printable version of this section on service learning as well as a list of lesson ideas, visit http://www.paulakluth.com/articles/servicelearning.html)

Project-Based Instruction

Project-based instruction is especially appropriate for students with diverse learning profiles because many needs and learning styles can be addressed; increased opportunities exist for peer support and the development of relationships; students can work in a range of environments including community settings, the school library, and outdoors; they can work at their own pace; and a number of skills and disciplines can be incorporated into any project (Kluth & Schwarz, 2008; Moursund, 2003; Winebrenner, 1996).

Projects are an ideal learning activity for those students with autism who need some time alone to work independently and those who thrive when given opportunities to immerse themselves in one topic. Donna Williams, a woman with autism, found that she could be academically successful when a favorite teacher believed in her abilities and let her pursue a topic of special interest, the American Civil Rights movement, in depth:

While the other teachers found me a devil, this teacher found me to be bright, amusing, and a pleasure to teach. At the end of the term, I handed her the most important piece of schoolwork any of my high school teachers had received.

. . . I told my teacher that what I wanted to do was a secret, and she agreed to extend my due date as I enthusiastically informed her of the growing length of my project. I had gone through every book I could find on the topic, cutting out pictures and drawing illustrations over my written pages, as I had always done, to capture the feel of what I wanted to write about. The other students had given her projects spanning an average of about three pages in length. I proudly gave her my special project of twenty-six pages, illustrations, and drawings. She gave me an A. (1992, p. 81)

Similarly, Betts, Betts, and Gerber-Eckard (2007) reported on Madeline, a student with Asperger syndrome, who was able to successfully complete a genealogy project because the teacher created appropriate adaptations including meeting with her in advance, allowing her family to support her at different points, and giving all students leeway to use different materials (including various types of technology) to present their work. As a result,

Madeline's final project consisted of videotaped stories told by her parents, siblings, grandparents, and one great-grandparent. With the assistance of her brother, Madeline created a PowerPoint presentation using family pictures and favorite family music. [Her teacher] set up the computer and projection equipment and Madeline showed the video and the PowerPoint presentation to the students of the class. (p. 83)

Teachers working in diverse classrooms often turn to project-based instruction in order to provide interesting and appropriate instruction and to make sure that students have opportunities to address individual objectives. In project-based instruction (as in the example of Madeline above), any student can work on reading, writing, computer, videography, or interviewing skills while tackling challenging content. In addition, students with autism might be able to practice using a new communication device or develop new social skills (e.g., asking for help). One clever teacher allowed her student to do a project on his communication device itself. Credit was given both for studying uses of the device and for gaining competencies related to his system. See Table 10.3 for a list of other project ideas for individuals, small groups, or the whole class.

In managing projects, teachers should set clear timelines and teach students how to chart their own progress, develop regular reports, and produce a final product or products. Harmin and Toth (2006) suggested that teachers steer students away from projects that involve copy work and passive learning and point them toward those activities that will inspire higher order thinking and meaningful engagement. In order to prevent students from engaging in excessive pencil and paper work, teachers could ask them to design a model, compare ideas, or produce a mural (Harmin & Toth, 2006). Instead of asking them to do a report on school discipline policies, then, teachers could ask them to summarize the opinions of two experts, interview four local school administrators, and invent a model policy to present to the school board.

Desktop Teaching

Desktop teaching is an active learning strategy designed to give students the opportunity to act as both teachers and learners (Draper, 1997; Parker, 1990). Desktop teaching involves giving students individual topics and having them prepare mini-lessons based on those topics. Students prepare a short lesson lasting from 5 to 10 minutes based on the topic that is assigned to them or on the one they have chosen.

The students teach one another in a fair-like atmosphere; approximately 10 students have materials set up on their desks for desktop teaching, while the remaining students move from "teacher" to "teacher," participating in the lessons. The students who are teaching rotate with the students who are learning so as to have the opportunity to participate in the lessons prepared by their peers. The students continue rotating around the room until each member of the class has attended the lessons prepared by all of the other members of the class.

> **Table 10.3.** Project ideas for individuals, small groups, or the whole class
>
> Write and produce a movie.
>
> Collect oral histories.
>
> Develop a business plan and/or start a small business.
>
> Design a pamphlet, develop a newspaper or magazine, or write a book.
>
> Propose and launch a new school club.
>
> Plan and create a permanent mural or sculpture for the school.
>
> Study a community or school problem and write a proposal with possible solutions.
>
> Design and implement a school or community survey.
>
> Create a mini-museum for your school or neighborhood library.
>
> Develop a manual for your school (e.g., "What every new student should know").
>
> Create a computer program.
>
> Make your own podcast with material created by class members.
>
> Create board games related to content, complete with illustrations and rules (e.g., "Fun with Fractions").

Students can include visual aids, hands-on materials, short activities, and examples in their lessons. A student in one classroom taught her classmates about the coordinate grid and graphing lines using an ocean theme. She made a large blue coordinate grid to represent the sea and she had students plot points to represent the fish and lines to represent the seaweed. Another student in the group taught how to graph inequalities and intervals using string and M&Ms (Draper, 1997).

Any student with a special skill or interest can incorporate it into the presentation. For instance, Richard, a student with autism, was very gifted in mathematics and was especially good at working out his own algorithms. Instead of presenting typical class content at his desktop, Richard asked students to suggest math problems. He then solved each problem while showing his peers at least two different ways to tackle every one.

Community Research Teams

Still another way to challenge all students in inclusive classrooms is to have them work in heterogeneously grouped research teams (Brown et al., 2000; Kluth, 2000; Tomlinson, 1999). Instead of using the school library as the primary base of information, students can go "straight to the source" and pursue their questions through interviews, observations, and the community artifacts.

Group research offers "something for everybody" in that students have choices about which topics they want to pursue and which group roles they want to adopt. This structure also enhances student collaboration and learning. Sharan and Sharan (1992) found that group research and investigation promotes cooperation and mutual assistance among students with diverse learning profiles. They also found that students engaged in group research demonstrated higher levels of academic achievement than did their peers taught in a more traditional whole-class method.

Because library research requires fairly sophisticated reading and writing skills, some students may not be able to perform the task acceptably. Therefore, many students stand to learn very little, if anything, from this type of research alone. Investigative research in the community, conversely, allows students to take in information visually, kinesthetically, auditorially, and otherwise experientially. Using the entire community as a resource base gives students with diverse learning profiles opportunities to pursue topics and explore environments in which they are most interested; the range of topics can be as diverse as the students themselves.

This type of research is ideal for a diverse group of learners; every student can easily find his or her niche. One research project alone involves a wide range of skills and competencies, including generating provocative questions; designing plans; securing information about community environments and activities; making contacts; developing interviewing skills; and learning to use cameras, computers, and, potentially, new types of software (e.g., movie-making programs).

Such opportunities to interact in the community also provide communication and social opportunities for all students. Miller, Shambaugh, Robinson, and Wimberly (1995) found that students gained confidence in communications skills by interviewing experts and fielding questions from community members. These opportunities may be especially important for students with autism who need practice in these areas. Although interacting with peers is a useful way to practice taking turns and making small talk, having an opportunity to interview a local politician or college sports star can provide special motivation to learn new greetings or try a new joke.

An example of a meaningful research project comes from an elementary school in Ferndale, Wisconsin, where students put their investigative skills together to study airplanes. They sought the expertise of many community members including a local flying club, a pilot, and a building supply store. Part of their community-referenced experience allowed them to spend a $500 voucher in the Boeing Company's warehouse. Students built their own replica of an airplane based on their research experience and exhibited their knowledge at the Paine Field Air Fair in Everett, Washington. They also attended the show as exhibitors and shared their knowledge of aviation with the audience members (Morehouse, 1995). Thus, students not only honed their research skills but also were able to share their work in an authentic way.

Stations

Using stations involves setting up different spots in the classroom where students work on various tasks simultaneously (Cook & Friend, 1995). These stations (or centers, as some teachers call them) invite flexible groupings because not all students need to go to all stations all of the time, and each station houses a task or activity that will appeal to a different type of learner (Lieberman, Lytle, & Clarcq, 2008). This format is appropriate for any class and any age and is ideal for co-teaching (one teacher can support groups; the other can assess or work with individual students).

According to Cook and Friend, "in station teaching, teachers divide instructional content into two, three, or more segments and present the content at separate locations within the classroom" (1995, p. 6). By using this model, teachers are able to offer activities that engage all students in challenging content while freeing themselves to pause at different stations to listen and assess learning, provide more information about a topic, prompt a more complex discussion, ask a question, or reinforce information from lecture or readings.

Stations should focus on important learning goals, contain materials that promote individual students' growth toward those goals; use materials and activities addressing a wide range of reading levels, learning profiles, and student interests; provide clear directions (if some students do not read, this will mean including auditory or pictorial instructions); include instructions about what a student should do when he or she completes the work at the center; and include a record-keeping system to monitor what students do at each station.

Stations might be student or teacher led and any number of activities (e.g., reading, working on a skill, participating in a mini-lesson with a teacher) might be used in this format. For instance, in a secondary classroom, learners in a math class might rotate through several different stations, including the following:

- Working with the teacher to learn about probability

- Solving probability problems from the textbook

- Generating a list of real-world applications for probability

- Working on web games with a partner (Probability Central: http://library.thinkquest.org/11506)

- Completing a review worksheet from the last unit

A teacher could also allow students to move fluidly between these stations based on their interests or needs.

Station teaching is ideal for use in the inclusive classroom because it allows teachers to work with individual students or small groups without having to use a more restrictive "pull-out" model. A special education teacher can be teaching new vocabulary to the student with autism while a general educator can be circulating around the room making sure other students are engaged. Or, a general educator can work with a student with autism and a peer without identified needs on a collaborative writing project while the special educator works at another center with a small group of students who are editing their work. The adults and students in both scenarios are engaged in meaningful ways and all learners are getting what they need.

One adaptation to stations (a format that can be a bit busy and chaotic at times) that may be helpful for some students is to use visual supports (Cohen & Sloan, 2007; Earles-Vollrath et al., 2006). A visual can be created to communicate to students where they should be stationed (see Figure 10.4) and, if needed, to help students engage in the individual tasks at each station as well.

Figure 10.4. Visual support that helps students learn which centers they need to visit.

Another way to individualize instruction in this format is to utilize technology. Amy Benjamin (2005), author of *Differentiated Instruction Using Technology: A Guide for Middle and High School Teachers,* suggests, for instance, that teacher-created PowerPoint presentations can be used as a center. This center can be personalized in that different learners can be assigned to watch different versions of the same presentation (provided more than one computer is available). Students can also be encouraged at such a station to add a few slides of their own to the teacher's presentation. Again, this allows opportunities for differentiation; some students will be able to add a lot of text including thoughts, opinions, and facts. Those unable to type long sentences or generate ideas in writing may be able to add graphics, links to web sites, or single words.

Step 5: Use Multiple Assessments

Finally, teachers need some way of evaluating and making sense of student progress and continued challenges. A myriad of tools and techniques should be employed for this purpose, including those that are formative (i.e., assessment that takes place during the process of learning and teaching) and those that are summative (i.e., assessment used at the end of a period or after the completion of certain activities to determine the level of skill or concept mastery). Here, I explore ideas for testing students on the spectrum as well as provide ideas for using authentic assessment tools.

Testing

Traditionally, student learning has been assessed by a collection of tests and quizzes. Although these tools are sometimes appropriate for learning about student progress, it is only one strategy among many that should be used to understand the needs, learning, and academic growth of all students.

As Wendy Lawson (1998), a woman on the autism spectrum, explained, testing can be a very confusing and stressful experience when the proper supports are not offered. In the following passage, she recounts the frustration she felt when directed to take a placement exam for secondary school:

> I was accompanied into a small room not far from Sister's office. It had only one desk and one chair in it, plus a loud ticking clock on the wall directly opposite where I sat. I was given a pencil and several sheets of paper and told it was important to my education that I concentrate and work to the best of my ability. Whatever "important to my education" meant, being in that office with those bits of paper did not feel very important to me.
>
> I drew on paper, played "[Tic Tac Toe]" and felt very anxious—I had told one of the nurses earlier that I would roll some bandages for her and I felt that really was important. (p. 42)

Not surprisingly, Lawson did not pass the exam. In reflecting on this experience, she offered suggestions for how the situation might have been more supportive:

> Maybe if the exam had been explained to me and I had been told to read the information sheet accompanying the writing paper, I might have attempted to answer the questions. It would have been very helpful if the exam had been broken down into smaller chunks of information so that I could have worked without being overwhelmed by so many words all lumped together. (pp. 42–43)

As Lawson illustrated, tests can be real obstacles for students with unique learning profiles (Salend, 2009). Tests are a reality, however, and nearly every teacher gives one at some point during the year. For this reason, all teachers should have general knowledge of how to make tests as fair and as stress-free as possible. Some of the most common ways to do this are as follows:

- Make the students comfortable; for longer tests, in particular, give learners seating choices (e.g., with a study carrel, in a favorite room).

- Be sure the student has plenty of experience with the types of questions featured on the test and with the testing format used.

- Make it efficient for the learner (Wormeli, 2006); put all matching items on one page and have students circle *T* or *F* instead of having to write *true* or *false,* for instance.

- Be very clear in your directions; highlight and underline key words (Salend, 2009).

- Provide a sample question and completed answer in each new section to illustrate how students should respond.

- Provide a layout that is uncluttered and user friendly; provide appropriate margins, group like items together, and use borders to draw attention to directions or to examples that are provided.

If following these guidelines still will not provide enough support for your students, the content, format, or even objectives of the test can be changed. Teachers might, for instance, have students take the test with a partner, allow some or all learners to use crib sheets, or allow learners to take two tests and accept the highest score. See Figure 10.5 for a test created for a learner needing adapted content and less complex language.

A final suggestion for testing students with autism (especially those with motor problems) is to assess "off the page." In other words, find a way to assess the same or similar content while minimizing or eliminating the pencil and paper portion. Some ways to adapt "off the page" include interviewing the student, having him or her arrange items instead of writing them out (e.g., arrange cards in order to show the life cycle of the butterfly), or even having the learner act out or otherwise demonstrate knowledge.

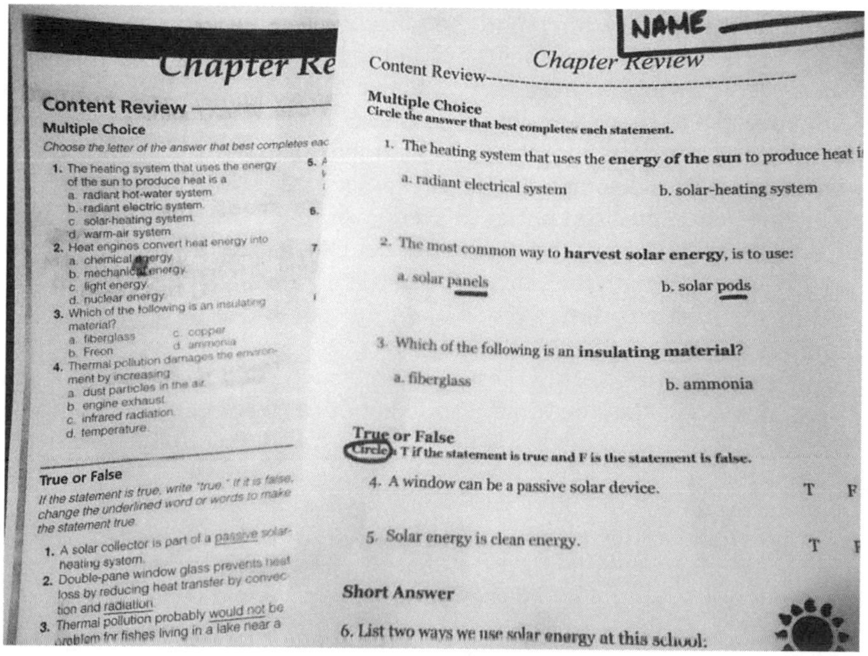

Figure 10.5. Adapted test with fewer items, more work space, and less complex content.

Authentic Assessments

Even with several adaptations in place, some students with autism will never be able to demonstrate understanding by taking a pencil and paper test. The most effective way to gather information about what students know and can do is to use a wide range of authentic assessment strategies.

Darling-Hammond suggested that assessments be based on "meaningful performances in real-world contexts" and that these performances should be so "closely entwined as to be often inseparable" from the curriculum itself (1997, p. 115). This proposal is a far stretch from the teach-test-teach-test model so often used in schools today. Despite the prevalence of the testing culture, however, many teachers are moving toward these more meaningful ways of assessing students. In one middle school classroom, a teacher who wanted to move to more authentic ways of assessing student learning eliminated her unit test on drugs and alcohol. Instead, she had students develop a PowerPoint presentation and create a brochure related to content learned. Students then worked with peers to edit these materials and enhanced content by talking to community professionals (e.g., nurses). At the unit's end, students gave presentations to other classes and elicited feedback about the content presented and their presentation skills. And Richardson (2006) reported on a teacher who introduced his students to Web publishing and taught them to turn writing assignments into podcasts and into their own student blogs (http://www.mrmayo.typepad.com/). Other assessment ideas for the inclusive classroom include portfolios, exhibitions and presentations, checklists, projects, essays, reflections, and journals; anecdotal reports, interviews, observations, models, artwork and selected work samples.

Authentic assessments offer a fuller picture of student learning in that they are linked directly to what students are learning (Luongo-Orlando, 2003), are continuous and cumulative, occur during real learning experiences, are collaborative, and are easily communicated to all stakeholders (Pike & Salend, 1995; Valencia, 1990). Perhaps most important, authentic assessments are student-centered. That is, students engaged in authentic assessments often evaluate themselves, have choices in how to be assessed, and participate in designing criteria. A carefully constructed assessment system can provide all students access to academic opportunities (Layton & Lock, 2007).

Using authentic assessments may be especially crucial when teaching students with autism because of the difficulties some of these individuals experience in reading, writing, or communicating. These difficulties might prevent them from adequately completing a traditional assessment (e.g., quiz) and may lead a teacher to believe that these students are less knowledgeable or capable than they are. For instance, one of my former students, Gail, hated to write. When the first-grade teacher asked students to get out their notebooks or workbooks, she visibly cringed and sometimes cried. She seemed especially distressed when it was time for math instruction. She did not or could not complete the easiest math worksheets and she appeared confused when the teacher asked her to solve simple math problems (e.g., "What is 2 + 2?"). When I met with the teacher, she reported that she was enjoying having Gail in class but that the math curriculum seemed inappropriate for the child. The teacher reported that Gail could not count or even identify numbers.

A different picture of this learner emerged when I visited Gail's home 2 weeks later. When I arrived, Gail's mother asked her to get three coffee cups out of the cupboard and two spoons from the drawer. She then asked Gail to go and play in the basement and "come back upstairs in a half hour." Gail followed these directions with ease (returning exactly 30 minutes later), and I went back to school with news for the classroom teacher; we would need to assess Gail in context and pay more attention to her actions and the real work she performed in the classroom; not only did she have math skills we had not seen but she had at least one (telling time) that other 6-year-olds did not!

Summary

When I began teaching, I felt my job as a special educator was to get lesson plans from general educators and create adaptations that would ensure the participation of students with disabilities in the classroom. Of course, this approach had many flaws. Because I did not work with the teachers very closely, I didn't know the curriculum well enough to make meaningful adaptations. And once lessons were planned it was difficult to make changes to them or to invent creative assignments or strategies that might facilitate the involvement of students with unique learning characteristics.

As teachers move toward using more collaborative teaching models and developing pedagogy that is inclusive and that supports and responds to all learners, it is less likely that they will need to engage in impromptu adaptation creation and lesson planning and more likely that students will be able to gain access to curriculum, instruction, and assessment that is carefully planned and thoughtfully implemented. It is also more likely that students will see each other as capable and as learners.

A popular teaching mantra is "If they can't learn the way we teach them, let's teach them the way they learn." This philosophy is especially important for today's inclusive classrooms. By choosing content that matters, using flexible groupings, offering a wide range of materials, mixing up lesson formats, and designing a variety of assessments, teachers set all students up for success and give those with and without autism opportunities to learn with and from one another in the inclusive classroom.

FOR MORE ANSWERS AND INFORMATION

 Books

Benjamin, A. (2005). *Differentiated instruction using technology: A guide for middle and high school teachers.* Larchmont, NY: Eye on Education.

Gent, P. (2009). *Great ideas: Using service learning and differentiated instruction to help your students succeed.* Baltimore: Paul H. Brookes Publishing Co.

Lewis, B. (2009). *The kid's guide to service projects: Over 500 service ideas for young people who want to make a difference* (2nd ed.). Minneapolis, MN: Free Spirit Publishing.

Salend, S. (2009). *Classroom testing and assessment for ALL students: Beyond standardization.* Thousand Oaks, CA: Corwin Press.

Schwarz, P., & Kluth, P. (2007). *"You're welcome": 30 innovative ideas for inclusive classrooms.* Portsmouth, NH: Heinemann.

Silberman, M. (1996). *Active learning: 101 strategies to teach any subject.* Boston: Allyn & Bacon.

Udvari-Solner, A., & Kluth, P. (2007). *Joyful learning: Active and collaborative learning in the inclusive classroom.* Thousand Oaks, CA: Corwin Press.

(continued)

(continued)

Web Sites

The Access Center

http://www.k8accesscenter.org

> The Access Center is a national technical assistance (TA) center. You will find articles, forms, and PowerPoint presentations on differentiated instruction.

Authentic Assessment Toolbox

http://jonathan.mueller.faculty.noctrl.edu/toolbox/

> Compiled by professor Jon Mueller, this site includes a lot of FAQs about authentic assessment and features several examples of authentic tasks, rubrics, and portfolios.

CAST

http://www.cast.org/pd/index.html

> The CAST web site offers hundreds, if not thousands, of ideas for expanding learning opportunities for all. Technology is a special focus of this site.

Differentiation Daily

http://differentiationdaily.com/

> I created this site specifically to reach teachers in inclusive schools who are seeking new ideas for differentiation. Every day (except Saturdays and Sundays), I post a link to a new teaching or lesson planning idea on the web.

National Service Learning Clearinghouse

http://www.servicelearning.org

> A one-stop shop for everything related to service learning. Find project ideas, recommended reading, and resources for both kids and their teachers.

NOTES: _____

_____

_____

_____

_____

_____

_____

_____

_____

_____

11

Teaching Strategies

with Christi Kasa-Hendrickson

I was amazed when I started fifth grade and [my teacher] seemed
to understand my problems. She let me complete the Scholastic Reading
Achievement tests at my own pace. When I finished them, she let me choose my own
reading material and write book reports. She never criticized my bad penmanship. She allowed
me to start and edit a class poetry journal called *Writers on the Wing*. (Prince-Hughes, 2004, p. 47)

In a study conducted by the second author of this chapter, Lisa Tyler, a teacher, shared the process she uses to ensure participation of all students in the classroom:

> Here are some questions I ask myself when I am thinking of how all kids can participate: Is this student able to share his opinions and thoughts about the activity? Can the student ask a question when they need help? Does the student have peers around to work on the subject with? Is the relationship equal, do the [students] seek each other out? Is the work area and environment supporting the students' attention? These are just some but I think there are many more. But this is what I do. I have to answer these questions because it is not ok for the student to just sit there. I want the students to participate, to interact with their own learning. (Kasa-Hendrickson, 2002, p. 57)

Lisa and the other teachers who participated in this study (which focused on supporting students with autism in inclusive classrooms) used a range of strategies to meet the needs of students with and without disabilities. As Lisa pointed out, they were reflective about their practice and constantly thought about how students would use the classroom space, communicate and interact, gain access to curriculum and instruction, and work with each other.

Teachers in the study also shared that they felt comfortable trying different strategies for different students and taking risks with new strategies when one particular teaching approach was not effective. As another teacher in the study commented, "If you get hit with a problem there's always a way to make it work. Nothing is insurmountable . . . but that's what I love, the problem-solving piece of teaching" (2002, p. 117).

This chapter is our attempt to help teachers engage in some of the problem solving described by Lisa Tyler and her colleagues. We hope that our strategies raise helpful questions, provide answers, and perhaps even inspire teacher creativity, in general. The chapter is divided into three sections. First, we offer strategies that can be used to prepare for the arrival of a student with autism. The second section details strategies that can be used in the general education classroom to benefit all students; and the third section includes strategies that individual students with autism may find helpful. Because teaching is a dynamic process, the strategies that work for one student may or may not work for another. Having expressed that, it is also true that certain strategies are often successful with some students with autism as well as with many students without identified disabilities. Many of these strategies, in fact, are simply suggestions for good teaching that can support students with a range of needs, strengths, and abilities in inclusive classrooms.

Getting Ready for Inclusive Schooling: Strategies to Support Students and Teachers

This section offers suggestions for helping teachers and students prepare for inclusive schooling. These strategies are designed to prepare the learner with autism for a new school or a new schooling experience and can be used days or months before the student arrives in the inclusive school or classroom. Any of these strategies also can be used throughout the school year. The strategies discussed are information, ideas, and inspiration; student or family surveys; personal portfolios; planning in reverse; school preview; and Making Action Plans (MAPS).

Information, Ideas, and Inspiration

Perhaps the best "strategy" that teachers can use to ensure success is to collect information, ideas, and inspiration about autism and their student. If an educator needs more information on autism itself, there are many ways to learn. For instance, many autobiographies have been published in the last 2 decades (see Table 11.1). These books, without question, serve as the best source of information on autism. There are autobiographies that are appropriate for any audience and any purpose, including some written for young people, some written for people on the spectrum, and some written for families or teachers of those on the spectrum. Many helpful sources of information about inclusion also are available. If you started this journey of inclusive schooling in the early 1980s, there would have been little professional literature to guide you. Today, however, there are web sites, books, and articles aplenty on the topic, including resources aimed specifically at preschool, elementary, and secondary audiences (see For More Answers and Information at the end of this and other chapters for book and web site recommendations).

Teachers might also look for support and information from parent groups, local and national conferences, and other teachers who have successfully educated students with diverse needs and abilities in an inclusive classroom. If a student has been educated previously in an inclusive classroom, it might be helpful to talk to the teachers who supported that student. Teachers who have specific teaching roles might find it helpful to talk to others who share their responsibilities; for instance, an English teacher might find it very helpful to talk to the student's previous English or reading teacher.

Observing the student in his or her current classroom setting also can be useful. If the teacher knows that she will have a certain student in the classroom for the next school year, she should take time to observe the learner, if possible. In particular, these observations should focus on the student's successes: What can this student do well? What has worked to

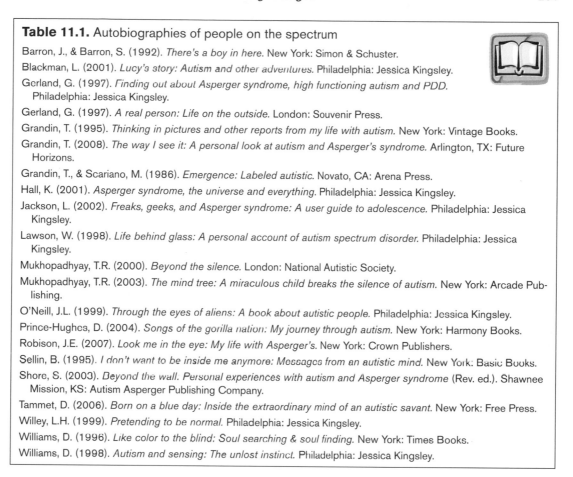

Table 11.1. Autobiographies of people on the spectrum

Barron, J., & Barron, S. (1992). *There's a boy in here.* New York: Simon & Schuster.

Blackman, L. (2001). *Lucy's story: Autism and other adventures.* Philadelphia: Jessica Kingsley.

Gerland, G. (1997). *Finding out about Asperger syndrome, high functioning autism and PDD.* Philadelphia: Jessica Kingsley.

Gerland, G. (1997). *A real person: Life on the outside.* London: Souvenir Press.

Grandin, T. (1995). *Thinking in pictures and other reports from my life with autism.* New York: Vintage Books.

Grandin, T. (2008). *The way I see it: A personal look at autism and Asperger's syndrome.* Arlington, TX: Future Horizons.

Grandin, T., & Scariano, M. (1986). *Emergence: Labeled autistic.* Novato, CA: Arena Press.

Hall, K. (2001). *Asperger syndrome, the universe and everything.* Philadelphia: Jessica Kingsley.

Jackson, L. (2002). *Freaks, geeks, and Asperger syndrome: A user guide to adolescence.* Philadelphia: Jessica Kingsley.

Lawson, W. (1998). *Life behind glass: A personal account of autism spectrum disorder.* Philadelphia: Jessica Kingsley.

Mukhopadhyay, T.R. (2000). *Beyond the silence.* London: National Autistic Society.

Mukhopadhyay, T.R. (2003). *The mind tree: A miraculous child breaks the silence of autism.* New York: Arcade Publishing.

O'Neill, J.L. (1999). *Through the eyes of aliens: A book about autistic people.* Philadelphia: Jessica Kingsley.

Prince-Hughes, D. (2004). *Songs of the gorilla nation: My journey through autism.* New York: Harmony Books.

Robison, J.E. (2007). *Look me in the eye: My life with Asperger's.* New York: Crown Publishers.

Sellin, B. (1995). *I don't want to be inside me anymore: Messages from an autistic mind.* New York: Basic Books.

Shore, S. (2003). *Beyond the wall: Personal experiences with autism and Asperger syndrome* (Rev. ed.). Shawnee Mission, KS: Autism Asperger Publishing Company.

Tammet, D. (2006). *Born on a blue day: Inside the extraordinary mind of an autistic savant.* New York: Free Press.

Willey, L.H. (1999). *Pretending to be normal.* Philadelphia: Jessica Kingsley.

Williams, D. (1996). *Like color to the blind: Soul searching & soul finding.* New York: Times Books.

Williams, D. (1998). *Autism and sensing: The unlost instinct.* Philadelphia: Jessica Kingsley.

create success for the student? The observing teacher might also record questions for the student's current teacher that can be answered in a short meeting or via e-mail. See Figure 11.1 for a sample observation form.

Student or Family Surveys

Consider the way a teacher might feel after reading this excerpt from a report:

> Michael's behavior has continued to escalate this year and now is directed toward almost everyone. . . . His whole program is in jeopardy. As his aggression has increased less positives can be implemented and there is general frustration about him. Peers avoid him. (Kluth, 1998, p. 73)

Contrast this report with an account of how Michael understood those same behaviors:

> I never got to learn in a classroom that taught academics but I was all ready to learn. The classroom was called self-contained because they wouldn't let us out. It made me feel so sad and angry and I was doing a lot of kicking. (Kluth, 1998, p. 73)

This perspective can be incredibly helpful and can give teachers ideas for working with Michael and for creating an ideal program for him. When educators have only test scores and clinical reports to inform their teaching, they may be puzzled by how to translate that infor-

Student Observation Form

Student: _____ Date: _____

Setting (grade level/type of classroom): _____

Lesson/activity: _____

Observable student strengths:

_____

_____

Observable struggles or challenges	Teacher response to or support for the challenge, if any

Adaptations used:

Comments or suggestions from the current teacher:

_____

_____

_____

Questions for the current staff:

_____

_____

Questions for the family:

_____

_____

Figure 11.1. Inclusive schooling Student Observation Form.

"You're Going to Love This Kid!" Teaching Students with Autism in the Inclusive Classroom, Second Edition, by Paula Kluth
Copyright © 2010 by Paul H. Brookes Publishing Co. All rights reserved.

mation into practice. A teacher reading Michael's school record might feel anxious about having him in the classroom. After reading Michael's own account, however, a teacher would have a more meaningful understanding of the behavior and might have some ideas on how to support him. She might, for instance, engineer opportunities for him to receive more challenging instruction and talk to him about his frustration and sadness.

Personal surveys can help to fill in gaps left by formal school reports (Udvari-Solner, 2007). Before the school year begins or during the first couple of weeks of classes, some teachers ask students and their families to complete a survey. This tool can help the teacher become better acquainted with learners and their families. Some teachers may choose to administer different surveys to students and parents, whereas other teachers may design a survey that families and students complete together. Although a survey would undoubtedly help a teacher learn more about his or her student with autism, many teachers choose to use them with every student in the class.

Surveys are a nice way to begin the school year for a student with autism, especially because so many with this label have been diagnosed, assessed, and otherwise evaluated by dozens of professionals during their schooling career. In many cases, teachers who meet a learner with autism for the first time are introduced to him or her through these records. In some cases, records include descriptions of and data suggesting what students *cannot* do. A survey can give a student and his or her family an opportunity to provide information about what the student *can* do; it elicits information that is positive and personal and can give the teacher a unique first-hand account of the individual's life.

Udvari-Solner (2007) provides an example of how survey information can be integrated into curriculum and instruction. She writes about an English teacher who developed an "expertise profile" of his students based on questions such as, "What do you do well?" and "What have you learned from your family?" He discovered that his students had interests ranging from clothing design to hip-hop music to botany. He also found out that Julie, a student with Down syndrome, had lived in South Africa at one point in her life. The teacher was then able to use this information when the class studied folklore. Julie shared tribal artifacts and stories from her own childhood in Africa and was able to contribute to the class in a way that might otherwise have been overlooked.

When considering what to include on a survey, teachers should focus on learning styles, interests, needs, strengths, and even the student's ideas for the classroom. If one or more students cannot write, the teacher, parent, or support person can ask these learners to submit graphic or visual surveys. Students might draw pictures; create a collage; or submit photographs, a video clip, or audio recording in response to the survey questions. See Figure 11.2 for a survey you could adapt or use in your K–12 classroom. You can find additional copies of surveys on Paula's Facebook fan page in the photos section.

Personal Portfolios

Portfolios are another way students with unique needs and abilities can introduce themselves to teachers and peers. Portfolios may include photographs, artwork, writing or schoolwork samples, and even lists of favorite things. Although using a portfolio is a good idea for a student with autism, it also can be fun for the entire class. In one school, all students created portfolios to share with their classmates and school personnel and used them to get to know each other better and to educate teachers about their lives outside of school.

A portfolio can be an especially helpful tool for students who do not speak or use a reliable communication system. I worked with one young man, J.D., to assemble a portfolio he would use as he made the transition from middle school to high school. This student did not speak, and those who met him for the first time often struggled to connect with him. When his teachers first accompanied him to his new school, J.D.'s peers began asking them ques-

Student Survey

Instructions: This form should be completed by the student or by the student and his or her family.

What words describe you best?

What hobbies do you have?

What do you want to learn this year?

What is your favorite part of the school day?

What is your favorite thing to do at school?

What are your talents or areas of expertise (e.g., karate, babysitting, collecting bugs, drawing)?

What else do you want me to know about you?

Figure 11.2.   Example of a Student Survey.

 From Kluth, P., & Schwarz, P. (2008). *"Just give him the whale!" 20 ways to use fascinations, areas of expertise, and strengths to support students with autism* (pp. 11–12). Baltimore: Paul H. Brookes Publishing Co.; adapted by permission. Copyright © 2008 by Paul H. Brookes Publishing Co. Inc.

In *"You're Going to Love This Kid!" Teaching Students with Autism in the Inclusive Classroom, Second Edition,* by Paula Kluth. (2010, Paul H. Brookes Publishing Co., Inc.)

tions about him: Did he understand them? Did he have any interests? Why did he flap his arms like that? The teachers decided that J.D. needed a way to represent himself so that they didn't need to serve as his voice and liaison. In order to facilitate this process, the teachers worked with J.D. to create a portfolio that he could use to introduce himself to new people and to interact with those he already knew. J.D.'s portfolio included the following:

- Four pages of photographs (J.D. with family, J.D. playing soccer, J.D. working on a biology experiment, J.D. visiting the Rock and Roll Hall of Fame in Ohio)

- A short "résumé" outlining some of the classes he took in middle school

- A list of his favorite movies and songs

- A "Learning About Autism" pamphlet J.D. got at a conference

- A glossy picture of the Green Bay Packers, J.D.'s favorite football team

Although it took a few weeks for J.D. to initiate conversations using the portfolio, he soon became comfortable approaching his classmates to share the book. Individuals who saw J.D.'s portfolio now had a way to interact with him and learn more about his life. Two of J.D.'s classmates even developed their own portfolios to share with him.

All of J.D.'s new teachers had opportunities to review his book before he started their classes; this helped the instructors become acquainted with J.D. and to understand something about his needs and strengths. One of J.D.'s teachers even used one of his favorite movies in her English class as a result of reviewing his portfolio, and another teacher helped him to create some watercolor landscape paintings to include in his growing album.

Portfolios can be in paper, audio, or video form; formal or informal; and composed of a few pages or dozens of pages. They can include only current information and artifacts or serve as a cumulative record of the student's life. One student I know keeps his formal portfolio at home and carries a four-page condensed copy with him at all times. Another student, a young woman with Asperger syndrome, developed a creative video portfolio complete with clips of her sisters reading poetry that she wrote. See Figure 11.3 for a glimpse of a personal portfolio.

Planning in Reverse

Planning in reverse is most useful when working with students who need the most unique supports. Planning in reverse means looking first at "what works" and building from there instead of looking at a typical school day and asking, "How will this student fit in to the day or schedule as it exists?" The process begins with a teacher or teachers brainstorming about all of the student's strengths, preferences, and abilities and generating ways to include the student using these ideas. Teachers beginning the process of planning in reverse should first ask themselves the following questions:

- In what contexts, school situations, or environments is the student successful?

- When does the student perform well?

- What opportunities does the student have to present his or her knowledge or understanding of age-appropriate content?

- When does the student successfully interact with peers in meaningful ways?

The following is an example of planning in reverse:

Preshanth, a nearly nonverbal student with autism, loved to learn but had a difficult time with the seatwork and quiet study time that dominated many of his high school classes. His

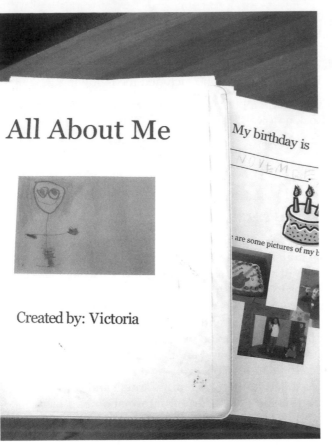

Figure 11.3. A third grader's personal portfolio.

speech was very limited, but he could interact with others by using his communication board. Preshanth was able to sit for approximately 10 minutes at a time and needed a lot of engagement to stay connected to a task. Preshanth also loved to swim. He felt at ease in the water and could move independently in the pool.

Planning in reverse for Preshanth involved capitalizing on his strength in swimming. Preshanth's team arranged for him to swim twice a day. His high school had a swimming pool, so this adaptation to the day was fairly easy. The pool was often occupied with PE classes, however, so involving Preshanth in swimming meant getting permission from the PE teacher and arranging a way for Preshanth to participate in the classes. The teacher agreed to give Preshanth room to swim independently while working to incorporate him into classroom drills and activities when possible.

Next, the team examined Preshanth's need for active learning and targeted classes in which he could be successful and active. We gave him a list of possible classes and he chose biology, family and consumer education, and English (with a teacher who often asked students to act out stories and plays). Teachers of these classes agreed to let Preshanth stand or pace in the back of the classroom during lectures. They also built errands into their lessons so Preshanth had a constructive reason to take a break each day. One day, for example, the biology teacher asked Preshanth and a friend to go outside and get a soil sample. During another lesson, he asked Preshanth and a classmate to go to the office and call a local fish hatchery to ask a question.

Similar adaptations were made in Preshanth's English class. Students in that class were typically given long periods of time to do silent reading and writing. Although we did implement several different supports that allowed Preshanth to read and write at his desk, he struggled to participate in this activity for more than 10 minutes. The teacher, using the planning in reverse strategy, began thinking about Preshanth's strengths and abilities; she considered what he *could* do instead of dwelling on what he couldn't do and decided to offer him the chance to use the classroom computers at any time during the reading and writing time. She found some literacy-based computer programs he could work on during this time and eventually allowed some other students in the classroom to work on literacy-based software programs during the independent reading and writing time.

The key to planning in reverse, of course, is to always look for opportunities to create a more typical experience for the learner when possible. A student who starts the year needing physical education more than once a day may be ready to return to just one class by the second quarter. And a learner who can't sit still for lectures and must have alternative activities may be able to engage in more traditional classroom tasks over time.

School Preview

Many students with autism will profit from seeing, experiencing, and learning about the school before they show up on the first day. This is an effective strategy for students who are changing schools or for those who will be going to a certain classroom for the first time. A student can preview the school using many different tools. Some learners might appreciate a DVD of the school and its rooms, complete with short interviews with their new teachers (e.g., "Hi, I'm Ms. Thiel, and I'm going to be your fifth-grade teacher. We always start our day with humor, so feel free to bring your favorite joke book. We also use a lot of cooperative learning so you will get to know and work with all of the students in the classroom throughout the year."). Other students like to meet teachers face to face before school officially starts. Still others may want to hear siblings, parents, or friends tell them about the school. Here are a few other ways students can experience a preview:

- Send them brochures of the school and other paperwork (e.g., school calendar, student handbook).

- Send them school newsletters from the previous year.

- Show them the school's web site and have them take a "tour" by visiting the different areas of the site, reading information, and looking at pictures.

- Have them construct questions about the school and/or new classes and ask teachers to answer those questions in writing, or perhaps via a Skype phone call.

Some students need more than a video or brochure to introduce them to a new school. One of our former students visited his new school once a week during the summer. On every visit, he saw a different room. By September, when the school year began, he was able to make the transition with ease.

Making Action Plans (MAPS)

Making Action Plans (MAPS; Forest & Lusthaus 1990; Forest & Pearpoint; 1992; Forest, Pearpoint, Vandercook, & York, 1989; Pearpoint, Forest, & O'Brien, 1996) addresses the question, "What does the child and family want?" The MAPS process is a tool teams can use to "think big" for a particular learner; it is especially appropriate for those students who are new to inclusive education because the process can help teachers generate adaptations and supports as well as serve as a starting point for a new IEP (Pearpoint et al., 1996).

MAPS brings together key individuals in a student's life. The student, his or her family and teachers, and others who are significant in the person's life meet to discuss dreams and goals and to brainstorm ways of making them a reality. The team then creates an action plan for the general education classroom (Pearpoint et al., 1996).

MAPS is different from some other assessment or planning tools because the process is centered on the strengths, potential, and uniqueness of the learner instead of on weaknesses or deficit areas. MAPS is based on the following core beliefs:

- All students belong in general classrooms—no ifs, ands, or buts.

- General education teachers can teach all students.

- Necessary supports will be provided as needed.

- Quality education is a right, not a privilege.

- Outcomes must be success, literacy, and graduation for all.

- Creative alternatives will be available for populations who do not succeed in typical ways (Pearpoint et al., 1996).

To use the MAPS process, stakeholders assemble and generate ideas for including the individual in schooling and in community life. Participants typically include the student; his parents; other family members of the student (e.g., grandmother, sister); classroom teachers (both general and special education); an administrator; and other school professionals such as a social worker, a favorite coach, or even a playground assistant. The student's peers also are invited to the meeting and are central to the process.

A MAPS session also requires two facilitators who guide the team through questions and ensure the comfort and participation of all. One facilitator, the process facilitator, explains the collaborative planning process and asks the questions. The other facilitator functions as a recorder; he or she takes notes using visuals; colored markers; and, typically, many sheets of chart paper. For technology-oriented teams, PowerPoint slides projected on a screen can also serve as a structure for note taking.

Hospitality is also a part of the MAPS process. The atmosphere should be personal and informal. To achieve this, the facilitator might put motivational posters on the wall, provide beanbag chairs for the younger participants, tack up favorite photos of the participant, or ask members of the group to bring a treat to share.

To begin the MAPS process, the family members answer the question, "What is _____'s history and story?" Then, each of the individuals present at the MAPS session focus on the remaining five questions and the plan that make up the MAPS process. These questions include the following:

- What are your dreams for _____? The facilitator should encourage the participants to think big. She might remind them that this is an opportunity to share their wishes without thinking about the constraints of money or time. In other words, participants should share what they truly dream for the student of focus, not what they think they can get or what they think is reasonable.

- What are your nightmares for _____? This can be a hard question to ask and an emotional one to answer. This question is used to generate a profile of what to avoid.

- Who is _____? Or, What are some words that describe _____ best?

- What are _____'s gifts, strengths, and talents? This is usually an enjoyable and easy part of the process. Some team members find they view the student differently after seeing the extensive list of strengths, gifts, and talents forming.

- What is _____ good at doing? What are his or her needs? The latter part of this question is when the team considers the person's struggles. The team also considers the different types of supports the individual receives or needs. Needs listed can range from concrete resources such as money or a new piece of assistive technology to abstract ideas such as love or happiness.

In order for the meeting to qualify as MAPS, the team must make a decision to assemble again and the meeting must end with the formation of a concrete plan of action. Participants should leave with actual tasks to address immediately. For instance, a parent may need to contact the drama teacher about getting the student involved in the school play. A school principal might work on a student's course schedule, making sure he or she can take classes with some friends. A general educator might go back to her classroom and move the student's desk to the front of the room. A friend might make a date with the student to go shopping.

After the process is over, the MAPS facilitator may also ask participants to think of ways in which the student has been described on other assessments. For instance, when I facilitated a MAPS session with a young woman named Crystal, she was described by the team as "a good listener," "a true friend," "always smiling," "loves art class," "Beach Boys fan," "a dancer," and "a trendy dresser." Then, the group brainstormed labels she had been given in her records. Figure 11.4 includes details about Crystal's MAPS session. That list included the

MAPS: for Crystal

What are your dreams for _Crystal_ ?

- Traveling to South Padre Island
  Winning the lottery and having all the money she will need
  Falling in love
- Driving a car
- Going to dance school
- Being able to talk

What are _Crystal's_ gifts?

- Loving
- Good listener
- Great smile
- Sensitive
- Graceful
- Active and a fast runner

What are your nightmares for _Crystal_ ?

- She will never have a boyfriend.
- She won't be able to live in her own house.
- She won't finish high school.

What are some of _Crystal's_ needs?

- Daily quiet time
- Soft clothes
- Access to her baseball cards at all times
- Friends around her
- Time to read her favorite books

Crystal is . . . (What are some words that describe _Crystal_ best?)

- Jolly
- A sister
- A daughter
- Animal lover
- Animated
- A night owl
- Family-oriented
- Funny
- Shy
- A true friend
- A Beach Boys fan
- A trendy dresser
- A dancer

IDEAS FOR A PLAN: What would an ideal day look like for _Crystal_ ?

- She would get to watch a few minutes of CNN before school.
- She would walk to school with a friend and go to the cafeteria to hang out before classes begin.
- She would go to general education classes with her peers.
- She would get to take two art classes including one course related to sculpture (her friend Robby would be in the class with her).
- She would have lunch with a group of friends, and she would get to eat hamburgers at least once a week.
- She would get to take a 10-minute walk with one of these friends before heading back to classes.
- She would get to take a physical education class in the afternoon—hopefully with Mr. Dyson, her favorite teacher. She would get to help to manage the equipment during class.
- She would get to have some trail mix as a snack in the afternoon.
- She would stay after school and attend track practice.
- She would get to dance.
- She would get to listen to the Beach Boys at some point.

Figure 11.4. An example of MAPS for Crystal

following descriptors: "mentally retarded," "disabled," "slow," "manipulative," "autistic," and "aggressive." As a group, we contrasted these two sets of descriptions. This part of the process is important because it helps participants see that the discourse of special education often overshadows the individual's strengths and uniqueness.

Supporting Teaching and Learning: Strategies to Use with the Whole Class

Many strategies that seem effective for students with autism are also useful to use with all students in the inclusive classroom. In this section, we highlight several strategies that teachers can use to support students with autism and their peers as they plan lessons and organize instruction. These strategies are routines and schedules; transition tools; checklists, guides, and rules; organization support; choices; nonverbal supports and cues; and "stay put" boxes.

Routines and Schedules

Many students benefit from the development and implementation of written schedules, picture calendars, or daily planners. As one of our former students with autism explained to us, "School is very stimulating and a lot of noises and disorganization for me. So I need to get used to new places and have a schedule." Likewise, Daniel Tammet, a man on the spectrum, recalls that he craved order and would became upset if school events were announced on short notice: "Predictability was important to me, a way of feeling in control in a given situation, a way of keeping feelings of anxiety at bay, at least temporarily" (2006, p. 67).

Obviously, teachers should talk often to students with autism about how time will be used in the classroom. They also should try to give them as much warning as possible when they are going to alter the class schedule or when a substitute will be teaching the class.

All students, in fact, in a given classroom may benefit from knowing more about the schedule. Having information about what content will be taught and what activities will take place on any given day or week can help any student become a better planner and time manager. Teachers can make going over the daily schedule a part of the routine in any classroom; even taking a few seconds to review this information can make a difference in the learning of some students. Students with autism may even want to copy the agenda or schedule into an individual notebook so they can peek at it throughout the day and be reminded of the hour-by-hour events.

Martha Kaufeldt (1999) writes her daily agenda on a tablet of chart paper that she keeps on a stand. She flips the chart over daily, but old schedules are handy at any time. This system ensures that students who are absent can independently learn about work they need to start or finish. Kaufeldt pointed out that this system also serves as a planning tool for the teacher. At any time, a teacher can see how much time has been dedicated to certain activities and when units of study were started or finished.

It is sometimes surprising to discover how many students seem to appreciate knowing "what comes next." In our current roles as college professors, we often observe students highlighting their syllabi, carefully crossing off each topic as it is covered in class. We also occasionally have students approach us at the beginning of a class to ask, "Can you tell me what we will do today?" Although some students may want to know what activities and transitions are happening at what specific times, others may be satisfied with even a simple description of events, or what we call a *checklist schedule* (see Figure 11.5 for an example). A checklist schedule is a good option for a secondary education teacher or for any instructor who will

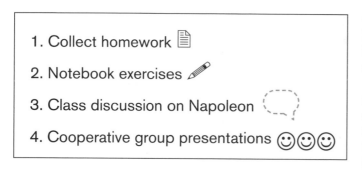

1. Collect homework

2. Notebook exercises

3. Class discussion on Napoleon

4. Cooperative group presentations ☺☺☺

Figure 11.5.   Example of a checklist schedule used in a high school social studies classroom.

teach for a short period of time and knows what will be covered but can't be sure how much time each topic or activity will take.

Keep in mind that students can be responsible for creating the schedule or presenting it to the class. The teacher might use this opportunity to teach any number of skills or competencies. For example, when students are more actively involved in the schedule tasks, the schedule itself becomes a literacy activity. Students can enhance reading, writing, speaking, and listening skills while learning how to plan time and follow an agenda. A teacher might even ask students to come up and cross the items off the list as they are accomplished.

Consider that younger learners (or those with a lot of anxiety about time or transitions) may want to keep a personal schedule at their desks. Students or teachers can use pictures symbols such as those from the Boardmaker software program to represent the day's schedule. Then small pieces of Velcro can be placed on the back of each symbol and the student can move each piece of the schedule as activities are completed. This type of schedule also can be posted at the front of the room; the student with autism or any other student can be responsible for managing (e.g., arranging, taking off) the symbols or pictures as the day passes. See Figure 11.6 for a sample schedule used by an elementary student on the spectrum.

Transition Tools

Students with autism struggle with transitions. Some students are uncomfortable changing from environment to environment, whereas others have problems moving from activity to activity. Individuals with autism report that changes can be extremely difficult, causing stress and feelings of disorientation.

Teachers can minimize the discomfort students may feel when making transitions by providing cues and supports. For instance, a teacher we know plays a transition song ("What a Wonderful World" by Louis Armstrong) every time her third graders need to switch activities in the classroom. After the first few weeks, students know they have 2 minutes and 17 seconds to get where they are going—whether it is to line up at the door or to grab clipboards and get to the rug area (and Diane, the teacher, claims that the transition also helps *her* keep organized and change activities smoothly and without delays). Other ways teachers can support transitions include the following:

- Give first 5- and then 1-minute reminders to the class before big transitions.

- Provide the class with a transitional activity such as writing in a homework notebook or, for younger students, singing a short "clean up" song (Feldman, 2000).

- Use a timer to show students how many minutes they have until the next activity. If you have access to a computer and projector in the classroom, you can use some of the great free visual timers found at these websites:

  ○ http://www.timeme.com

  ○ http://www.vickiblackwell.com/timer.html

  ○ http://www.online-stopwatch.com

Figure 11.6. Student assembling her picture schedule for the day.

- Ask peers to help during transition time. In elementary classrooms, teachers can ask all students to transition with a partner. In secondary classrooms, students with autism might choose a peer to walk with during passing time.

- Create transition rituals (e.g., always begin English class with a poem, always end the day by having students write in journals).

- Give the student a transition aid. Some students need to carry a toy, object, or picture to facilitate their movement from one place to the next. One student we know carries a rabbit's foot from class to class. He leaves it at the door and picks it up again when he needs to move to a new room. Some students need an object that helps them specifically focus on the next environment or activity. A student might, for instance, carry a tennis ball when he goes to the playground.

Using simple strategies like these can limit challenges during transitions throughout the school day. Students will, in many cases, become more relaxed and feel more prepared. Teachers may also find that the classroom, in general, becomes more peaceful and orderly when students who are more aware of upcoming transitions may find time to clean their work space, organize materials, and otherwise prepare to finish their work.

Checklists, Guides, and Rules

Many students with autism feel comforted when they can see and be informed about procedures, steps, or expectations. Written information is concrete and can be used even when the teacher is unavailable. For instance, Dennis Debbaudt, a safety expert who works with law enforcement organizations across the country, put a list of rules on his refrigerator to teach his son, Brad, how to stay safe. The list reads as follows:

- You can't push or hit other people.

- You can't destroy your property or the property of others.

- You can't say you are going to hit or destroy property.

Debbaudt discusses the rules with his son, reminds him of the consequences of violating the rules (but not in the "heat of the moment"), and models the rules as well. For this family, this simple set of rules has worked beautifully. According to his dad, Brad follows the rules religiously (Debbaudt & Debbaudt, 2008).

Not every student will respond to every list or set of rules, but we do know that many learners with autism find such lists helpful. Checklists, rules, and guidelines can help students feel organized and calm and increase their success on tasks and assignments (Myles,

2005). These tools might be created for any number of situations. Checklists, for example, might be created for finishing long assignments, packing a backpack, getting ready for a field-trip, or checking out a library book. Guides might be created for having fun at the prom or surviving the first day of school. Written rules might be generated for riding the bus safely, using and sharing playground equipment, playing after-school kickball, and using lab equipment. See Figure 11.7 for an example of a checklist used to help a student check a book out of the classroom library and Figure 11.8 for an example of rules that students generated about working in the computer lab.

Organization Support

Although some students with autism are ultraorganized, others need support to find materials, keep their locker and desk areas neat, and remember to bring their assignments home at the end of the day. Wendy Lawson, a woman with the autism spectrum label, remembered her schooling experience as a mess of papers, schedules, and expectations:

 Secondary school posed many problems for me . . . I would get class timetables and rooms muddled and was often unprepared for lessons. Homework was usually forgotten or badly done. School was a confusing place to be and I dreaded having to go. (1998, p. 55)

For students who feel as Lawson does, look for strategies and methods that help the individual manage time and work space while learning new skills that will help them become more independent in negotiating environments, materials, and their daily schedule. For example, a teacher might help a student clean out his homework folder but then work with him to devise a system that can be used to keep it orderly. Other ways teachers can inspire students to get and stay organized include the following:

- *Asking all students to do 5-minute clean-up and organization sessions throughout the week.*

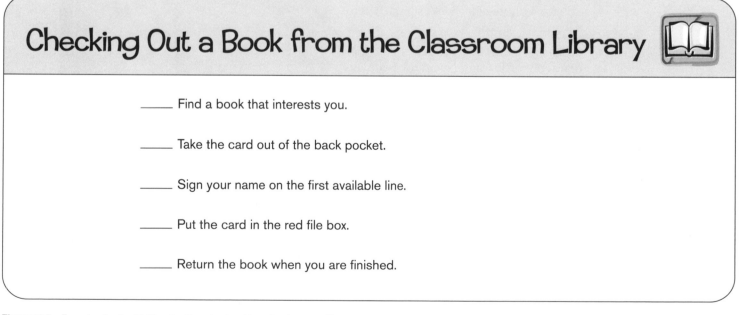

Checking Out a Book from the Classroom Library

_____ Find a book that interests you.

_____ Take the card out of the back pocket.

_____ Sign your name on the first available line.

_____ Put the card in the red file box.

_____ Return the book when you are finished.

Figure 11.7. Example of a checklist for checking a book out from the classroom library.

"You're Going to Love This Kid!" Teaching Students with Autism in the Inclusive Classroom, Second Edition, by Paula Kluth
Copyright © 2010 by Paul H. Brookes Publishing Co. All rights reserved.

Computer Lab Rules

1. No food or drink.

2. No cell phones.

3. No games.

4. Leave the workstation as you found it (keyboard in center, monitor on, chair pushed in).

5. Report all problems to Ms. Long. Do not try to fix computer problems on your own!

Figure 11.8.   List of rules for working in the computer lab.

- *Having students copy down assignments, pack book bags, put materials away, and clean work spaces as a class.* Specific skills even can be taught during this time (e.g., creating to-do lists, setting priorities for tasks).

- *Using the method employed by the Internal Revenue Service* (Goodman, 1995). The flap on tax envelopes prompts taxpayers to review materials and reminds them of certain elements of their forms that should be double-checked (e.g., Did you sign your name?). Such a checklist can be placed near an assignment "in box" (e.g., Is your name on the paper? Did you check your work?) or on the door (e.g., Do you have a pencil? Homework?). Reminders also can be attached to student materials. See Figure 11.9 for a photo of a checklist attached to a learner's backpack.

- *Following the leader.* Students who depend on order and seem to have no problems keeping materials together and work areas neat might be called on to help others and even to lead the class in organizing activities. For instance, a student might share tips for using cell phones as an organizational tool.

- *Going by the book.* Older students might be given how-to books on organization so they have concrete tips they can read again and again and use as a resource. Good choices for teens include *Organizing from the Inside Out for Teenagers* (Morgenstern & Morgenstern-Colon, 2002) and *"Where's My Stuff?": The Ultimate Teen Organizing Guide* (Moss & Schwartz, 2007).

Figure 11.9.   Example of a "traveling" checklist.

Choices

Every day and throughout the year, all students should be given choices about the type of work they do, their activities, and the ways in which they spend their time. Choice can be built into almost any part of the school day. Students can choose which assessments to complete, which role to take in a cooperative group, which books to read or which problems to solve, and how to receive personal assistance. Choice may not only give students a feeling of control in their lives but may also present them with an opportunity to learn about themselves as workers. Students themselves usually know best during which times of the day they are most creative, productive, and energetic; what materials and supports they need; and in what ways they can best express what they have learned.

Choice can be integrated into almost any activity. One teacher gives her students a choice of shaking hands or giving a high-five as they walk out of the classroom each day. Another teacher gives her second graders a choice of seven different ways to practice spelling words, including writing them in shaving cream, tracing them on a friend's back using a finger, or "writing" them out using rubber stamps. A high school biology teacher lets students choose some of the labs they will conduct. Table 11.2 includes some ways teachers can offer choices to students.

Nonverbal Supports and Cues

Some students feel overwhelmed by verbal interactions. We know one young man with autism who has told us he cannot understand our words when we "talk them." He finds conversations especially challenging when the speaker is too loud or speaks too quickly. Another friend, Kathy Xenia Grant, says that, during verbal exchanges with others, words often "drop out" and become hard to decipher (Hussman, Kluth, Strong, & Tweedy, 2009). Tito Rajarshi Mukhopadhyay, a young man with autism, also has problems with verbal interactions but has been strategic in coping with these problems:

> Any new voice is frightening to me and it takes time for me to adjust to it. Usually people get frustrated and give up. However, if the person is persistent and maintains the same pitch, I can slowly get used to the voice. (2000, p. 72)

Table 11.2.   Choices that can be offered to students in the inclusive classroom

Work alone or with a peer.

Read quietly, listen to a book on tape, or read an electronic book on the computer.

Take a seat anywhere in the room.

Use a pencil, pen, or marker.

Conduct your research in the library or stay in the room and work.

Type on the computer, write in your notebook, or use a typewriter.

Use a calculator, count on your fingers, use manipulatives, or solve problems in your head.

Choose any topic for your research paper.

If you know the answer, raise your hand, give me the thumbs-up sign, or sit on your desk.

Start your homework or find an educational game to play.

Of the 10 problems on the sheet, complete any 5.

Take "regular" notes on the lecture or take notes by drawing pictures of the concepts I present.

Stand or sit in your chair.

Choose any two ways to be assessed in this unit.

Pick your favorite piece of work for the bulletin board.

Let me check your paper or have a friend do it.

Write the problem down or solve it in your head.

Tito's revelations are helpful in stressing how important it is to respect the ways in which students support themselves. This young man's words also should serve as a reminder to interpret student behaviors and reactions with caution. Tito, and undoubtedly other students with autism, need teachers to be patient and work to understand their specific communication needs and preferences.

Because spoken words are hard for some students to process, teachers should also experiment with other ways to supplement their speech. Consider the following:

- Sign language can be integrated into classroom instruction and routines. Signs and speech together can be used when giving simple directions (e.g., asking students to stand, sit, or stop talking).

- Gestures can be incorporated throughout the day. A teacher can use his or her fingers when giving directions: [Hold up one finger] "First, you need to," [Hold up two fingers] "Second, you should," and so forth. Thumbs up can communicate a job well done. A finger to the lips can signal "quiet."

- PowerPoint slides or an overhead projector can be utilized. During lectures and whole-class discussions, students can listen *and* see related words and pictures.

Perhaps the easiest way to create nonverbal support for a learner is to use the written word. If students are given directions verbally, the same information can be written on the chalkboard or whiteboard or typed on a computer that is hooked up to a projector.

Writing also can be a useful tool for calming a student. When a student is upset or confused, writing can be a way to communicate when other types of interaction seem too overwhelming. One of us used to work with a fifth-grade student named Mickey. Mickey would get very nervous when changes occurred during the day (e.g., the announcements were late, a favorite peer was absent). To calm him, a teacher or peer simply would sit down next to Mickey, ask him for a notebook, take out a pen, and begin writing a message to him. For example, if a friend of his was out sick, a teacher might sit down and write, "Hi Mickey, it seems like you are upset this morning—I'm sorry to see you so upset. I wonder if you are upset because Maggie is out sick today. Don't worry about her, though. I heard that she is doing fine but needs to rest for one more day. Maybe later you could write an e-mail note to her when we go to computer class." Mickey would then be handed the notebook to provide a response.

Stay-Put Box

Often, learners with autism struggle to stay seated or to remain in the classroom for extended periods of time. Although allowing learners to move frequently is one way (and certainly an important way) to approach this need, having desktop sensory supports available also can make seatwork and class work, in general, more manageable for the learner. Furthermore, by using these materials for all students in the classroom, students with specific sensory needs are not singled out and all students, regardless of their learning profile or needs, learn what their bodies require in order for them to be effective learners (Prestia, 2004).

In one elementary school classroom, students could visit a box with "staying put" resources at any time during the day. The box contained Koosh balls, small stuffed toys, stress balls, weighted "snakes," seat cushions, and other similar items. Students borrowed the objects when they needed them and returned them when they were finished. None of these interactions with objects bothered the teachers or created a stir in the class, and the teachers found that allowing students to use the box gave them insight into their individual learning needs and helped them remain focused and on task. See Figure 11.10 for a photo of a stay-put or sensory box that was used in a sixth-grade classroom.

As one teacher explained, having this type of simple support can make the difference between a student's presence in the classroom and his or her engagement in an activity:

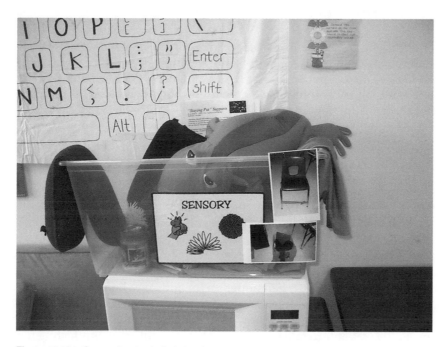

Figure 11.10.   Sensory box for the inclusive classroom.

At the beginning of the year Sam could not stay seated through morning meeting and his mom suggested that we give him something to hold. She sent in the Koosh ball. Ever since then he has sat through meeting just fine. We started the box because some of the other kids said that they would like to try holding something too. (Kasa-Hendrickson & Kluth, 2005, p. 8)

Allowing students to doodle or draw can be another effective "staying put" strategy. Many learners with and without identified needs appear better able to concentrate on a lecture or activity when they are given the opportunity to doodle on a notepad, draw on their folders, or sketch in a notebook. One of our student teachers reported that a student without an identified disability in her high school U.S. history class often filled in the pictures of a coloring book during lectures. Although the student teacher was initially skeptical of the young man's behavior, by the end of the semester she was convinced that he not only was able to sit and listen longer when he used the coloring book but also seemed to process the lectures and learn the content better when he used the crayons. As a way to honor the student's need, the teacher brought a "Heroines of the Civil War" coloring book into the classroom and offered it to the young man to use as a resource for an upcoming unit.

Helping Students with Autism: Individual Strategies

Although many strategies offered in this chapter will be appropriate for all students, some may be necessary only for the learner with autism or for other students with similar characteristics. To determine the need for any one of these strategies, it is typically best to follow the lead of the student or to consult with the student's family. The strategies featured are as follows: Autism 101, breaks and movement, visual supports, connections to fascinations, safe space, and help with movement differences.

Autism 101

Teaching students about their own label can result in many benefits. Students on the spectrum may feel relief at having a name for and an understanding of their differences ("I'm not alone"). Others may experience a sense of validation ("I knew something about me was different"). And still others may feel some excitement about the positive changes that might occur because of the new information (Attwood, 2007; Attwood & Willey, 2000; Hussman, Kluth, Strong, & Tweedy, 2009). Furthermore, if a student is given information about others with autism (e.g., autobiographies, web sites), he or she might get ideas about coping with challenges such as sensory sensitivity or find practical tips for dating, dealing with stress, or making friends.

Staff members may also benefit when learners know about their diagnosis. Teachers, for example, may be able to get specific feedback about supports as a learner becomes more sophisticated in talking about and interpreting his or her own needs and abilities. Furthermore, when the teacher and the student share a language about the label, the teacher may have another tool to use to help students cope with difficulties. One of us (Paula), for example, was able to calm a student by sharing information about autism. As the story goes, Paula was waiting for a school bus with Jay, her student with autism, when the bus company called to say that they were behind schedule. As the two waited, Jay became increasingly agitated and began to whimper as if in pain. Every time the bus was late, Jay had the same reaction, but this time Paula was able to talk to him about how his autism was affecting his reaction because she had been reading him small excerpts from the autobiographies of people with autism. "Remember that book we read about the guy who hated to wait for the bus? He sure hated waiting, too. His autism made it hard for him to wait. This is your autism acting up again, huh? It must be hard to handle, but you are doing a great job. How do you manage?" Although the wait was still noticeably uncomfortable for Jay, he was able to have a short conversation about how he was handling the situation. Later, we put this conversation on paper and made it into a story about autism, waiting, and how to cope with a "misbehaving bus."

As Paula did with Jay, teachers might read autobiographies of people with autism to their older students, whereas very young students might enjoy picture books on the topic. Teachers might also take students to local conferences on autism and help them to understand the social and even political implications of having a disability label. For instance, a student we know attended an autism conference one weekend and came back to school with renewed self-confidence, wearing an "Autistic and Proud" button. This student later presented his life story at a local teachers' meeting, getting a real confidence boost from serving as an expert on autism and, for once, on his own life.

In a study Paula conducted with high school students (Kluth, 1998), a paraprofessional used a two-person book club to support Candy, a teen with significant disabilities. The pair often read books written by Donna Williams, a woman on the spectrum who writes about living with autism. The two would go to a quiet space and Ms. Colton, the paraprofessional, would read aloud. They would also have long, serious conversations (via Candy's typed communication) about Candy's disabilities. These experiences were very different from the types of conversations that had filled Candy's school career. She had never before been informed about autism and had not previously been told by teachers that living with it could be hard sometimes, that she was doing a good job managing her needs, or that others in the world were experiencing some of the same things she was.

Another Autism 101 strategy is to ask students to write about their experiences and share their stories with peers or professionals through student magazines, newspapers, or even through national publications. Writing can be a cathartic experience, serving as a way for students to learn about themselves and educate others. We know at least three students who have written their own books about life on the spectrum and several others who have written speeches, newsletter columns, and even pamphlets about their experiences. We also know

Table 11.3. Personal and professional web sites of individuals on the spectrum

Temple Grandin
  http://www.templegrandin.com

Brian King
  http://www.imanaspie.com

Wendy Lawson
  http://www.mugsy.org/wendy

Bradley Olson
  http://www.paulbunyan.net/users/cbsolson/BOlson1

John Elder Robison
  http://jerobison.blogspot.com

Stephen Shore
  http://www.autismasperger.net

Sarah Stup
  http://www.sarahstup.com

Lianne Holliday Willey
  http://www.aspie.com

Donna Williams
  http://www.donnawilliams.net

one young man who saves his writing skills for the IEP process; he likes to "write back" to comments made on his formal education reports, often refuting the ways professionals have interpreted his needs and abilities.

Still another way students are learning about themselves and honing advocacy skills is through blogging or through the creation and maintenance of personal web pages. See Table 11.3 for a list of web sites created by people with autism; perhaps these sites will serve as an inspiration for learners in your classroom.

Breaks and Movement

Some students work best when they can pause between tasks and take a break of some kind. Depending on the needs and the ages of your individual students, breaks will vary in quantity and length. And different students will need different types of breaks as well. Some will simply need to rest and stop working for a few moments. Others will need to stretch and perhaps even stand. Many others will need to take a walk or pace.

Walking breaks are among the most common offered to students with autism in inclusive schools. Breaks can last anywhere from a few seconds to 15–20 minutes. Some individuals will need to walk up and down a hallway once or twice; others will be fine if allowed to move around a bit in the classroom. For example, Teo, a fifth-grader on the spectrum needed to stand and pace constantly during classroom lessons. His teacher was warned that this student was likely to crouch at his desk (both feet on the seat), stand up during teacher lectures, and pace for a minute or more every half hour. The teacher's response was to give the student a seat in the back row and to surround him with other students who indicated on a learner profile questionnaire that they wouldn't be distracted by movement.

Another student, Mike, needed time to unwind when he arrived at school. Because Mike's school was a quarter mile from the district's middle school, he started each day by walking down to the school and back with a peer. As part of the walk, Mike started taking "kid mail" (students from the elementary school could write notes to siblings or peers in the middle school) from one school to the next. Classmates from his second-grade class took turns working with Mike to deliver the mail.

If students in the classroom need frequent breaks and are able to communicate this to the teacher, passes can be created for them so they can independently indicate the need for a break without disturbing the class. For instance, in an environmental science class, the teacher gave all of his students a punch card (kept in a box on his desk) that they could use for breaks. Every student had six "free" breaks per semester; to use one students simply pulled their card and punched it. At the end of the semester, most of the students had used only one or two breaks but a few had used more. Ben, a student with Asperger syndrome, was allowed 20 breaks and, therefore, had a special card created to reflect this accommodation.

In another classroom, J.R., a third grader, required several breaks per day to be successful. His teachers, therefore, created a board full of break cards that he could use throughout the day. Each time he needed to leave the classroom, he was required to hand the teacher one of his cards. In the fall, J.R. needed 16 breaks a day. By February, however, he was using only about 6. By year's end, he was using only two cards per day—one for the morning and one for the afternoon.

Visual Supports

Because individuals with autism have strong visual skills and—at the same time—struggle with auditory skills, visual supports can be very effective as a teaching tool (Arwood & Kaulitz, 2007; Cohen & Sloan, 2007; Dyrbjerg & Vedel, 2007; Savner & Myles, 2000). Because written words, pictures and objects stay put and do not "disappear" like speech, visuals allow cues and information to remain available to the student and, therefore, reduce stress and anxiety. Furthermore, when a student has the use of visuals, there is an increased chance of success and independence on tasks. The types of visuals that may be helpful to a student on the spectrum include diagrams, schedules, pictures, photographs, labels, words, objects, and models.

Once you decide what you need a visual support for, you will need to choose what type of visual will work best. Do you need just a line drawing, or will a photograph be necessary? Will the photo be sufficient, or might the child need an actual object to see or hold? After you determine use, you can decide on where to keep or use the support. Should the steps for the packing up for the day be available in a binder or stuck right to the locker door? Should a picture schedule be at a learner's desk or near the chalkboard with the classroom schedule? The answers to these questions will depend on your student's comfort level, preferences, and abilities.

One example of a visual support is an activity schedule (see Figure 11.11); an activity schedule teaches a skill through a set of pictures or written words, which are used to cue the student to complete the task or activity as independently as possible. The number of activities and steps per activity can be adjusted based on the needs and abilities of the learner. For some students, activities will need to be depicted step by step in order for the child to complete the activity independently. For others, a few words on an index card might be sufficient.

First/then boards (see Figure 11.12) are another popular adaptation used in inclusive classrooms; this support is really the most basic type of picture schedule you can provide, but it can be useful for any student, no matter the age or need. The first/then board is simply a piece of paper or laminated board that helps the student quickly understand the order of two activities and, specifically, what task or activity must be completed before a preferred task or activity can be started.

Choice menus are also used frequently for learners on the spectrum. Menus may offer students just a handful of choices or, as in the example in Figure 11.13, they can have several. Menus are sometimes provided because students cannot look at an environment and see what the options are; they, therefore, need a tangible representation of these options (e.g., a menu of exercises appropriate during physical education warm-ups). Teachers may also make menus for things that are tangible or in sight (e.g., indoor recess games); the purpose of a menu in this case would be to narrow options, quickly allow students to see what is available, and supplement any verbal explanation by the classroom teacher about what is available.

Finally, written words/cues also can be used as visual supports for learners on the spectrum. Written words can be produced on the spot, or you can create word or phrase cards to use across contexts and environments. Some teachers even carry a memo pad or small wipe board for the purpose. Writing can work to deal with major issues, such as writing or drawing an explanation of why a peer is absent (this can be more comforting than having the

Figure 11.11. Visual activity schedule for showering after gym class.

Figuro 11.12.   Example of a first/then board.

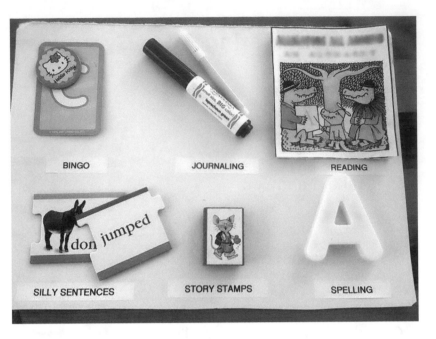

Figure 11.13. Picture of a student choice board.

teacher simply explain it). Words and cues also can work to help students navigate the day. One student who struggles to finish his artwork at the bell (he likes to make drawings "perfect") has a much easier time transitioning to his next class if his art teacher places a card next to him that says, "STOP. Finish tomorrow."

Connections to Fascinations

In *"Just Give Him the Whale!" 20 Ways to Use Fascinations, Areas of Expertise, and Strengths to Support Students with Autism,* a book that Paula wrote with her colleague, Patrick Schwarz (2008), she shared a story that illustrates our philosophy on responding to student fascinations. We share it here to frame our way of thinking and our recommendations:

> Pedro, a little boy with autism, was screaming in his kindergarten classroom on the first day of school. Ms. Gomez, the principal, heard the child's cries and walked into the room. She observed two colleagues discussing the appropriate way to deal with the situation. It appeared that Pedro had started crying because the kindergarten teacher had taken away his favorite whale toy. Believing that her new student would be more successful without the "distraction" of his favorite possession, she had decided to try and hide it from him. The teacher's co-teaching partner, a special education teacher, had a different perspective on the situation. "What do you want him to do?" she asked her colleague. "I want him to do his work. I want him to participate," answered the kindergarten teacher. The special education teacher thought for a minute and replied, "Then just give him the whale." (p. xii)

We have worked with students interested in vacuum cleaners, Toyotas, screwdrivers, fences, world governments, traffic signs, churches, weathervanes, polka dots, monster movies, construction workers, Barack Obama, and salvage yards. Like the teachers in the story, we believe that instead of trying to seize or fade out these items or interests, they should, in most cases, be used as tools for inspiring learners and teaching standards-based content (Kluth & Schwarz, 2008; Winter-Messiers, 2007).

A student who loves trains might be asked to write a story about riding on a caboose, research different railroads on the Internet, or do an independent research project on ground transportation in America. A learner who is crazy about Hannah Montana could read magazine stories about her, write her letters, estimate the ticket sales and projected revenue for a concert tour, and replace the lyrics of favorite songs with content that he or she needs to know for an upcoming science or social studies test.

Both of these examples illustrate how a learner's passion can be a stepping stone for learning about new content and acquiring new skills. Too often, teachers are timid about encouraging a student's fascination; however, if this is done with some creativity and planning, the student's interest can be honored while the teacher's need to move beyond the interest is also answered. For example, Freddie, a sixth grader, loved to study the calendar and answer questions about holidays and special days throughout the year. Although this interest wasn't hurting Freddie's education, it also wasn't helping him to grow as a learner. To enhance Freddie's learning and to challenge all learners in the classroom, we developed a calendar activity appropriate for older students. Although all of the students in the classroom knew the days of the week and the months of the year, none of them knew that December 7th was the anniversary of the bombing of Pearl Harbor or that President Kennedy was assassinated on November 22nd in Dallas, Texas. The teachers had all of the students work in small groups to find important dates in American and world history. Freddie was responsible for presenting the "event of the day" each morning. All students—including Freddie—learned something new, and Freddie was thrilled to have a calendar activity incorporated into the daily classroom routine. See Table 11.4 for more examples of how fascinations can be used to meet the needs of students in your inclusive classroom.

Safe Space

Teachers should make quiet study or relaxation areas available for any student who seems to need a safe haven. The library might be used, or a few chairs might be set up in the hallway for any student who needs a break from the chaos of the classroom. Donna Williams stated, "Allowing me privacy and space was the most beneficial thing I ever got" (1992, p. 218). Many individuals with autism reported a need to retreat into a safe space at times. Liane Holliday Willey, a woman with Asperger syndrome, suggested that even college students will need to find a place to "relax and re-group" somewhere on campus (1999, p. 132). In addition, Pyles quotes a parent as saying that her son needed "a haven when things get to be too much" (2003, p. 248). This parent noted that the haven identified for her son was the nurse's office. Although the young man preferred the more anonymous option of hanging out in the library throughout his entire high school career, his mother shares that it was always a comfort to her son to know the more private option was available.

The most important part of creating a safe space is ensuring that the area will not be used or viewed as a place of punishment. Consider Becky, a fourth grader who often needed to take a break from the classroom. Teachers were unsure of how to give Becky a private space without stigmatizing her and making her feel like she had done something wrong. Teachers worked with Becky to give her both a dignified place to unwind and a natural way to learn relaxation skills. They started by using a small office that was used for testing. In this room, Becky seem agitated; she flipped the chair over and tried to stand on the desk. Her teachers took this as a sign that Becky was not comfortable in the room so they continued to look for an alternative space:

> Outside the special education resource room, a smaller room served as an entryway for students to get to the resource room. We (the special educator, the teaching assistant, and the consultant) decided that Becky might like working in this little room because other students came into this room to work each day. Because Becky also liked music and books about kittens and ballerinas, we placed these items in the room. Whenever Becky left the classroom, it was not viewed as a punishment, but as a way for Becky to "take a break" and then return when she was ready. The next

Table 11.4. Ten ways to use fascinations and passions to teach, support, and include

Use fascinations and passions . . .	Examples
To calm	Mason, a middle school student with a love of cockroaches, struggled with social anxiety. His teacher found a plastic roach that Mason could keep in his pocket at all times and wrote "I will survive" on the insect's back in permanent marker. Then he taught Mason that cockroaches have an unbelievable ability to survive, even in the most daunting conditions and circumstances.
To comfort	Ms. Cooney, aware that her student, Mary Chris, struggled during fire and tornado drills, used the child's passion—the music of Patsy Cline—to keep her calm during these stressful times. When the drill began, Ms. Cooney pulled Mary Chris near her and softly sang "Walking After Midnight" as the class marched to their designated emergency spot.
To build classroom expertise	Matt, a middle school student, loved to read and draw maps. When his teachers learned of Matt's gift, they had him bring his work into the classroom and to teach his peers a few skills related to map reading and map making.
To facilitate connections between students	Patrick, an eighth grader, had few friendships and seldom spoke to his classmates until a new student came into his English classroom wearing a Star Wars T-shirt. This connection eventually led to a friendship, which then led to the students forming a science fiction game club.
To encourage in-depth study	Devon particularly liked the movie *Young Frankenstein*, so his speech therapist, Ms. Rice, programmed information about the movie into his communication device and showed Devon how to hit the keys to share this information.
To teach manners and social norms	Kelly became interested in learning more about etiquette when his teacher gave him manners guides and hiking literature and asked him to create an etiquette guide that hikers could use on the Appalachian Trail (one of his many fascinations).
To teach literacy	Jem, a student who loved reading about rats and other rodents, often groaned when his teachers asked him to read fiction or explore about other topics. During the first weeks of school, Mr. Mueller did not hound Jem about adding new topics to his reading list and instead chose to focus on other literacy objectives during this time (e.g., fluency, comprehension of informational texts).
To teach mathematics	Tova, a fan of competitive swimming and diving, was always more willing to engage in the daily lesson if the teacher mentioned swimming. Fractions lessons were enhanced by discussions of how many lanes of the pool were filled with swimmers from a certain team or how much of a race a swimmer had completed when he or she had finished a certain number of laps.
To connect students to career paths	Eric felt very passionate about fire trucks. An insightful teacher, aware of the joy that fire trucks brought to Eric's day, arranged an apprenticeship for him. He was given high school credit to volunteer at the firehouse as part of the school's service learning curriculum.
To help students make sense of a confusing world	During a high school football game, Blake's fascination with tools helped him decipher the world of sports. The Grizzlies (wearing blue and gold) were playing the Eagles (wearing green and yellow). Throughout the first half of the game, Blake's mom would explain plays to him, but Blake showed little interest. Suddenly, Blake took a second glance at the game and smiled. He pointed and said, "Woodtech versus Delta." Woodtech is a power tool company whose primary colors are green and yellow, and Delta tools are painted blue and silver. That evening, Blake "cracked the code" of the game and enjoyed football for the first time.

From Kluth, P., & Schwarz, P. (2008). *"Just give him the whale!" 20 ways to use fascinations, areas of expertise, and strengths to support students with autism.* Baltimore: Paul H. Brookes Publishing Co.; adapted by permission.

day when Becky became loud, we walked her to the room that we called "Becky's room." (Hedeen, Ayres, Meyer, & Waite, 1996, pp. 154–155)

The authors recall that in "Becky's room," their young student sat down and began reading books and listening to music. Becky seemed to like the room at once and was, therefore, able to relax and quietly return to her classroom after the break was over. The new space was a success, but the authors point out that not every educator may see it in this way. They explain, for instance, that traditional learning theory might understand the provision of safe space for Becky as a "reward," in which case negative behaviors may have escalated. This, however, was not the case, leading these educators to challenge the notion that they did anything other than sensitively respond to the needs of their student:

> We believe that, to borrow a phrase from [a teacher], Becky had given us the "best behavior she could" under the present circumstances—she wasn't trying to manipulate us directly, although she was telling us that she needed a break. When we responded to her needs by giving her a break rather than a punishment, she was apparently able to recoup and return to work. It seemed to us that this is the same kind of strategy that many of us follow when we are frustrated with something and cannot take another minute! When we treated Becky as we would want to be treated, her behavior improved. (pp. 154–155)

Help with Movement Differences

As stated in Chapter 1, many individuals with autism experience significant difficulties with movement. People with autism and other disabilities often report that they cannot get their bodies to do what they want them to (Donnellan & Leary, 1995). The problems can be exacerbated when people supporting the individual with autism believe that the student could control or change his movement or behavior "if he really wanted to." For instance, we know a student who can move over the monkey bars and the rest of the jungle gym with ease, but he often finds it difficult to cross a room on his own. His teachers are sometimes confused by this contrast and find it hard to understand how some actions are so easy for him while others remain so challenging.

Students with movement differences may be supported in several ways. Here, we offer five different categories of ideas. Specific student examples also are given in Table 11.5. As you review all of the examples we provide, keep in mind that the supports that work for one person may create difficulties when applied to another person. In other words, remember that when it comes to helping those with movement problems, "One man's meat is another man's poison" (Donnellan & Leary, 1995). Five categories that can be considered with any movement problem are touch or tactile supports, cognitive tools, rhythm and music, modeling, and imagery and visualization.

Touch or Tactile Supports

When a student seems unable to move, a touch cue might be administered to the back of the hand, on the arm, on the leg, or on any part of the body that seems "stalled." For example, a teacher might tell a student that she can take a muffin from the snack tray. If the child does not respond, the teacher might try reminding the student again while touching (or providing counter pressure to) her hand. To help students move; communicate; initiate; transition; or change a posture, action, or behavior, you might try the following:

- Make physical contact or keep in contact with the person.
- Provide resistance or counterpressure.
- Provide a squeeze or gentle pressure.
- Give a quick wrist, hand, or shoulder massage.

Cognitive Tools

Any number of cognitive strategies might also be used to support someone with autism. Using cognitive tools involves teaching students about their own thinking and the power of

Table 11.5. Examples of accommodations for movement differences

Movement problems	Ideas for accommodations
Jason struggled to sit at his table in his classroom. He often left the table or pushed back on his chair and tipped over.	Jason's teacher found that if she sat him near the wall, then he could lean against it. She also gave him (and a few other students) a choice to sit in a beanbag chair or in his seat for certain activities. Jason was also allowed to take 5-minute walking breaks around the room whenever he asked for them.
Walking down the carpeted hallway became hard for Trey, who seemed unable to leave strings and fuzz on the floor—he had to pick up these things when he noticed them.	Trey and his classmates made keychains out of sturdy string. Trey carried his keychain with him at all times so he could wind it through his fingers and fidget with it when needed. This seemed to decrease his need to seek other pieces of string. Trey also walked in between two favorite peers when transitioning from class to class. The peers gave him gentle input on each arm (leaned on him a bit) as they walked. This pressure seemed to distract him from staring at the floor and helped him to keep his head up.
Barb had a hard time moving through the cafeteria line. She would sometimes run through the line without picking up her lunch. Other times, she would sit down on the floor when she was halfway through the line	Barb's teacher videotaped her walking through the lunch line for four consecutive days. She then edited the tape, taking out all "scenes" during which Barb ran, sat down, or otherwise struggled. She then put the footage together until the tape showed Barb successfully walking all the way through the line, getting her lunch, and sitting down. Seeing this "model day" was exactly what Barb needed. She was able to imitate the video perfectly within days.
Lindsay struggled to get from the classroom to the bus and from the bus to the classroom; she sometimes refused to walk and occasionally wept. Once Lindsay had made the transition, she became almost instantly calm but teachers needed a way to get her more comfortably through the transition.	As she stepped off the bus each day, Lindsay's teachers gave her a picture of Ms. Holloway, the school secretary. Lindsay took the picture to the office, where she started her day by greeting Ms. Holloway. At the day's end, the teachers gave her a picture of her mother to take to the bus. Her transitions became increasingly easier and more peaceful.
Vang had problems going up and down stairs. He often got "stuck" halfway up the staircase and would not (or could not) come down.	A paraprofessional in Vang's classroom told the young man to imagine that he was climbing a mountain when he was on the stairs. The two wrote a story about "Vang the Mountain Climber," and Vang read the story on Thursday mornings before he had to climb the stairs to get to his music lesson.
Clay often chewed on his watch band when he felt anxious.	Clay's friends learned to rest their hand on his back when he seemed stressed out; this seemed to help him relax. The teacher also gave Clay gum when he started chewing on his band.

Sources: Donnellan and Leary (1995); Kluth (2000).

their thinking. A student might, for example, be taught a mantra or slogan to cope with a particular situation and to "talk" him- or herself into trying, completing, or even stopping a particular action or state of being. Or, the teacher can tap into a learner's memory and remind him of another time when he was able to succeed in the past. To help students move; communicate; initiate; transition; or change a posture, action, or behavior, you might try the following:

- Teach how to use self-talk (even nonverbal students can be taught this strategy) and specifically how to use calming or inspiring mantras.

- Introduce meditation.

- Use redirection.

- Provide intellectual stimulation (e.g., read the person an age-appropriate book; talk to the person, tell the person stories, share information and humor).

Rhythm and Music

For some, movement is facilitated by certain music, chants, or rhymes. One student with autism we know performed sluggishly at his hotel laundry work site until his boss began playing music by Billy Joel at the start of the day. The music had such an impact on him that his teacher bought him a digital audio player so he could use different types of music to help him through the day. To help students move; communicate; initiate; transition; or change a posture, action, or behavior, you might try the following:

- Integrate music into daily activities or use music as a cue.

- Use auditory cues instead of speech (e.g., a chime to signal transition).

- Sing the directions or bits of the conversation.

- Teach the student a chant (e.g., to start the day, to get into the pool).

Modeling

Some students need to see a task performed before they can actually do it. One former student would watch peers play basketball for half of the recess period and then would join in for the second half. It also can be helpful to move *with* a student. A teaching assistant we know told us a story about a young woman named Molly who dropped to the floor one day and seemed unable to get up. The teaching assistant dropped to the floor with Molly and then said, "Maybe this will help. I'll get up with you." Molly immediately stood up with the assistant. To help students move; communicate; initiate; transition; or change a posture, action, or behavior, you might try the following:

- Have students watch you model a task or activity before they attempt it.

- Have students watch other students.

- Have students watch a video of the task or activity (e.g., a child watches a video of his brother's soccer game before he plays soccer for the first time).

Imagery and Visualization

Reed (1996) shared an example of how a man with autism, Mac, used imagery to ease transitions. Mac, who often became "stuck" when he tried to transition from room to room, devised a mental image to break his "feeling of confusion and disorientation." In order to get his body to move at will, Mac imagines that he is playing for the Minnesota Twins. In this visualization, it is the bottom of the ninth inning, there are two outs, and Mac is up to bat. He cracks a home run, runs the bases, and is met at home plate by his excited teammates. To help students move; communicate; initiate; transition; or change a posture, action, or behavior, you might try the following:

- Teach visualizing techniques (e.g., tell the student to "see himself" being calm during the SAT and walk him through the entire test in his mind).

- Teach students imagery techniques (e.g., when the student gets very upset he is allowed to listen to his "Sounds of the Sea" songs and take a "mini-vacation" to the coast).

- Provide inspiring or helpful pictures (e.g., a preschool teacher painted a basket on her wall so students could put any bad feelings into it throughout the day).

Summary

In a teacher workshop we gave, one teacher described how Kelly, a young man in her classroom, coped with his need for movement by scooting around on the floor occasionally. One day, the teacher was teaching about the oceans when a school administrator walked into the room. The teacher asked the students to name the oceans surrounding the United States. Kelly popped up from his spot between two rows of desks and shouted "the Pacific." The teacher asked for other answers, and after a brief pause, Kelly popped up again, this time from another area, and shouted, "the Atlantic." The principal, disapproving of this unconventional teaching and learning behavior, frowned and left the room. Later, when the teacher was confronted by the principal, she explained that Kelly did some of his best work on the floor and that although she was doing her best to give him a wide range of more typical ways to participate, right now this was the most effective way to engage him in learning.

Teachers such as those featured in this chapter realize that working in an inclusive classroom involves employing a huge variety of strategies—some of which may be very unique. As Sylvia Ashton-Warner (1963), a teacher who brought unconventional methods to Maori children in rural New Zealand, found, a teacher may need to be bold in creating supports that work and advocate for those that seem effective. Even Ashton-Warner, today a celebrated figure in the field of education, worried about how her administrators would view her unusual, student-centered, culturally rich strategies, but she implemented them anyway in order to give students every opportunity to learn and succeed:

> If only I kept workbooks and made schemes and taught like other teachers I should have the confidence of numbers. It's the payment, the price of walking alone. If you saw the reading scheme I have been making the last few days you'd know why I speak of walking alone. Yet I must present it. I've got to do what I believe. And I believe in all I do. It's this price one continually pays for stepping out of line. I'm feeling too old to pay it. But I must do what I believe in or nothing at all. Life's so short. What other people call their timetables. . . . In mine, the children, might get up and dance in the middle of their sums. (p. 198)

Surely, it is the teacher's job to respond to student needs in the classroom and to adjust his or her personal style to fit the classroom population each year. In other words, we need educators like Lisa Tyler, featured in the beginning of the chapter, who speaks of constantly interrogating her own practice; Kelly's teacher, who builds on her student's strengths and does her best to follow his lead; and Ashton-Warner, who will meet students "where they are" instead of expecting learners to adjust to typical instructional approaches. Although students with autism need a welcoming school and great curriculum to be successful, nothing may be more important to a student's success than the willingness of the educator to take some risks, treat students as individuals, and keep learning as they teach.

FOR MORE ANSWERS AND INFORMATION

Books

Brower, F. (2007). *100 ideas for supporting pupils on the autistic spectrum.* New York: Continuum.

Feldman, J. (2000). *Transition tips and tricks for teachers.* Lewisville, NC: Gryphon House.

(continued)

(continued)

Kluth, P., & Danaher, S. (2010). *From tutor scripts to talking sticks: 100 ways to differentiate instruction in K–12 inclusive classrooms.* Baltimore: Paul H. Brookes Publishing Co.

Kluth, P., & Schwarz, P. (2008). *"Just give him the whale!" 20 ways to use fascinations, areas of expertise, and strengths to support students with autism.* Baltimore: Paul H. Brookes Publishing Co.

Myles, B.S. (2006). *Simple strategies that work! Helpful hints for all educators of students with Asperger syndrome, high-functioning autism, and related disabilities.* Shawnee Mission, KS: Autism Asperger Publishing Company.

 Web Sites

Edupics.com
http://www.edupics.com

For K–12 students who love to doodle, check out this site for realistic coloring pages on such topics as history, space exploration, and pollution.

Index of Learning Styles Inventory
http://www.engr.ncsu.edu/learningstyles/ilsweb.html

Created by Dr. Richard Felder and Dr. Barb Soloman, this inventory will give teachers ideas for discussion and planning (e.g., "I am more likely to be considered a) careful about my work or b) creative about my work").

LD Online
http://www.ldonline.org

This site, focused on learning disabilities, has a lot of great content—as well as many teaching tips—that will be of interest to teachers of those on the spectrum.

Person-Centered Planning Education Site
http://www.ilr.cornell.edu/edi/pcp

If you are interested in conducting MAPS, you will want to visit this site sponsored by Cornell University. You will find an overview of the person-centered planning process and a self-study course on person-centered planning.

NOTES: _____

_____

_____

_____

_____

_____

_____

Collaboration and
Cooperation in the Inclusive School

They need to work together. Each one–the home and school–knows that if they don't work together then we can't learn together. We have to learn to treat each other with respect. We really need to trust each other. (Pat Wilson, parent of a child with autism, as cited in Kluth, 1999, p. 1)

When I started teaching in an inclusive school, I felt it was enough for me to facilitate the involvement of my students in their general education classrooms and coach the teachers on how best to support these learners. After a few weeks, however, my vision of my job and my secure position behind the scenes were shattered when Peg, a sixth-grade teacher, asked for my input about her science lesson. She had one student with an identified disability in her classroom, one with significant emotional needs, two students needing speech and language support, and three others who were learning English as a second language. On top of all of this, Peg had 36 students in her classroom that year—an all-time high number. She needed help.

During a team meeting, I reviewed Peg's lessons with her and suggested that she try a cooperative learning structure to teach the concept of the food chain. "Okay," she agreed, "when can you come in and teach it with me?" I was stunned and silently tried to figure out Peg's request. I wondered, "Why doesn't this veteran teacher understand the system? Doesn't she know that I give the suggestions and she implements them?" After staring at her blankly for a few moments and stuttering something about not knowing much about food or chains, she told me to come to her room the next day to start planning.

I met Peg in her classroom, and we planned a cooperative lesson on the functions of the food chain. We divided students into groups and assigned them an animal to study. Groups were then provided with materials to research their animal's place and function in the food chain. The students were charged with creating a poster to illustrate how their animal fit into the cycle of life. Students then had to defend their position and their drawing to the rest of the class in the form of a short, informal class presentation. Peg and I served as judges in "Survival Court" and determined whether the groups had proved that their animal was a necessary part of the ecosystem.

Peg and I decided that I would begin the lesson by giving a mini-lecture on ecology, and she would assist by passing out materials and giving directions for the activity. I was nervous in my debut as a general educator but eager to earn my stripes at the front of the classroom. Although I made a lot of rookie mistakes (such as talking too fast and failing to assess whether students were understanding the information as I was providing it), Peg and I were pleased with the lesson. I had a chance to experience the difficulties and pleasures of presenting a lesson I had crafted, and Peg finally had a chance to talk to individual students, work with small groups, and observe her classroom without having to be at the helm.

The students seemed to love the busy, active lesson and participated enthusiastically. Most important, we felt confident that students understood the content; through informal assessments (e.g., observations, short interviews), we deemed that learners were grasping the vocabulary and concepts we had introduced through the activity.

The food chain lesson was the end of my special education isolation and the beginning of my life as a co-teacher and true collaborative team member. This does not mean that I started co-teaching full time in Peg's classroom and that I never played a behind-the-scenes consulting role again. Because I was responsible for supporting six students in six different classrooms in five different grades, I was not actually able to engage in a lot of cooperative teaching, but my participation in the science lesson communicated to my colleague that I was willing to take on new and unfamiliar roles in my job as inclusion facilitator. And Peg communicated that she trusted me to do more than make observations and suggestions.

In this chapter, I will explore more about the kind of collaboration, cooperation, and team teaching Peg and I experienced. I begin the chapter by discussing collaboration essentials; this section highlights the five components necessary for any team to succeed. This is followed by a listing of team members; here I explain the role and the function of everyone from parent to therapist. Finally, I share information about how team members can work together most effectively and answer questions about how much support students need, how teachers can teach collaboratively, and how roles and responsibilities can be shared and shifted to best meet the needs of every student in the classroom.

Collaboration Essentials

In the past decade, considerable attention has been given to the benefits of collaboration among K–12 classroom teachers. In particular, general education and special education teachers have been exploring ways to work together with other service providers and families to create inclusive classrooms for students with a wide range of abilities (Lipsky & Gartner, 1996; Maanum, 2009; Murawski, 2009; Villa, Thousand, & Nevin, 2008). Given the tremendous diversity in U.S. classrooms—in ability, ethnicity, and culture, for example—teachers are finding that it is difficult to deliver effective instruction in isolation. Responsive and appropriate instruction, particularly in inclusive classrooms, requires cooperation, teaming, and shifts in roles and responsibilities for many school personnel. Therefore, schools committed to inclusive schooling must encourage and value collaboration and the "inclusion" of adults as well as students. In this section, I will explore how teams can come together to meet the needs of all students in their diverse, inclusive classrooms. The five essentials include common goals, values, and mission; parity and role sharing; structures for planning and communication; shared leadership; and shared responsibility for students.

Common Goals, Values, and Mission

Members of any collaborative team should share goals (Appley & Winder, 1977; Coleman & Levine, 2008; Thousand & Villa, 2000) and a framework or mission of some type (Schwarz &

Table 12.1.   Philosophy and recommended practice statement from Kruse Education Center

That students of diverse abilities and educational background need to learn from one another.

Our purpose is to find the "best way" of making education work well for students with individual differences.

We can meet the needs of all students with diverse needs by individualizing the curriculum for the range of students' abilities.

Modeling for students from one another is essential in learning.

Support means more than just supervision: It means preparing to make informed, educational decisions for all students.

We own all students: Boundaries are minimized in our model.

Most school- and community-based objectives for students with disabilities in primary and intermediate grades can be met in the settings of same-age peers without disabilities.

We need to empower students to be in general education settings whenever possible based on their individual needs and the degree they can tolerate the expectations or adapted expectations in the classroom.

The focus of related service support is to provide expertise within their area to successfully integrate and enhance the general education curriculum.

Every student is an "individual." Individual goals and objectives come first.

The focus of learning is to make students more independent and empower everyone to be an effective learner and citizen.

From Schwarz, P., & Bettenhausen, D. (2000). You can teach an old dog new tricks. In R. Villa, & J. Thousand (Eds.). *Restructuring for caring and effective education: Piecing the puzzle together* (2nd ed., p. 478). Baltimore: Paul H. Brookes Publishing Co.; reprinted by permission.

Bettenhausen, 2000; Schwarz & Kluth, 2007; Villa, Thousand, Nevin, & Malgeri, 1996). In one of the schools in which I served as an inclusion facilitator, an entire philosophy was drafted in order to focus team members as they made decisions and to communicate the school's beliefs and values to new staff and community members (Schwarz & Bettenhausen, 2000; see Table 12.1). Goals might be centered on specific students (e.g., "Teach Kenny to read") or related to the school or staff (e.g., "We will all co-teach at least one class next year"; "We will eliminate pulling students out and provide all services within general education settings"). Educators in Vermont, for instance, formed a task force just to define their philosophy around students with autism. The philosophy emphasizes their commitment not only to a range of services and supports but also to providing an educational environment that welcomes and understands the unique qualities of students with autism labels (Godek, 2008).

Although team members will undoubtedly come to the group with different levels of commitment to supporting students with and without disabilities together, individuals must share some core values if inclusive schooling is to become a part of school culture. Team values in inclusive schools typically include the fundamental belief that all students can learn and that those learners have a right to be educated with their peers. These values, to be translated to student outcomes, should be advertised—in a sense—to the entire school community.

Parity and Role Sharing

In inclusive classrooms, the adults shift and share roles and responsibilities in order to expand their own skills, further their own knowledge, and give students access to a wider range of supports. In inclusive schools, lesson planning involves not only teachers but also, in some cases, therapists and paraprofessionals. Designing classroom rules and establishing guidelines for the school community originates from all team members as well, including students and their families, and both special and general educators are responsible for individualized education program (IEP) development and implementation.

Educators may experience some confusion and anxiety when these roles initially shift. In such cases, up-front planning and discussion about changes can be helpful. In a study conducted by Udvari-Solner and Keyes, Jennie Allen, a principal of an elementary school, shared how she helped teachers prepare for their shifts in roles and responsibilities:

> Before team-taught classrooms came about we had some very lengthy discussions. [Discussions] about simple things like, "How do you feel about having a roommate? Essentially, you are getting a roommate. So, how do you feel about sharing a room, having somebody else's desk in that room, and their stuff and their mess? What are you going to do the first time there is a behavior problem in the classroom? Who is going to do the disciplining? Who is going to make the telephone call home? How are you going to decide that? During planning time, do you co-plan? How many weekdays a week are you going to co-plan? How many days are you going to go separately and plan? Who will teach which learning groups?" Those are the kinds of discussions that we need to take place. The message [behind those questions] was that I was not going to allow [one person] to act as an educational assistant in this classroom and the other person as the teacher. (2000, p. 443)

As Allen pointed out, collaboration also requires parity between participants; this means that team members demonstrate their willingness to work together as classroom equals (Kohler-Evans, 2006). For example, in a study that focused on universal design in high school science classes, Dymond and her colleagues interviewed one teacher who articulated this clearly:

> The general educator needs to be speaking with all the students and trying to teach them. I don't think we should segregate students to teachers. In my opinion, all the students on our class lists are mine and all of them are [my co-teacher's]. We're both responsible for all of them. (2006, p. 298)

Cook and Friend suggested that adults working together in schools send parity signals in order to communicate their cooperation to students, families, and other staff members. Parity signals are "visual, verbal, and instructional signals" that convey equality (1995, p. 11). Parity signals teachers might employ include hosting an open house night as a team; putting both teachers' names on communication that goes home to families; having both teachers deliver instruction, design curriculum, and assess students; and giving both teachers the same (or nearly the same) amount of workspace in the classroom.

Structures for Planning and Communication

Effective collaboration, although incredibly valuable and so often enjoyable, is neither easily nor quickly achieved. Effective and productive collaborative relationships develop from time spent together exchanging ideas and information and solving problems. Time and practice are necessary to build trust and develop the informal and formal structures and procedures that enable teams to work together effectively (Larson & LaFasto, 1989).

Successful inclusive education demands that teachers have opportunities to meet face to face and plan for individual students and to develop whole-class lessons for all students. Ideally, teachers should meet weekly with all team members to plan instruction and develop curriculum. In addition, team meetings—no matter how often they occur—must be designed for maximum effectiveness. Often, teachers have no more than 20 or 30 minutes to plan lessons and solve problems, so these meetings need to be well planned, orderly, and productive. Notes should be used so that team members can see what was discussed in previous meetings and where the conversation should begin in the next gathering. (See Figure 12.1 for a set of completed notes from an elementary school team meeting and Figure 12.2 for a template that can be used for your team meetings.) For those groups who cannot find time to meet weekly, longer monthly sessions can be used to engage in long-term planning and other types of tools

Team Meeting Notes

Date: __4/12/09__

Team members present and roles:

Facilitator: __Erin__

Recorder: __Jen__

Timekeeper: __Amy__

Snacks: __Ping__

Team members absent:

__Elinor__

This week's good news/success story: Jade gave her report in front of the class and read her index card independently; Will's documentary made it to state finals!

Agenda items	Status (FYI: information; JD: just discussion; ND: needs decision)	Time required	Action(s) required	Individual(s) responsible	Timeline
Field trip to Wisconsin Historical Society	ND—do we want to book this?; bus $ is more than planned.	o 5 min ☒ 10 min o ____	* Confirm/book the trip—ask about special lesson on the Civil War letters * Book the bus—new company?	Jen Ping	By next meeting By next meeting
Lessons on Mathew Brady photos	ND—finish designing lessons and make decisions about supports	o 5 min ☒ 10 min o ____	* Students will work in pairs (or groups of three)—group the students (Jade w/ Cy) * Jade will need support generating story ideas—(create choice board) and writing (provide assistive tech)	Ping (group) Erin (assistive tech)	Wed. Wed.
Lesson on cost of war	JD	☒ 5 min o 10 min o ____	* NOTE: Amy will include challenge questions for Henry, Seth, Ro		
Upcoming unit: Reconstruction	FYI	☒ 5 min o 10 min o ____			

Agenda items for next meeting:

• Co-teaching for final unit; who will take the lead on which pieces of Reconstruction unit?
• Exhibitions—updates; adapting assessment (maybe new rubric) for Jade, Rio, Sam, and Tamika

Figure 12.1. Team meeting notes example.

Team Meeting Notes

Date: _____

Team members present and roles: Team members absent:

Facilitator: _____   _____

Recorder: _____

Timekeeper: _____

Snacks: _____

This week's good news/success story:

Agenda items	Status (FYI: information; JD: just discussion; ND: needs decision)	Time required	Action(s) required	Individual(s) responsible	Timeline
		o 5 min o 10 min o _____			
		o 5 min o 10 min o _____			
		o 5 min o 10 min o _____			
		o 5 min o 10 min o _____			
		o 5 min o 10 min o _____			

Agenda items for next meeting:

Figure 12.2. Team meeting notes template.

"You're Going to Love This Kid!" Teaching Students with Autism in the Inclusive Classroom, Second Edition, by Paula Kluth
Copyright © 2010 by Paul H. Brookes Publishing Co. All rights reserved.

Table 12.2. Structures for planning and collaboration

Team meetings	Teachers can meet every week, every other week, or work together for several hours at the end or beginning of each month.
Mini-team meetings	Team meets 15 minutes before school every week. Teachers typically plan to cover only one or two issues at these meetings. The topic is usually shared beforehand, and participants come to the meeting with ideas. Having a facilitator can keep members on task.
Lunch meetings	One or two team members or a whole team might plan to share a meal together a few times a month. Some teams use this time the same way they would any other meeting. Other teams engage in these meeting just to socialize and share stories of success.
"Stolen" meetings	Some of the team members meet in the back of the classroom or in an adjacent room when students are watching a movie, listening to a guest speaker, or engaging in independent work.
Dialogue notebook	Some teams communicate by dialoguing on paper. One team member shares ideas and thoughts and passes them to their colleague. This individual responds, adds his or her own ideas and thoughts, and passes it back. This format can be used between just two educators or more.
E-mail	E-mail can be used to ask simple questions (e.g., Is Emi going to join chess club?) or to plan lessons. One teacher can make notes on an upcoming lesson and mail it to another; she can then make adjustments and suggestions and send it back to her colleague.
Lesson binder	Some teams keep all plans in one big binder that can be accessed by all. Teachers, therapists, and paraprofessionals who have ideas to add or materials to contribute can do so by adding to the binder. An "electronic binder" can be posted on a web site and used in the same way.
Communication forms	In some schools (especially in secondary schools where team members may not see each other every day), teams communicate by filling out a communication form. The best forms have checklists, scales, or short answer options that make them easy to use. For instance, in one school, general education teachers filled in a form every other week that asked them to answer a number of questions, including the following: – On a scale of 1 to 10, how well do you feel student IEP goals are being addressed in the general education classroom? – On a scale of 1 to 10, how well do you think you are meeting the needs of all students? – How do you feel about the amount of paraprofessional support students are receiving (circle one): not enough just right too much – Explain any gains individual students have made recently:

and structures can be used for daily and weekly communication (see Table 12.2 for ideas for structures for planning and collaboration).

Shared Leadership

Effective teams use a distributed functions theory of leadership (Johnson & Johnson, 1999; Thousand & Villa, 2000) in which "task and relationship functions of the traditional lone leader are distributed among all members of the group" (Thousand & Villa, 2000, p. 257). This means that the different team members take turns completing certain tasks (e.g., leading meetings, calling the family, completing paperwork related to a student's IEP) and that all participate in discussions and decision making. It may be initially challenging to move away from traditional roles, especially if an administrator or a certain teacher has done a lot of preliminary work to initiate collaborative work. In order to facilitate the transition to shared leadership, teams might delegate specific roles for members and then systematically switch those roles. For instance, a teacher may serve as the team facilitator (responsible for running meetings and following up on agenda items) one month and then move to being the team trouble shooter (responsible for checking in with members, gauging the team's progress, and clearing up communication problems) the next month.

Shared Responsibility for Students

A student shoves a student with autism, and the student with autism shoves back. Does the teacher speak to both students and help them to negotiate their shared problem, or does she speak to the student without an identified disability and tell the young man with autism that he needs to talk to "his teacher" about the incident?

Some teachers new to inclusive schooling may feel responsible for those without disabilities but think that those with disabilities "belong" to someone else. This longstanding and deeply entrenched practice of seeing some students as "other" occurs in many ways in our schools every day.

In inclusive schools, however, all adults are responsible for all students and demonstrate this responsibility actively. They show care and concern for all learners, they work hard to get to know students, and they take part in providing instruction. For example, a speech-language therapist might teach a small reading group including students with and without identified disabilities, a special educator might work on an independent project with a student without disabilities, a general educator might work one to one with a student with autism, and a social worker might teach social skills to an entire second-grade class.

In classrooms where responsibilities for students are shared, language may also change. For instance, when all educators teach and support all students, the language of "yours" and "mine" is eradicated. This language can be transforming; as teachers begin to use words such as "us" and "ours," separating responsibilities and seeing students as belonging to a program or teacher often feels awkward and unnatural.

The Team: Roles and Contributions

One day, I walked into the school library and saw a paraprofessional from my team quietly reading a book with a 6-year-old boy. I watched them for at least 20 minutes, completely stunned. I had never seen the student, who was nonverbal and very active, sit still for more than 6 minutes. No teacher, therapist, or administrator had been able to help him relax so completely. After school, I had only one question for my colleague: "How did you do that?" She sat me down and told me the story of how the two came to be sitting sharing *Miss Spider's Tea Party* (Kirk, 1994) on that afternoon. She told me about the soft voice she used to read and the way she allowed him to look at the book even if that meant that he would tilt it sideways and page through it at breakneck speed. She also told me about the way she talked to this student: "I tell him about things. I tell him stories when we are walking around the building. Sometimes I tell him about my kids."

This talented woman did not have much experience working in education; in fact, she had only been working as a paraprofessional for a few weeks when this incident occurred. What she did have was a knowledge of and respect for children and a belief that all students were learners. This colleague not only gave me some concrete strategies to try but also demonstrated that the student could be successful if his educators taught him the way he needed to learn. She also demonstrated that everyone on our team has something very valuable to offer.

As a young teacher, I learned a lot from working closely with seven paraprofessionals in my first teaching job and from all others on my team. From the physical therapist, I learned how to increase a student's range of motion; from the administrators, I learned how to conduct sensitive staff evaluations; and from the physical education teacher, I learned how to incorporate kinesthetic activities into daily classroom lessons. Clearly, every team member is critical to the success of students and to the professional development of other team members. Every individual on the team has a different area of expertise as well as a different set of experiences to share. For example, some members may have more experiences working in inclusive schools whereas others may be more familiar with community resources or curriculum and instruction. Therefore, it is critical that teams take advantage of the contributions of all members.

In this section, I describe some of the roles and contributions typically made by different team members. It should be noted that every possible team member (e.g., school nurse, student mentor) is not and could not be listed here. Instead, I have tried to outline the roles of those who most often have membership on teams in inclusive schools: students with autism and their families; classmates of students with autism; administrators; general education teachers; special education teachers; paraprofessionals; therapists; social workers, school counselors, and psychologists; and professional consultants.

Students with Autism and Their Families

The most important members of the collaborative team are the student with autism and his or her family. Although these members may not participate in teaching lessons or delivering services, their ideas, preferences, and needs should be constantly fielded, considered, and integrated into the child's program.

The student with autism can offer the insider perspective and can provide the team with the best information on "what works." For this reason, learners should be formally and informally involved in developing their own IEPs and crafting their own supports. For example, a student might write a letter to the team to make them aware of his preferences, needs, or requests (see Figure 12.3 for an example) or, if possible, even lead his own IEP meeting. See Table 12.3 for a variety of ways students of all ages can take a more central role in the IEP process.

Keep in mind that the student on the spectrum may need help in learning about the process before she can begin serving as a self-advocate. Teachers and families will need to teach the student about her label, needs, strengths, and abilities. Stephen Shore, in his edited book *Ask and Tell: Self-Advocacy and Disclosure for People on the Autism Spectrum* (2004), suggests that educators have their students study the IEP in detail. One tool that Shore has used for this purpose is the IEP worksheet (see Figure 12.4); this tool asks students to review their educational

---

Dear IEP team members:

Before you make any decisions about my plan for next year, please keep the following in mind:

    I love math! I love math! I love math!
    I detest writing without my computer!
    I think the art room smells and I need help if I am going to sit in there for 55 minutes.

Your student at Red Road Middle,

        Byron

Figure 12.3. Letter to IEP team members from a student.

Table 12.3.   Ideas for including the student with autism in the IEP process

Prekindergarten and early elementary school

- Have the child come in and introduce himself (verbally or using AAC).
- Have the child hand out a few photographs or show a few objects that help the team understand more about him (e.g., something he does well, an interest).
- Have the child hand out materials that parents have brought (e.g., an outside evaluation).

Late elementary and middle school

- Have the child give a short "report" on likes, dislikes, needs, and strengths.
- Have the child suggest goals for the IEP (you may need to provide options to choose from).
- Have the student prepare an "about me" poster, slogan, or even music video.
- Have the student run a PowerPoint presentation of a photo essay that illustrates "present level of performance," current abilities, needs, and/or progress and updates.

Secondary school

- Have the student attend as much of the meeting as possible and have her contribute her own "report" as well as facilitate some of the meeting.
- Have the student bring a classmate to talk about the goals and needs of teens.
- Help the student submit suggested goals for the IEP either in writing, verbally, or perhaps by pointing to pictures of favorite materials, people, and activities.
- Help the student create formal advocacy-related products (e.g., "published" pamphlets, short documentary, auto-biography) to share with IEP team and, perhaps, with others in her life.

plan and learn about the various pieces of the process and resources related to their label and educational needs.

Families also must be at the center of the planning process. The importance of family–school collaboration and partnership has been so consistently supported by research that it is no longer considered an option but rather a professional obligation (Corrigan & Bishop, 1997; Grant & Ray, 2009). In practice, however, families are too often relegated to the margins of their child's education (Kluth, Biklen, English-Sand, & Smukler, 2007). For example, parents may be asked to attend meetings in which large numbers of professionals tell them about their child without asking for their input or soliciting advice or ideas from them. This outdated model must be replaced by one in which families are viewed as equal partners in the educational process and provided with opportunities to share their knowledge.

Classmates of the Students with Autism

Classmates are ideal team members in that they are consumers of education in the same schools and classrooms as the students with autism. Every student certainly experiences his or her education differently; however, peers can provide a general report on the effectiveness of certain types of curriculum or instruction. In one classroom, for instance, two students were asked to help in constructing a daily schedule for a peer with autism. When the team suggested that the student take a certain art class because of the student's interest in painting, both students groaned. One piped up, "That class is so boring. The teacher talks too much. We should sign Tressa up for ceramics. I'm taking that and so are other kids she knows." Because Tressa did not have a reliable way to communicate, the team decided to listen to the students and value their input over the ideas of the adults. In matters of school culture, the team assumed that the students might be more "in the know" than any professional or member of Tressa's family.

In some districts, peers may even take on more formal roles of support (Carter, Cushing, Clark, & Kennedy, 2005; Carter & Kennedy, 2006). Carter, Cushing, Clark, and Kennedy, for

My IEP

Question	Answer
Where is my name located?	
When is the date of my next review?	
What does the "present level of educational performance" tell me?	
What are my measurable annual goals?	
Are there any short-term objectives, and what do they say?	
What special education and related services am I provided?	
Why was I given these services?	
What supplementary aides and services are provided?	
What are they used for?	
What steps am I taking to prepare for life after graduation?	

Figure 12.4. My IEP worksheet.

From Shore, S. (2004). *Ask and tell: Self-advocacy and disclosure for people on the autism spectrum* (pp. 87–88). Shawnee Mission, KS: Autism Asperger Publishing Co.; adapted by permission. Copyright © 2004 by Autism Asperger Publishing Co.

In *"You're Going to Love This Kid!" Teaching Students with Autism in the Inclusive Classroom, Second Edition,* by Paula Kluth. (2010, Paul H. Brookes Publishing Co., Inc.)

instance, have studied the impact of support interventions in which peers are trained to adapt class activities, contribute to the attainment of IEP goals, and facilitate interactions with other students in the class. They have found that middle and high school students with significant disabilities maintained high levels of engagement in instructional activities when working with one or two peer supports in their core academic classrooms. Increases in social interactions also have been documented in such arrangements (Kennedy & Itkonen, 1994; Shukla, Kennedy, & Cushing, 1999). These findings challenge the idea that paraprofessionals are the only way to provide direct, one-to-one support to students in inclusive classrooms.

Despite all of the potential benefits of peer support, students are often overlooked as team members, perhaps because of their age or lack of experience. Although students may not have formal knowledge of disabilities, teaching, or curriculum, they certainly do have the wisdom that their own experience provides, and they also have the "expertise" of knowing and being educated with the student with autism and understanding what it is like to be a young person in that particular setting. These experiences and the wisdom that grows from them are sometimes as helpful or even *more* helpful than the textbook knowledge and professional experiences of educators or even the lived experiences and insider wisdom possessed by families.

Students can be asked to help in several ways, including making scheduling choices, suggesting curricular supports, and crafting social opportunities as well as voicing their opinions about any other decision or idea. If peers are enlisted for these or other ways of helping, the individual with autism should surely be the one to select them. If the student with autism does not have a reliable way to communicate, educators should observe the student to determine with whom he or she seems most comfortable. Families also can help in selecting appropriate peer team members; parents and siblings will be able to identify those peers who the student with autism knows from the neighborhood or from church, for instance.

Administrators

Educators in leadership positions, especially principals, directors of pupil services, supervisors, and department heads, are critical members of collaborative teams (Goor, Schwenn, & Boyer, 1997; Keyes, 1996; Udvari-Solner & Keyes, 2000; Causton-Theoharis, 2009; Villa & Thousand, 1990). Administrators serve as the philosophical backbone of an inclusive school. It is very difficult—but not impossible—to provide all students with an education that is appropriate, challenging, engaging, motivating, and inclusive if administrators are not informed about the federal laws as they relate to inclusive education and aware of the tools and practices needed to grow an inclusive school. Dramatic changes in both teaching behavior and student learning are possible when administrators communicate support and empowerment to educators (Felner, Kasak, Mulhall, & Flowers, 1997).

Although placement decisions for students with disabilities are made by each student's IEP team, the behavior and perceptions of the principal strongly influence these decisions. Furthermore, a principal's support is necessary for the successful implementation of inclusion. As Praisner (2003) found when she surveyed 408 elementary school principals, principals with more positive attitudes toward inclusion were more likely to believe that less restrictive placements were most appropriate for students with disabilities.

It is very important that administrators communicate their commitment to inclusive education clearly. In fact, the school may want to state its position in a mission statement or slogan to ensure that all stakeholders understand the importance of such a commitment. One of the administrators in my school had a banner over his desk reading, "Special education is not a place." Everyone who visited his office understood his dedication to students and to inclusive education.

As part of this commitment to inclusion, administrators might attend team meetings, assist with staff schedules and other structures that support inclusion, monitor classroom enrollment, supervise special education processes, work with parents, encourage educators, and serve in supportive capacities with students. Principals and other leaders also will help with troubleshooting and improving inclusive programming in the school.

General Education Teachers

Although general education teachers may be new to some of the language and practices of inclusive education, most have "done inclusion" without realizing it by simply responding to the diversity that has always existed in their classrooms. General education teachers are important members of the team because they are the experts on general education curriculum and instruction. For example, a general educator is a good resource for learning about how the school's math program might intersect with a learner's IEP goals or for suggesting ways in which the occupational therapist might be able to work with the student during art instruction.

The general educator is one of the team members (and sometimes the only member) responsible for planning lessons for an inclusive classroom. Thus, he or she should be a primary decision maker in creating supports and adaptations for those lessons. The general education teacher also can help the team understand the rituals, routines, and traditions of a grade level. For instance, he or she knows what games their students play at recess and what field trips they will take during the year; this team member can, therefore, help the team plan for such events.

Because the general educator is sometimes the least experienced in implementing inclusive schooling, he or she may appreciate guidance. Teachers who are completely unfamiliar with disability may appreciate a mini–in-service on special education jargon, the IEP, or the role of related services in the student's education. Furthermore, the teacher will need to receive information about autism. This can come from the student, the student's family, the special educator, therapists, books, and/or the Internet. Some teachers want to know a lot about the label of autism before they begin teaching the student. Others prefer to get to know the student before learning about his or her label.

Special Education Teachers

Special educators are also key members of the team; these professionals often have very different roles in inclusive schools than they do in other settings. In most cases, special education teachers in inclusive schools shift from being classroom teachers to facilitators, consulting teachers, and co-teachers. This can be a rocky transition for some teachers, especially if they have become accustomed to being "in charge" of their own classroom and students. The process is often easier when general educators welcome their colleagues and work with them to reinvent classroom space, teacher roles and responsibilities, and curriculum and instruction.

The role of the special educator in inclusive classrooms is to ensure that the students with disabilities are able to participate in and benefit from the general education curriculum and instruction; however, he or she also should be attending to the learning needs of students without disabilities. Just as the general educator is expected to take responsibility for all students, so should the special educator support and serve those with and without disabilities.

Paraprofessionals

Paraprofessionals play many diverse educational roles, depending on the needs of individual teachers and the hiring guidelines and requirements of each program, school, and district. Many schools employ paraprofessionals as classroom assistants or to help individual students with personal care, academic tasks, and life skills. Those hired to support students with disabilities should have roles and responsibilities explicitly defined by the program and by their supervisors. Many positions occupied by paraprofessionals are not so clearly defined, however, and at times, these individuals may be pulled in different directions by those who direct and supervise them. At the very least, paraprofessionals should be informed about the educational needs (e.g., IEP goals and objectives) and characteristics of the students with whom they work as well as classroom and school practices and routines.

Paraprofessionals also should have opportunities to contribute to the development of the educational programs and instructional plans but should not be given sole responsibility for these and related activities. This point is critical. Too often, paraprofessionals are asked to design curriculum or instruction, conduct formal and informal assessments, create adaptations for students, and make a range of other instructional decisions on their own (Downing, Ryndak, & Clark, 2000; Giangreco, 2009; Giangreco, Broer, & Edelman, 1999; Marks, Schrader, & Levine, 1999).

In one classroom I visited, the paraprofessional made decisions related to the student's curriculum and instruction all day long. The general educator in this classroom told me that the student with autism, Keith, was included in lessons only when the paraprofessional "decided the activity would benefit him." The paraprofessional didn't necessarily want this responsibility, but she was not given direction beyond "Use your best judgment." This system of decision making is problematic on many levels, but one of the most egregious mistakes made is the lack of up-front planning around Keith's education. A paraprofessional should never be in the position to make such a significant decision regarding a student's participation. Although many paraprofessionals may be quite able to engage in these activities, it is the teachers' professional and legal responsibility to do so.

Teachers, special educators, and related service providers (e.g., speech-language pathologists, occupational therapists) have the ultimate responsibility for ensuring the appropriate design, implementation, and evaluation of instruction carried out by paraprofessionals; therefore, it is critical that these professionals find time and create structures and materials that will help the paraprofessional do his or her job. For instance, if a speech therapist wants a paraprofessional to take data on a certain behavior or skill, then that therapist must take the time and provide the necessary training to allow the paraprofessional to do so accurately.

Because they are such central members of the collaborative team, paraprofessionals must also be given ample opportunities to voice concerns, ask questions, and share ideas. If they cannot be included in regular team meetings due to time or scheduling constraints, then other tools and structures for communicating must be designed and implemented. When I was charged with supervising and collaborating with nine paraprofessionals, I tried to keep them informed through individual 15- or 20-minute meetings scheduled during the school day a few times each month. Our group also communicated by posting notes and suggestions on a community chalkboard in our shared office. Because everyone came into the office to store personal belongings and take coffee breaks, all members of our group had some opportunity to give and get news of the day and updates on happenings related to individual students or classrooms. In today's schools, e-mail or text messages can also be used, as can electronic message boards.

During busy days, a paraprofessional may feel quite overworked and underappreciated. They are often the busiest adults in the building and are often given too little recognition and compensation for their creativity and hard work. In order to pull paraprofessionals into the team and to make them feel more comfortable and valued, teachers and other team members must be sure to recognize and mine all of the talents that paraprofessionals bring to the classroom. If a paraprofessional is a history buff, teachers should look for opportunities for that person to share favorite stories or to help the teaching team design a lesson on a history topic. If a paraprofessional is really skilled at supporting a student who often gets upset, he or she might be asked to talk to other paraprofessionals about the strategies that he or she uses. Table 12.4 includes more tips on working with paraprofessionals.

Table 12.4.   Tips for working with paraprofessionals

Communication

- Make sure that paraprofessionals get to attend as many meetings as possible. If they cannot attend key meetings, take notes to share.

- Keep important team information in a three-ring binder, on a bulletin board, or even on a group web page so that paraprofessionals can regularly check information on adaptations, lesson plans, student therapies, and so forth.

- Try to meet weekly with each paraprofessional. Even if the meetings are short, this time together is critical.

- Provide time and structures for idea sharing and problem solving. For instance, you can maintain a suggestion box or board or have a monthly coffee chat.

- Share the good news. If you get feedback about a student or situation that is positive, be sure to pass it on. In addition, always discuss what is going well.

Teaching and learning

- Assess the skills and competencies of each paraprofessional before making assignments. Is the person extremely organized? Playful? Collaborative? Interested in mathematics? Active? Gathering this type of information will be critical for making the right matches between the job and the paraprofessional.

- Provide plenty of time for learning new skills, and never ask a paraprofessional to do something that you would not or have not done yourself; he or she should not be expected to perform a task or engage in an activity that has not been modeled for them and practiced under supervision.

- Write it all down. If paraprofessionals are teaching lessons to individuals or groups of students, they need written plans to follow. If a particular learner has a behavior protocol, the paraprofessional needs a copy of it to read and follow.

- Take time to observe the work of paraprofessionals and provide opportunities for paraprofessionals to observe you as you support students on the spectrum. Give feedback and support as needed.

Staff development

- If you have a highly qualified veteran paraprofessional in your building, you might use this person as a coach for other paraprofessionals.

- Look for formal learning opportunities for your paraprofessionals. Keep in mind any upcoming conferences, seminars, or even webinars that might be helpful and interesting to the person.

- As you read your teaching magazines, journals, and newsletters, clip out articles that your paraprofessionals might find interesting. Likewise, when you find a new web site that is helpful in your teaching or in your understanding of autism, share it.

- Provide catch-as-catch-can learning opportunities. For example, a few times a year, you might show a documentary film on autism, inclusion, or teaching during staff lunch breaks or download podcasts on key topics and play them as your paraprofessional is setting up the classroom in the morning.

- Have a book club or even an article club! Periodically, invite paraprofessionals to join you in reading something that will help all of you in your daily work. An autobiography of a person on the spectrum is always a good choice, but a relevant journal article or book chapter could also be the subject of discussions.

Therapists

School therapists traditionally provided their services in private offices that often were in the basements or back hallways of schools. This support was typically quite disconnected from classroom teaching and learning. Teachers found that many students receiving therapy in this model were not able to generalize their new skills to the classroom.

Educators now understand that learning skills and competencies in isolation is often an exercise in futility; students must practice new skills and competencies in the environments in which they are most likely to use them (Downing, 2005; Giangreco, Edelman, & Dennis, 1991; Rainforth & England, 1997; Rainforth & York-Barr, 1997). Today, many speech-language therapists, occupational therapists, physical therapists, vision and mobility instructors, and even some art and music therapists (Aldridge, 2005) work in the inclusive classroom alongside general and special educators. These individuals might support students and classrooms in any number of ways, including by providing ideas for environmental accommodations, adaptive equipment and adaptive technology needs, and activities that would help students meet individual goals (Berkey, 2009). For example, a physical therapist might give the physical education teacher ideas for including a student with limited movement in a game of basketball; a speech-language therapist might teach a student with autism and his peers how to use a new communication system during a discussion group; and an occupational therapist might visit the classroom during journal-writing time and give a student with autism (and perhaps others) help with her writing posture and pencil grip.

Therapists also serve as the teachers of teachers; every therapist must educate his or her colleagues about the language and strategies related to therapy. Teachers, paraprofessionals, and all others expected to address therapeutic goals in the general education classroom should be given enough information to understand why they are supporting a certain skill or behavior. For example, if an occupational therapist wants a student to change his posture or start using a certain piece of assistive technology, then all of the adults in the classroom should know why these changes are important, understand how to help the student to do those things, and learn how to talk to the student about making those changes.

Social Workers, School Counselors, and Psychologists

Social workers, school counselors, and psychologists can offer a lot of support to the team in terms of how to meet the social and emotional needs of the student with autism while helping all students to understand appropriate ways to interact with their classmate with autism. Individuals in these roles may spend a lot of time evaluating students, but these professionals work with students in a variety of other capacities as well. These professionals may provide direct services to a student with autism by offering counseling or helping the learner with transition planning. They might also help the student and the student's team address scheduling, social supports, learning needs, and family–school communication.

Another role social workers, counselors, and psychologists might adopt is to teach students about self-advocacy and help them hone related skills. For example, a school psychologist I know worked with a young man with Asperger syndrome on creating a product about his educational needs. During her time with him, they visited web sites on Asperger syndrome, read articles written by people with Asperger syndrome, and worked on a personal portfolio of the young man's life. Using ideas from the Internet and from the articles, the young man was able to construct an autobiographical portfolio that he then used to teach his family and friends about his label and diagnosis. The psychologist, meanwhile, used the portfolio as a way to connect with the young man and to talk to him about his needs and his goals.

Mental health professionals can also help teams get connected with community resources. A social worker might, for instance, encourage a student to join a community club, group, or team or help families find outside tutoring support.

Finally, these individuals also can serve an important function in supporting staff members who are experiencing major changes in job responsibilities. Mental health professionals can offer ideas for dealing with stress, negotiating conflicts among staff members, or helping team members assess their struggles and their successes.

Professional Consultants

In some instances, schools may want to call on the services of a professional who specializes in educating students with autism. Some districts have in-house support available to teachers; in other instances, schools need to find help from local nonprofit agencies, colleges and universities, or independent consultants.

Outside consultation can offer the team a fresh perspective and new ideas or, in some cases, a welcome affirmation that they are on the right track. Teams might seek input from such an individual if they need more information about autism, the family seems unable to provide the expertise they need, and/or both the team and the student feel undersupported and in need of new answers. A consultant may be able to offer new materials, strategies, or information. The support from this person, however, will be temporary in most cases, so the team will want to have a plan for getting support after the consultant is gone.

One caution related to the use of consultants and outside support must be given: Teams should not assume that any individual has expertise that will be helpful to his or her particular team just because that person has a certain set of credentials or title. Team members should be sure that the consultant shares the values of the team and that he or she understands that the school has an inclusive ideology. The consultant also should be attentive and respectful to all members of the team including the student and his or her family and should consider the needs and skills of the entire group when offering suggestions.

Working Together

Many teachers are thrilled to have help in the classroom and relieved to have colleagues with whom to share successes and frustration, yet some are puzzled about how to handle all of the support. I have even heard teachers lament that they have too much support and too many adults in the classroom!

In actuality, there is seldom, if ever, a situation in which a classroom or a school has too much support. In almost every case, students profit from lower student–teacher ratios; therefore, it is beneficial to have access to as much adult power as possible. It is critical, however, that these supports are used in the most efficient and effective ways. If team members are not used wisely, valuable human resources are wasted and students may suffer. By assessing proximity, using a range of co-teaching structures, and carefully planning the roles and responsibilities of everyone working in the classroom, all students can benefit from additional support and all adults can participate meaningfully in classroom life.

How Much? Assessing Proximity, Cues, and Support

One day, a friend called and asked me to visit her classroom. For the first time in her career as a seventh-grade teacher, she was going to have a student with autism in her class and was looking for ideas. I walked into the classroom as students were conducting a science experiment and was able to spot her new student immediately; he was sitting at a table in the back of the room surrounded by three adults. I learned later that two of the women were therapists and the other was a paraprofessional. Although his educators were likely engaged in what they considered to be an important teaching moment, the exchange looked more like a summit than a science lesson.

I use this vignette to illustrate how critical it is to consider the impact that adult proximity has on student learning. In one study, researchers identified eight significant problems that resulted from paraprofessionals' proximity to students (Giangreco, Edelman, Luiselli, & MacFarland, 1997). Although study participants indicated that some level of close proximity between students with disabilities and paraprofessionals was desirable and sometimes quite necessary (e.g., tactile signing, personal care), they also recognized that adult support and proximity was not always needed and could, in fact, be detrimental to students. As one special educator in the study shared,

Sometimes I think it inhibits her relationship with her peers because a lot is done for Holly and Holly doesn't have the opportunity to interact with her peers because there is always somebody hovering over her, showing her what to do or doing things for her. I'd like to get

the instructional assistant away from Holly a little bit more so that peers will have a chance
to get in there and work more with Holly. (Giangreco et al., 1997, p. 217)

Specifically, the findings of the study suggest that too much adult proximity results in interference with general education teacher ownership and responsibility, separation from
classmates, dependence on adults, decreased peer interactions, limitations on receiving competent instruction, loss of personal control, loss of gender identity, and interference with the
instruction of others. It should be noted that although these researchers specifically focused
on the behaviors of paraprofessionals, this study and its results offer an important message
for any adult who works with students with disabilities, including teachers, therapists, and
classroom volunteers. This research is not so much about the work of paraprofessionals as it
is a critique of how all adult time, energy, and talent might be used or misused in inclusive
classrooms.

Clearly, too much adult support and the wrong type of adult support can rob students of
critical social opportunities as well as have a negative impact on learning. For instance, one of
my former students, Thomas, needed a lot of support. Thomas had a hard time sitting for any
period of time. He would leap out of his chair every few minutes unless someone sat near
him. Furthermore, he couldn't examine materials very effectively unless they were held for
him. For these reasons, Thomas always had a paraprofessional sitting or standing at his side.
Although this arrangement enhanced his participation in some ways, it also robbed him of
social opportunities and forced him to be unfailingly "on task" at all times. For instance, if
Thomas giggled at a friend's "inappropriate" joke, his support person would reprimand
him. Students such as Thomas, who get a lot of personal support, are constantly being super-
vised; therefore, they do not have the same opportunities as others to pass notes, gossip, tell
jokes, doodle, daydream, or fidget. Although none of these "offenses" are encouraged by
teachers, they are, if nothing else, *normal* student behaviors and are part of life in the classroom. Behaviors such as fidgeting and doodling might even help some learners stay seated
and attentive during class. Others such as passing notes and whispering to friends undoubtedly help students build and maintain social connections. So, losing the opportunity to engage in these ways is not unimportant.

In this section, you will find stories of success as well as ideas for fading adult support
and encouraging independence. As you read, consider how you might change the supports
for students in your classroom or school. Also, keep in mind that supports must be evaluated
constantly as student needs and abilities change over time. Therefore, even if a particular student needs a lot of proximal support now, the team can reassess a few weeks later to update
the types of assistance provided.

Fading Adult Support: Two Stories of Success

Fading adult proximity prompts teachers to consider ways in which students can be provided
with supports that are more natural and unobtrusive. For example, one of my former students, Tim, seemed to need a lot of reassurance to stay with a large group. For this reason, his
teacher put him in the back of the classroom so a paraprofessional could sit next to him and
the two could leave the room easily if Tim needed a break. When we noticed that this arrangement was isolating Tim from his peers, we put his desk in the middle of the room and put his
seat in between two students he knew and liked. Both of the students were able to offer the
supportive comments Tim needed, and he immediately responded to the arrangement. Over
time, he needed fewer breaks and, ultimately, very few encouraging comments to stay with
the group and participate in lessons. Meanwhile, the paraprofessional who had previously
supported Tim was freed to create new adaptations for Tim, to float around the classroom and
give support to all, and to act as a co-teacher for pieces of whole-class lessons (e.g., taking

graphic notes during a whole-class discussion so Tim and other students can see as well as hear the information).

Another student, Garren, was fairly independent during the school day but was always supported by a paraprofessional during lunchtime. This bothered Garren's mother because lunch was a time for socializing and the presence of a paraprofessional seemed to block Garren's engagement in typical lunchtime activities such as sharing news and reporting on the school day. When Garren's mother asked if he could go to the lunchroom alone, his teachers pointed out that he needed help getting ready for lunch. He often dropped his heavy tray if he had to balance it on his own. He was also unable to open his food containers. Furthermore, the staff pointed out, he scarcely made efforts to interact with other students. Having an adult there, they reasoned, would help him make connections with his peers. When Garren's mother persisted, the team agreed to reexamine the strategies they employed.

The team decided that Garren understood how to go through the lunch line and retrieve his lunch but that he didn't have the strength or coordination to do so. The team, therefore, decided that Garren could choose between having a cafeteria worker put his tray out on the table for him or coming a little early to the lunch room to get his lunch items one at a time. The staff then taught Garren how to punch his straw into the top of his milk carton instead of opening the spout and to ask a peer to open his hot lunch. Peers were happy to help; some of them even asked Garren to open their milk in the cool new "straw-punch" way. After only a few days of the new routine, Garren was independently enjoying his lunch experience and getting to know peers without the support of an adult. Interestingly, Garren no longer needed an adult to "facilitate social interactions" when one was not sitting next to him separating him from his classmates! See Table 12.5 for ideas for fading support in the inclusive classroom.

Encouraging Independence

The various ways in which students are supported in the classroom should be evaluated constantly. In most cases, physical supports and proximity should be faded as students gain skills and become more able to work independently. When I encourage teachers to think about

---

Table 12.5.   Ideas for fading adult support and proximity

In most cases, direct support should only be considered if a student cannot be supported using other methods, materials, or human resources. Try these ideas:

- Talk to the general educator about fading support and ask him or her for ideas.
- Constantly encourage interactions between students with and without disabilities.
- Allow the student to walk to classes with peers; follow as far behind as possible.
- Have the student sit with peers without disabilities at lunch without direct support. Stand at a distance, if possible, and help the lunch aides supervise the room.
- If you need to sit next to a student with a disability to get him or her started on work, immediately stand up and move away after the student is engaged in that work.
- Provide adapted materials so the learner can work without extra cues or support.
- Refrain from sitting next to the student and repeating directions and/or information during lectures. Teach the student to ask the teacher to repeat directions if needed.
- Support all students in the class; after providing assistance to a student with autism, move to another student in the classroom and provide help to him or her.
- Structure opportunities for the learner to be independent. For some students, you may actually need to find or make excuses to leave the room (e.g., make copies for the class) at first to communicate the message that you will not always be available.
- Look for situations that do not require adult support. Keep trying to expand the number of situations that require little or no support.

proximity and, in some cases, to fade direct support from learners with disabilities, they sometimes tell me that a particular student "can't do anything" independently. It is certainly true that many students with autism have significant needs and that some of these individuals need intensive support, but it is also true that students with such needs can get support in many ways, not just through the presence of an adult. In fact, all other adaptations should be considered before implementing a model involving adult support because it is not only costly but also difficult to fade.

In some cases, "support" may simply mean teaching the student to take risks, learn new skills, and develop new competencies. For instance, a student who relies on an adult to organize his or her materials for each class can be taught to use a checklist and a written course schedule. A student who needs help dressing for recess can be given boots without complicated snaps and buttons and can ask peers to help, if needed. And a student who relies on adult support to communicate with peers might be taught to use sign language or a communication device.

Of course, some students will unequivocally need adult support and teachers and paraprofessionals may need to offer direct instruction, one-to-one tutoring, or physical support, but, even in these instances, educators should carefully evaluate when students need such supports and how much is appropriate. In many instances, an adult pulls a chair up to a student's desk and fails to leave this position for large periods of time. This arrangement is stigmatizing and represents an inefficient use of human resources. Even when students need a lot of personal support, educators should problem solve how to minimize the use of this model. For example, if a learner needs several cues to get started on an assignment, the adult can provide these cues and step back from the student's desk (even if it is just for a minute or a few seconds). Or the adult can sit with the learner but help other students as well; he or she might pull up a chair and reteach a piece of a lesson to the learner with autism and two "neighboring" classmates. Both of these options give the student with autism the support he or she needs while providing opportunities for independence.

One of the most important reasons to change the ways in which we support students is related to cost–benefit analyses. Teachers are charged with doing the impossible on a daily basis; increasingly, they are being asked to take on new responsibilities and to change their roles. In other words, they need all of the help they can get! Thinking critically about how adults will work in the classroom can not only prompt better instruction for students but it can make the work of all adults more manageable and enjoyable. When teachers and other adults who are working in the classroom move away from giving a student intensive, one-to-one support, they are free to support that individual indirectly (e.g., creating adaptations, working with small groups of students)—in ways that often profit not only the learner on the spectrum but his or her peers as well.

Using a Range of Co-Teaching Structures

When I started co-teaching in an inclusive classroom, my colleague, Bea, claimed to know nothing about autism. She seemed apprehensive about having students with disabilities in her classroom and encouraged me to plan curriculum and instruction for "my kids." In only a matter of weeks, however, she was creating and teaching lessons with me, questioning my decisions, and demanding to be a part of the IEP planning for "her" students! Through our partnership, she learned about autism, reading and implementing IEPs, and teaching diverse learners. As the special education teacher, I learned about general education curriculum and gained confidence teaching whole-class lessons. Bea also taught me how to design thematic instruction and performance assessments and how to plan challenging science and math lessons.

Co-teaching typically involves a specialist and a classroom teacher jointly planning, instructing, and evaluating heterogeneous groups of students in general education classrooms (Murowski, 2009; Walther-Thomas, 1997; Walther-Thomas, Korinek, McLaughlin, & Williams, 2000). By intentionally varying their roles, the co-teachers share responsibility for their classes more fully. Studies conducted since 1990 have applauded the use of co-teaching between special education and general education professionals in preschool through high school settings (Dieker, 2001; Meyers, Gelzheiser, & Yelich, 1991; Pugach & Wesson, 1995; Scruggs, Mastropieri, & McDuffie, 2007; Walther-Thomas, 1997). In a study by Meyers and colleagues (1991), for instance, general education teachers reported that they preferred in-class support models to pull-out models because the more collaborative model seemed to inspire a greater focus on instructional issues for students with unique learning needs. In another related study, educators in co-taught classrooms described themselves as confident about meeting the needs of all students in the classroom (Pugach & Wesson, 1995). In addition, Walther-Thomas (1997) found that both special and general education teachers in co-teaching teams reported that professional growth and enhanced teaching motivation resulted from their collaboration. In this same study, students claimed that they received more teacher time and attention in their co-taught classrooms. And Dieker interviewed more than 50 secondary level students with and without disabilities and reported that all of them claimed that they benefited from their cotaught class, except for one student with emotional disabilities who reported, "You can't get away with anything" (2001, p. 19).

For co-teachers to succeed and achieve these types of positive outcomes, however, more than shared space and students are required. Teachers need some common goals, a mutual understanding of responsibilities, and open lines of communication. One tool that teams may find helpful for addressing the development of these elements is the self-assessment checklist (see Figure 12.5) from Villa, Thousand, and Nevin (2008). This form not only helps individual teachers articulate where they are in philosophy and knowledge but serves as a great tool for conversation, problem solving, and planning.

Another way educators can optimize success is to use a wide range of co-teaching structures throughout the week, month, and year. Doing so optimizes expertise, increases interactions with students, and give adults opportunities to build skills and learn from one another. In this section, I outline six different structures that can be used by two or more teachers or other adults.

Duet Teaching

Duet teaching simply involves two adults working together to provide instruction. These "duet" presentations (Greene & Isaacs, 1999) typically involve both adults engaging in primary teaching roles in the class; for example, instructors may take turns leading class discussion, answering student questions, and facilitating lectures and activities.

One Teach/One Assist

When teachers use the one teach/one assist model, they typically share lesson delivery responsibilities; one leads the lesson while the other supports in some way (Cook & Friend, 1995). The lead person is usually in charge of the content while the assisting teacher adds examples; shares humor or anecdotes; takes notes on a chalkboard, or uses a computer program that is then projected on a screen. Or, one instructor can act as lead teacher while the other floats throughout the classroom, providing individual assistance and facilitating small-group activities. For example, one instructor may provide instruction on geography while the other instructor writes important points on a whiteboard and points out different features on the classroom map.

Self-Assessment Checklist: Are We Really Co-Teachers?

Instructions: Check *Yes* or *No* for each of the following statements to determine your co-teaching score at this point in time.

Yes	No	In our co-teaching partnership. . . .
		We share ideas, information, and materials.
		We identify the resources and talents of the co-teachers.
		We teach different groups of students at the same time.
		We share responsibility for deciding what to teach.
		We share responsibility for deciding how to teach.
		We identify student strengths and needs.
		We share responsibility for differentiating instruction.
		We agree on discipline procedures and jointly carry them out.
		We communicate freely our concerns.
		We celebrate the process of co-teaching and the outcomes and successes.
		We have fun with the students and each other when we co-teach.
		We have regularly scheduled time to meet and discuss our work.
		We use our meeting time productively.
		We can effectively co-teach even when we don't have time to plan.
		We are each viewed by our students as their teacher.
		We can use a variety of co-teaching approaches (i.e., supportive, parallel).
		We seek and enjoy additional training to make our co-teaching better.

Figure 12.5.   Self-Assessment Checklist: Are We Really Co-Teachers?

From Thousand, J. Villa, R., & Nevin, A. (2008). *A guide to co-teaching: Practical tips for facilitating student learning* (2nd ed.). Thousand Oaks, CA: Corwin Press; adapted by permission. Copyright © 2008 by Corwin Press.

In *"You're Going to Love This Kid!" Teaching Students with Autism in the Inclusive Classroom, Second Edition,* by Paula Kluth. (2010, Paul H. Brookes Publishing Co., Inc.)

One teach/one assist is easy to implement and can be arranged "on the spot." Because of this ease of implementation, teachers can naturally shift into one teach/one assist when one drifts into the classroom for unplanned co-teaching or stays in the classroom past a planned co-taught lesson. In using one teach/one assist, teachers should, as much as possible, trade roles so that both teachers have opportunities to lead instruction and provide the assistance.

One Teach/One Observe

In some instances, teachers and paraprofessionals may want to take turns acting as a classroom observer—the one teach/one observe method. An observer might study whole-class dynamics (e.g., how students solve problems in collaborative groups) or individual student behaviors (e.g., how often and how effectively a student uses a piece of assistive technology). Teachers can use this observational data to improve their planning and teaching and to learn about students in meaningful ways. For example, it might be difficult to assess how a nonverbal student initiates social interactions until you have an hour to watch him work with a small group of peers.

Teachers also can learn a lot about each other through the one teach/one observe structure. One of my colleagues observed me several times when I was learning to teach whole-class lessons; she helped me to improve my teaching by showing me how to pace a lesson and manage 30-plus learners at a time. She claimed that she learned as much from me and complimented me regularly on the various differentiation techniques I used. For teachers who want to fine-tune this kind of observation, consider narrowing the focus of attention during the lesson. That is, instead of having a colleague observe and provide feedback, ask him or her to look for specific teaching behaviors during an observation. For instance, a paraprofessional who is unaccustomed to teaching a small group of students might ask a teacher to give feedback specifically on the organization of her instruction.

One teach/one observe also can be used to evaluate how much and what types of support a learner needs. In one classroom, the general education teacher was convinced that her student, a young man with Asperger syndrome, was receiving too much personal support from a paraprofessional. The teacher believed the student could do more of his classroom work on his own and felt he would take more initiative if allowed to work independently. In response to these concerns, the team decided that they should observe the student and collect information on what type of assistance he needed throughout the day. The paraprofessional agreed to collect the data. She spent an entire day observing the teacher and the classroom, making notes every time the student needed help or struggled with a task or activity. The team was somewhat surprised to find that the student actually needed very little direct support. Although he was confused a few times (especially when the students learned a new game), students were able to coach him through these rough spots.

After the team was presented with the information from the observation, they asked the paraprofessional to support the student in new ways. Instead of sitting near his desk at all times, the paraprofessional engaged in spot checks on the young man, taught him how to become more independent by showing him tricks for organizing and soliciting help, facilitated interactions between him and his peers, and helped the classroom teacher meet the needs of all students in the classroom.

One Teach/One Assess

Similar to one teach/one assist and one teach/one observe, the two educators in this model work together but have different roles. In one teach/one assess, one teaching partner is evaluating students formally or informally as the other teacher is conducting a lesson. The assessment might involve a formal tool or product (e.g., checklist) that the teacher completes after talking to or observing a student or it may be less structured and only involve casual observation or an informal conversation with a student or group of students. Further, the teacher doing the assessment might be evaluating the skills, knowledge, or abilities of individual students or may simply be conducting a general assessment of the progress or knowledge of the group. Examples of one teach/one assess include the following:

- One teacher conducts a whole-class discussion while another teacher takes data on how many students participate, how many boys versus girls participate, and how many contributions individual students make. This data is then used to plan future discussions and to design ways to involve more students in whole-class lessons.

- One teacher facilitates a whole-class chemistry lab (students working in groups to separate the pigments found in markers) while another rotates from group to group interviewing individual students about the lab. One by one, the assessing teacher pulls students aside and asks them, "What is an Rf value?" and, "What is one thing you learned from this lab?"

- One teacher works with small reading groups while the other teacher pulls several students aside (two students with IEPs and two English language learners) one by one to conduct a fluency assessment.

Station Teaching

As Cook and Friend noted, "In station teaching, teachers divide instructional content into two, three, or more segments and present the content at separate locations within the classroom" (1995, p. 6). For instance, teachers might create four stations; one for listening to recordings of African drum music, one for collaboratively composing a few lines of music (e.g., eight measures per group), one for learning a new drumming skill, and one for researching African dance drumming on the Internet.

Station teaching is a smart way to use the expertise and energy of all of the adults in the classroom, especially in those environments that are served by several adults at certain points in the day. One way to engage those adults efficiently is to have them circulate around the classroom and offer support and instruction for students at all stations. Although this model can be effective, many teaching teams find that lessons are richer when adults have specific roles. For instance, one teacher may be anchored at a station in order to provide small-group instruction to five or six students at a time while a paraprofessional moves from station to station interviewing individual students about their knowledge of key concepts. At the same time, a special educator might teach mini-lessons to a few learners who need enrichment for that particular lesson.

Parallel Teaching

Parallel teaching (Cook & Friend, 1995) involves splitting the class into equal sections and providing each group with the same lesson or activity. This structure lowers the student–teacher ratio and, therefore, "is useful when students need opportunities to respond aloud, to engage in hands-on activities, or to interact with one another" (Cook & Friend, 1995, p. 7). Parallel teaching also can be used when teachers want to introduce smaller groups to two different activities, concepts, or ideas; the two instructors teach different content for some part of the class and then, typically, switch groups and repeat the lesson with the other half of the class. Finally, parallel teaching can be used when teachers want to provide individual instruction for certain students or when they are completing a project with different roles or tasks. In this version of the structure, group sizes may not be equal and may be determined based on the types of activities being assigned. For instance, in a high school Food Science class, most of the students worked with their teacher to bake bread and make soup for the local food pantry. A small group of students worked with a paraprofessional to assemble the baskets. In this example, one group was smaller because of the task itself; more students were needed to make food than to assemble baskets. The following are additional examples of parallel teaching:

- A fifth-grade class is split into two groups of equal size. A special educator teaches one group about the Democratic Party while a general educator teaches the other group about the Republican Party. The students can then come back into a whole-class format and teach the content to each other.

- A general educator and a speech-language therapist each work with half of a first-grade class; both educators give students a mini-lesson on phonics.

- A paraprofessional reviews for a test with half of the class while the classroom general educator teaches all the students new study and test-taking skills (e.g., skimming text, reading questions carefully, organizing materials). Halfway through the class period, students switch groups.

- Students in a high school computer class are divided into two heterogeneous groups. Sixteen students work on creating a class web page under the direction of the computer teacher while the remaining six students work with the special education teacher to write copy for the page and generate ideas for populating the web site.

Assigning Specific Roles and Responsibilities

During visits to classrooms, I often see adults underused and misused. In one classroom, the general education teacher was reading a story to the class while 18 kindergarten students, 1 paraprofessional, and 1 special educator sat on the floor watching her. Although the paraprofessional and the special educator were undoubtedly trying to serve as role models and offering support to the students with autism in the classroom, I wondered whether this was the best type of support for the students and wisest use of human resources.

At times, this may, in fact, be the very best model to use. Without question, having all students and all adults meeting together as a group can build a sense of community in the classroom. In many other instances, however, students can get more effective and individualized supports when teachers evaluate the lesson or activity, assess student needs and lesson demands, and creatively design the most appropriate and meaningful ways to use the skills and talents of the available adults. Table 12.6 includes some of the meaningful ways paraprofessionals and other adults can support the whole classroom when they are not providing direct support to students.

Table 12.6. How adults can help all students in the inclusive classroom

Conduct performance assessments.

Observe individual students or whole-class behaviors (e.g., turn taking, giving feedback).

Make telephone calls to families.

Connect with other team members.

Create adaptations.

Complete administrative tasks (e.g., making copies, setting up a meeting).

Plan or set up for a lesson.

Engage in a short meeting with a team member.

Program a communication device.

Gather materials for a lesson.

Ask students enrichment questions.

Collect data on individualized education program objectives.

Video- or audiorecord classroom interactions for future observation and reflection.

In some instances, educators may purposely choose to keep their roles ambiguous, but oftentimes teachers can differentiate instruction more easily and create more learning opportunities for students when they take on specific responsibilities. For example, instead of having a special and general educator both walk around the room offering assistance to various groups during a chemistry lab, these professionals could split responsibilities by having the special educator circulate and answer general questions while the general educator focuses specifically on giving mini-lessons to small groups of students and offering a daily "challenge" question to those learners who need it. Or, the general educator could circulate and manage the lesson while the special educator carries a clipboard, rotates to each group, and takes notes on students' understanding of safety and emergency equipment in the room (e.g., safety shower, eyewash, first-aid kit). Other ideas for sharing roles are illustrated by Wendy Murawski in Table 12.7.

When educators find themselves in a slump, when they have been doing business in the same ways for years without trying different ways, or when they have wanted to do something differently but have not yet taken the opportunity to do so, it is especially important to consider these different roles and responsibilities. It is also a signal to switch roles and responsibilities when educators feel overworked or underchallenged. A teacher is probably in need of a new approach if they find themselves in the following situations:

- The only role of the paraprofessionals in the classroom is to offer one-to-one support to a student with a disability.

- The general educator never has a chance to work individually with any student.

Table 12.7.   Ways for collaborative team member to share roles and work together

If one of you is doing this…	The other can be doing this…
Lecturing	Modeling notetaking on the board or overhead
Taking roll	Collecting and/or reviewing last night's homework
Passing out papers	Reviewing directions
Giving instructions orally	Writing down instructions on the board
Checking for understanding with large heterogeneous group of students	Checking for understanding with small heterogeneous group of students
Circulating, providing one-to-one support as needed	Providing direct instruction to the whole class
Prepping half of the class for one side of a debate	Prepping the other half of the class for the opposing side of the debate
Facilitating a silent activity	Circulating, checking for comprehension
Providing large-group instruction	Circulating, using proximity control for behavior management
Running last-minute copies or errands	Reviewing homework
Reteaching or preteaching with a small group	Monitoring a large group as they work on practice materials
Facilitating sustained silent reading	Reading aloud quietly with a small group; previewing upcoming information
Reading a test aloud to a group of students	Proctoring a test silently with a group of students
Creating basic lesson plans for standards, objective, and content curriculum	Providing suggestions for modifications, accommodations, and activities for diverse learners
Facilitating stations or groups	Also facilitating stations or groups
Explaining new concept	Conducting role play or modeling concept
Considering modification needs	Considering enrichment opportunities

From Murawski, W. (2009). *Collaborative teaching in secondary schools: Making the co-teaching marriage work!* Thousand Oaks, CA: Corwin Press; adapted by permission.

- The special educator has never taught a lesson or worked with students without disabilities.

- Therapists are not invited to develop curriculum or teach in the classroom.

- Students do not have leadership roles and are never asked to present lessons with each other or with their teachers.

Certainly, I do not mean to suggest that teachers must change every role and responsibility they have adopted. It is important, however, that the roles and responsibilities of all team members be reviewed and assessed continuously. A model that works during one semester may not work the next, and a team member who takes on certain responsibilities one year may want to try new ones the next year.

Summary

Teachers truly committed to an inclusive schooling agenda will seek the expertise and support of others, including students with autism and their families. They will be reflective. They will take risks and be willing to share ideas with others. Collaborative educators will question their own practices, attitudes, and knowledge and constantly consider how they might learn from the practices, attitudes, and knowledge of others. In inclusive schools, educators also continuously question and evaluate collaborative structures. When a model of service delivery doesn't seem to work, stakeholders think about how they are supporting students, design ways to team teach more effectively, or consider shifts in roles and responsibilities.

Increasingly, the business world has moved toward models that are more collaborative and team oriented (DeNucci, 2005; Edwards, Edwards, & Benzel, 1997; Stieber, 1999). Why? Because big business realizes that teaming increases productivity and creativity; the quality of the work is better when it is done through teams. In other words, teaming is not something that is done because it is trendy or because educators have not yet learned enough about inclusive education to make it on their own. Educators collaborate because it forces them to grow and learn and because it ultimately results in better outcomes for students.

FOR MORE ANSWERS AND INFORMATION

Books

Causton-Theoharis, J. (2009). *The paraprofessional's handbook for effective support in inclusive classrooms.* Baltimore: Paul H. Brookes Publishing Co.

Doyle, M. (2008). *The paraprofessional's guide to the inclusive classroom: Working as a team* (3rd ed.). Baltimore: Paul H. Brookes Publishing Co.

Murawski, W. (2009). *Collaborative teaching in secondary schools: Making the co-teaching marriage work!* Thousand Oaks, CA: Corwin Press.

Schwarz, P., & Kluth, P. (2007). *"You're welcome": 30 innovative ideas for the inclusive classroom.* Portsmouth, NH: Heinemann.

Tamm, J.W., & Luyet, R.J. (2004). *Radical collaboration: Five essential skills to overcome defensiveness and build successful relationships.* New York: HarperCollins.

(continued)

(continued)

Villa, R., Thousand, J., & Nevin, A.I. (2008). *A guide to co-teaching: Practical tips for facilitating student learning* (2nd ed.). Thousand Oaks, CA: Corwin Press.

Villa, R., Thousand, J., & Nevin, A. (2010). *Collaborating with students in instruction and decision-making: The untapped resource.* Thousand Oaks, CA: Corwin Press.

Web Sites

Circle of Inclusion
http://www.circleofinclusion.org
> This site is a favorite of educators trying to maintain energy around inclusive schooling. The "methods and practices" section is the most relevant to those interested in collaboration.

Collaboration by Eduscapes
http://eduscapes.com/sessions/butter/collaborate.htm
> Eduscapes is a web site that allows teachers and students to develop web pages to share collaborative ideas around the world.

Co-Teaching Connection
http://www.marilynfriend.com
> Dr. Marilyn Friend's web site focuses on collaboration and provides co-teaching resources. Innovative practices are highlighted.

Mike Giangreco's web site
http://www.uvm.edu/~mgiangre
> There are many useful resources on Dr. Giangreco's web site but the hidden gems of this page are the full text PDF files of his many articles on paraprofessionals.

2 Teach, LLC
http://www.2teachllc.com
> Wendy Murawski's site has a great collection of K–12 co-teaching lesson plans that users can access free of charge.

NOTES: _____

_____

_____

_____

_____

_____

_____

_____

Bibliography

References

Adams, M., Foorman, B., Lundberg, I., & Beeler, K. (1997). *Phonemic awareness in young children: A classroom curriculum.* Baltimore: Paul H. Brookes Publishing Co.

Allen, J. (2002). *On the same page: Shared reading beyond the primary grades.* Portland, ME: Stenhouse.

Aldridge, D. (2005). *Case study designs in music therapy.* Philadelphia: Jessica Kingsley.

Alvermann, D.E., Hinchman, K.A., Moore, D.W., Phelps, S.F., & Waff, D.R. (Eds.). (1998). *Reconceptualizing the literacies in adolescents' lives.* Mahwah, NJ: Lawrence Erlbaum Associates.

American Psychiatric Association. (1994). *Diagnostic and statistical manual of mental disorders* (4th ed.). Washington, DC: Author.

American Psychiatric Association. (2000). *Diagnostic and statistical manual of mental disorders* (4th ed., text rev.). Washington, DC: Author.

Anderson, J. (2005). *Mechanically inclined: Building grammar, usage, and style into a writer's workshop.* Portland, ME: Stenhouse.

Appley, D.G., & Winder, A.E. (1977). An evolving definition of collaboration and some implications for the world of work. *Journal of Applied Behavioral Science, 13,* 279–291.

Armstrong, R.V. (1997). *Teaming up for excellence.* Hardy, VA: Armstrong Publishing.

Armstrong, T. (1987). *In their own way.* Los Angeles: Tarcher.

Armstrong, T. (1994). *Multiple intelligences in the classroom.* Alexandria, VA: ASCD.

Aronson, E., & Patnoe, S. (1997). *The jigsaw classroom: Building cooperation in the classroom* (2nd ed.). New York: Addison-Wesley Longman.

Arwood, E.L., & Kaulitz, C. (2007). *Learning with a visual brain in an auditory world.* Shawnee Mission, KS: Autism Asperger Publishing Co.

Ashton-Warner, S. (1963). *Teacher.* New York: Simon & Schuster.

Asperger, H. (1991). Die autistischen psychopathen im kindesalter. In U. Frith (Ed. & Trans.), *Autism and Asperger syndrome* (pp. 37–92). New York: Cambridge University Press. (Original work published 1944)

Attfield, R. (1993, February). Letter. *Facilitated Communication Digest, 1*(2), p. 11.

Attwood, T. (1998). *Asperger's syndrome: A guide for parents and professionals.* Philadelphia: Jessica Kingsley.

Attwood, T. (2007). *The complete guide to Asperger's syndrome.* Philadelphia: Jessica Kingsley.

Attwood, T., & Willey, L.H. (2000). *Crossing the bridge* [Video]. Higganum, CT: Starfish Specialty Press.

Atwell, N. (1998). *In the middle: New understandings about writing, reading, and learning.* Portsmouth, NH: Heinemann.

Ayers, W. (2001). *To teach: The journey of a teacher.* New York: Teachers College Press.

Bailey, B. (2001). *Conscious discipline: 7 basic skills for brain smart classroom management.* Oviedo, FL: Loving Guidance.

Baker, J. (2001). *The social skills picture book: Teaching play, emotion, and communication to children with autism.* Arlington, TX: Future Horizons, Inc.

Baker, J. (2005). *Preparing for life.* Arlington, TX: Future Horizons.

Baker, J. (2008). *No more meltdowns: Positive strategies for managing and preventing out-of-control behavior.* Arlington, TX: Future Horizons, Inc.

Barron, J., & Barron, S. (1992). *There's a boy in here.* New York: Simon & Schuster.

Bauby, J-D. (1997). *The diving bell and the butterfly.* New York: Vintage.

Baumann, J., Jones, L., & Seifert-Kessell, N. (1993). Using think-alouds to enhance children's comprehension monitoring abilities. *The Reading Teacher, 47,* 184–193.

Baumgardner, J., & Richards, A. (2005). *Grassroots: A field guide for feminist activism.* New York: Farrar Straus Giroux.

Bayer, D. (2008). My journey with Jacob. In R. Parish (Ed.), *Embracing autism: Connecting and communicating with children in the autism spectrum.* San Francisco: Jossey-Bass.

Beaudoin, M., & Taylor, M. (2004). *Creating a positive school culture: How principals and teachers can solve problems together.* Thousand Oaks, CA: Corwin Press.

Beck, I., McKeown, M., & Kucan, L. (2002). *Bringing words to life: Robust vocabulary instruction.* New York: Guilford Press.

Bedrosian, J., Lasker, J., Speidel, K., & Politsch, A. (2003). Enhancing the written narrative skills of an AAC student with autism: Evidence-based research issues. *Topics in Language Disorders, 23*(4), 305.

Bellini, S., & Akullian, J. (2007). A meta-analysis of video modeling and video self-modeling interventions for children and adolescents with autism spectrum disorders. *Exceptional Children, 73,* 261–284.

Bellini, S., Akullian, J., & Hopf, A. (2007). Increasing social engagement in young children with autism spectrum disorders using video self-modeling. *School Psychology Review, 36,* 80–90.

Bennett, B., Rolheiser, C., & Stevahn (1991). *Cooperative learning: Where heart meets mind.* Ajax, Ontario, Canada: Bookation.

Berkey, S.M. (2009). *Teaching the moving child: OT insights that will transform your K–3 classroom.* Baltimore: Paul H. Brookes Publishing Co.

Betts, S., Betts, D., & Gerber-Eckard, L. (2007). *Asperger syndrome in the inclusive classroom: Advice and strategies for teachers.* Philadelphia: Jessica Kingsley.

Beukelman, D., & Mirenda, P. (2006). *Augmentative and alternative communication: Management of severe communication disorders in children and adults* (3rd ed.). Baltimore: Paul H. Brookes Publishing Co.

Biancarosa, G., & Snow, C. (2004). *Reading next: A vision for action and research in middle and high school literacy: A report to the Carnegie Corporation.* Washington, DC: Alliance for Excellence in Education. Retrieved May 26, 2006, from http://www.all4ed.org/publications/ReadingNext/ReadingNext.pdf

Biever, C. (November, 2009). *Steven Laureys: How I know 'coma man' is conscious.* Retrieved December 1, 2009, from http://www.newscientist.com/article/dn18209-steven-laureys-how-i-know-coma-man-is-conscious.html

Bigelow, B. (1994). Getting off the track: Stories from an untracked classroom. From *Rethinking our classrooms: Teaching for equity and justice* (pp. 58–65). Milwaukee, WI: Rethinking Schools.

Biklen, D. (1990). Communication unbound: Autism and praxis. *Harvard Education Review, 60,* 291–314.

Biklen, D. (1992). *Schooling without labels: Parents, educators, and inclusive education.* Philadelphia: Temple University Press.

Biklen, D. (1993). *Communication unbound: How facilitated communication is challenging traditional views of autism and dis/ability.* New York: Teachers College Press.

Biklen, D. (2005). *Autism and the myth of the person alone.* New York: NYU Press.

Biklen, D., & Burke, J. (2006). Presuming competence. *Equity & Excellence in Education, 39,* 1–10.

Biklen, D., & Cardinal, D. (1997). *Contested words, contested science.* New York: Teachers College Press.

Biklen, D., Saha, S., & Kliewer, C. (1995). How teachers confirm the authorship of facilitated communication: A portfolio approach. *Journal of The Association for Persons with Severe Handicaps, 20,* 45–56.

Biklen, D., & Shubert, A. (1991). New words: The communication of students with autism. *Remedial and Special Education, 12,* 46–57.

Bishop, K.D., Jubala, K.A., Stainback, W., & Stainback, S. (1996). Facilitating friendships. In S. Stainback & W. Stainback (Eds.), *Inclusion: A guide for educators* (pp. 155–169). Baltimore: Paul H. Brookes Publishing Co.

Blachman, B. (2000). Phonological awareness. In M. Kamil, P.B. Mosenthal, P.D. Pearson, & R. Barr (Eds.), *Handbook of reading research* (Vol. III, pp. 483–502). Mahwah, NJ: Lawrence Erlbaum Associates.

Blachman, B.A., Ball, E.W., Black, R., & Tangel, D.M. (2000). *Road to the code: A phonological awareness program for young children.* Baltimore: Paul H. Brookes Publishing Co.

Blackburn, J. (1997). *Autism? What is it?* Retrieved January 14, 2009, from http://www.autistics.org/library/whatis.html

Blackman, L. (2001). *Lucy's story: Autism and other adventures.* Philadelphia: Jessica Kingsley.

Bober, S. (1995). Nicholas. In A. Stehli (Ed.), *Dancing in the rain: Stories of exceptional children by parents of children with special needs* (pp. 114–115). Westport, CT: The Georgiana Organization.

Bondy, A., & Frost, L. (2002). *A picture's worth: PECS and other visual communication strategies in autism.* Bethesda, MD: Woodbine House.

Boulineau, T., Fore, C. J., Hagan-Burke, S., & Burke, M.D. (2004). Use of story map instruction to increase story grammar text comprehension for elementary school students with learning disabilities in a resource setting. *Learning Disability Quarterly, 27,* 105–121.

Broderick, A., & Kasa-Hendrickson, C. (2001). "SAY JUST ONE WORD AT FIRST": The emergence of reliable speech in a student labeled with autism. *Journal of The Association for Persons with Severe Handicaps, 26,* 13–24.

Broderick, A. Mehta-Parekh, H., & Reid, D. K. (2005). Differentiating instruction for disabled students in inclusive classrooms. *Theory into Practice, 44,* 194–202.

Brophy, J., & Evertson, C. (1981). *Student characteristics and teaching.* Boston: Addison Wesley.

Broun, L.T. (2004). Teaching students with autism spectrum disorders to read: A visual approach. *Teaching Exceptional Children, 36*(4), 36–40.

Brown v. Board of Educ. 347 U.S. (483). 1954.

Brown, L., Kluth, P., Suomi, J., Causton-Theoharis, Houghton, L., & Jorgensen, J. (2000). *Research team experiences for students with and without disabilities.* Durham: University of New Hampshire, Institute on Disability.

Burke, J. (1999, December). The school of my dreams. *Facilitated Communication Digest, 8*(1), 4.

Burke, J. (2002, December). *TASH: Our quest: Opportunity, equality, justice.* Keynote presentation at the meeting of The Association for Persons with Severe Handicaps, Boston.

Burke, J. (2005). The world as I'd like it to be. In D. Biklen (Ed.), *Autism and the myth of the person alone* (pp. 248–253). New York: New York University Press.

Burns, N. (1998, October). Equality. *TASH Newsletter, 24*(10).

Cafiero, J. (2001). The effect of an augmentative communication intervention on the communication, behavior, and academic program of an adolescent with autism. *Focus on Autism and Other Developmental Disabilities, 16,* 179–189.

Calculator, S., & Singer, K. (1992). Letter to the editor: Preliminary validation information on facilitated communication. *Topics in Language Disorders, 13,* ix–xvi.

Calkins, L. (1986). *The art of teaching writing.* Portsmouth, NH: Heinemann.

Cardinal, D., Hanson, D., & Wakeman, J. (1996). Investigation of authorship in facilitated communication. *Mental Retardation, 34,* 231–242.

Carter, E. (2007). *Including people with disabilities in faith communities: A guide for service providers, families, and congregations.* Baltimore: Paul H. Brookes Publishing Co.

Carter, E.W., Cushing, L.S., Clark, N.M., & Kennedy, C.H. (2005). Effects of peer support interventions on students' access to the general curriculum and social access. *Research & Practice for Persons with Severe Disabilities, 30,* 15–25.

Carter, E., & Kennedy, C.H. (2006). Promoting access to the general curriculum using peer support strategies. *Research & Practice for Persons with Severe Disabilities, 31*(4), 284–292.

Causton-Theoharis, J. (2009). *The paraprofessional's handbook for effective support in inclusive classrooms.* Baltimore: Paul H. Brookes Publishing Co.

Cautela, J., & Groden, J. (1978). *Relaxation: A comprehensive manual for adults, children, and children with special needs.* New York: Research Press.

Centers for Disease Control and Prevention (2009, October 5). *CDC statement on autism data.* Retrieved November 8, 2009, from http://www.cdc.gov/ncbddd/autism/data.html

Chandler-Olcott, K., & Hinchman, K. (2005). *Tutoring adolescent literacy learners: A guide for volunteers.* New York: Guilford Press.

Cohen, M.J., & Sloan, D.L. (2007). *Visual supports for people with autism.* Bethesda, MD: Woodbine House.

Cole, R.W. (2008). (Ed.). *Educating everybody's children: diverse teaching strategies for diverse learners* (2nd ed.). Alexandria, VA: ASCD.

Coleman, D., & Levine, S. (2008). *Collaboration 2.0: Technology and best practices for successful collaboration in a web 2.0 world.* Cupertino, CA: Happy About.

Coles, G. (1987). *The learning mystique: A critical look at "learning disabilities."* New York: Fawcett Columbine.

Contract Consultants, Inc. (1997). *What we are learning about autism/pervasive developmental disorder: Evolving dialogues and approaches to promoting development and adaptation.* New Cumberland, PA: Contract Consultants and Temple University Institute on Disabilities.

Corbett, B.A., & Abdullah, M. (2005). Video modeling: Why does it work for children with autism? *Journal of Early and Intensive Behavior Intervention: 2*(1), 2–8.

Cortiella, C. (2008). Excusing IEP team members: Why, when, who, and how. *The Exceptional Parent, 38*(5), 83–84.

Cook, L., & Friend, M. (1995). Co-teaching: Guidelines for creating effective practices. *Focus on Exceptional Children, 28,* 1–15.

Copeland, S.R., & Keefe, E.B. (2007). *Effective literacy instruction for students with moderate or severe disabilities.* Baltimore: Paul H. Brookes Publishing Co.

Coppola, F.F. (Director). (1979). *Apocalypse now* [Motion picture]. United States: Paramount Pictures.

Corrigan, D., & Bishop, K.K. (1997). Creating family-centered integrated service systems and interprofessional educational programs to implement them. *Social Work in Education, 19*(3), 149–163.

Crossley, R. (1997). *Speechless: Facilitating communication for individuals without voices.* New York: Dutton.

Crowther, I., & Wellhousen, K. (2003). *Creating effective learning environments.* Florence, KY: Delmar Cengage Learning.

Cummins, J. (1996). *Negotiating identities: Education for empowerment in a diverse society.* Ontario: California Association for Bilingual Education.

Cunat, M. (1996). Vision, vitality, and values: Advocating the democratic classroom. In L.E. Beyer (Ed.), *Creating democratic classrooms: The struggle to integrate theory and practice.* New York: Teachers College Press.

Cunningham, P.M., & Cunningham, J.W. (1992). *Making words: Enhancing the invented spelling-decoding connection. Reading Teacher, 46,* 106–115.

Cutler, R. (1998). *Ask Rob: The communicator.* North Plymouth, MA: Autism National Committee.

Dahl, K., & Farnan, N. (1998). *Children's writing: Perspectives from research.* Newark, DE: International Reading Association and National Reading Conference.

Danaher, S., Price, J., & Kluth, P. (2009). Come to the fair! *Educational Leadership, 66*(5), 70–72.

Danforth, S., & Rhodes, W.C. (1997). Deconstructing disability: A philosophy for inclusion. *Remedial and Special Education, 18,* 357–365.

Daniels, H., & Zemelman, S. (2005). *Subjects matter: Every teacher's guide to content-area reading.* Portsmouth, NH: Heinemann.

Darling-Hammond, L. (1997). *The right to learn.* San Francisco: Jossey-Bass.

D'Ateno, P., Mangiapanello, K., & Taylor, B.A. (2003). Using video modeling to teach complex play sequences to a preschooler with autism. *Journal of Positive Behavior Interventions, 5*(1), 5–11.

Davern, L. (1996). Building partnerships with parents. In M.F. Giangreco (Ed.), *Quick-guides to inclusion: Ideas for educating students with disabilities* (pp. 29–55). Baltimore: Paul H. Brookes Publishing Co.

Debbaudt, G., & Debbaudt, D. (2008). North of the border. In R. Parish (Ed.), *Embracing autism: Connecting and communicating with children in the autism spectrum* (pp. 49–60). San Francisco: Jossey-Bass.

Delpit, L. (1995). *Teaching other people's children: Cultural conflict in the classroom.* New York: New Press.

DeNucci, P. (2005). *Commander and crew: The human factors approach to teambuilding and leadership.* Charleston, SC: BookSurge Publishing.

Dewey, J. (1910). *How we think.* Boston: Heath.

Dieker, L.A. (2001). What are the characteristics of "effective" middle and high school co-taught teams for students with disabilities? *Preventing School Failure, 46,* 14–23.

Diller, D. (2007). *Making the most of small groups: Differentiation for all.* Portland, ME: Stenhouse Publishers.

Dole, J., Duffy, G., Roehler, L., & Pearson, P.D. (1991). Moving from the old to the new: Research on reading comprehension instruction. *Review of Educational Research, 61,* 239–264.

Donnellan, A., & Leary, M. (1995). *Movement differences and diversity in autism/mental retardation: Appreciating and accommodating people with communication and behavior challenges.* Madison, WI: DRI Press.

Dougherty, P. (2006). Through the looking glass. In C.N. Ariel & R.A. Naseef (Eds.), *Voices from the spectrum* (pp. 36–39). Philadelphia: Jessica Kingsley.

Downing, J. (2005). *Teaching communication skills to students with severe disabilities* (2nd ed.). Baltimore: Paul H. Brookes Publishing Co.

Downing, J. (2005). *Teaching literacy to students with significant disabilities: Strategies for the K–12 inclusive classroom.* Thousand Oaks, CA: Corwin Press.

Downing, J., Ryndak, D., & Clark, D. (2000). Paraeducators in inclusive classrooms: Their own perspective. *Remedial and Special Education, 21,* 171–181.

Doyle, M.B. (2008). *The paraprofessional's guide to the inclusive classroom: Working as a team* (3rd ed.). Baltimore: Paul H. Brookes Publishing Co.

Draper, R. (1997). Active learning in mathematics: Desktop teaching. *Mathematics Teacher, 90,* 622–625.

Dugan, E., Kamps, D., Leonard, B., Watkins, N., Rheinberger, A., & Stackhaus, J. (1995). Effects of cooperative learning groups during social studies for students with autism and fourth-grade peers. *Journal of Applied Behavior Analysis, 28,* 175–188.

Dymond, S.K., Renzaglia, A., Rosenstein, A., Chun, E.J., Banks, R.A., Niswander, V., et al. (2006). Using a participatory action research approach to create a universally designed inclusive high school science course: A case study. *Research & Practice for Persons with Severe Disabilities, 31*(4), 293–308.

Dyrbjerg, P., & Vedel, M. (2007). *Everyday education: Visual support for children with autism.* Philadelphia: Jessica Kingsley.

Dyson, B., & Grineski, S. (2001). Using cooperative learning structures in physical education. *Journal of Physical Education, Recreation & Dance, 72,* 28–31.

Earles-Vollrath, T.L., Cook, K.T., & Ganz, J.B., (2006). *How to develop and implement visual supports.* In R.L. Simpson (Series Ed.), *PRO-ED series on autism spectrum disorders.* Austin, TX: PRO-ED.

Eckert, T.L., Lovett, B.J., Rosenthal, B.D., Jiao, J., Ricci, L.J., & Truckenmiller, A.J. (2006). Class-wide instructional feedback: Improving children's academic skill development. In S.V. Randall (Ed.), *Learning disabilities: New research* (pp. 271–285). Hauppauge, NY: Nova Sciences.

Education for All Handicapped Children Act of 1975, PL 94-142, 20 U.S.C. §§ 1400 *et seq.*

Edwards, E., Heron, A., & Francis, M. (2000, April). *Toward an ideological definition of literacy: How critical pedagogy shaped the literacy development of students in a fifth-grade social studies class.* Paper presented at the meeting of the American Education Research Association, New Orleans.

Edwards, P., Edwards, S., & Benzel, R. (1997). *Teaming up.* Los Angeles: Tarcher.

Egel, A.L. (1989). Finding the right educational program. In M.D. Powers (Ed.), *Children with autism: A parent's guide* (pp. 169–202). Bethesda, MD: Woodbine House.

Epstein, K.K. (2005). The whitening of the American teaching force: A problem of recruitment or a problem of racism? *Social Justice, 32*(3), 89–102.

Erickson, K., & Koppenhaver, D. (2007) *Children with disabilities: Reading and writing the Four-Blocks Way*®. Greensboro, NC: Carson-Delosa.

Ernst, K. (1994). *Picturing learning: Artists and writers in the classroom.* Portsmouth, NH: Heinemann.

Esquith, R. (2007). *Teach like your hair's on fire: The methods and madness inside Room 56.* New York: Penguin.

Evanski, J. (2004). *Classroom activators.* San Diego, CA: The Brain Store.

Faber, A., & Mazlish, E. (1995). *How to talk so kids can learn—at home and at school.* New York: Avon Books.

Falvey, M., Givner, C., & Kimm, C. (1995). What is an inclusive school? In R. Villa & J. Thousand (Eds.), *Creating an inclusive school* (pp. 1–12). Alexandria, VA: ASCD.

Farlow, L. (1996). A quartet of success stories: How to make inclusion work. *Educational Leadership, 53,* 51–55.

Farmer, S. (1996). Finding Amy's voice: A case for inclusion. *Voices from the Middle, 3*(4), 27–31.

Farnan, N., & Dahl, K. (2003). Children's writing: Research and practice. In J. Flood, D. Lapp, J. Squire, & J. Jensen (Eds.), *Handbook of research on teaching the English language arts* (2nd ed., pp. 993–1007). Mahwah, NJ: Lawrence Erlbaum Associates.

Feldman, J. (*2000*). *Transition tips and tricks.* Beltsville, MD: Gryphon House.

Felner, R.D., Kasak, D., Mulhall, P., & Flowers, N. (1997). The Project on High Performance Learning Communities: Applying the Land-Grant Model to School Reform. *Phi Delta Kappan, 78*(7), 520–527.

Ferguson, D., Ralph, G., Meyer, G., Lester, J., Droege, C., Guoôjônsdôttir, H., et al. (2001). *Designing personalized learning for every student.* Alexandria, VA: ASCD.

Fihe, T. (2000, November). *Speech in an Abnormal Psychology class.* Paper presented at University of California, Santa Cruz.

Fisher, D., & Frey, N. (2001). Access to the core curriculum. *Remedial and Special Education, 22,* 148.

Fling, E. (2000). *Eating an artichoke: A mother's perspective on Asperger syndrome.* London: Jessica Kingsley.

Forest, M., & Lusthaus, E. (1990). Everyone belongs with MAPS action planning system. *Teaching Exceptional Children, 22,* 32–35.

Forest M., & Pearpoint, J.C. (1992, October). Putting all kids on the MAP. *Educational Leadership, 26*–31.

Forest, M., Pearpoint, J.C., Vandercook, T., & York, J. (1989). The McGill Action Planning System (MAPS): A strategy for building the vision. *JASH, 14*(3), 205–215.

Fox, B. (2003). Word recognition. In B. Guzzetti (Ed.), *Literacy in America: An encyclopedia of history, theory, and practice, volume two* (pp. 678–682). Santa Barbara, CA: ABC-Clio.

Frank, L.S. (2004). *Journey toward the caring classroom: Using adventure to create community.* Oklahoma City, OK: Wood 'N' Barns Publishing & Distribution.

Freedom Writers, & Gruwell, E. (1999). *The freedom writers' diary.* New York: Doubleday.

Freire, P. (1970). *Pedagogy of the oppressed.* New York: Continuum.

Fullan, M., & Hargreaves, A. (1996). *What's worth fighting for in your school?* New York: Teachers College Press.

Gallagher, P.A. (1997). Promoting dignity: Taking the destructive D's out of behavior disorders. *Focus on Exceptional Children, 29,* 1–19.

Gallego, M., & Hollingsworth, S. (2000). *What counts as literacy: Challenging the school standard.* New York: Teachers College Press.

Ganz, J.B., Kaylor, M., Bourgeois, B., & Hadden, K. (2008). The impact of social scripts and visual cues on verbal communication in three children with autism spectrum disorders. *Focus on Autism and Other Developmental Disabilities, 23,* 79–94.

Gardner, H. (2006). *Multiple intelligences.* New York: Basic Books.

Gent, P. (2009). *Great ideas: Using service-learning and differentiated instruction to help your students succeed.* Baltimore: Paul H. Brookes Publishing Co.

Gent, P., & Gurecka, L.E. (2001). Service learning: A disservice to people with disabilities? Michigan *Journal of Community Service Learning, 8*(1), 36–43.

Gere, A.R., Christenbury, L., & Sassi, K. (2005). *Writing on demand: Best practices and strategies for success.* Portsmouth, NH: Heinemann.

Gerland, G. (1996). *A real person.* London: Souvenir Press.

Giangreco, M.F. (2009). *Critical issues brief: Concerns about the proliferation of one-to-one paraprofessionals.* Arlington, VA: Council for Exceptional Children, Division on Autism and Developmental Disabilities.

Giangreco, M.F., Broer, S.M., & Edelman, S.W. (1999). The tip of the iceberg: Determining whether paraprofessional support is needed for students with disabilities in general education settings. *Journal of The Association for Persons with Severe Handicaps, 24,* 280–290.

Giangreco, M.F., Edelman, S.W., & Dennis, R. (1991). Common professional practices that interfere with the integrated delivery of related services. *Remedial and Special Education, 12*(2), 16–24.

Giangreco, M.F., Edelman, S., Luiselli, T.E., & MacFarland, S.Z.C. (1997). Helping or hovering? Effects of instructional assistant proximity on students with disabilities. *Exceptional Children, 64,* 7–18.

Gibbs, J. (1995). *Tribes: A new way of learning and being together.* Sausalito, CA: Center Source Systems, LLC.

Giberson, (2007). *The guy in the wheelchair: God & Stephen Hawking.* Retrieved December 3, 2009, from http://www.christianitytoday.com/bc/2007/sepoct/16.20.html

Gilles, R. (2007). *Cooperative learning: Integrating theory and practice.* Thousand Oaks, CA: Sage Publications.

Gillingham, G. (1995). *Autism: Handle with care.* Edmonton, Alberta, Canada: Tacit Publishing.

Gillingham, G. (2000). *Autism: A new understanding.* Edmonton, Alberta, Canada: Tacit Publishing.

Gilroy, D.E., & Miles, T.R. (1996). *Dyslexia at college.* New York: Routledge.

Ginott, H. (1972). *Teacher and child: A book for parents and teachers.* New York: Macmillan.

Glover, D.R., & Anderson L.A. (2003). *Character education: 43 fitness activities for community building.* Champaign, IL: Human Kinetics.

Godek, J. (2008). Inclusion for students on the autism spectrum: A Vermont district commits to serving the unique needs of children in their home communities. *The School Administrator, 65*(8), 32.

Gomez, M.L. (1996). Prospective teachers' perspectives on teaching "other people's" children. In K. Zeichner, S. Melnick, & M.L. Gomez (Eds.), *Current reforms in preservice teacher education* (pp. 109–132). New York: Teachers College Press.

Goodman, G. (1995). *I can learn! Strategies & activities for gray-area children, grades K–4.* Peterborough, NH: Crystal Springs Books.

Good Tracks, J. (1973). Native American non-interference. *Social Work, 18,* 30–35.

Goor, M.B., Schwenn, J.O., & Boyer, L. (1997). Preparing principals for leadership in special education. *Intervention in School and Clinic, 32,* 133–141.

Gould, S.J. (1981). *The mismeasure of man.* New York: Norton.

Graff, H. J. (2001). The nineteenth-century origins of our times. In E. Cushman, E. Kintgen, B. Kroll, & M. Rose (Eds.), *Literacy: A critical sourcebook* (pp. 211–233). New York: Bedford/St. Martins.

Graham, S., Harris, K., & Larsen, L. (2001). Prevention and intervention of writing difficulties for students with learning disabilities. *Learning Disabilities Research & Practice, 16*(2), 74–84.

Graham, S., & Perin, D. (2007). *Writing next: Effective strategies to improve writing of adolescents in middle and high schools—A report to the Carnegie Corporation of New York.* Washington, DC: Alliance for Excellent Education.

Grandin, T. (1995). *Thinking in pictures and other reports from my life with autism.* New York: Vintage Books.

Grandin, T. (1996a). *Emergence: Labeled autistic.* Boston: Warner Books.

Grandin, T. (1996b). *Interview with Temple Grandin.* Retrieved January 1, 2010, from http://www.autism.com/individuals/temp_int.htm

Grandin, T., & Barron, S. (2005). *Unwritten rules of social relationships.* Arlington, TX: Future Horizons.

Grant, K., & Ray, J. (2009). *Home, school, and community collaboration: Supportive family involvement practices.* Thousand Oaks, CA: Sage Publications.

Grassi, E., Hanley, D., & Liston, D. (2004). Service-learning: An innovative approach for second language learners. *Journal of Experimental Education, 22*(1), 87–110.

Graves, D. (1983). *Writing: Teachers and children at work.* Portsmouth, NH: Heinemann.

Gray, C. (1994). *Comic strip conversations.* Arlington, TX: Future Horizons Inc.

Gray, C. (2000). *The new social story book: Illustrated edition.* Arlington, TX: Future Horizons.

Gray, C. (2010). *The new social story book: 10th anniversary edition.* Arlington, TX: Future Horizons.

Gray, C., & White, A. (2002). *My social stories book.* Philadelphia: Jessica Kingsley.

Green, G., & Shane, H. (1994). Science, reason and facilitated communication. *Journal of The Association for Persons with Severe Handicaps, 19,* 173–184.

Greene, M., & Isaacs, M. (1999). The responsibility of modeling collaboration in the university education classroom. *Action in Teacher Education, 20,* 98–106.

Hall, K. (2001). *Asperger syndrome, the universe and everything.* Philadelphia: Jessica Kingsley.

Hamrick, D. (2001, May). *Living with the challenges of autism.* Keynote presentation handout from the meeting of the Autism Society of Wisconsin, Green Bay.

Harmin, M., & Toth, M. (2006). *Inspiring active learning: A complete handbook for today's teachers* (2nd expanded ed.). Alexandria, VA: ASCD.

Harmon, A. (2004). *How about not curing us, some autistics are pleading.* Retrieved December 12, 2007, from http://www.nytimes.com

Harrison, L. (2000, May). *Breaking away. Crossing dis/ABILITY borders: Beyond the myth of normal.* Paper presented at the meeting of the Facilitated Communication Institute, Syracuse University, New York.

Harris, S.L., Handleman, J.S., Gill, M.J., & Fong, P.L. (1991). Does punishment hurt? The impact of aversives on the clinician. *Research in Developmental Disabilities, 12,* 17–24.

Harry, B. (1992). Restructuring the participation of African American parents in special education. *Exceptional Children, 59*(2), 123–131.

Harry, B. (1995). Communication versus compliance: African American parents' involvement in special education. *Exceptional Children, 64*(4), 364–377.

Harvey, S., & Goudvis, A. (2007). *Strategies that work: Teaching comprehension to enhance understanding* (2nd ed.). Portland, ME: Stenhouse.

Hedeen, D.L., Ayres, B.J., Meyer, L.H., & Waite, J. (1996). Quality inclusive schooling for students with severe behavioral challenges. In D. Lehr & F. Brown (Eds.), *People with disabilities who challenge the system* (pp. 127–171). Baltimore: Paul H. Brookes Publishing Co.

Henderson, J. (1992). *Reflective teaching: Becoming an inquiring educator.* New York: Macmillan.

Henderson, W. (2001). *Inclusion: A catalyst for whole school improvement.* Retrieved November 21, 2009, from http://www.wholeschooling.net/WS/WSPress/ARTInclCatalyst.html

Henke, N.R. (2003). *A teacher training program on reflection. IPP Collection. Paper 383.* Retrieved December 12, 2009, from http://digitalcollections.sit.edu/ipp_collection/383/

Hernandez, H. (1989). *Multicultural education.* Columbus, OH: Charles E. Merrill.

Hertz-Lazarowitz, R., Kagan, S., Sharan, S., Slavin, R., & Webb, C. (Eds.). (1985). *Learning to cooperate: Cooperating to learn.* New York: Plenum.

Hess, R.H., Molina, A., & Kozleski, E.B. (2006). Parental perceptions of their children's special education services. *British Journal of Special Education, 33,* 148–157.

Hill, A. (2009). *Doctors are failing to spot Asperger's in girls.* Guardian News and Media. Retrieved April, 12, 2009, from http://www.guardian.co.uk/lifeandstyle/2009/apr/12/autism-aspergers-girls.

Hindley, J. (1996). *In the company of children.* Portland, ME: Stenhouse.

Hirshorn, A., & James, G. (1995). Further negative findings on facilitated communications. *Psychology in the Schools, 32,* 109–113.

Hitzing, W. (1994, November). Facilitated communication: Communication and black box psychology. *Facilitated Communication Digest, 3*(1), 2–3.

Holt, J. (1967). *How children fail.* New York: Pitman.

Howard, P. (2004). The least restrictive environment: How to tell? *Journal of Law & Education, 33,* 167–180.

Howard, G.R. (2007). As diversity grows, so must we. *Educational Leadership, 64,* 16–22.

Howlin, P. (1998). *Children with autism and Asperger syndrome: A guide for practitioners and carers.* New York: Wiley.

Hoyt, L. (1999). *Revisit, reflect, retell: Strategies for improving reading comprehension.* Portsmouth, NH: Heinemann.

Hughes, R. (2003). *Running with Walker: A memoir.* Philadelphia: Jessica Kingsley.

Hussman, J., Kluth, P. (Director), Strong, B., & Tweedy, J. (Producers). (2009). *"We thought you'd never ask": Voices of people with autism* [Video]. United States: Landlocked Films.

Hutchinson, J.N. (1999). *Students on the margins: Education, stories, dignity.* Albany: State University of New York Press.

Hyatt, K.J., DaSilva Iddings, A.C., & Ober, S. (2005). Inclusion: A catalyst for school reform. *TEACHING Exceptional Children Plus, 1*(3) Article 2. Retrieved November 23, 2009, from http://escholarship.bc.edu/education/tecplus/vol1/iss3/2

Individuals with Disabilities Education Act (IDEA) Amendments of 1997, PL 105-17, 20 U.S.C. §§ 1400 *et seq.*

Individuals with Disabilities Education Act (IDEA) of 1990, PL 101-476, 20 U.S.C. §§ 1400 *et seq.*

Institute for the Study of the Neurologically Typical. (2002, March). http://isnt.autistics.org/

Irvin, J. (Director). (1987). *Hamburger hill* [Motion picture]. United States: Avid Home Entertainment.

Jackson, L. (2002). *Freaks, geeks, and Asperger syndrome: A user guide to adolescence.* Philadelphia: Jessica Kingsley.

Jacobson, J.W., Mulick, J.A., & Schwartz, A.A. (1995). A history of facilitated communication: Science, pseudoscience, and antiscience. *American Psychologist, 50*, 750–765.

Jensen, E.P. (2008). *Brain-based learning: The new paradigm of teaching (2nd ed.).* San Diego: Corwin Press.

Johnson, D.W., & Johnson, R.T. (1999). *Cooperation and competition: Theory and research.* Edina, MN: Interaction Book Company.

Johnson, M. (Producer), & Levinson, B. (Director). (1988). *Rain man* [Motion picture]. United States: United Artists.

Jolliffe, W. (2007). *Cooperative learning in the classroom: Putting it into practice.* London: Paul Chapman Publishing.

Jorgensen, C. (1998). *Restructuring high schools for all students: Taking inclusion to the next level.* Baltimore: Paul H. Brookes Publishing Co.

Jorgensen, C., Sonnenmeier, R.M., & McSheehan, M. (2009). *The Beyond Access model: Promoting membership, participation, and learning for students with disabilities in the general education classroom.* Baltimore: Paul H. Brookes Publishing Co.

Kagan, S. (1992). *Cooperative learning: Resources for teachers.* San Juan Capistrano, CA: Kagan Cooperative Learning.

Kallem, M., Hoernicke, P.A., & Coser, P.G. (1994). Native Americans and behavioral disorders. In R.L. Peterson, & S. Ishii-Jordan (Eds.), *Multicultural issues in the education of students with behavioral disorders* (pp. 126–137). Boston: Brookline Press.

Kamps, D.M. (1995). Cooperative learning groups in reading: An integration strategy for students with autism and general classroom peers. *Behavioral Disorders, 21*(1), *89–109*.

Karagiannis, A., Stainback, S., & Stainback, W. (1996). Historical view of inclusion. In S. Stainback & W. Stainback (Eds.), *Inclusion: A guide for educators* (pp. 17–28). Baltimore: Paul H. Brookes Publishing Co.

Kasa-Hendrickson, C. (2002). *Participation in the inclusive classroom: Successful teachers for non-verbal students with autism.* Unpublished manuscript, Syracuse University, New York.

Kasa-Hendrickson, C., Broderick, A., & Hanson, D. (2009). Sorting out speech: Understanding multiple methods of communication for persons with autism and other developmental disabilities. *Journal of Developmental Processes, 4*(2), 116–133.

Kasa-Hendrickson, C., Broderick, A., Biklen, D. (Producers), & Gambell, J. (Director). (2002). *Inside the edge* [Video documentary]. (Available from Syracuse University, 370 Huntington Hall, Syracuse, NY)

Kasa-Hendrickson, C., & Kluth, P. (2005). "We have to start with inclusion and work it out as we go": Successful inclusion for non-verbal students with autism. *Journal of Whole Schooling, 2*, 2–14.

Kaufeldt, M. (1999). *Begin with the brain: Orchestrating the learner-centered classroom.* Tucson, AZ: Zephyr Press.

Keefe, E., Moore, V., & Duff, F. (Eds.). (2006). *Listening to the experts: Students with disabilities speak out.* Baltimore, MD: Paul H. Brooks Publishing Co.

Keller, H. (1954). *The story of my life.* Garden City, NJ: Doubleday.

Kennedy, C.H., & Itkonen, T. (1994). Some effects of regular class participation on the social contacts and social networks of high school students with severe disabilities. *Journal of the Association for Persons with Severe Handicaps, 19*, 1–10.

Kennedy, M. (2002). Creating ideal facilities. *American School & University, 74*(5) 30–33.

Kern, J.K., Trivedi, M.H., Garver, C.R., Grannemann, B.D., Andrews, A.A., Savla, J.S., et al. (2006). The pattern of sensory processing abnormalities in autism. *Autism, 10*, 480–494.

Kephart, B. (1998). *A slant of sun.* New York: Norton.

Keyes, M.W. (1996). *Intersections of vision and practice in an inclusive elementary school: An ethnography of a principal.* Unpublished doctoral dissertation, University of Wisconsin–Madison.

King-Sears, M.K. (1996). *Curriculum-based assessment in special education.* Baltimore: The Johns Hopkins University.

Kinney, J., & Fischer, D. (2001). *Co-teaching students with autism K–5.* Verona, WI: IEP Resources.

Kirby, D., Liner, T., & Vinz, R. (1988). *Inside out: A developmental approach to teaching writing* (2nd ed.). Portsmouth, NH: Heinemann.

Klein, R. (2000). Fighting disaffection. *Improving Schools, 3*(1), 18–22.

Klewe, L. (1993). An empirical evaluation of spelling boards. *Journal of Autism and Developmental Disorders, 23*(3), 559–566.

Kliewer, C. (1998). *Schooling children with Down syndrome.* New York: Teachers College Press.

Kliewer, C., & Biklen, D. (2000). Democratizing disability inquiry. *Journal of Disability Policy Studies, 10,* 186–206.

Kliewer, C., & Biklen, D. (2001). School's not really a place for reading: A research synthesis of the literate lives of students with severe disabilities. *The Journal of The Association for Persons with Severe Handicaps, 26,* 1–12.

Kliewer, C., Biklen, D., & Kasa-Hendrickson, C. (2006). Who may be literate? Disability and resistance to the cultural denial of competence. *American Educational Research Journal, 43,* 163–192.

Kliewer, C., & Landis, D. (1999). Individualizing literacy instruction for young children with moderate to severe disabilities. *Exceptional Children, 66,* 85–100.

Kluth, P. (1998). *The impact of facilitated communication of the educational lives of students: Three case studies.* Doctoral dissertation, University of Wisconsin–Madison, Special Education Department.

Kluth, P. (1999, December). Developing successful schooling experiences for FC users: An interview with Franklin and Pat Wilson. *Facilitated Communication Digest, (8)*1, 7–11.

Kluth, P. (2000). Community-referenced instruction and the inclusive school. *Remedial and Special Education, 21,* 19–26.

Kluth, P. (2004). Autism, autobiography, and adaptations. *Teaching Exceptional Children, 36*(4), 42–47.

Kluth P., Biklen, D., English-Sand, P., & Smukler, D. (2007). Going away to school: Stories from families who move to find inclusive schools. *Journal of Disability Policy Studies, 18*(1), 43–56.

Kluth, P., Biklen, D., & Straut, D. (2003). *Access to academics: Critical approaches to inclusive curriculum, instruction, and policy.* Mahwah, NJ: Lawrence Erlbaum Associates.

Kluth, P., & Chandler-Olcott, K. (2008). *"A land we can share": Teaching literacy to students with autism.* Baltimore: Paul H. Brookes Publishing Co.

Kluth, P., Diaz-Greenberg, R., Thousand, J.S., & Nevin, A.I. (2002). Teaching for liberation: Promising practices from critical pedagogy. In J.S. Thousand, R.A. Villa, and A.I. Nevin (Eds.), *Creativity and collaborative learning: The practical guide to empowering students, teachers, and families* (pp. 71–84). Baltimore: Paul H. Brookes Publishing Co.

Kluth, P., & Schwarz, P. (2008). *"Just give him the whale!" 20 ways to use fascinations, areas of expertise, and strengths to support students with autism.* Baltimore: Paul H. Brookes Publishing Co.

Kluth, P., & Shouse, J. (2009). *The autism checklist: A practical reference for parents and teachers.* San Francisco, CA: Jossey-Bass.

Kluth, P., & Straut, D. (2001, September). Standards for diverse learners. *Educational Leadership, 59,* 43–46.

Kluth, P., Straut, D., & Biklen, D. (2003). *Access to academics for all students: Critical approaches to inclusive curriculum, instruction, and policy.* Mahwah, NJ: Lawrence Erlbaum Associates.

Kluth, P., Villa, R., & Thousand, J. (2001, December/January). "Our school doesn't offer inclusion" and other legal blunders. *Educational Leadership, 59,* 24–27.

Knight, T. (2003). Academic access and the family. In P. Kluth, D. Straut, & D. Biklen (Eds.), *Access to academics: Critical approaches to inclusive curriculum, instruction, and policy* (pp. 49–68). Mahwah, NJ: Lawrence Erlbaum Associates.

Kochmeister, S.J. (1997). Excerpts from SHATTERING WALLS. *Facilitated Communication Digest, 5*(3), 10–12.

Kohler-Evans, P.A. (2006). Co-teaching: How to make this marriage work in front of the kids. *Education, 127*(2), 260–264.

Koliba, C.J., Campbell, E.K., & Shapiro, C. (2006). The practice of service learning in local school–community contexts. *Educational Policy, 20*(5), 683–717.

Kooy, M. (2006). *Telling stories in book clubs: Women teachers and professional development.* New York: Springer.

Koppenhaver, D., Coleman, P., Kalman, S., & Yoder, D. (1991). The implications of emergent literacy research for children with developmental disabilities. *American Journal of Speech and Language Pathology, 1,* 38–44.

Kozleski, E.B., Engelbrecht, P., Hess, R.S., Swart, E., Eloff, I., Oswald, M. Molina, A., & Jain, S. (2008). Where differences matter: A cross-cultural analysis of family voice in special education. *Journal of Special Education, 42,* 26–35.

Kozol, J. (1967). *Death at an early age*. Boston: Houghton-Mifflin.

Kurtz, L. (2006). *Visual perception problems in children with AD/HD, autism and other learning disabilities: A guide for parents and professionals*. Philadelphia: Jessica Kingsley.

Krystal, S. (1998/1999). The nurturing potential of service learning. *Educational Leadership*, January, 58–61.

Labbo, L., Eakle, J., & Montero, K. (2002). Digital Language Experience Approach: Using digital photographs and software as a Language Experience Approach innovation. *Reading Online*, 5(8). Retrieved April 2, 2007, from http://www.readingonline.org/electronic/elec_index.asp?HREF=/electronic/labbo2/index.html

Ladson-Billings, G. (2009). *The dreamkeepers* (2nd ed.). San Francisco: Jossey-Bass.

Lapkoff, S., & Li, R. (2007). *Five trends for schools*. Educational Leadership, 64, 8–15.

Larson, C.E., & LaFasto, F.M.J. (1989). *Teamwork: What must go right, what can go wrong*. Thousand Oaks, CA: Sage Publications.

Lasley, T.J., Matczynski, T.J., & Rowley, J.B. (2002). *Instructional models: Strategies for teaching in a diverse society*. Belmont, CA: Wadsworth.

Lawson, W. (1998). *Life behind glass: A personal account of autism spectrum disorder*. London: Jessica Kingsley.

Layton, C., & Lock, R. (2007). Use authentic assessment techniques to fulfill the promise of no child left behind. *Intervention in School Clinic*, 42(3), 169–173.

Leary, M.R., & Hill, D.A. (1996). Moving on: Autism and movement disturbance. *Mental Retardation*, 34, 39–53.

Lieberman, L., Lytle, R.K. & Clarcq, J. (2008). Getting it right from the start: Employing the universal design for learning approach to your curriculum. *The Journal of Physical Education, Recreation & Dance*, 79(2), 32–40.

Lipsky, D., & Gartner, A. (1996). Inclusion, school restructuring, and the remaking of American society. *Harvard Educational Review*, 66, 762–796.

Loomans, D., & Kohlberg, K. (2002). *The laughing classroom: Everyone's guide to teaching with humor and play* (Rev. ed.). Tiburon, CA: H J Kramer.

Lovaas, O.I., Schaeffer, B., & Simmons, J.Q. (1965). Experimental studies in childhood schizophrenia: building social behavior in autistic children by the use of electric shock. *Journal of Experimental Research Personnel*, 1, 99–109.

Lovett, H. (1985). *Cognitive counseling & persons with special needs*. Westport, CT: Praeger.

Lovett, H. (1996). *Learning to listen: Positive approaches and people with difficult behavior*. Baltimore: Paul H. Brookes Publishing Co.

Luongo-Orlando, K. (2003). *Authentic assessment: Designing performance-based tasks*. Markham, Ontario, Canada: Pembroke Publishers.

Maanum, J. (2009). *The general educator's guide to special education* (3rd ed.). Thousand Oaks, CA: Corwin Press.

MacArthur, C., Graham, S., & Fitzgerald, J. (Eds.). (2006). *Handbook of writing research*. New York: Guilford Press.

Mahaffey, H., & Newton, C. (2008). *Restorative solutions: Making it work*. United Kingdom: Inclusive Solutions UK Ltd.

Marcus, E. (1998, June). On almost becoming a person. *Facilitated Communication Digest*, 6(3), 2–4.

Marcus, E. (2002, Spring). Compulsion and yes, freedom too. *Facilitated Communication Digest*, 10(1), 7–10.

Marks, S.U., Schrader, C., & Levine, M. (1999). Paraeducator experiences in inclusive settings: Helping, hovering, or holding their own? *Exceptional Children*, 65, 315–328.

Martin, R. (1994). *Out of silence: An autistic boy's journey into language and communication*. New York: Penguin.

Martin, R. (2001). *Disability rights are "civil rights" too*. Retrieved February 2, 2003, from http://www.reedmartin.com/specialeducationarticles.htm

Marzano, R.J. (2010). Using games to enhance student achievement. *Educational Leadership*, 67(5), 71–72.

Matthews, J. (1988). *Escalante: The best teacher in America*. Austin, TX: Holt, Rinehart & Winston.

McClannahan, L.E., & Krantz, P.J. (2005). *Teaching conversation to children with autism: Scripts and script fading*. Bethesda, MD: Woodbine House.

McCoy, K., & Hermansen, E. (2007). Video modeling for individuals with autism: A review of model types and effects. *Education & Treatment of Children, 30*, 183–213.

McCutcheon, D. (2006). Cognitive factors in the development of students' writing. In C. MacArthur, S. Graham, & J. Fitzgerald (Eds.), *Handbook of writing research* (pp. 115–130). New York: Guilford Press.

McIntyre, T. (2002). *Are behaviorist interventions inappropriate for culturally different youngsters with learning and behavior disorders?* Retrieved from http://maxweber.hunter.cuny.edu/pub/eres/html

McLeskey, J., & Waldron, N. (2006). Comprehensive school reform and inclusive schools: Improving schools for all students. *Theory into Practice, 45*(3), 269–278.

McMaster, K.L., Fuchs, D., & Fuchs, L.S. (2002). Using peer tutoring to prevent early reading failure. In J. Thousand, R. Villa, & A. Nevin (Eds.), *Creativity and collaborative learning: The practical guide to empowering students, teachers, and families* (2nd ed., pp. 235–246). Baltimore: Paul H. Brookes Publishing Co.

McNabb, J. (2001). *I don't want to be a pioneer I just want to be me.* Retrieved from http://www.autistics.org/library/nopioneer.html

Meier, D. (2002). *The power of their ideas: Lessons from a small school in Harlem* (2nd ed.). Boston: Beacon Press.

Meyers, J., Gelzheiser, L.M., & Yelich, G. (1991). Do pull-in programs foster teacher collaboration? *Remedial and Special Education, 12*, 7–15.

Michie, G. (1999). *Holler if you hear me.* New York: Teachers College Press.

Miller, L., & Opland-Dobs, D. (2001). Students blow the whistle on toxic oil contamination. In *Rethinking our classrooms: Teaching for equity and justice* (Vol. 2, pp. 144–147). Milwaukee, WI: Rethinking Schools.

Miller, P., Shambaugh, K., Robinson, C., & Wimberly, J. (1995). Applied learning for middle schoolers. *Educational Leadership, 52*, 22–25.

Mirenda, P. (2005). Augmentative and alternative communication techniques. In J.E. Downing (Ed.), *Teaching communication skills to students with severe disabilities* (pp. 119–138). Baltimore: Paul H. Brookes Publishing Co.

Mirenda, P. (2003). "He's not really a reader . . . ": Perspectives on supporting literacy development in individuals with autism. *Topics in Language Disorders, 23*, 270–282.

Mirenda, P. (2008). "A back door approach to autism and AAC." *Augmentative and Alternative Communication, 24*, 219–233.

Molloy, H., & Vasil, L. (2004). *Asperger syndrome, adolescence and identity: Looking beyond the label.* Philadelphia: Jessica Kingsley Publishers.

Molton, K. (2000). Paper presented at the Annual General Meeting of the National Autistic Society (UK), Cheshire, England.

Mooney, J., & Cole, D. (2000). *Learning outside the lines: Two Ivy League students with learning disabilities and ADHD give you the tools for academic success and educational revolution.* New York: Simon & Schuster.

Moursund, D. (2003). *Project-based learning using information technology* (2nd ed.). Eugene, OR: ISTE.

Morehouse, P. (1995). The building of an airplane (with a little help from friends). *Educational Leadership, 52*, 56–57.

Morgenstern, J., & Morgenstern-Colon, J. (2002). *Organizing from the inside out for teenagers.* New York: Holt.

Morris, R. (Ed.). (1992). *Solving the problems of youth at-risk: Involving parents and community resources.* Lancaster, PA: Technomic.

Moses, R.P., & Cobb, C.E. (2001). *Radical equations: Math literacy and civil rights.* Boston: Beacon.

Moss, S., & Schwartz, L. (2007). *"Where's my stuff?": The ultimate teen organizing guide.* San Francisco: Zest Books.

Mukhopadhyay, T. (2000). *Beyond the silence.* London: National Autism Society.

Mukhopadhyay, T. (2003). *The mind tree: A miraculous child breaks the silence of autism.* New York: Arcade Publishing.

Murawski, W. (2009). *Collaborative teaching in secondary schools: Making the co-teaching marriage work!* Thousand Oaks, CA: Corwin Press.

Myles, B.S. (2004). *The hidden curriculum: Practical solutions for understanding unstated rules in social situations.* Shawnee Mission, KS: Autism Asperger Publishing Company.

Myles, B.S. (2005). *Children and youth with Asperger syndrome: Strategies for success in inclusive settings*. Thousand Oaks, CA: Corwin Press.

Myles, B.S., Cook, K.T., Miller N.E., Rinner, L., & Robbins, L. (2000). *Asperger syndrome and sensory issues: Practical solutions for making sense of the world*. Shawnee Mission, KS: Autism Asperger Publishing Co.

Myles, B.S., Hagiwara, T., Dunn, W., Rinner, L., Reese, M., Huggins, A., & Becker, S. (2004). Sensory issues in children with Asperger syndrome and autism. *Education and Training in Developmental Disabilities, 3*(4), 283–290.

Myles, B.S., & Simpson, R. (1994). Facilitated communication with children diagnosed as autistic in public school settings. *Psychology in the Schools, 31*, 208–220.

Myles, B.S., Swanson, T., Holverstott, J., & Duncan, M. (Eds.). (2007). *Autism spectrum disorder: A handbook for parents and professionals*. Westport: CT: Praeger Publishers.

National Council on Disability. (2000). *Back to school on civil rights*. Washington DC: Author.

Nagy, W., Herman, P., & Anderson, R. (1985). Learning words from context. *Reading Research Quarterly, 20*, 233–253.

National Education Association. (1992). *Status of the American public school teacher*. New Haven, CT: Author.

National Institute of Child Health and Human Development. (2000). *Report of the National Reading Panel. Teaching children to read: An evidence-based assessment of the scientific research literature on reading and its implications for reading instruction* (NIH Publication No. 00-4769). Washington, DC: U.S. Government Printing Office.

Nayate, A., Bradshaw, J.L., & Rinehart, N.J. (2005). Autism and Asperger's disorder: Are they movement disorders involving the cerebellum and/or basal ganglia? *Brain Research Bulletin, 67*, 327–334.

Newport, J. (2001). *Your life is not a label: A guide to living fully with autism and Asperger's syndrome for parents, professionals, and you*. Arlington, TX: Future Horizons, Inc.

Newport, J., Newport, M., & Dodd, J. (2007). *Mozart & the whale: An Asperger's love story*. New York: Touchstone.

Nichols, S., Moravcik, G.M., & Tetenbaum, A.P. (2009). Girls growing up on the autism spectrum: what parents and professionals should know about the pre-teen and teenage years. London: Jessica Kingsley Publishers.

Nieto, S., & Bode (2008). *Affirming diversity: The sociopolitical context of multicultural education*. New York: Longman.

Noddings, N. (1984). *Caring: A feminine approach to ethics and moral education*. Berkeley: University of California Press.

Notbohm, E., & Zysk, V. (2004). *1001 great ideas for teaching and raising children with autism spectrum disorders*. Arlington, TX: New Horizons.

O'Brien, D. (2001, June). "At-risk" adolescents: Redefining competence through the multiliteracies of intermediality, visual arts, and representation. *Reading Online, 4*. Retrieved March 2, 2007, from http://www.readingonline.org/newliteracies/obrien/

O'Brien, C., & Dieker, L.A. (2008). Effects of video modeling on implementation of literature circles by students with learning disabilities and their peers in inclusive content classrooms. *Journal of Curriculum and Instruction, 2*(2), 52–73.

O'Connor, I.M., & Klein, P.D. (2004). Exploration of strategies for facilitating the reading comprehension of high-functioning students with autism spectrum disorders. *Journal of Autism and Developmental Disorders, 34*(2), 115–127.

Oczkus, L. (2009). *Interactive think aloud lesson: 25 surefire ways to engage students and improve comprehension*. New York: Scholastic Teaching Resources.

Olmedo, I.M. (1997). Challenging old assumptions: Preparing teachers for inner city schools. *Teaching & Teacher Education, 13*, 245–258.

Olney, M. (1995). Reading between the lines: A case study on facilitated communication. *Journal of The Association for People with Severe Handicaps, 32*, 109–113.

Olney, M. (1997). A controlled study of facilitated communication using computer games. In D. Biklen & D. Cardinal (Eds.), *Contested words, contested science: Unraveling the facilitated communication controversy* (pp. 96–114). New York: Teachers College Press.

Olson, M.W., & Gee, T. (1991). Content reading instruction in the primary grades: Perceptions and strategies. *The Reading Teacher, 45*(4), 298–307.

O'Neill, J. (1997, Spring). A place for all. *The Pennsylvania Journal on Positive Approaches, 1*(2). Retrieved from http://www.quuxuum.org/~greg/journal/o_neill.html

O'Neill, J. (1999). *Through the eyes of aliens: A book about autistic people.* Philadelphia: Jessica Kingsley.

Onosko, J., & Jorgensen, C. (1998). Unit and lesson planning in the inclusive classroom: Maximizing learning opportunities for all students. In C. Jorgensen (Ed.), *Restructuring high schools for all students* (pp. 71–105). Baltimore: Paul H. Brookes Publishing Co.

Oyler, C. (2001). Democratic classrooms and accessible instruction. *Democracy & Education, 14,* 28–31.

Paley, V. (1979). *White teacher.* Cambridge, MA: Havard University Press.

Paley, V. (1990). *The boy who would be a helicopter.* Cambridge, MA: Harvard University Press.

Paley, V. (1992). *You can't say you can't play.* Cambridge: Harvard University Press.

Palincsar, A.S., & Brown, A.L. (1984). Reciprocal teaching of comprehension-fostering and comprehension-monitoring activities. *Cognition and Instruction, 1,* 117–175.

Parker, D. (1997). *Jamie: A literacy story.* York, MD: Stenhouse Publishers.

Parker, J. (1990). *Workshops for active learning.* Vancouver, British Columbia, Canada: JFP Productions.

Patterson, M. (1997). *Every body can learn.* Tucson, AZ: Zephyr.

Paul, P. (2006). New literacies, multiple literacies, unlimited literacies: What now, what next, where to? *Journal of Deaf Studies and Deaf Education, 11*(3), 382–387.

Pearpoint, J., Forest, M., & O'Brien, J. (1996). MAPs, Circles of friends, and PATH: Powerful tools to help build caring communities. In S. Stainback & W. Stainback (Eds.), *Inclusion: A guide for educators* (pp. 67–86). Baltimore: Paul H. Brookes Publishing Co.

Peterson, K. (2002). Positive or negative? *Journal of Staff Development, 23*(3), 10–15.

Peterson, K.D., & Deal, T.E. (2009). *The shaping school culture fieldbook* (2nd ed.). San Franciso: Jossey-Bass.

Pike, K., & Salend, S.J. (1995). *Authentic assessment strategies: Alternatives to norm-reference testing, 28,* 15–20.

Pinnell, G.S., Pikulski, J., Wixson, K., Campbell, J., Gough, P., & Beatty, A. (1995). *Listening to children read aloud.* Washington, DC: U.S. Department of Education, Office of Educational Research and Improvement.

Pitonyak, D. (2005). *10 things you can do to support a person with difficult behaviors.* Retrieved May 21, 2009, from http://www.dimagine.com/10Things.pdf

Powell, J., & Azrin, N.H. (1968). The effects of shock as a punisher for cigarette smoking. *Journal of Applied Behavior Analysis, 1,* 63–71.

Praisner, C.L. (2003). Attitudes of elementary school principals toward the inclusion of students with disabilities. *Exceptional Children, 69*(2), 135–145.

Pressley, M. (2000). What should comprehension instruction be the instruction of? In M. Kamil, P.B. Mosenthal, P.D. Pearson, & R. Barr (Eds.), *Handbook of reading research* (Vol. III, pp. 545–561). Mahwah, NJ: Lawrence Erlbaum Associates.

Prestia, K. (2004). Incorporate sensory activities and choices into the classroom. *Intervention in School & Clinic, 39,* 172–175.

Prince-Hughes, D. (2004). *Songs of the gorilla nation: My journey through autism.* New York: Harmony Books.

Pritchett, P. (1993). Try something different. In J. Canfield & M.V. Hansen (Eds.), *Chicken soup for the soul: 101 stories to open the heart and rekindle the spirit.* Deerfield Beach, FL: Health Communications Inc.

Prizant, B.M., & Duchan, J.F. (1981). The functions of immediate echolalia in autistic children. *Journal of Speech and Hearing Disorders, 46,* 241–249.

Pugach, M., & Warger, C. (2001). Curriculum matters: Raising expectations for students with disabilities. *Remedial and Special Education, 22*(4), 192–196.

Pugach, M.C., & Wesson, C. (1995). Teachers' and students' views of team teaching of general education and learning-disabled students in two fifth-grade classes. *The Elementary School Journal, 95,* 279–295.

Purcell-Gates, V. (2002). Multiple literacies. In B. Guzzetti (Ed.), *Literacy in America: An encyclopedia of history, theory, and practice, volume one* (pp. 376–380). Santa Barbara, CA: ABC-Clio.

Putnam, J. (1997). *Cooperative learning in diverse classrooms.* Upper Saddle River, NJ: Prentice Hall.

Pyles, L. (2003). Education and the adolescent with Asperger syndrome. In L.H. Willey (Ed.), *Asperger syndrome in adolescence* (pp. 243–282). Philadelphia: Jessica Kingsley.

Quinlan, T. (2004). Speech recognition technology and students with writing difficulties: Improving fluency. *Journal of Educational Psychology, 96*(2), 337–46.

Rainforth, B., & England, J. (1997). Collaboration for inclusion. *Education and Treatment of Children, 20*(1), 85–104.

Rainforth, B., & York-Barr, J. (1997). *Collaborative teamwork for students with severe disabilities: Integrating therapy and educational services* (2nd ed.). Baltimore: Paul H. Brookes Publishing Co.

Rajapatirana, C. (1998). On being mute. *Facilitated Communication Newsletter, 7*(1), 6.

Rashotte, C.A., & Torgesen, J.K. (1985). Repeated reading and reading fluency in learning disabled children. *Reading Research Quarterly, 20,* 180–188.

Rasinski, T. (2003). *The fluent reader: Oral reading strategies for building word recognition, fluency, and comprehension.* New York: Scholastic.

Reed, D. (1996). *Paid for the privilege: Hearing the voices of autism.* Madison, WI: DRI Press.

Regal, R., Rooney, J., & Wandas, T. (1994). Facilitated communication: An experimental evaluation. *Journal of Autism and Developmental Disorders, 24,* 345–355.

Reid, R., & Maag, J. (1998). Functional assessment: A method for developing classroom-based accommodations for children with ADHD. *Reading and Writing Quarterly, 14,* 9–42.

Rethinking Schools. (2000). *Failing our kids: Why the testing craze won't fix our schools.* Milwaukee, WI: Author.

Richardson, W. (2006). *Blogs, wikis, podcasts, and other powerful web tools for classrooms.* Thousand Oaks, CA: Corwin Press.

Riehl, C.J. (2000). The principal's role in creating inclusive schools for diverse students: A review of normative, empirical, and critical literature on the practice of educational administration. *Review of Educational Research, 70*(1), 55–81.

Ringman, J., & Jankovic, J. (2000). Occurance of tics in Asperger's syndrome and autistic disorder. *Journal of Child Neurology, 15,* 394–400.

Ritter, C.L., Michel, C.S., & Irby, B. (1999). Concerning inclusion: Perceptions of middle school students, their parents, and teachers. *Rural Special Education Quarterly, 18*(2), 10–17.

Robb, L. (2004). *Nonfiction writing from the inside out: Writing lessons inspired by conversations with leading authors.* New York: Scholastic.

Robillard, A.R. (1997). Communication problems in the intensive care unit. In R. Hertz (Ed.), *Reflexivity and voice* (pp. 229–251). Thousand Oaks, CA: Sage Publications.

Robison, J.E. (2007). *Look me in the eye: My life with Asperger's.* New York: Crown Publishers.

Robinson, W. (2003). *Gentle giant.* London: Vega, Chrysalis Books.

Rocco, S. (1996). Toward shared commitment and shared responsibility. In S.J. Meisels & E. Fenichel (Eds.), *New visions for the developmental assessment of infants and children.* Washington, DC: ZERO TO THREE: National Center for Infants, Toddlers, and Families.

Roncker v. Walter, 700 Fd. 1058 (6th Cir. 1993).

Rosinski, D. (2002, June). Literacy on the autism spectrum. *The Spectrum.* Available from the Autism Society of Wisconsin.

Routman, R. (1994). *Invitations: Changing as teachers and learners K–12.* Portsmouth, NH: Heinemann.

Rubin, S. (1998, December). *Castigating assumptions about mental retardation and low functioning autism.* Paper presented at The Association for Persons with Severe Handicaps National Conference, Seattle, WA.

Rubin, S. (1999, December). Independent typing. *Facilitated Communication Digest, 1*(8), 5–6.

Rubin, S., Biklen, D., Kasa-Hendrickson, C., Kluth, P., Cardinal, D.N., & Broderick, A. (2001). Independence, participation, and the meaning of intellectual ability. In *Disability & Society, 16*(3), 415–429. (http://www.tandf.co.uk)

Russell, D. (2006). Historical studies of composition. In P. Smagorinsky (Ed.), *Research on composition: Multiple perspectives on two decades of change* (pp. 243–276). New York: Teachers College Press.

Russo, C.J., & Osborne, A.G. (2007). *School based cases in special education law.* Thousand Oaks, CA: Corwin Press.

Ryder, R.J., & Graves, M. (1998). *Reading and learning in content areas* (2nd. ed.). Upper Saddle River, NJ: Merrill.

Ryndak, D.L., Morrison, A.P., & Sommerstein, L. (1999). Literacy before and after inclusion in general education settings: A case study. *Journal of The Association for Persons with Severe Handicaps, 24*, 5–22.

Sacks, O. (1973) *Awakenings*. New York: Vintage Books.

Sacramento City School District v. Rachel H., 14 F.3D 1398 (9th Cir. 1994).

Samuels, S.J. (1979). The method of repeated readings. *The Reading Teacher, 32*, 403–08.

Sapon-Shevin, M. (1999). *Because we can change the world*. Boston: Allyn & Bacon.

Sapon-Shevin, M. (2001). Making inclusion visible: Honoring the process and the struggle. *Democracy & Education, 14*, 24–27.

Sapon-Shevin, M. (2007). *Widening the circle: The power of inclusive classrooms*. Boston, MA: Beacon Press.

Sapon-Shevin, M., & Kluth, P. (2003). In the pool, on the stage, and at the concert. In P. Kluth, D. Straut, & D. Biklen (Eds.), *Access to academics for all students: Critical approaches to inclusive curriculum, instruction, and policy*. Mahwah, NJ: Lawrence Erlbaum Associates.

Sarokoff, R.A., Taylor, B.A., & Poulson, C.L. (2001). Teaching children with autism to engage in conversational exchanges: Script fading with embedded textual stimuli. *Journal of Applied Behavior Analysis, 34*, 81–84.

Savarese, R. (2007). *Reasonable people: A memoir of autism and adoption*. New York: Other Press.

Savner, J.L., & Myles B.S. (2000). *Making visual supports work in the home and community*. Shawnee Mission, KS: Autism Asperger Publishing Company.

Scarlett, W.G., Ponte, I., & Singh, J. (2009). *Approaches to behavior and classroom management: Integrating discipline with care*. Thousand Oaks, CA: Sage Publications.

Schine, J., & Halsted, A. (1997). Alienation or engagement? Service learning may be an answer. In S. Totten & J. Pederson (Eds.), *Social issues and service at the middle level* (pp. 195–210). Boston: Allyn & Bacon.

Schlosser, R.W., & Blischak, D.M. (2004). Effects of speech and print feedback on spelling by children with autism. *Journal of Speech, Language, and Hearing Research, 47*(4), 848–862.

Schmidt, J. (1998). Where there's a will there's a way: The successful inclusion of a child with autism. B.C. *Journal of Special Education, 21*, 45–63.

Schneider, E.R. (2003). *Living the good life with autism*. Philadelphia: Jessica Kingsley.

Schwarz, P. (2006). *From disability to possibility*. Portsmouth, NH: Heinemann.

Schwarz, P., & Bettenhausen, D.L. (2000). You can teach an old dog new tricks. In R.A. Villa, & J.S. Thousand (Eds.), *Restructuring for caring and effective education: Piecing the puzzle together* (2nd ed., pp. 469–483). Baltimore: Paul H. Brookes Publishing Co.

Schwarz, P., & Kluth, P. (2007). *"You're welcome": 30 innovative ideas for the inclusive classroom*. Portsmouth, NH: Heinemann.

Scruggs, T.E., Mastropieri, M.A., & McDuffie, K.A. (2007). Co-teaching in inclusive classrooms: A meta-synthesis of qualitative research. *Exceptional Children, 73*, 392–416.

Selden, S. (1999). *Inheriting shame: The story of eugenics and racism in America*. New York: Teachers College Press.

Sellin, B. (1995). *I don't want to be inside me anymore: Messages from an autistic mind*. New York: Basic Books.

Shapiro-Barnard, S. (1998). Preparing the ground for what is to come: A rationale for inclusive high schools. In C. Jorgensen (Ed.), *Restructuring high schools for all students: Taking inclusion to the next level* (p. 12). Baltimore: Paul H. Brookes Publishing Co.

Sharan, Y., & Sharan, S. (1992). *Expanding cooperative learning through group investigation*. New York: Teachers College Press.

Shaw, D. (2005). *Retelling strategies to improve comprehension: Effective hands-on strategies for fiction and nonfiction that help students remember and understand what they read*. New York: Scholastic.

Shevin, M. (1987). *The language of us and them* [Poem]. Unpublished manuscript.

Shevin, M. (1999, September). On being a communication ally. *Facilitated Communication Digest, 7*(4), 2–13.

Shevin, M., & Chadwick (Eds.). (2000). *Facilitated communication training standards*. Syracuse, NY: Facilitated Communication Institute.

Shore, S. (2003). *Beyond the wall: Personal experiences with autism and Asperger syndrome* (2nd ed.). Shawnee Mission, KS: Autism Asperger Publishing Co.

Shore, S. (Ed.). (2004). *Ask and tell: Self-advocacy and disclosure for people on the autism spectrum.* Shawnee Mission, KS: Autism Asperger Publishing Company.

Shore, S., & Rastelli, L. (2006). *Understanding autism for dummies.* San Francisco: Jossey Bass.

Shukla, S., Kennedy, C.H., & Cushing, L.S. (1999). Intermediate school students with severe disabilities: Supporting their social participation in general education classrooms. *Journal of Positive Behavior Interventions, 1,* 130–140.

Silberman, M. (1996). *Active learning: 101 strategies to teach any subject.* Boston, MA: Allyn & Bacon.

Simon, E., Toll, D., & Whitehair, P. (1994). A naturalistic approach to the validation of facilitated communication. *Journal of Autism and Developmental Disabilities, 24,* 647–657.

Simon, K.G. (2002). The blue blood is bad, right? *Educational Leadership, 60*(1), 24–28.

Sinclair, J. (1993). Don't mourn for us. *Our Voice, 1*(3), Autism Network International. Retrieved September 9, 2009, from http://ani.autistics.org/don't_mourn.html

Skinner, B.F. (1976). *About behaviorism.* New York: Random House.

Slaughter, E.L. (1976). *Indian child welfare: A review of the literature.* Denver, CO: Denver Research Institute.

Sleeter, C.E. (1986). Learning disabilities: The social construction of a special education category. *Exceptional Children, 53,* 46–54.

Smagorinsky, P. (Ed.). (2006). *Research on composition: Multiple perspectives on two decades of change.* New York: Teachers College Press.

Smith, C., & Strick, L. (1997). *Learning disabilities: A to Z.* New York: Fireside.

Smith, P. (2007). Have we made any progress? Including students with intellectual disabilities in regular education classrooms. *Intellectual and Developmental Disabilities, 45*(5), 297–309.

Smith, W.E. (2002). Reading readiness. In B. Guzzetti (Ed.), *Literacy in America: An encyclopedia of history, theory, and practice* (Vol. 2, pp. 526–527). Santa Barbara, CA: ABC/Clio.

Sonnenmeier, R., McSheehan, M., & Jorgensen, C. (2005). A case study of team supports for a student with autism's communication and engagement within the general education curriculum. *Journal of Augmentative and Alternative Communication, 21,* 101–115.

Sorrell, A.L. (1990). Three reading comprehension strategies: TELLS, story mapping, and QARS. *Academic Therapy, 25*(3), 359–367.

Sprenger, M. (2008). *Differentiation through learning styles and memory.* Thousand Oaks, CA: Corwin Press.

Stainback, S.B. (2000). If I could dream: Reflections on the future of education. In R.A. Villa & J.S. Thousand (Eds.), *Restructuring for caring and effective education: Piecing the puzzle together* (2nd ed., pp. 503–512). Baltimore: Paul H. Brookes Publishing Co.

Stauffer, R.G. (1970). *The language-experience approach to the teaching of reading.* New York: Harper & Row.

Stehli, A. (1991). *The sound of a miracle.* New York: Avon Books.

Stevensen, C.L., Krantz, P.J., & MClannahan, L.E. (2000). Social interaction skills for children with autism. A script-fading procedure for nonreaders. *Behavioral Interventions, 15,* 1–20.

Stieber, W. (1999). *Teaming for improvement: Building business profits.* Wilsonville, OR: BookPartners.

Stone, O. (Director). *Platoon* [Motion picture]. (1986). United States: MGM Studios.

Stoner, J.B., Beck, A.R., Bock, S.J., Hickey, K., Kosuwan, K., & Thompson, J. R. (2006). The effectiveness of the Picture Exchange Communication System with nonspeaking adults. *Remedial and Special Education, 27*(3), 154–163.

Strickland, D., & Schickendanz, J. (2004). *Learning about print in preschool: Working with letters, words, and beginning links with phonemic awareness.* Newark, DE: International Reading Association.

Strong, W. (2006). *Write for insight: Empowering content area learning, grades 6–12.* New York: Pearson.

Strully, J., & Strully, C. (1996). Friendships as an educational goal: What have we learned and where are we headed? In S. Stainback & W. Stainback (Eds.), *Inclusion: A guide for educators* (pp. 141–154). Baltimore: Paul H. Brookes Publishing Co.

Szempruch, J., & Jacobson, J. (1993). Evaluating facilitated communication of people with developmental disabilities. *Research in Developmental Disabilities, 14,* 253–264.

Tammet, D. (2006). *Born on a blue day: Inside the extraordinary mind of an autistic savant.* New York: Free Press.

Tanner, B.A., & Zeiler, M. (1975). Punishment of self-injurious behavior using aromatic ammonia as the aversive stimulus. *Journal of Applied Behavior Analysis, 8,* 53–57.

Tashie, C., Shapiro-Barnard, S., & Rossetti, Z. (2006). *Seeing the charade: What we need to do and undo to make friendships happen.* Nottingham, UK, Inclusive Solutions.

Tavalaro, J., & Tayson, R. (1997). *Look up for yes.* New York: Kondansha International.

Taylor, D., & Dorsey-Gaines, C. (1988). *Growing up literate: Learning from inner-city families.* Portsmouth, NH: Heinemann.

Theoharis, G. (2009). *The school leaders our children deserve: Seven keys to equity, social justice, and school reform.* New York: Teachers College Press.

Thousand, J.S., & Villa, R.A. (2000). Collaborative teaming: A powerful tool in school restructuring. In R.A. Villa & J.S. Thousand (Eds.), *Restructuring for caring and effective education: Piecing the puzzle together* (2nd ed., pp. 254–291). Baltimore: Paul H. Brookes Publishing Co.

Thunberg, G., Sandberg, A. D., & Ahlsén, E. (2009). Speech-generating devices used at home by children with autism spectrum disorders: A preliminary assessment. *Focus on Autism and Other Developmental Disabilities, 24*(2), 104–114.

Tomlinson, C. (1995). *How to differentiate instruction in a mixed-ability classroom.* Alexandria, VA: Association for Supervision and Curriculum Development.

Tomlinson, C. (1999). *The differentiated classroom: Responding to the needs of all learners.* Alexandria, VA: ASCD.

Tomlinson, C., & Strickland, C. (2005). *Differentiation in practice: A resource guide for differentiating curriculum, Grades 9–12.* Alexandria, VA: Association for Supervision and Curriculum Development.

Tovani, C. (2000). *I read it but I don't get it: Comprehension strategies for adolescent readers.* Portland, ME: Stenhouse.

Treacy, D. (1996, Spring). A meditation. *The Communicator, newsletter for the Autism National Committee, 7*(1), 8.

Trivedi, B. (2005). Autistic and proud of it. *New Scientist,* 36–40.

Trump, G., & Hange, J. (1996). *Teacher perceptions of and strategies for inclusion: A regional summary of focus group interview findings.* Charleston, WV: Appalachia Education Laboratory (ERIC Document Reproduction Service No. ED 397 576).

Udvari-Solner, A. (1995). A process for adapting curriculum in inclusive classrooms. In R.A. Villa, & J.S. Thousand (Eds.), *Creating an inclusive school* (pp. 110–124). Baltimore: Paul H. Brookes Publishing Co.

Udvari-Solner, A. (1996). Examining teacher thinking: Constructing a process to design curricular adaptations. *Remedial and Special Education, 17,* 245–254.

Udvari-Solner, A. (1997). Inclusive education. In C.A. Grant, & G. Ladson-Billings (Eds.), *Dictionary of multicultural education* (pp. 141–144). Phoenix, AZ: Oryx Press.

Udvari-Solner, A. (2007). Co-designing responsive curriculum. In M. Giangreco & M.B. Doyle (Eds.), *Quick-guides to inclusion: Ideas for educating students with disabilities* (2nd ed., pp. 151–164). Baltimore: Paul H. Brookes Publishing Co.

Udvari-Solner, A., & Keyes, M.W. (2000). Chronicles of administrative leadership toward inclusive reform: "We're on the train and we've left the station, but we haven't gotten to the next stop." In R.A. Villa, & J.S. Thousand (Eds.), *Restructuring for caring and effective education: Piecing the puzzle together* (2nd ed., pp. 428–452). Baltimore: Paul H. Brookes Publishing Co.

Udvari-Solner, A., & Kluth, P. (2007). *Joyful learning. Active and collaborative learning in the inclusive classroom.* Thousand Oaks, CA: Corwin Press.

Valencia, S. (1990). A portfolio approach to classroom reading assessment: The why, whats, and hows. *The Reading Teacher, 43,* 338–340.

VanSciver, J. (2005). Motherhood, apple pie, and differentiated instruction. *Phi Delta Kappan 86*(7), 534–535.

Van der Klift, E., & Kunc, N. (2002). Beyond benevolence: Supporting genuine friendships in inclusive schools. In J.S. Thousand, R.A. Villa, & A.I. Nevin (Eds.), *Creativity and collaborative learning: A practical guide to empowering students and teachers* (2nd ed., pp. 391–401). Baltimore: Paul H. Brookes Publishing Co.

Van Dyke, R., Stallings, M.A., & Colley, K. (1995). How to build an inclusive school community: A success story. *Phi Delta Kappan, 76*(6), 475–479.

Vargo, R., & Vargo, J. (2000). In the mainstream: A confirmation experience. In R.A. Villa & J.S. Thousand (Eds.), *Restructuring for caring and effective education: Piecing the puzzle together* (2nd ed., pp. 242–248) Baltimore: Paul H. Brookes Publishing Co.

Vicker, B. (2009). *Functional categories of immediate echolalia.* Bloomington, IN: Indiana Resource Center Autism. Retrieved December 3, 2009, from: http://www.iidc.indiana.edu/irca/communication/echolaliImmed.html

Villegas, A., & Lucas, T. (2007). The culturally responsive teacher. *Educational Leadership, 64,* 28–33.

Villa, R.A., & Thousand, J.S. (1990). Administrative supports to promote inclusive schooling. In W.C. Stainback & S.B. Stainback (Eds.), *Support networks for inclusive schooling: Interdependent integrated education* (pp. 210–218). Baltimore: Paul H. Brookes Publishing Co.

Villa, R.A., & Thousand, J.S. (Eds.). (2000). *Restructuring for caring and effective education: Piecing the puzzle together* (2nd ed.). Baltimore: Paul H. Brookes Publishing Co.

Villa, R., Thousand, J., & Nevin, A. (2008). *A guide to co-teaching: Practical tips for facilitating student learning* (2nd ed.). Thousand Oaks, CA: Corwin Press.

Villa, R., Thousand, J., & Nevin, A. (in press). *Collaborating with students in teaching, decision-making, and instruction: The untapped resource.* Thousand Oaks, CA: Corwin Press.

Villa, R. Thousand, J., Nevin, A., & Malgeri, C. (1996). Instilling collaboration to inclusive schooling as a way of doing business in public schools. *Remedial and Special Education, 17,* 169–181.

Wagstaff, J.M. (1999). Word walls that work. *Instructor, 110*(5), 32–34.

Waites, J., & Swinbourne, H. (2001). *Smiling at shadows: A mother's journey raising an autistic child.* Berkeley, CA: Ulysses.

Walther-Thomas, C.S. (1997). Co-teaching experiences: The benefits and problems that teachers and principals report over time. *Journal of Learning Disabilities, 30,* 395–407.

Walther-Thomas, C., Korinek, L., McLaughlin, V., & Williams, B.T. (2000). *Collaboration for inclusive education: Developing successful programs.* Boston: Allyn & Bacon.

Weatherbee, I. (1999, March). The view from Huntington College. *Facilitated Communication Digest, 7*(2), 2–6.

Webb, T. (Director). (1995). *A is for autism* [Film]. (Available from National Autistic Society, 393 City Road, London EC1V 1NE, 44 Tel:44-171-833-2299.)

Webster-Heard, S. (2008). God's special child. In The Healing Project (Ed.), *Voices of autism: The healing companion* (pp. 121–124). Brooklyn, NY: LaChance Publishing LLC.

Weiss, M., Wagner, S., & Bauman, M. (1996). A validated case study of facilitated communication. *Mental Retardation, 34,* 220–229.

Weiss, N. (1999). It may be non-aversive, but is it non-coercive?: The ethics of behavior change. *TASH Newsletter, 25*(11), 20–22, 27.

Whalon, K. (2004). *The effects of a reciprocal questioning intervention on the reading comprehension of children with autism.* Unpublished manuscript, Florida State University, Tallahassee.

Whalon, K.J., & Hanline, M.F. (2008). Effects of a reciprocal questioning intervention on the question generation and responding of children with autism spectrum disorder. *Education and Training in Developmental Disabilities, 43*(2), 367–387.

Wheelock, A. (1992). *Crossing the tracks: How "untracking" can save America's schools.* New York: The New Press.

Wiggins, G., & McTighe, J. (2005). *Understanding by design.* Alexandria, VA: ASCD.

Wilhelm, J., Baker, T., & Dube, J. (2001). *Strategic reading: Guiding students to lifelong literacy, 6–12.* Portsmouth, NH: Heinemann.

Willey, L.H. (1999). *Pretending to be normal: Living with Asperger's syndrome.* Philadelphia: Jessica Kingsley.

Willey, L.H. (2001). *Asperger syndrome in the family: Redefining normal.* Philadelphia: Jessica Kingsley.

Willey, M., & Willey, L.H. (2003). The importance of occupational therapy for adolescents with Asperger syndrome. In L.H. Willey (Ed.), *Asperger syndrome in adolescence* (pp. 129–147). Philadelphia: Jessica Kingsley.

Williams, D. (1992). *Nobody nowhere: The extraordinary biography of an autistic.* New York: Avon Books.

Williams, D. (2007). *Putting autism on trial: An interview with Amanda Baggs by autistic author Donna Williams.* Retrieved from http://www.americanchronicle.com/articles/view/31329

Williams, D. (1996). *Autism: An inside-out approach.* Philadelphia: Jessica Kingsley.

Williams, D. (1998). *Autism and sensing: The unlost instinct.* Philadelphia: Jessica Kingsley.

Williams, D. (1994). *Somebody, somewhere: Breaking free from the world of autism.* New York: Times Books.

Winebrenner, S. (1996). *Teaching kids with learning difficulties in the regular classroom*. Minneapolis, MN: Free Spirit.

Winter-Meissiers, M.A. (2007). From tarantulas to toilet brushes: Understanding the special interest areas of children and youth Asperger syndrome. *Remedial and Special Education, 28,* 140–152.

Winebrenner, S., & Espleland, P. (1996). *Teaching kids with learning difficulties in the regular classroom: Strategies and techniques every teacher can use to challenge and motivate struggling students.* Minneapolis, MN: Free Spirit Publishing.

Winner, E. (1996). *Gifted children: Myths and realities.* New York: Basic Books.

Winter-Messiers, M.A. (2007). From tarantulas to toilet brushes: Understanding the origin and development of the special interest areas of children and youth with Asperger's syndrome, *Remedial and Special Education, 28*(3), 140–152.

Wormeli, R. (2006). *Fair isn't always equal: Assessing and grading in the differentiated classroom.* Portland, ME: Stenhouse.

Yack, E., Aquilla, P., & Sutton, S. (2005). Sensory and motor differences for individuals with Asperger syndrome: Occupational therapy assessment and intervention. In K.P. Stoddart (Ed.), *Children, youth, and adults with Asperger syndrome: Integrating multiple perspectives.* Philadelphia: Jessica Kingsley.

Yell, M. (1995). The law and inclusion: Analysis and commentary. *Preventing School Failure, 39*(2), 45–49.

Yoder, D.I., Retish, E., & Wade, R. (1996). Service learning: Meeting student and community needs. *Teaching Exceptional Children, 28,* 14–18.

Literacy References

Bloom, J. (1972). *Tales of a fourth-grade nothing.* New York: Dutton Juvenile.

Carle, E. (1969). *The very hungry caterpillar.* New York: Putnam.

Cisneros, S. (1991). *The house on Mango Street.* New York: Vintage Books.

Hoyt-Goldsmith, D. (1998). *Lacrosse: The national game of the Iroquois.* New York: Holiday House.

Kirk, D. (1994). *Miss Spider's tea party.* Danbury, CT: Scholastic.

O'Dell, S. (1960). *Island of the blue dolphins.* New York: Yearling.

Peterson, J. (1969). *Mystery in the night woods.* New York: Scholastic.

Rey, M., & Rey, H.A. (1973). *Curious George goes to the hospital.* New York: HMH Books.

Wakely, M. (2005). *An audience for Einstein.* Cincinnati, OH: Mundania Press, LLC.

Walker, A. (1982). *The color purple.* New York: Pocketbooks.

Discussion Questions

These questions can be used for book clubs, study groups, or staff development activities. For a more comprehensive version of this list with more questions and "in the field" activity suggestions, see http://www.paulakluth.com

Chapter 1: Defining Autism

QUESTIONS

- What did you know about autism before reading this chapter? What did you learn after reading the chapter?

- Students with autism have communication, sensory, movement, and social differences. How do these differences affect your students?

- The social construction of autism is described in this chapter. Have you seen examples of the social construction of autism in your teaching experience?

IN THE FIELD

- Interview a student about his or her autism. Find out how the student understands his own label and how he or she labels him or herself.

Chapter 2: Understanding Inclusive Schooling

QUESTIONS

- What is your definition of inclusive schooling?

- Administrative support is key to the success of inclusive schools. In your opinion, in inclusive schools, what is the role of the principal, the director of pupil services, the director of curriculum and instruction, and the superintendent?

- Do you think inclusive schooling inspires education reform, in general? If so, how?

IN THE FIELD

- Complete the "Is Your School Inclusive?" checklist with your colleagues. Decide which actions are needed to support all students more effectively

Chapter 3: The Role of the Teacher

QUESTIONS

- Which of these "roles of the teacher" do you feel are most critical? Which do you already adopt? Which do you feel you need to further explore or develop?

- What roles would you add to this list of 10?

- One of the roles listed in this chapter is that of the advocate. What barriers do teachers face when they act as advocates for their students or teach advocacy?

IN THE FIELD

- To learn more about autism and inclusion, start a book club at your school.

Chapter 4: Connecting with Families

QUESTIONS

- Chapter 4 is full of parent stories. What stories have you heard from the parents of your students? What are their experiences with inclusion? Support? Participation?

- One parent is quoted as saying, "Somehow, somewhere, an invisible barrier has been built between the school and home." Have you seen any of these invisible barriers? If so, how can teachers work to dismantle them?

- Many families tell stories of meetings that are overwhelming (e.g., too many people attending, communication that is ineffective). How can teachers change the nature of these meetings? How can we make them more collaborative?

IN THE FIELD

- Conduct a home visit for a student who challenges you; observe the child in the home and interview family members to gather information and ideas.

Chapter 5: Creating a Comfortable Classroom

QUESTIONS

- This chapter opens with a discussion of my ideal writing environment. What is your ideal work environment? What changes have you made to your home office area or desk area at school to inspire productivity and provide comfort?

- How do you deal with students who fidget or move around a lot? Would any of the ideas in this chapter work for your students?

- Are you currently satisfied with the way your classroom looks and feels? How could you make your classroom more cozy? Inspired? Organized?

IN THE FIELD

- Using the checklist provided, choose a student who has sensory needs, complete the list, and share the information with key team members.

Chapter 6: Friendships, Social Relationships, and Belonging

QUESTIONS

- Community building is a central part of the inclusive classroom. Do you use any structures or strategies to help kids give and get support from one another? Discuss the ways you inspire students to connect to one another.

- In this chapter, I recommend using peers to teach and support one another. How do you ask peers to work together? Do your students formally support one another in any way? Tutor one another? Turn to each other to solve problems?

- Have you ever used role play to help students learn rules, solve problems, or interact more effectively and respectfully with one another? If so, how? Do you think you should try this technique for any of the students you have now?

IN THE FIELD

- With help from your students, create a social secrets guidebook for students in your classroom. Then find a way to share it with any student who will need it or, simply share it with all of the learners in the class.

Chapter 7: Building Communication Skills, Competencies, and Relationships

QUESTIONS

- Before reading this chapter, what did you know about echolalia? What did you learn that helped you to better understand your student and his or her communication?

- A large part of Chapter 7 is dedicated to being a supportive communication partner. How can you become a better communication partner for your student on the spectrum? For any student?

- Teachers often write IEP objectives about eye contact. After reading quotes from people with autism about eye contact, how do you feel about targeting it as an objective?

IN THE FIELD

- Is there a student at your school in need of a more comprehensive communication system? Talk to team members about steps that can be taken to provide better supports for this person. Is a new evaluation needed?

Chapter 8: Teaching Literacy to Students with Autism

QUESTIONS

- Luke Jackson's story opens this chapter. What does that story mean to you as a teacher?

- Why do you think my coauthor and I included the section on defining literacy? How might understanding the two frameworks we list affect teacher practice?

- The last part of this chapter is about students with significant disabilities. What barriers do teachers face in teaching literacy to these students? What types of literacy experiences do these students have in your school?

IN THE FIELD

- In this chapter, we provided a list of ideas for including a student in the read-aloud. Create your own list of ways to include students in other literacy structures such as partnered reading, guided reading, or writing workshop. Share this list with your colleagues.

Chapter 9: Rethinking Behavior

QUESTIONS

- Reread the section titled "Is the Behavior a Problem?" Can you think of an instance when you created a problem that didn't need to be created?

- Building a relationship is one of the most important pieces of supporting behavior. How do you build relationships with students?

- I suggest that you ask students about their behaviors if you can. What barriers might you face in doing this? Would your student have the language and awareness to explain his or her behavior? If not, how could you learn more about his perspective?

IN THE FIELD

- Bring your team together and complete a Strengths and Strategies assessment on a student in your classroom. Share the results with your team.

Chapter 10: Inclusive Pedagogy

QUESTIONS

- In Chapter 10, I recommend planning lessons *with* students when possible. Do you ever plan with your students? If so, how?

- Are there any formats mentioned in Chapter 10 that you would like to try or use more often? Which ones?

- Service learning is a very powerful tool for teaching students with and without disabilities. What kinds of projects do you think your students would enjoy? How would using service learning help you to differentiate instruction?

IN THE FIELD

- Try one of the games described in this chapter. Adapt it for your student or students on the spectrum. Then ask them about their experience: Do they enjoy active learning? Do they have ideas for adapting the activity for the class?

Chapter 11: Teaching Strategies

QUESTIONS

- Which of the ideas in the "Getting Ready for Inclusive Schooling" section sound helpful or appealing to you? Which are most appropriate for your students and grade level? Discuss one you are willing to implement immediately.

- In looking over the strategies recommended for the entire classroom, which ones do you feel would most benefit or work for your students? Discuss one you are willing to implement immediately.

- In looking over the strategies recommended specifically for students on the spectrum, which ones do you feel would most benefit or work for your students? Discuss one you are willing to implement immediately.

IN THE FIELD

- Create a survey for your students. After you get them back, review the results. Do you need to make changes in curriculum or instruction? Do you need to group students differently? Are there interests you will want to integrate into lessons?

Chapter 12: Collaboration and Cooperation in the Inclusive School

QUESTIONS

- The story that opens this chapter is about my own experience learning about collaboration and co-teaching. What is your story?

- Some teams co-teach but don't "shake up" or experiment with their individual roles very much. Are there roles you would like to take on in your co-teaching partnership, but haven't? What are they and how could you go about doing so?

- Several pages of this chapter are dedicated to the roles and responsibilities of paraprofessionals. How do paraprofessionals support students in your classroom? Do you need to adapt the type of support paraprofessionals provide?

IN THE FIELD

- Conduct a series of observations of the paraprofessionals on your team, then consider the following: Are there new roles he or she should adopt? In what areas does he or she need more training, do well, or excel? Share these notes in an informal meeting or review.

Index

Page numbers followed by *f* indicate figures; those followed by *t* indicate tables.